THE
GODDESS
WITHIN

THE GODDESS WITHIN

A GUIDE TO
THE ETERNAL MYTHS
THAT SHAPE
WOMEN'S LIVES

JENNIFER BARKER
WOOLGER AND
ROGER J. WOOLGER

FAWCETT COLUMBINE · NEW YORK

A portion of this text was originally published in *Quadrant: Journal of the C.G. Jung
Foundation for Analytical Psychology*.

Grateful acknowledgment is made to the following for permission to reprint previously
published material:

Beacon Press: Excerpt from *The Kabir Book* versions by Robert Bly. Copyright ©
1971, 1977 by Robert Bly. Reprinted by permission of Beacon Press.

Molly Malone Cook Literary Agency Inc.: "The Grandmothers" from *No Voyage and
Other Poems* by Mary Oliver. Copyright © 1963 by Mary Oliver. Reprinted by permission
of the Molly Malone Cook Literary Agency.

Daimon Verlag: Excerpts from "Strukturformen der weiblichen Psyche" from
Studien zu C.G. Jungs Psychologie by Toni Wolff, second edition, Copyright © 1981 by
Daimon Verlag, Zurich. ISBN: 3-85630-006-6. English edition in preparation by Daimon
Verlag, Einsiedeln, Switzerland.

E.P. Dutton: Excerpt from *Shamanic Voices: A Survey of Visionary Narratives* by Joan
Halifax, Ph.D. Copyright © 1979 by Joan Halifax, Ph.D. Reprinted by permission of the
publisher, E.P. Dutton, a division of Penguin Books USA Inc.

East West: The Journal of Natural Health and Living: Excerpt from an interview with
Robert Bly. Reprinted by permission of *East West: The Journal of Natural Health and
Living*, Brookline, Mass.

Faber and Faber Ltd: Excerpt from "Prayer Before Birth" from *The Collected Poems of
Louis MacNeice* by Louis MacNeice. Reprinted by permission of Faber and Faber Ltd.

Farrar, Straus, & Giroux, Inc.: Excerpt from "Women" from *The Blue Estuaries* by
Louise Bogan. Copyright 1923, 1951, © 1968 by Louise Bogan. Reprinted by permission
of Farrar, Straus, & Giroux, Inc.

Harcourt Brace Jovanovich, Inc. and Faber and Faber Ltd: Excerpt from "Little
Gidding" from *Four Quartets* by T.S. Eliot. Copyright 1943 by T.S. Eliot. Renewed 1971
by Esme Valerie Eliot. Rights in the United States administered by Harcourt Brace
Jovanovich, Inc. Rights in all other territories administered by Faber and Faber Ltd.
Reprinted by permission of Harcourt Brace Jovanovich, Inc. and Faber and Faber Ltd.

Page 483 constitutes a continuation of the copyright page.

Library of Congress Catalog Card Number: 87-91870
ISBN: 0-449-90287-0

Cover design by James R. Harris
Cover photograph: *Venere Vencitrice*, National Museum, Naples
(Bettmann Archive)
Text design by Holly Johnson

Manufactured in the United States of America

First Edition: October 1989
10 9 8 7 6 5 4 3 2 1

To all the goddesses,
born and unborn

CONTENTS

PREFACE

Our meditations on the goddesses go back many years. For Roger they began in Oxford in the late sixties with a disturbing dream about pigs and labyrinths that prompted John Layard to lend him his own copiously and intriguingly annotated copy of Erich Neumann's *The Great Mother.* For Jennifer, it was the feminist ferment of the early seventies and stumbling across Jung and Kerényi's great essays on the Kore and the goddesses. Since then our readings, personal encounters, and dreams have been too numerous for us to recall accurately, though we have quoted in boxes extracts from our favorite sources and have put many more in our bibliography. For those who want a scholarly bird's-eye view of the field we provide our "Brief History of Goddess Psychology" in appendix B.

We have learned most profoundly of the goddesses from those of our women clients and students who have so generously shared their dreamwork, journaling, painting, sculpture, weaving, and music with us. From them, too, we have glimpsed so much about the transformative power of the goddess energies in so many memorable performances and Goddess Wheel interactions. Many of you will recognize pieces of your stories in our reconstructions throughout the book.

But we particularly want to thank all the many individuals and groups that have sponsored and encouraged this work over the years: Tom Verner at Burlington College, Vermont; Paul Kugler and the Buffalo Analytical Psychology Society; Patricia King-Edwards and the Ottawa Jung Society; Alice Johnstone and the Montreal Jung Society; Rebecca Browning and the TARA Foundation in Boulder; Sue and Larry Anderson in Chapel Hill; Mary Leue and the folks at Rainbow Camp Association in Albany; Sean McEvenue of Lonergan College at Concordia University, Montreal, and Marilyn Taylor also at Concordia; Beth Darlington of Vassar College.

Special thanks for all their support and help when we took the show on the road—with baby Claire—to Rosemarie Delahaye and Jannis Toussulis in San Francisco, Rebecca Browning in Boulder, Carol Steiner and (in spirit) the late Connie Stafford in Buffalo. Any many thanks too for encouragement, inspiration and ideas in our conversations, short and long, with: Brewster and Sandy Beach, Mary and Ted

Brenneman, Hyla Cass, Norma Churchill, Guy Corneau, Irene Friel, Alice O. Howell, Mary Jaquier, David Joy, Robin and Steven Larsen, Rux and Luther Martin, David Miller, Ginette Paris, Sylvia Brinton Perara, Charles Ponce, Laura Simms, June Singer, Cheryl Southworth, Pat Taylor, Suzanne Toomy, Jim and Alison Van Dyck, Edith Wallace, Leslie Wheelock, and Alice Wright.

A special place of honor belongs here to the memories of two wonderful women who passed into Persephone's realm before the completion of the book, but who lived and embodied its spirit: Katherine Whiteside Taylor and Connie Stafford. *Ave et vale!*

Additional thanks to our editors at Ballantine, Michelle Russell, Jane Bess and Virginia Faber, for encouraging us to let the goddesses really speak through, thus expanding the book into its present form; to Leslie English for her meticulous proofreading and last of all to John Brockman and Katinka Matson for their initial enthusiasm and for supporting us all the way.

Jennifer and Roger Woolger

THE
GODDESS
WITHIN

WHAT IS GODDESS PSYCHOLOGY?

The motif of the return of the Great Goddess and her consort is encountered over and over again in the dreams and unconscious fantasies of people who seek psychological help to overcome the deadness of their lives. Art, films, literature, and political upheavals also reflect increasingly the same dynamics. The changes they demand entail new understandings of masculinity and femininity in both men and women and the relations between the sexes, as well as new views of reality.
—EDWARD C. WHITMONT, *RETURN OF THE GODDESS*

Throughout the world, but most prominently in Westernized countries, we are witnessing a reawakening of the feminine, a profound upheaval within the consciousness of women. Many men fear it and discount it, others are challenged by it. Radical commentators have called it figuratively a "return of the Goddess," because it seems to suggest the very antithesis of patriarchal society.

Slowly, but irrevocably, this ferment inside women, and the reaction going on in men, is starting to affect every aspect of our lives and thinking. All our assumptions about ourselves, our values, our politics, our sexual relationships, our place in the universe, are being challenged by this awakening.

In response to it, radical new ways of understanding the feminine in our society are starting to emerge. Feminist writings and books such as Jean Shinoda Bolen's popular *Goddesses in Everywoman* and Monica Sjöö and Barbara Mor's *The Great Cosmic Mother* offer us insights, both ancient and new, to feed the huge spiritual hunger we feel. With them, we believe it is time to begin writing a new psychology of the feminine, a psychology that returns women to their ultimate roots—a goddess psychology.

When the authors began teaching workshops about the return of the Goddess in her many forms several years ago, we were not prepared for the variety and intensity of the reactions we received everywhere from the women and men we met. After an evening slide-show lecture women would report staying up half the night talking passionately about their love lives, what it meant to have children, and the frustrations of their careers. "You gave me a whole new way of talking about myself," they would say. "I have never before been so clear."

One female student, after hearing us talk about the moon and menstruation at the beginning of a twelve-week class, came up to us at the end of the course to tell us quietly how her periods, previously so troublesome, were now completely regular and in tune with the moon cycle.

A man who had never managed to understand his attraction to and failure with certain women told us how our goddess types had enabled him to stop making wrong choices and had revolutionized his love life.

Women have made major career changes, moving out of or into cities, upon learning certain fundamentals that will be explained in the pages that follow. Other women have made radical life adjustments in regard to having or not having children or getting married or divorced, once they understood how the goddess energies worked within them.

Nevertheless, we don't want to give the impression that working with this new language of the feminine is simply about having intellectual insights. What it really entails is engaging deeply and courageously with these feminine forces as they live within and through us. We have to get to know them as spiritual and psychological presences— what psychologist Carl Jung called *archetypes*, which is to say, living transformers of our lives and our consciousness.

Even as we wrote this book, we both felt the very different energies of each of six major goddesses—all aspects of the supreme Mother Goddess, as we will explain—coming into our lives in powerful and sometimes disruptive ways. It was not easy to write about the goddess

Athena as solely the principle of wisdom, for example. We found ourselves arguing endlessly about our text until we realized that Athena is a *warrior* goddess who loves competitiveness and fights. When it came to Hera, the matriarch among the goddesses, the disputes tended to shift to "who knows best" and "who is really in charge"!

When we wrote about Demeter, the mother goddess, we found ourselves quieter and more placid—but we both found we were tending to overeat. As for invoking Aphrodite, the love goddess, we leave the reader to deduce how and where our creative energies often got distracted.

But we are getting ahead of ourselves. To understand the revolution that we see happening, the reader will need to learn the fundamentals of a new psychological language and be introduced to certain historical facts about the development of our culture. This is the purpose of what follows in this chapter.

AN INNER AWAKENING

If we look around, there are more than a few outer signs of this emergence of new feminine awareness. Whether it is feminism and the Deep Ecology movement in America and Europe, las Madres de la Plaza de Mayo protesting dictatorship in Argentina, the political emergence of women in West Africa, or visionary women artists in China and Russia, many women are manifestly responding to deep and urgent forces within themselves.

But what are the origins of this reawakening of the feminine? How did such a revolution in consciousness start? Is it mostly political?

Feminism is of course one of the main contemporary sources of this momentous change. However, the vast majority of women are not as intellectually or as politically inclined as most feminists. As this book shows, the feminist outlook speaks for only a small, but still highly significant proportion of women as a whole. The majority of women, whether they work or not, feel most fulfilled in their primary roles as wives, partners, and mothers.

There is, however, another extremely important segment of the female population. These are the many women who live (often alone) as little-known poets or artists, writers or musicians, as well as those who live quietly in the background as healers, therapists, community wise women, and mystics. They, too, are all feeling the inner rumblings of this revolution, and even if they are not as vocal as their articulate feminist sisters, their contributions are of immense importance. A goddess psychology must include all these women.

Given the rich variety of experience among so many different types of women, it is hard to pinpoint the origins of these transformations in feminine consciousness. Many factors have contributed to women's new self-awareness and growing self-esteem, especially in Western society, where these changes are most prominent. Birth control, for instance, has freed many women from the restrictive round of continual childbearing. Better health care and the opening of the urban marketplace to women has meant independence, real careers, and some degree of power sharing in the formerly all-male world. Freer divorce laws have enabled women to escape from destructive marriages without extreme social stigma.

Many of these blessings have been mixed, as we know only too well, but they have altered the face of the modern world. Some changes—women's suffrage, for example—have indeed been won through feminist political struggle. But by no means all. Some, such as birth control, are due to advances in science. But other developments, such as the growing demand for women ministers in the Christian church, reflect unprecedented changes in the deeper psychic structures that underlie our culture, in what Jung named the collective unconscious.

Our shifting attitudes toward sexuality are yet another example. The changes we have seen in the last hundred years—Freudianism, free love, open marriage, the epidemic of pornography, the demand for easy divorce—cannot be attributed to any single event and are hard to account for. They are as much symptoms of our changing sexual mores as they are their causes.

Why, then, is our contemporary experience of sexuality so confused? In the authors' view, we are witnessing the return of a crucial aspect of the forgotten feminine, a transcendent power that used to be called, in symbolic language, the goddess of love. Banished many centuries ago, this goddess and her inescapable charms can be discerned within the much larger pattern of emerging feminine consciousness.

Spiritual and sexual longings that lead us to question our religious institutions and our patterns of relationship are not imposed from out-side. These stirrings felt so powerfully by women and in a different way by men are surely coming from within. They may eventually lead to social and political movements, but they are first experienced as compelling inner pressures. In fact, the dreams and inner experiences of women and men in psychotherapy and the themes taken up by novelists, media writers, and artists everywhere all show both ancient and radically new images of the feminine pushing toward conscious-ness. This is the observation of Jungian psychotherapist Edward C. Whitmont, as the quote heading this chapter attests. And as we try to show in this book, these forces are fermenting within all of us, poten-tially transforming the most fundamental ways we think about our-selves. We call these powerful inner forces and the images and changes they bring "the goddesses."

WHAT IS A "GODDESS"?

By *goddess* we mean a psychological description of a complex female character type that we intuitively recognize both in ourselves and in the women around us, as well as in the images and icons that are every-where in our culture. For example, the smartly dressed, intelligent young career woman we see everywhere in our cities is the living em-bodiment of a goddess type we call *the Athena woman*, named after the Greek goddess who was patroness of the ancient city of Athens. Mag-azines, movies, and novels all reproduce her as a stereotype because she is so prevalent today.

Yet a goddess type such as Athena is much more than just a media stereotype or cliché. Athena also represents a complex and highly evolved style of consciousness that characterizes everything about the way this type of woman thinks, feels, and acts. The most prominent features of the Athena woman are that she is hardworking, achieve-ment-oriented, independent, and intellectual. She values education, a high degree of political and social awareness, and generally puts her career before her children and husband.

There is a fundamental *dynamic* behind the behavior of such a woman that makes her unique as a type. Part of it is socially acquired and part seems to be innate. When such a psychological dynamic is observed in a whole group of individuals, it is what Jung called an archetype. He was the first to observe that dynamic types of this sort are to be found in their purest forms in mythology and literature and that they show up, in disguise, in everyone's dream and fantasy life. Today they can easily be observed in movies, television soap operas, and the way the media treats the lives of prominent people. Thus Marilyn Monroe became a tragic love goddess both on and off the screen; Oliver North enacts a frustrated patriotic hero during congressional hearings. The well-known book *Man and His Symbols*, edited by Jung, gives hundreds of contemporary as well as historical examples.

A *goddess*, then, is the form that a feminine archetype may take in the context of a mythological story or epic. In a fairy tale this archetype may appear as a princess, a queen, or a witch. When we ourselves dream or fantasize, our unconscious mind may draw upon the common pool of archetypal images in our culture (Jung called this pool the *collective unconscious*). Instead of a queen or goddess like the Hera of Greek myth to represent the feminine archetype of power, we may dream of Margaret Thatcher or a soap opera matriarch like Jane Wyman.

When the goddess Athena appears in Homer's *Iliad*, she is the divine protectress and companion of the young warrior heroes, but she also had many other functions for the Greeks, as we will show later. Her image actually sums up a highly complex feminine energy dynamic that emerges among aggressive, ambitious, and highly civilized peoples, whether they are ancient Greeks or modern urban women. In this sense we believe that Athena is very much alive today. As a goddess, she incarnates that psychic energy field we see inspiring and informing the common attitudes, behavior, and ideals of many women in contemporary society.

THE MAJOR GODDESS TYPES

In this book we have selected six major Greek goddess archetypes that strike us as the most active in the lives of modern women and in contemporary society.

The basic characteristics of all six types can be summarized as follows:

- **The Athena woman** is ruled by the goddess of wisdom and civilization and is concerned with achievement, career, education, intellectual culture, social justice, and politics.

• **The Aphrodite woman** is ruled by the love goddess and her chief concerns are relationships, sexuality, intrigue, romance, beauty, and the inspiration of the arts.

• **The Persephone woman** is ruled by the goddess of the underworld; she is mediumistic and is attracted to the spirit world, to the occult, to visionary and mystical experience, and to matters associated with death.

• **The Artemis woman** is ruled by the goddess of the wilds; she is practical, athletic, adventurous; she likes physical culture, solitude, the outdoors, animals, and is concerned with the protection of the environment, alternative life-styles, and women's communities.

• **The Demeter woman** is ruled by the corn goddess; she is an earth mother who loves bearing, nurturing, and raising children; she is concerned with all aspects of childbirth and women's reproductive cycles.

• **The Hera woman** is ruled by the queen of heaven; she is concerned with marriage, partnerships with men, and with issues of power wherever women are rulers and leaders.

As an aid to learning and remembering the goddess types, the reader may wish to refer to the diagram we call *the Goddess Wheel*, which summarizes details found in the individual chapters about each goddess. This diagram also helps to illustrate aspects of the dynamics *between* the goddess types, which we will explain later. There is also a detailed questionnaire in part 3 to help women discover how the goddess types are distributed in their personality and to enable men to see which goddess types they are naturally drawn to in relationships.

What we want to emphasize in this book is that not just one but several of these goddess types, in various combinations, underlie every woman's behavior and psychological style. Unlike sun-sign astrology, in which one is fixed as a Pisces or a Leo, every woman is a complex mixture of all the goddess types. To know oneself more fully as a woman is to know which goddesses one is primarily ruled by and to be aware of how different goddesses influence the various stages and turning points of one's life.

Men, too, are influenced by the goddess types. The goddesses most certainly mirror feminine energies in the male psyche, although men usually experience them as being more external to themselves in the

shape of women they are either attracted to or else have strong reactions to. Psychologically we would say that men experience the goddesses *projected* onto the women around them as well as onto particular
media images that arouse or repel them.

All of men's relationships with women are, we believe, determined
by one or more of the goddess energies and the particular archetypal
patterns that belong to each. One man may unconsciously look for
Demeter in a woman; another may want Hera to take power in their
partnership; and so on.

To a limited degree we will naturally mention the complementary
god and hero archetypes that interact with each of the goddesses. The
main emphasis of this book, however, is on the goddesses, since they
have received far less attention in psychological literature. To help men
understand their age-old problems in relationships from the perspective of goddess psychology, we devote a chapter to these issues (see
chapter 10).

THE POWER OF GODDESS LANGUAGE

According to Jungian theory the goddesses are archetypes, which is to
say, they are the ultimate sources of those emotional patterns in our
thinking, our feelings, our instincts, and our behavior that we might
call "feminine" in the broader sense of the word. All creative and
inspirational thinking, all nurturing, mothering and gestating, all passion, desire and sexuality, all urges towards connectedness, social cohe-
sion, union and communion, all merging and fusion as well as impulses
to absorb, to destroy, to reproduce, and to replicate belong to the
universal archetype of the feminine. Modern academic psychology,
however, with its love of masculine abstractions prefers to use the
rational and spiritually deadening language of "instincts," "drives," and
"behavior patterns"—words that produce no images in the imagination,
no flash of recognition in the soul. As archetypal psychologist James
Hillman once put it: "the language of psychology is an insult to the
soul."

But the Greeks and all ancient cultures perceived these energies
not as soulless abstractions but instead as spiritually vital forces—forces
or energies that are constantly exerting powerful influences upon our

psychological processes. When they were able to recognize the spiritual forces that activated and informed particular aspects of human behavior and experience, they called these phenomena "the compulsion of the gods and goddesses." It is for this reason that Jung was moved to remark that "there is a god or goddess at the heart of every complex." The names and stories that the ancients gave to these forces therefore—Aphrodite, Athena, Demeter, and so on—reflect how they saw them as living, personified forms of what today we call complexes. The goddesses personify in their myths the many and varied, but nevertheless *typical* ways any woman may be moved to act and feel when in love (Aphrodite), when inspired by an ideal (Athena), or absorbed in her role as mother (Demeter), for example.

When a goddess energy appears in our lives, we often find everything we are doing turned upside down; suddenly we are madly in love, passionately campaigning for some cause, brooding over our coming child, and so on. This turbulent upsurge or radical change of behavior was observed by Jung and led him to note that archetypes don't just pattern behavior, they *transform* it as well. The poet Robert Bly, paraphrasing Jung, calls archetypes like the goddesses *transformers*, because they often appear at important changes in our life—adolescence, marriage, bereavement—and totally alter our feelings, our perceptions, and the way we behave.

Because of the strongly rationalistic bias of our education we tend, in our superior way, to regard ancient myths—the stories of the gods, goddesses, and heroes—as superstitious nonsense. Actually they are highly sophisticated psychology. It is simply that they are not couched in the mechanistic abstractions of academic psychology, but rather in the poetic language of image, story, and drama. We have been sold an arbitrary distinction between the "hard" language of science (masculine) and the "soft" language of literature, the arts, and religion (feminine).

Let us take sexuality, for example. When behavioral psychologists describe sexual patterns in humans and animals, they use terms such as "courtship rituals," "innate releasing mechanisms," and so on. Freudians, who should know better, resort to clumsy talk of "erogenous zones," "polymorphous perversity," and the like. The ancients, by contrast, would tell an exemplary story of what happened when "Aphrodite, the love goddess, came down to earth one time . . ."

Instead of reducing falling in love entirely to the prosaic influence of hormones or "narcissistic object choice," the ancients would tell a story of how the spirit of Aphrodite changed a certain person's mood, sleeping habits, dreams, and possibly his basic sanity. The story would illustrate how people in love are "starry-eyed," forgetful, sleepless, obsessed with one thing only; how their dreams are erotic and sensuous; how they may be inspired to both creative and quite absurd behavior; in fact how they seem to observers more than a little crazy and how this craziness can affect everyone around them.

When two people are in love, it sometimes happens that whole institutions, such as marriage, governments, even kingdoms, get overturned. Lunatics, lovers, and poets, as Shakespeare observed in *A Midsummer Night's Dream*, are all possessed by the same feverish imagination of the beloved. They make "asses" of themselves, as Bottom does with Queen Titania in Shakespeare's hilarious story of the chaos wrought by an aphrodisiac love potion.

Some "masculine" terminology can be helpful, so long as it isn't alienating and demeaning of the true archetypal wisdom of the poetic or mythic image. It would be wrong to call Aphrodite, who loves to sit in front of a mirror making herself lovely, "narcissistic," for instance. For one thing, this would be to incorrectly attribute her behavior to a different archetypal character: Narcissus, who was foolish enough to fall into the water and drown when admiring himself. Aphrodite is much more self-aware than that; she's busy preparing her persona to offer it to others for *their* pleasure, not just her own.

We will inevitably fall back on some of the terminology used by Freudians, Jungians, and Reichians from time to time when describing the goddesses, but sparingly, we hope, and always backed up with stories, case histories, living examples, poems, and of course the myths themselves, which are the case histories of the goddesses.

GODDESSES, POLYTHEISM, AND CHRISTIANITY

Why do we use Greek goddesses and not archetypal figures from Celtic or Hebrew or African or Native American traditions?

Mainly because the imagery of the Greek archetypes is already quite familiar to us from literature, art, and astrology. The characters of Mars, Venus, Mercury, and so on survived as psychological shorthand in the Middle Ages because the Arabs, who had retained much of Greek culture, later imported astrology to Europe. Then, during the Renaissance, there was the revival of classical learning and the rediscovery of many of the myths and religious images of the Greeks and their romanized versions. Stories contained in books such as Ovid's influential collection, the *Metamorphoses*, and translations of Plutarch and Homer passed into educated culture. Shakespeare, for example, drew on all these authors, as did painters and musicians—Botticelli and Monteverdi, for example.

Most of us today are superficially familiar with mythic themes and characters, such as the birth of Venus, the labors of Hercules, the war fought for Helen of Troy, the revels of Bacchus, or the tale of Orpheus and Euridyce. We know them in a variety of forms ranging from paintings and opera to comic books and Hollywood movies. Judging by the continued publication of illustrated collections of Greek myths and books on mythology in general by scholars such as Joseph Campbell, there is an unabated hunger for stories of heroes, heroines, gods, and goddesses.

In addition to their myths, the civilizations of Greece and Rome have repeatedly provided models for Western secular culture. On the surface many of our institutions; our style of government, imperialism, architecture; our art forms, drama, and philosophy; even our science— all bear the stamp of the early Greek and Roman genius.

Yet classical culture runs in tandem with another major cultural stream that has shaped the West spiritually, namely the Judeo-Christian tradition. Indeed, we could say, very broadly, that Western civilization has arisen out of a remarkably complex dialectic between the *secular* values and models of classical Greece and Rome and the *religious* values of Judaism and its offspring, Christianity.

This is a rather crude division, we realize, but it does pinpoint a significant thing about how the enlightened modern mind views mythology. Despite the fact that mythology deals with gods, goddesses, creation stories, destiny, and universal justice, among other things, most people do not regard it as religious or spiritual in any way. As master mythographer Joseph Campbell once put it rather sardonically, "Myths are *other people's* religions" [our emphasis].

The fact is that the Greek gods and goddesses were long ago robbed of their original spiritual power and transcendent meaning and were reduced to literary stereotypes and the subjects of courtly art and theater. Thanks to Christianity, so the official view goes, Western man (and woman) outgrew the childish polytheism of the Greeks and Romans, to discover a mature monotheism in the belief in one God.

However, it is by no means certain that monotheism is all that psychologically "healthy." One major loss, as feminist critics such as Mary Daly and Naomi Goldenburg observe, is that Christianity has restricted our image of ultimate divinity to a *father*. In doing so, it has reinforced and further authorized the patriarchal domination that was already well under way among the Greeks and Hebrews.

Another serious loss—this is the view of Jung and archetypal psychologist James Hillman—is that we have denied the psyche its craving for healthy variety in its spiritual life, a craving once amply satisfied by *polytheism*, with its many gods, goddesses, nymphs, fairies, demons, nixies, and local spirits. When the multiplicity of the gods is denied to us, Jung once remarked, "they become diseases."[1]

THE RETURN OF THE GODDESS

In referring to Greek goddess archetypes as the cornerstones of a new psychology of the feminine, following the Jungian and feminist lead, we are resurrecting more than just a colorful and vaguely familiar set of names and mythic stories. As will become apparent from each goddess chapter, we are raising the question of the whole *psychospiritual imbalance* in our culture—a profound disharmony we and many others cannot help but perceive between the masculine and feminine life forces, those fundamental archetypal energies that nourish and inspire each one of us.

Jung once described a neurotic person as one-sided, by which he meant someone who overemphasizes one side of his personality to

[1] For a discussion of this whole issue by a historian of religion and culture, see David Miller's *The New Polytheism*, which also contains James Hillman's seminal statement "Psychology: Monotheistic or Polytheistic." For a feminist discussion of Hillman and Jung, see Naomi Goldenburg's *The Changing of the Gods: Feminism and the End of Traditional Religions*.

avoid dealing with the other, less agreeable side. What is true of individual neurotics is also true of whole cultures. This is where archetypal and feminist thinking converge. They are in agreement that our whole culture—with its endless violence, homeless people on the streets, colossal nuclear arsenals, and global pollution—is sick. It is sick because it is out of harmony with itself; it suffers from what the Hopi Indians call *koyaanisqatsi*, which is rendered in English, "crazy life, life in turmoil, life out of balance."[2] What is missing is the feminine dimension in our spiritual and psychological lives; that deep, mystical sense of the earth and her cycles and of the very cosmos as a living mystery. We have lost our inner connection to that momentous power that used to be called the Great Mother of us all.

Historians of religion agree that at those times in human history when the Great Mother was worshipped, human beings were very much in harmony with themselves and with the life force. In ancient Mesopotamia, for example, where the Mother Goddess was known as Inanna (in Assyria she was Ishtar), she was worshipped as the very source of life itself. She was the power manifest in all fertility and all its forms, whether human, animal, or vegetable. Annually she mated with the shepherd-god Dumuzi (or Tammuz), who incarnated the creative powers of spring. His autumnal death symbolized the seasonal decline, and their reunion in the spring enacted the renewal of the earth. But the young god was only the agent of renewal. It was the Mother Goddess herself who resuscitated him. In the words of E. O. James, "she was the embodiment of creative power in all its fullness." As a divine principle, she also came to preside over "all deaths and resurrections in whatever plane they might occur."

What we find when we investigate the matriarchal cults is a certain harmony and deep security in the sacred union between the Mother and her Son Lover. Archaeological relics of matriarchal worship, which stretch back thousands of years into Neolithic times, suggest centuries of uninterrupted change in many settlements. It is hard to estimate today the deep degree of confidence in life these ancient peoples must have felt.

Despite the rise of warrior cultures, which thrived more by conquest and enslavement, we know that cults of the Mother Goddess

---

[2] We take this concept from the stunning film by Godrey Reggio, *Koyaanisqatsi*.

survived and flourished right up until Roman times. Local goddesses were easily assimilated into her worship—Cybele in Asia Minor; Isis, first in Egypt, then Rome; Gaia in Greece—because they were essentially the same divinity, "the goddess of many names." But increasingly, as we show in detail later in this chapter, the conflict between the patriarchal warrior gods and the Goddess became intense. The triumph of modern times becomes the triumph of Christianity and a supreme Father God. By the end of the Roman Empire in the West, the cults of the Mother have become scattered, suppressed, assimilated, distorted. Gone is the deep sense of trust and belonging her cults once gave.

Seen from the larger perspective of world religion, the cultures of Western civilization are like the children of a family that has suffered a terrible divorce. The children now live only with the father and are forbidden to mention their mother's name or remember those warm and happy times they once spent in her embrace. With only a father to guide us, despite his love, we have become hardened, relentlessly heroic, and grimly puritanical in our effort to forget the lost security and sensual trust in the earth the Mother once gave us. Long ago, we dimly sense, there was a primordial unity, when an Earth Mother *and* a Spirit Father enjoyed happy and harmonious union. But that paradise is lost, and in our estrangement we have been forced to swallow the embittered propaganda of a guilty, yet all-powerful Father. The Mother herself is disempowered; her cults scattered, divided, unattended, persecuted.

THE WOUNDED GODDESS IN US ALL

When Mary Daly writes in *Beyond God the Father* of the way the Christian "father image" of God has distorted and tyrannized our view of women in the West, she is also describing what Jung would call the distorting power of a single archetype. Archetypes can possess whole cultures and make them neurotic in just the same way as a personal "father complex" can drive an individual to be neurotically slavish to authority, for example.

What Daly and other feminist writers attack as the sickness of "patriarchy" is precisely what Jungians criticize as the way in which Western civilization has been one-sidedly overshadowed by the Father archetype, to the exclusion of the Mother archetype. By worshipping the father principle alone and suppressing or belittling the feminine, we have done serious damage to our individual and collective psychic health. And this is to say nothing of the physical health of our bodies and that of the planet earth.

But the signs are that, both spontaneously and consciously, the balance is actually shifting. Patriarchal supremacy is manifesting symptoms of spiritual bankruptcy, and everywhere— in the arts, in literature, in politics, in the churches—there are the signs of a huge resurgence of the feminine, of matriarchal consciousness. Such an auspicious "return of the Goddess" is surely under way.

It is urgent, therefore, that we understand the nature and condition of the feminine archetypes that are currently reemerging from the collective unconscious of our culture. The first thing we notice is that, like anyone who has been imprisoned, exiled, reviled, and misrepresented, the goddesses, when they are restored to consciousness as psychospiritual principles, often appear weak, confused, and wounded. This woundedness is due to the harsh treatment they have received at the hands of patriarchal repression: Aphrodite is ashamed of her sexuality; Athena questions her own ability to think; Hera doubts her own power; Demeter mistrusts her fertility; Persephone denies her visions; Artemis misunderstands her instinctive bodily wisdom. This, and much, much more, is the legacy of the psychic exile of the feminine.

When we begin to look at the psychology of each of the goddesses in detail in their individual chapters, we shall have to pay careful attention to what we call *the goddess wound* in each of them. These are wounds that have been sustained over the long history of the psychological battle for supremacy waged by the masculine forces in Western culture. And whether these wounds were first inflicted by the warrior supremacy of the early Greeks, the imperialism of the Romans, or the puritanical fear of the feminine and the body among certain factions in Christianity, we shall need to ask why every modern woman carries within her residues of that particular goddess's wound that have been festering for nearly three millennia.

CONFLICTED GODDESSES ANCIENT
AND MODERN

The goddess wounds are by no means new. They arose nearly three thousand years ago, in the period when patriarchal cultures first began to wrest control from the older "matriarchal" cultures.[3] Indeed, when we look closely at the origins of the individual goddesses' wounds as recorded in their mythic biographies in ancient Greece, we find the very same conflicts behind the attitudes, values, and priorities that undermine the power and confidence of women today.

There are, for example, certain psychosocial oppositions between the goddesses that seem almost impossible to reconcile. When Hera is totally identified with marriage and with her powerful mate, she will always be scandalized by Aphrodite's constant stream of affairs. Likewise an Athena careerwoman will often undergo agonies at the mere thought of pregnancy and confinement in the home raising children. These conflicts were already present either in the social life of the Greeks or in the collective unconscious of the time as it was projected into their myths.

It is highly illuminating to look at ancient Greece as a kind of "distant mirror," in historian Barbara Tuchman's phrase. In this mirror we can discern quite clearly how many of our current conflicts arose from that civilization's growing need to impose patriarchal values. But we can also see how their solutions differ from ours. For despite the rise of patriarchy, most of the original cults of the goddesses did survive, along with an uncontaminated collection of myths. As a result, a considerable degree of matriarchal consciousness was kept alive in ancient Greece.

When we compare the evolution of Greek myth and religion with that of Christianity or Judaism, with their one Father God, we find a very different situation. Greek religion retained both father and mother divinities, as well as a whole host of other gods and goddesses. Even

---

[3] Here, and throughout this book, we do not use *matriarchal* to mean "rule by women." We do not believe there is any solid evidence of an era when women were the sole rulers of any culture, much wishful historical thinking notwithstanding. By *matriarchal* we refer to cultures that worshipped the Mother Goddess, in one or more of her forms, as the supreme divinity. Matriarchal religion seems to us perfectly compatible with polytheism.

if Zeus did rule Olympus as supreme Sky Father, he nevertheless consented to share his sacred mount with Athena, Apollo, Artemis, Hermes, Demeter, Hephaistos, Poseidon, Hestia, Aphrodite, Ares, and of course, Hera. This constituted in fact, an equal distribution of gods and goddesses. The heroes of myth, too, had constant intercourse, literal and figurative, with the gods.

It seems that in the absence of any early unified state religion or tribal monotheism, both the male and the female divinities had to co-exist in the religious universe of the Greeks. It is true that their relationships were often far from amicable, as exemplified by the stormy marriage of Zeus and Hera on Olympus. Nevertheless, it was still possible for the early Greeks to live with these continual tensions without completely repressing them, as we have learned to do. We can only conjecture that the dream stories of their myths or the magico-spiritual hygiene of their cults helped relieve at least some of the pressures arising from the conflicting matriarchal and patriarchal strains in their culture.

But despite the accommodation of the feminine on the Olympian level, life in ancient Greece was far from wonderful for women; there was little choice between being a homebound matron, a hetaera or high-class prostitute, and a slave. Yet the mere existence of the various cults to goddesses as individual as Aphrodite, Artemis, Demeter, and Athena provided many rich possibilities for women's psychic and spiritual life, many more than were later retained in Christianity or Judaism. The great temples to Artemis at Ephesus, to Hera on Samos, to Aphrodite on Paphos, for example, were enormously popular and in continuous use throughout antiquity. And most famous of all were the Mysteries of Demeter and her daughter Persephone, celebrated in the little town of Eleusis, outside Athens. For nearly two thousand years this rite, the most complete later flowering of the more ancient cults of the Mother Goddess, held sway and was as influential during the classical era as was Christianity.

In their myths, their drama, and their epics we can see the Greeks agonizing, sometimes bloodily, with the wrenching inner tug-of-war between patriarchal and matriarchal loyalties—one thinks of Orestes' guilty matricide or of Oedipus's regressive incestuous entanglement with his mother. But at least the Greeks did not sweep the whole problem under the carpet as Christianity was to do some time later.

They seemed aware, however dimly, of the perils of denying the feminine, as well as of the fact that when both sides of a problem are present, there is at least the possibility of working toward some creative resolution.

When, by contrast, the early Christian fathers, in reaction to the sexual decadence of imperial Rome, attempted to drive out everything that the love goddess Venus-Aphrodite stood for, they lost that possibility for consciousness. What followed was nearly two thousand years of guilt and shame about our bodily functions, a collective repression that has led directly to the sorry mess we are in today with our sexuality.

THE GODDESS DIVIDED

In taking a closer look at the overall history of each of the goddess's cults, as we do in each goddess chapter, we begin to see quite clearly how each goddess's wounds in the struggle with the patriarchy are reflected directly in her particular myths. In fact, *we can read the myths as the archetypal case histories of individual goddesses.* Each collection of myths, when taken with what is known about the cults of each goddess, contains not only suggestive remnants of the older Mother religions but also clear indications of the opposition and manipulation of the goddesses by the more favored male gods.

Zeus's forced marriage to Hera is an obvious example. Hera was one of the names for the original Mother Goddess of pre-Hellenic Greece. In fact, one of the oldest known shrines to any divinity in Greece is the temple of Hera on the island of Samos. Patriarchal invaders from the north took over her holy places and imposed a husband upon her, namely their sky god, Zeus. The "marriage," as we know from their myths, was far from happy, but it clearly symbolizes this uncomfortable fusion of matriarchal and patriarchal cultures.

It is our strong belief that such mythic "case histories" have psychological, social, and political ramifications that we are still struggling with today. The history of Greek religion shows very clearly how the patterns of matriarchal (that is, Mother Goddess worshipping) society slowly ceded and came to terms with the patriarchal warrior tribes who conquered them. It shows, as well, how the goddesses—which is to say, the fullness of feminine self-awareness—became compromised and deeply wounded in the process. And yet, when we study the evolution of the goddess myths, we can still discern something of the original power and glory of the Great Mother who was once worshipped everywhere.

Robert Graves, who thought deeply about these matters, writes as follows in the introduction to *The Greek Myths*:

> A study of Greek mythology should begin with a consideration of what political and religious systems existed in Europe before the arrival of the Aryan invaders from the distant North and East. The whole of neolithic Europe, to judge from surviving artifacts and myths, had a remarkably homogeneous system of religious ideas, based on worship of the many-titled Mother-goddess, who was also known in Syria and Libya. (p. 13)

Recent researches into the prehistory of Europe by archaeologists such as Marija Gimbutas show that the Mother Goddess was worshipped everywhere many thousands of years ago. But the period that saw the most evolved form of her worship was roughly between 3000 and 1200 B.C., in Sumer, Egypt, and the Mediterranean basin. There she was known as Inanna, Ishtar, and Isis, among other names. Reigning supreme as the Great Mother, she was honored with a glorious profusion of epithets: "Lady of Plants," "Lady of Beasts," "Mother of All," "Goddess of Love," "Protectress," and many more. This is why Graves refers to her as "many-titled." What these worshipful designations tell us is that as the supreme divinity, she encompassed all the possibilities of being—life, death, power, youth, age, wisdom, as well as the masculine and the feminine.

Although evidence of her worship has long since disappeared in Greece, we can get some idea of how she was thought of in the following "Hymn to the Goddess" from the matriarchal cult of Tantrism that has survived in India:

> Pure One
> Essence of All
> Knowledge
> Action
> The Supreme One

Giver of Buddhi [enlightenment]
Who Art All
Whose Love is Unbounded
Existence
Holder of Many Weapons
Virgin
Maiden
Youthful
Ascetic One
Old Mother
Giver of Strength . . .

The awesome totality and all-inclusiveness of the cosmic Goddess invoked here who is virgin *and* mother seems very alien to us today, (unless perhaps we reflect that in Christian theology it is permissible to think of God as *both* Father *and* Son), but this was indeed the way in which all the Mother goddesses of the high matriarchal era were regarded. And despite the fact that she had many names—Isis, Ashtoreth, Inanna, Gaia, Atana Potinija—she was everywhere essentially the same goddess (see figure 1).

In Greece the oldest goddess was Gaia, whose name means "earth." Except for the myths collected in Hesiod's *Theogony*, which tell of her marriage to the sky god, Ouranos, and her many progeny (the later gods), we know nothing of her cult as Great Mother. This unitive level of Greek religion disappeared pretty much without trace; we can only guess at it from looking at what did remain of the cult of Isis in Egypt, the worship of Inanna in Sumer or Cybele in Asia Minor, and other survivals.

But the complex history of Greek religion (which we will sketch below) shows us another process, an extremely important one looked at psychosocially, namely *the division of the goddess.* For as the various northern and Aryan tribes imposed their more patriarchal gods upon the older Mother religions, the Great Goddess and her powers were split up. This process, which must have gone on for nearly a thousand years (roughly between 1600 and 700 B.C.), led to the retention of the goddess, *but in a weakened form.* They became, in the words of the great classical scholar Jane E. Harrison *"departmental goddesses."* Thus Aphrodite becomes solely a goddess of love, Artemis is consigned to

The unity and universality of the Goddess

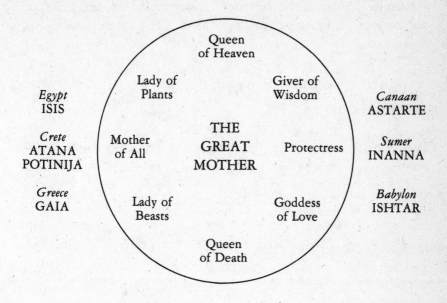

1. Matriarchal Religion in the Ancient World (c. 3000–1000 B.C.)

animals and the hunt, Hera is restricted to marriage, and so forth (see figure 2).

While this division gives these newer and more individual goddesses highly interesting archetypal personalities, it has one very far-reaching psychological consequence for the feminine. *Each of the departmental goddesses is now cut off from the original Mother, and they are from this point onward divided against themselves.* Here, very dramatically, is the historical origin of the deepest aspect of the goddess's wounds. Naturally the incursion of the patriarchal tribes and their suppression of the Mother cults was hardly a premeditated stratagem, but what it ultimately amounted to was the *de facto* imposition of a religious policy of "divide and rule." Individualized goddesses are tolerable to the extent that they function separately and even compete with other. So, for example, Aphrodite's character trait of promiscuity is set against Hera's patronage of matrimony. The result is that the fuller, more ancient solutions to marital and sexual relations that belonged to matriarchal consciousness, namely polyandry and polygamy, are lost and the feminine impulse is divided against itself.

EARLY GREEK RELIGION: A SYNOPSIS

Little is really known about the Neolithic Aegeans, the earliest inhabitants of the Greek peninsula, except that between 2500 and roughly

2. Patriarchal Conquest of Greece by Northern Tribes (1200–800 B.C.)

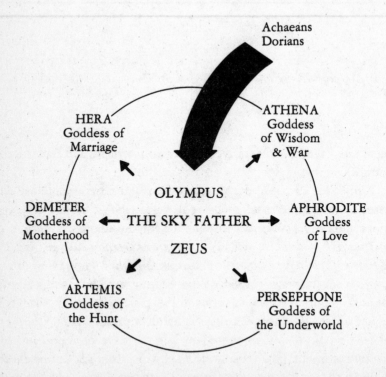

The division and dispersion of the Goddess

1600 B.C. they lived close to the land and were essentially a peasant culture, most likely matriarchal from the evidence of their artifacts. On the island of Crete a more advanced culture, the so-called Minoan civilization, flourished for nearly two thousand years, from roughly 3000 to 1000 B.C. Statuettes of priestesses (or goddesses?) have survived that, most experts believe, reflect aspects of a highly evolved form of Mother religion.

In the period between 2000 and 1600 B.C. numbers of Indo-European warrior tribes, called collectively the Aryans, migrated southward into the Aegean peninsula, bringing with them from the north their hunting gods and sky gods. Here is how the noted historian of religion E. O. James describes the arrival of these tribes:

> When the Indo-Europeans reached the pastures of Thessaly from southern Russia and the Balkans about 2000 B.C. and settled under the shadow of Mount Olympus, they brought with them their own sacred traditions and gods whom they installed on the misty Olympian heights under the leadership of Zeus. Having taken up their abode on the peninsula, they encountered the earlier inhabitants who had long been established not only in Greece but throughout the Aegean and its islands in the eastern Mediterranean. (*The Ancient Gods*, p. 41)

After a period of relatively peaceful integration with the indigenous races, the Indo-European tribes eventually arrived at a state of coexistence with them. A complex fusion of their cultures seems to have taken place, during which the matriarchal patterns and practices essentially became incorporated into, but not entirely suppressed by, the more patriarchal ways of the Aryans. Graves believes that the myths of Zeus seducing various nymphs refers to marriages between the Indo-European chieftains and local moon priestesses.

Out of this mixture of Aryan and Aegean there emerged a powerful warrior culture centered on the ancient fortified city of Mycenae, which flourished between 1600 and 1150 B.C. It was these proud warring and seafaring kings and their conquests that may have been the inspiration for Homer's *Iliad* and *Odyssey*. Homer called these people Achaeans. We know for certain that they rivaled the Minoans in maritime power.

The great Minoan palace of Knossos was destroyed in an earthquake around 1400 B.C., and either this or subsequent invasions brought to an end Minoan culture and with it any evolved form of matriarchal civilization. Many elements of their religious culture found their way to later classical Greece, probably exported by the Mycenaeans. The classicist Carl Kerényi believes that Dionysus derives from Crete, and the prototype of Athena may also be Cretan, according to Martin Nilsson.

Graves believes that the Achaeans (that is, the Mycenaeans) seriously weakened the matrilineal tradition whereby succession passed from *mother* to child. But its final death blow, according to him, came around 1200 B.C. from the Dorians, new invaders from the northwest who insisted on patrilineal succession and thereby set patriarchy firmly in place. The Dorians were militarily superior, driving the Achaeans to the outlying Ionian islands and farther afield. They were armed with iron weapons, and their warriors fought mounted on horseback against Achaean charioteers armed with bronze weapons. However, they left the social and religious culture essentially intact, except, of course, for reinforcing the supremacy of the patriarchal legacy.

How both the Dorians and, earlier, the Achaeans suppressed and depotentiated the old Mother Goddess cults is mirrored in numerous details of the mythic adventures of the gods and goddesses, as Graves shows in his copious notes in *The Greek Myths*. For example, the myth of Apollo slaying the monstrous snake, Python, is plainly a reference to the capture of the Cretan earth goddess's shrine. And when Perseus slays the serpent-haired Medusa, Graves sees behind this myth the destruction of an ancient cult of the goddess in which a monstrous Gorgon mask was worn to frighten away the uninitiated.

LATER GREEK POLYTHEISM

It is now generally agreed by scholars that male gods and heroes who belonged to the early invaders of Greece (such as Zeus, Apollo, Perseus, and Theseus) eventually supplanted many of the old Mother Goddess cults in eminence and authority. Nevertheless the matriarchal religious practices were never entirely suppressed, as we noted earlier. No edict ever went forth comparable to Yahweh's "Thou shalt have no other gods but me," by which the early Israelite fathers established their exclusive monotheism. Artemis, Demeter, Aphrodite, and the many other descendants of the Mother Goddess lived on in healthy profusion free of the kind of moral mudslinging the Hebrew prophets reserved for "the Whore of Babylon," as they called Ishtar. Hera's marriage to Zeus may well have symbolized the humiliating capitulation of the early Mother Goddess to the sky god intruder, but it does remain a marriage, even if a violent one.

Over the many centuries between the first northern invasions and the emergence of the city-states of Sparta and Athens in the sixth and fifth centuries B.C., the different but separate aspects of the more ancient Mother Goddess slowly evolved into the different cults we now associate with the preeminent goddesses we are discussing. And as Greek culture as a whole became more complex and diversified, so, it seems, did their gods and goddesses. It was during this essentially tolerant and pluralistic era that the goddesses became in many ways "departmentalized."

Since is was through military prowess and colonization that the city-state of Athens achieved its greatness, it was the martial aspects of their goddess, Athena, that the Athenians idealized. As Mother Goddess of their powerful city, her protectiveness, strength, brilliant resourcefulness, and love of warrior heroes were emphasized. The figure of Athena fully armed and dressed in armor was the spiritual guardian and inspiration of their culture. In many ways she was more of a consort to Zeus than was his official wife, Hera.

But if the city dwellers were devoted to a warrior maiden, always armed and ready for the fray, the peasants in the surrounding countryside continued to cherish Demeter. For Demeter was unquestionably the direct spiritual descendant of the Earth Mother, Gaia, and was thus indispensable to their lives because she sanctified the mysteries and cycles of the earth and nature that their agriculture so depended upon. Her cult is quite separate and distinct from Athena's. Because they ruled different areas of life in complex, evolving Greece, each of these two goddesses needed the other. Urban Athens needed food from the land, while the peasant economy needed military protection as well as supplemental foods imported by the Athenian sea merchants, since the Greek mainland was quite barren around Athens.

Nevertheless, despite all their complementarities, the way in which each of the major Greek goddesses actually survived to the present shows them all shorn, in one way or another, of their primordial power, which is to say, their all-encompassing power as Great Mother. Thus Artemis of Homeric epic becomes a rather charming adolescent goddess of the hunt, and, like Athena, is no longer a mother and is relatively powerless in the Olympian puppet government. Persephone, as benign mistress of the dead, has none of the awesome power of her more ancient predecessors in Sumer, Inanna and Ereshkigal. Demeter's agrarian functions and her dominion over the cycles of life and death are in many ways superseded by Athena's patronage—or rather matronage—of the Athenian warrior state. For Athenians, the warrior maid Athena was *he thea*, which means *the* goddess; motherhood as a feminine function has been lost in her image because it had come to mean less and less to a militaristic urban culture.

In sum, although the Mother Goddess was retained by the war-loving Greeks, her division into "departmental" roles left her weakened and seriously one-sided in her functions and powers. She was never her true self again. But in one way or another, the psychospiritual integrity of these goddesses, if not their actual cults, has survived throughout Western civilization. The Renaissance revived many of their icons and stories in countless paintings, such as Botticelli's Venus, and Shakespeare and later poets constantly invoked them. With extraordinary persistence the spirit of Athena reincarnates by changing her name to Britannia or Liberty and continuing to stand guard over the citadels of powerful nations. And despite her continued denigration, Aphrodite's spirit of love and beauty reemerges over and over again. If she had a temple today, it would probably be in Hollywood. Hera still lives among us in spirit too; she now runs the country club, an investment firm, or a chain of hotels. In fact, in one disguise or another the goddesses are still very much around, exercising their powerful influence in all of our lives.

And yet none of the goddesses, when they are rediscovered in the inner and outer lives of modern women, is entirely happy. None of them is complete in herself; each bears the wounds we have hinted at. The unified religion of the Mother Goddess has long since disappeared, but deep within every woman (and not a few men) is an unquenchable longing to return to the transcendent vision of wholeness, potency, and love the Great Mother once stood for.

HEALING THE FRACTURED GODDESSES

Obviously there is little chance of restoring the Great Mother to her primordial unified state. Indeed, it is highly debatable whether modern consciousness is really suited to that any longer. The compartmentalization of the Great Mother Goddess in many ways suits the complexity of our culture today, as it did that of ancient Greek civilization. But this does not mean that the separate functions each of the goddesses represents need to be forever alienated from one another, either in our collective social structures or in our individual psyches. It is surely time for the divide-and-rule setup that so suited patriarchal Greece to be abandoned.

The first thing the reader may notice is that the styles of each goddess chapter, as well as their contents, are very different. They were not planned that way. In fact we tried to impose a uniform shape upon each of them—but it didn't work! *It was as though the spirit of each goddess wanted to tell it from her perspective.* Once we honored this, we found that each chapter took on a unique flavor and structure. Aphrodite, for example, had a lot to say about relationships, while Athena gave them much less space. Hera insisted on talking at length about the male world and power, while Demeter ignored this entirely, favoring motherhood and children. All this was in character, so we just let it happen. Readers may notice a similar process going on in themselves. When you study a goddess deeply, you start to see and feel with her and through her. It is a powerful way of learning.

To summarize the characteristics and areas of influence of all six goddesses, we use the diagram we call the *Goddess Wheel*. In chapter 8 you will also find a *questionnaire* to help you explore the individual psychic mixes of the different goddess energies each of us has.

When we have a clear sense of which goddesses are dominant in us as women, and which strongly influence our lives as men, we then have a more difficult task. We need seriously to attend to those goddesses that are weak, neglected, or deeply wounded in us. Whether you feel inclined to or not, you will now need to read the goddess chapters you may have skimmed or avoided. (There is no particular order in which to read the six key chapters, although we have arranged them so that, as a sequence, one gains a cumulative picture of the archetypal division between matriarchal and patriarchal consciousness.)

As you read the chapters that are more alien to you, you may start to become aware of yet other areas in your life that are wounded. You will also naturally recognize in the goddess portraits your mother, sisters, lovers, and spouse and their issues.

Once you have some awareness of two or three goddesses that operate in you as women or draw you to them as men, you might want to experiment with observing your inner dialogues or even promoting some. Chapter 9, "Reconciling Your Inner Goddesses," was designed mostly for women and gives examples from our workshops of what such dialogues sound like. As you read them, you will most likely find yourself taking sides—a good starting point for your own dialogues. For men, we have a chapter specifically on relationships with the goddess types (chapter 10); this, of course, can be useful for women as well.

Dialoguing, either with friends or in a private journal, is the first stage in healing the goddess's wounds. If we can't get the Athena in us to at least acknowledge her alienation from our inner Demeter, what hope is there of solving our children-versus-career problems? Once we encourage the conflicted goddesses to consciously interact with one another within our own psyches or among our circle of friends, we can begin to stimulate enormous energy. Such energy can bring the goddesses out of those stagnant, hopeless, or isolated places where we carry them. It can create powerful opportunities for review and change. (In appendix A we suggest all kinds of ways of setting this in motion, based on the experience of workshops, group dynamics, and community celebrations.)

It is all too easy to develop and live by only one goddess in us. When we do this, we become one-sided, or what Jung would call neurotic. We are then caught in the compulsive "divisiveness" of the archetypal complex, which is what collectively we seem to have inherited from the Greeks.

A woman can get stuck in being only the matriarch of a family (Hera) by never working (neglecting Athena) and never addressing her sexuality (ignoring Aphrodite) or her inner world (Persephone). This invites the brittle, neurotic behavior and temperament of a one-sided goddess, a mere stereotype of Hera. Equally, a man who flees from intellectual women (Athena), avoids motherly women (Demeter) or strong women (Hera), and seeks only exciting sex partners is really stuck in a neurotic attachment to Aphrodite.

We all desperately need to listen to the goddesses in ourselves and learn to recognize them in others. We need to exchange the stories, laughter, tears, games, and celebrations of the goddesses. All the goddesses have stories to tell, contributions to make, wisdom to share: where Aphrodite risks all for love, Hera fears a broken marriage; where Demeter delights in her children, Persephone cherishes inwardness and visions; where Athena seeks upward mobility, Artemis longs for her cabin in the woods. Yet each knows something the others don't. Inwardly or outwardly the goddess energies can form a richly satisfying community of exchange among women and men.

As the various stories of the goddesses come alive while you reflect on them, you will notice different parts of your life becoming touched and activated. For example, if you attempt to open up a dialogue with your friends about their awareness of the different goddesses, you may suddenly find problem areas of your own life illuminated and freed as you start to see your world through the eyes of a different goddess, now incarnated in one of your friends or in some new acquaintance.

In this and many other ways we can bring the goddesses and the language of goddess psychology to life among our friends, our family, and our workmates. When we do, we may find that a powerful energy dynamic is slowly forming all around us and that all kinds of subtle changes are occurring. It is a cause for rejoicing: the lost goddesses are coming back into our lives!

PART ONE

THE GODDESS WHEEL

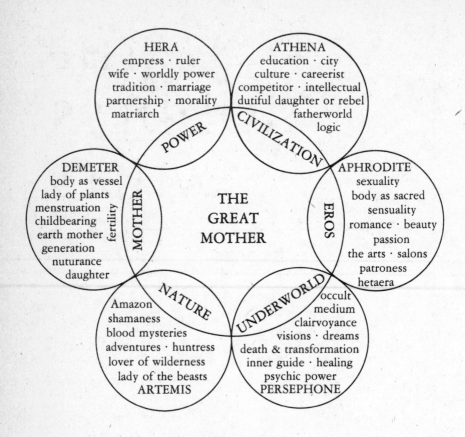

HERA
empress · ruler
wife · worldly power
tradition · marriage
partnership · morality
matriarch

ATHENA
education · city
culture · careerist
competitor · intellectual
dutiful daughter or rebel
fatherworld
logic

POWER

CIVILIZATION

DEMETER
body as vessel
lady of plants
menstruation
childbearing
earth mother
generation
nuturance
daughter

fertility

MOTHER

THE
GREAT
MOTHER

EROS

APHRODITE
sexuality
body as sacred
sensuality
romance · beauty
passion
the arts · salons
patroness
hetaera

NATURE

UNDERWORLD

Amazon
shamaness
blood mysteries
adventures · huntress
lover of wilderness
lady of the beasts
ARTEMIS

occult
medium
clairvoyance
visions · dreams
death & transformation
inner guide · healing
psychic power
PERSEPHONE

The Goddess Wheel

INTRODUCING THE GODDESS WHEEL: AN OVERVIEW

Throughout this book the reader will find repeated cross-references to different goddesses. Until you have studied each of the major goddess chapters in this section, this may be somewhat confusing. To help learn the six goddess types and their interrelationships, we suggest that you refer to the diagram of *the Goddess Wheel* for a quick overview of major themes. The purpose of this chapter is to sketch this overview and explain various concepts and the terms we use.

THE SIX MAJOR GODDESSES

Each section of the Wheel summarizes the attributes of a particular goddess and gives her major area of influence, her *rulership*. Here are the six goddesses described in terms of major areas and styles of life they pursue:

Athena rules everything to do with *civilization*, which is to say all aspects of cities, urban life, and what we call "civilized" pursuits, which may include anything that maintains the city or the nation-state it commands. Athena rules technology and science and all practical crafts, as well as the literary arts, education, and intellectual life in all its forms. For the modern woman living in the city, Athena would guide all aspects of her career, her profession, and how she relates to the patriarchal world of the city fathers.

Aphrodite rules *love and eros*, which is to say all aspects of sexuality, intimacy, and personal relationships. Because hers is the power to entice and attract the senses, she is the goddess of beauty and hence of all the visual arts, such as painting, sculpture, and architecture, as well as poetry and music. She is a "cultured" goddess like Athena in the sense that her influence is private, but she is individual rather than public and collective. Thus she rules salons, artistic inspiration, and all creative liaisons between the sexes.

As queen of the dead, **Persephone** rules over all aspects of contact with the *underworld*, the spirit world or the realm of the departed. She is consciously or unconsciously in contact with the greater transpersonal powers of the psyche traditionally called spirits, the ones Jung called the archetypes. In modern psychological terms we could say that she rules over the deeper unconscious mind, the dream world, and everything to do with paranormal or psychic phenomena and mysticism. She is thus concerned with mediumship or channeling, visionary capacity, occult matters, and areas of psychic healing covered by certain forms of psychotherapy. Because she is a goddess of the dead, she will be present in any event or situation where a death or tragic loss occurs. She also rules all minor losses, separations, and traumas.

As ruler of the wilds, **Artemis** is a goddess of *nature* in its virgin or untamed form. She stands in strict contrast to Athena, who represents nature tamed and civilized. Artemis is especially close to animals and the hunt and those cycles of nature that rule the animal as much as the human world; she is also a goddess of midwifery. A moon goddess, she rules over all instinctual life, emphasizing the body rather than the head (as Athena would) and living for all physical, practical, and outdoor activities, which today include athletics and dance. Since she is concerned with instinctual nature and hunting, she rules over killing and blood sacrifice. She complements and aids Persephone in regard to death: Artemis understands the death of the body; Persephone, the passage of its spirit. Artemis is related to the ancient practice of shamanism, which incorporates both.

The most direct descendant of the ancient Earth Mother goddess, **Demeter** is the goddess of *motherhood* and everything connected with the reproductive functions, particularly the inner experience of the menstrual and childbearing cycles. Because she rules seed and fruit, she is sometimes called the Lady of Plants. This symbolizes her deep connection to all aspects of food, growth, the cycles of the crops, and to harvesting and preserving. She is intimately bound up with nurturing and caring for the organic growth of the body. Most of her energy goes toward nurturing and caring for all infants, children, and growing creatures.

Hera is queen of heaven, or Olympus, and is concerned with *power and rulership.* As the wife of the god Zeus, she rules over marriage, partnership, and all public roles where a woman has power, responsibility, or leadership. Very much concerned with social morality and the upholding of the integrity of the family, she also oversees all aspects of tradition and the cohesiveness of the larger community. In this she shares something of Athena's vision of civilized life and the maintenance of patriarchal values, symbolized by her husband, Zeus. When her power is restricted only to the family arena, she becomes the undisputed family matriarch.

CONTRASTS AND COMMONALITIES: THE GODDESS DYADS

One clue to the basic perspectives of the six goddesses is that they arrange themselves very easily into opposite pairs on the Wheel, thus graphically suggesting certain common areas as well as major contrasts. We call these the three *Goddess Dyads.* As you get to know them, you will notice that these pairs have distinct complementary qualities.

One dyad that we have already noted is between **Artemis and Athena.** As goddesses of the wilds, on the one hand, and civilization, on the other, they are strongly contrasted. And yet they share two major qualities: both carry weapons in quite masculine warrior fashion, and neither has a consort or male lover. We call this opposing pair on the Goddess Wheel the **dyad of independence,** because these two goddesses are temperamentally much more inclined to live and work alone than with a mate. Even when married, they require very independent, unfettered styles of partnership. In the ancient world they were "virgin" goddesses, which simply meant *unmarried*. (Chastity as a component of virginity is largely an overlaid patriarchal value, as we explain in the Artemis and Aphrodite chapters.)

Their different worlds also reflect different styles of companionship. Athena is more extraverted, liking to work as part of a team of associates in the bustle and competition of the city; Artemis is more of an introvert, preferring to work alone, far from the madding crowd, with perhaps one or two close friends or in a specially chosen community of like-minded loners.

But because they are so temperamentally close in their independent spirits, both aspects of the Athena-Artemis dyad may show up in a woman. It is not uncommon to find a younger woman moving from the city to the country or vice versa in different phases of her life. On the other hand, if only one pole of this dyad is developed, many women find it relatively easy to develop the other.

A second contrasting pair of opposites is discernible in **Hera and Persephone,** though this is perhaps less immediately obvious. Their most extreme difference is how they relate to the outer and inner worlds. It is as though Hera, as supreme extravert, chooses to concern herself only with the outer world, whereas Persephone, as introvert, spurns the outer world for her inner psychic realm of the spirits. Yet, as queens of heaven and of the underworld they are both concerned with having control over their different worlds. Therefore we call theirs the **dyad of power.**

Because their worldviews are so different and their ego formations so opposite—Hera's ego is extremely strong, Persephone's weak to the point of permeability by her spirits—it is hard for them to appreciate and understand each other. Nevertheless they have much to learn from each other if they can let go of their individual prejudices. Hera often needs to go inward, Persephone to come out of her shell.

The remaining pair of contrasting opposites is that of **Demeter and Aphrodite.** Since they are both concerned with love in different ways, we call theirs the **dyad of love.** We can see in them a subtle contrast between how they express love and how they experience their bodies. Demeter reserves her love for her children, serving as a selfless container for all her loved ones both physically and spiritually. Aphrodite nurtures spiritually and physically, but not by containing or mothering those she loves. What she gives to her lover is his (or her) full maturity and otherness. She loves the adult rather than the child. Demeter's style of love is more introverted, carrying her loved ones always in her heart, no matter where they are, whereas Aphrodite, an extravert, is only fulfilled by the physical presence of her lover.

For Demeter the body is a sacred vessel, for Aphrodite it is a sacred love object, a thing of beauty. It is often difficult for an Aphrodite woman to fully enjoy her first pregnancy or for a Demeter woman to fully appreciate her body aesthetically, because they both experience and treat their body and its functions so differently. Nevertheless, they can both learn and share from the other's styles of loving and embodiment.

All three dyads arrange themselves broadly around the temperamental orientations of introversion and extraversion:

Dyad:	Independence	Power	Love
Extraverted:	Athena	Hera	Aphrodite
Introverted:	Artemis	Persephone	Demeter

In this respect the Wheel divides itself diagonally down the middle, the three goddesses concerned more with outer realities on the upper right, those goddesses inclined more toward inwardness on the lower left. Only Demeter does not entirely fit this scheme, being blessed with a healthy mixture of introverted love and extraverted energy to care for her children and family. We should also add that Aphrodite is very private, too, in her intimacy in that she often explores a form of soul-searching or mutual introversion with her lovers.

THE GODDESSES AND THEIR MASCULINE COMPLEMENTS: THE ANIMUS

Each goddess has a distinctly different relationship to the masculine, either in terms of the kind of male figures that appear in her individual myths or in terms of the particular form of masculine psychic energy that each goddess has harnessed within herself. Hera and Persephone both have husbands or consorts, which, ideally, suggests some kind of equal power sharing. Aphrodite and Demeter have relationships that are defined more by their styles of love. Although Artemis and Athena are "virgin" goddesses who have no marital or ongoing close relationships, they manifest masculine qualities as the huntress and the warrior woman.

In the following chapters we shall explore the way each of the goddesses relates to men and to the masculine as inner energy in varying degrees. However, there is more to say about certain goddesses—Aphrodite, for example—and less to say about others—Athena is a good example—so you can expect these sections of their chapters to be somewhat disproportionate. The patterns of all six goddesses are summarized in chapter 10, "Living with the Goddesses."

In the Goddess Wheel we refer in shorthand to the most typical relationship styles each goddess has with the opposite sex, calling the male counterpart her *animus*. This is Jung's term for the masculine element of every woman's psyche that is carried within her and that determines how she will be attracted to or repelled by certain kinds of men. Each of the goddesses is drawn to men who complement her style of femininity.

These, in brief are the common animus counterparts of each of the goddesses:

Athena relates to men as heroic "companions in arms," with whom she shares ideals, ambitions, career goals, and struggles. Frequently he will be an intellectual companion or friendly rival. She will not necessarily marry such men, maintaining instead close and enduring friendships. She is also drawn to father figures and usually has strong bonds to nonpersonal authority as invested in the institutions of the patriarchy or in spiritual ideals. She may also be in conflict with the fatherworld.

Her major animus counterparts are therefore the **companion hero** and the **father.**

Aphrodite admires the virility of a man. She engages the phallic power of the male as either **lover** or **warrior.** She admires success and combativeness in her men, but isn't too interested in being out there fighting with them, like Athena, since her chief area of engagement is the boudoir or the salon. She is happy with multiple relationships or extramarital affairs, but will marry (and divorce) as it suits her. She also attracts **creative men** and often acts as a patroness or inspirer of their artistic works.

Persephone is enamored more of the spirit than of incarnated males and will frequently have male **spirit guides** in her channeling or her mystical practices. Her deep and fatalistic involvement in the darker sides of life will mean that she unwittingly attracts destructive men—the **Dark Lord**—and will sometimes marry them, with disastrous results. To protect herself from this, she often chooses the safe, but unsatisfactory alternative of a younger or soft, nonthreatening man whose masculine side is underdeveloped and whom she can safely mother and manipulate. Her type of animus is best described as the **son lover.**

Artemis, in her independence, has so much masculine energy already integrated into her personality structure that she doesn't have strong needs for a man to complement her. Nevertheless, she, like Athena, enjoys a companionable male who will work alongside her in her practical pursuits. Marriage is not, as a rule, looked for, but is tolerated if her freedom is respected. Sexuality is often buried, and she can be quite shy, so she appreciates reserve and diffidence in a man. Her mythic brother, Apollo, models something of the distant friendship she wants from a man. **Friend, companion,** or **brother** best describes her animus counterpart.

Demeter is not particularly interested in sexuality or intellectual relationships, but she needs someone to bring home the bacon. She is best matched with a strong, reliable **earth father** as her mate. But since she has so much abundant mother energy, she has an irresistible tendency to mother all the men around her, regardless of their ages, and turn them into sons to idealize as heroes. Her other animus we describe as the **son hero.**

Hera wants a man to be her **partner** and ideally someone who will share his power equally with her. She wants only strong, successful men who are leaders or, if possible, **rulers,** as was Zeus, her mythic husband. Partnership for her means marriage, so she will usually only relate closely to one man, her husband. In this she is basically monogamous. She will always seek to marry a man for his worldly power and the social prestige he carries. She wants to pass his good name on to her children. Since she is attracted to the masculine energy of rulership, she herself will want either to rule her family as the matriarch or to rule some institution.

THE GODDESS WHEEL AS A LIVING DYNAMIC

This broad orientation should be helpful in understanding the pushes and pulls of the goddesses in your life. These are what we call the *dynamics* of the Goddess Wheel, the living energy that derives from the tension of opposites we all carry within us in infinite, individual combinations. As we become more open to these energies in our lives, we will find that we can harness them and not be torn apart by them. In part 3 of this book, we introduce dialogues between the goddesses to show how these dynamic tensions can be used creatively.

The Wheel is designed like a flower. The six goddesses, like petals, radiate from the Great Mother at the center, who symbolizes the transcendent unity of all the goddesses belonging to a broader, transpersonal level of being that we call archetypal or universal. Although this is a unity that a single individual can rarely achieve, we can catch glimpses of it from time to time. In addition, we need the diversity of experience that the different goddesses can bring us in our ordinary lives.

As we suggested in our introduction, each of the Greek forms of the goddess emanated originally from the Great Mother Goddess of more ancient times. Any psychological work that you undertake in getting to know a particular goddess may take you deeper into that goddess and *closer to the center of the Wheel.* What you may find is that at their deeper levels—which correspond to the older forms of the Goddess—they tend to overlap and merge with one another.

So, for example, in their deepest and oldest forms Artemis and

Demeter share regenerative earth power over all living things, be they animals, plants, or humans. Or, if we dig deeply into Persephone's connections to the death realm and into the fierce side of Artemis, the huntress, we find in both of them images of the ancient death goddess as Terrible Mother who destroys and demands blood sacrifice. Athena and Artemis also both share aspects of the avenger and the protectress of the Terrible Mother; after all, both bear arms as goddesses. And if we look at Hera and Aphrodite, we find that they share the same motif of uniting the masculine and the feminine energies, one in marriage, the other in sexual union. In their most ancient form they were united in these functions.

TWO

ATHENA:
WARRIOR WOMAN
IN THE WORLD

*There is no mother anywhere who gave me birth,
and, but for marriage, I am always for the male
with all my heart, and strongly on my father's side.*
—AESCHYLUS, *THE EUMENIDES*

RECOGNIZING ATHENA TODAY

It's easy to spot Athena in the modern world. She's out there in every sense of the word. Editing magazines, running women's-studies departments in colleges, hosting talk shows, making fact-finding tours to Nicaragua, producing films, challenging the local legislature.

The Athena woman is very visible because she is an extravert, she's practical, and she's intelligent. Men are often a little intimidated by her at first because she doesn't respond to the usual sexual gambits and she will push them to the wall in any intellectual argument. When they have won her respect, she can be the most loyal of companions, a lifelong friend, and a generous fund of inspiration. Understandably Athena was called the companion of heroes by the Greeks.

How different from the equally independent, but much shyer goddess Artemis, who shuns the busy world of the city in favor of the wild and natural places: the woods, the mountains, or the ocean. Since Athena's energy is almost wholly extraverted, her concerns are mostly worldly: people and ideas, the bustle of the marketplace, the arena of political debate, the creation and implementation of social reforms. As the companion of heroes she can be sensitive to the way men get along with each other and can help bind groups together. The companionate spirit that the Greek warriors fantasized in their myths is today a flesh-and-blood reality as she works alongside men in the fields of business, politics, or education.

In fact, Athena's ancient ability to bind the Athenian polis together under a common cause or ideal is now felt in a whole new way, a way that is slowly transforming contemporary society. No longer just a symbol of intellectual and social creativity, her spirit is everywhere embodied in the millions of women at work in all levels of society. Until recently our patriarchal society has given Athena little opportunity to develop and manifest herself fully. There have been notable, but rather rare cases of fully incarnate Athenas: Joan of Arc, Queen Elizabeth I, and Eleanor of Aquitaine, but even these latter two were assisted by some powerful Hera energy too. But until the eighteenth and nineteenth centuries, with the emergence of women writers and reformers, she was rarely allowed to be much more than a military emblem, as in England's Britannia, America's Liberty, or France's Marianne.

But even if women could not emerge in ancient Greece and take their place beside the heroes, as Athena did in the myths, the longing must have been there. The myth of the Amazons, a society of fierce warrior women who lived almost entirely without men, can be recognized as an expression of the longing born of frustrated Athena energy, which has, in the Amazons, fused with the spirit of her independent sister, Artemis, who embodies a love of the wilderness. The political and intellectual emergence of women that has been building so strongly since the beginning this century may well represent the rebirth of Athena, so long frustrated by the patriarchy.

ATHENA CONSCIOUSNESS TODAY

Though the battle has not been won on any front, Athena is far less a solitary voice crying in the wilderness today than was a lone George Eliot or a defiant suffragette like Mrs. Pankhurst. It no longer requires a private fortune or uncommon fortitude for a woman to publish a book or influence public policy. The days of unsung Athenas languishing in the suburbs or backwoods writing never-to-be-published novels, and being tyrannized like the heroines of Balzac, Ibsen, and Henry James are finally drawing to a close.

Greatly improved literacy and coeducation permit any Athena woman who is so inclined to enter and change "the system." So many women are in fact accepting this heroic challenge that a whole new psychology of the intelligent, creative woman in the world needs to be written. It is our belief that the inspiration for such a psychology is to be found in reflecting upon the images of wisdom, heroic courage, and practical creativity given to us in the transcendent feminine of Athena.

The Athena woman of today has amply demonstrated that she can be an excellent politician, social organizer, administrator, or researcher. Her fighting spirit enables her to be right at the forefront of new ventures, whether in business, education, or social work. She is tireless, courageous, and practical. She shares with men the heroic virtues of loyalty, perseverance, and single-mindedness; in modern terms she is successful and an achiever. Men are naturally a little in awe of her competence and sharp mind; accustomed to being looked up to for advice, they are having to recognize in the Athena woman of today independence and, often, superiority. For although she works well alongside men, she is not a girl Friday; she rightly requires respect, equal responsibility, and autonomy.

The Athena woman's independence of men is a quality she shares with her sister Artemis. Both figures in Greek myth are armed, and neither of them has a lover or consort. In fact, they were both regarded as virgin goddesses, which in the ancient world meant simply unmarried. Both embody masculine and feminine attributes in their archetypal characters. The fact that neither Athena nor Artemis ever married means, psychologically, that they have integrated the masculine within themselves and do not need a male partner or consort to reflect or bear contrasexual qualities such as aggressiveness, rationality, or authority (see box, "Jean Shinoda Bolen on Athena"). Hence, in the modern world, since they have worked so many things out for themselves, depending on a man is almost beyond their comprehension. Why Hera needs a mate or Aphrodite tolerates an immature lover is often a mystery to Athena.

If Athena has a partner at all, he will have to be a man who reflects her own androgynous independence, a man with a strongly integrated feminine component who takes care of his own emotional needs and prefers to share with her on an intellectual level or in doing projects together. Most of all, he must have the self-confidence not to be threatened by her autonomy and ambitions.

Yet despite her strength, brilliance, and independence, there is a paradox contained in the traditional image of a maid clad in armor. It seems to us that the more energy the Athena woman puts into developing her successful, worldly, armored self, the more she hides her maidenly vulnerability. So, within her androgyny Athena conceals a conflict, an unresolved tension between her tough outer self and her hidden, unexpressed self that can be a source of great insecurity with regard to her finding an integral feminine identity. We have found this to be present in almost all the Athena women we know and have worked with. We call it Athena's wound. It is a complex theme that we will return to later in this chapter.

ATHENA IN GREEK MYTH AND RELIGION

Who was Athena to the ancient Greeks?

In her closeness to the supreme god—her father, Zeus—the goddess Athena occupies a place of eminence in the Greek pantheon. As Pallas Athena, the Maiden Warrior and patroness of the city of Athens, she came to stand for the highest spiritual ideals and creations of fifth century B.C. Greek patriarchy. Her temple, the Parthenon (*parthenos* means "virgin"), still dominates the Acropolis in Athens, even though the enormous statue of her, complete with javelin, spear, and helmet has long since disappeared. Scholars disagree about her origins; most believe she was derived from a Mycenaean martial goddess whose func-

JEAN SHINODA BOLEN ON ATHENA

In her important psychological survey *Goddesses in Everywoman*, Jean Bolen challenges the Jungian assumption that thinking in a woman is somehow an inferior activity belonging to her masculine side, which Jungians call the *animus*. Athena for her is a powerful example of the autonomously thinking feminine:

> Athena is a feminine archetype: she shows that thinking well, keeping one's head in the heat of an emotional situation, and developing good tactics in the midst of conflict, are natural traits for some women. Such a woman is being like Athena, not acting "like a man." Her masculine aspect, or animus, is not doing the thinking for her—she is thinking clearly and well for herself. The concept of Athena as an archetype for logical thinking challenges the Jungian premise that thinking is done for a woman by her masculine animus, which is presumed to be distinct from her feminine ego. When a woman recognizes the keen way her mind works as a feminine quality related to Athena, she can develop a positive image of herself, instead of fearing that she is mannish (that is, inappropriate).
>
> When Athena represents only one of several archetypes active in a particular woman—rather than a single dominant pattern—then this archetype can be an ally of other goddesses. For example, if she is motivated by Hera to need a mate to feel complete, then Athena can help assess the situation and develop a strategy to get her man. Or, if Artemis is the guiding inspiration for a women's health collective or a women's studies center, the success of the project may depend on the political acumen of Athena. In the midst of an emotional storm, if a woman can call on Athena as an archetype in herself, rationality will help her to find or keep her bearings.

—*Goddesses in Everywoman*, pp. 78–79

tion was to defend the citadels in time of war, and some have claimed that her name etymologically means "vulva," which suggests that at one time she was none other than the Great Mother herself.

The most popular myth of her birth, however, makes it clear that Athena was later considered very much a father's daughter. One of the older mother goddesses, the Titaness Metis, was made pregnant by Zeus, and fearing lest she have a son who would depose him, he swallowed the goddess whole. Later a full-grown, fully armed warrior goddess emerged from Zeus's head (see box, "The Myth of Athena's Birth").

There is undoubtedly a political allegory in this myth of the way the more patriarchal invading tribes who worshipped their Father God, Zeus, assimilated the earlier matriarchal cults. But the name of this earlier goddess, Metis, is also very suggestive of the way men assume certain powers for themselves that are not necessarily their birthright. The word *metis* means "wise counsel," which is the attribute Athena is most valued for on Olympus. She confides to Odysseus: "Among all the gods, I boast of my intelligence [*metis*] and my skill" (*Odyssey*, book 13). Hesiod even considers her "equal to her father in strength and prudent wisdom" (*Theogony*, 896).

Athena was actually the only Olympian to have no true mother; instead she stands as supreme representative of the wisdom of the father born symbolically out of the Olympian head of state. In this sense she restores the wisdom (*metis*) that Zeus has digested and transformed, but which he still needs to manifest externally in female form. She is what Jung would call Zeus's anima, his creative feminine self. As such she symbolizes the highest inspiration for the amazing intellectual and spiritual fecundity that produced the sublime drama, philosophy, political institutions, and arts that we associate with the Golden Age of Athens.

If Athena's relationship to the life of the head is emphasized, her connection to her female body receives the opposite treatment. Whatever is soft and feminine about her maidenhood is hidden beneath layers of protective armor, and almost to make sure men get the "stay away" message, she carries the hideous skinned head of the Gorgon, Medusa, on her breastplate. This gruesome snake-haired relic comes from the adventure she inspired in one of her hero protégés, Perseus,

THE MYTH OF ATHENA'S BIRTH

A *Homeric Hymn* tells the story of Athena's birth, emphasizing her close connection to Father Zeus:

> I begin to sing about Pallas Athena, renowned goddess, with bright eyes, quick mind, and inflexible heart, chaste and mighty virgin, protectress of the city, Tritogeneia. Wise Zeus himself gave birth to her from his holy head and she was arrayed in her armor of war, all-gleaming in gold and every one of the immortals was gripped with awe as they watched. She quickly sprang forth from the immortal head in front of aegis-bearing Zeus, brandishing her sharp spear. And great Olympus shook terrible at the might of the bright-eyed goddess and the earth round about gave a dread groan and the dark waves of the deep seethed. But suddenly the sea became calm, and the glorious son of Hyperion halted his swift-footed horses all the while that the maiden Pallas took the divine armor from her immortal shoulders, and Zeus in his wisdom rejoiced. So hail to you, child of aegis-bearing Zeus; I shall remember both you and another song too.
> —*Homeric Hymn to Athena*, trans. Lang

Yet an earlier version of the myth by Hesiod adds an important dimension, namely that Athena had originally been fathered on a mother goddess, Metis:

> Zeus had gotten Metis the Titaness with child and fearing an oracle that it would be a boy child who would depose him he enticed Metis and swallowed her. But the child continued to grow inside Zeus and eventually he had such terrible headaches that he summoned Hephaistos, the smith, to cleave open his skull with an axe. With a wild battle cry, out leapt Athena, fully armed.
> —Hesiod, *Theogony*, 887–902

whose task it was to slay the monstrous female no man could look upon without turning to stone.

Given her preference for the company of young heroes and warriors in their war games and quests, Athena would be a tomboy were she a mortal. Actually, it is heroism, not warmongering, she truly admires, as she makes clear in her loathing of Ares, the war god of the *Iliad*. Perseus and Herakles (Hercules) are especially cherished by her, but it is Odysseus, the man "of many counsels" (*polymetis*) she most loves. Loves, that is, in the sense of intense sisterly friendship, for the goddess Athena rejects marriage and sexuality in any form. The goddess of love, Aphrodite, had no power over her, according to a Homeric hymn to Aphrodite. So we find her in Homer's epics as the loyal, ever-present, inspiring spiritual companion of the great heroes, urging them to quick-witted response and sharpening their practical intelligence.

[handwritten note in margin: like me when I was younger]

As in war, so, too, in peace, it is practical inventiveness she most inspires. In Athens she became a patroness of weavers, metalworkers, and joiners, in fact of all craftsmen. As the city and its dominions and colonies became more powerful, she became more and more of a spiritual force, along with her father, Zeus, behind the expansion of early Greek civilization (see box, "Athena, Patroness of the Athenian City-state").

ATHENA AND URBAN CIVILIZATION

Popular stories of Athena's close patronage of the restless masculine energy and activities of the early Athenians as well as the unmistakable symbol of her birth from her father's head clearly provided a valuable political expedient for an emerging but precarious patriarchy that was working to incorporate an older and more dispersed matriarchal tradition. It was also inevitable that the concentration of military power that created Athens as it moved from peasant to urban society would produce a new kind of esprit de corps, or group feeling, within this new society. Athena was thus an archetypal embodiment of the civic pride of the urban warrior state. The rise of Athens, as we know from history, owed its strength not to the land around it, but rather to its military prowess in conquest and colonization.

For the urban Athenians the agrarian Mother Goddess, Demeter,

ATHENA, PATRONESS OF THE ATHENIAN CITY-STATE

Carl Kerényi has given us a superb summary of Athena's many roles and benefices in ancient Athens, where she was the preeminent goddess of the city dwellers:

She is the rescuer from every danger and peril, the advisor for every tight spot, and the highest wisdom. The people's chiefs and leaders, as well as the whole people itself, are advised by her; she presides over all local, tribal, and national gatherings. She maintains life and health. She is the gracious, gentle nurse who takes the children of mankind to herself, who makes mothers fertile and children grow and develop, who increases the stock of the people through a strong younger generation. She preserves the divine order in nature, protects the seedlings and fruits from damage, sows and tends the noble and nourishing olive trees; she teaches men how to manufacture and plow, how to yoke oxen, and how to loosen up the hard ground with the rake. From her mankind receives the materials for all the arts that beautify life, and from her their skillfulness. She gave mankind the bridle so that he could master the horse for his own use. Shipbuilders work under her inspiration. She is enthroned protectively on the headlands, stirring up and stilling the storms. To her the sailor offers thanks as he happily steps to land at his desired goal. She guides the wanderer and the stranger safely over sea and land, and she accompanies the heroes on their adventures, fills them with courage, and saves them from danger. But she is also righteous, strictly recompensing Providence: seated beside Zeus, she is the only one who knows where the lightning bolts lie hidden, has the full right and power to use them, and also employs the aegis, the terrible shield of her father Zeus. With him she has many traits and epithets in common and she is frequently worshipped jointly with him, especially in the most ancient sites of her cult.

—*Athene: Virgin and Mother*, p. 8–9

receded in both social and psychological importance as their aggressive and mentally hyperactive culture continued to expand. ("They are adventurous beyond their power, and daring beyond their judgment . . . one might truly say that they were born into the world to take no rest themselves and to give none to others," Thucydides wrote of the Athenians.) Because she somehow focused and sublimated this powerful energy for them, the Athenians instituted their own major cult, the Panathenic Festival, to celebrate the power of the maiden goddess. Thousands eventually flocked from all around Athens to the Parthenon every four years.

Up to this time the major religious festival had been in the country town of Eleusis and was held in honor of Demeter and her daughter, Kore-Persephone. On this solemn occasion the whole populace would move in procession out of the city to join thousands of country folk at the sacred well in the tiny village where the goddess had bestowed her mysteries upon mankind (see Demeter chapter). This gradual reversal of the importance of sacred sites, particularly in the Athenian psyche, can be seen as a highly significant metaphor of the way Greek consciousness was beginning to shift toward the city. Traditionally it had been the custom to move away from the city to celebrate the earth as Mother. But now the movement was more and more *away* from the earth to the city and its values as Mother.

The Panathenic Festival of Athena and the Eleusinian Mysteries of Demeter were cultic expressions, then, of the psychic needs of the people for radically different kinds of goddesses: the first, for what has been called by anthroplogist John Layard a *culture mother*; the second for a *nature mother*. Whereas Demeter had satisfied the other and deeper needs of matriarchal consciousness to be connected to the cy-

clical mysteries of the earth and regeneration, Athena as culture mother
served to unite the city dwellers of Athens throughout the trials and
triumphs of both peace and war. In peacetime her "wise counsel"
helped them evolve those social, artistic, and intellectual institutions
that made Athens unique in the ancient world. In war her virginity and
strength symbolized the impenetrability and spiritual purity of the city
herself against all onslaughts:

> Dear city of men without master or lord.
> Fair fortress and fortress of sons born free.
> Who stand in her sight and in thine, O sun.
> Slaves of no man, subjects of none.
>
> —Swinburne, *Erectheus*

Even if, as the classicist Jane E. Harrison regretted, Athena became
"something of an abstraction, an unreality," her unifying power as
mother of the state (*metropolis* = *mater-polis*) has created an archetypal
personification of immense charisma and influence on men's and
women's imaginations ever since.

Whenever powerful city-states, and hence "civilization" (*cives*
means "city dweller"), arise, the spirit of Athena in myths, legends, or
her rare incarnations tends to emerge. In Joan of Arc she became a
martyr. Athena was present when thousands of English seamen cheered
young armor-clad Queen Elizabeth I when she rode to Tilbury docks
to rouse the English navy. Nor was Athena very far from the consciousness of Prime Minister Margaret Thatcher in her Falklands adventure of recent years. Though armor is no longer in fashion for such
occasions, the press, nevertheless, dubbed her "the Iron Lady" from
early on!

Whenever national or imperial unity is required or patriotic feelings need stirring up, Athena emerges in crude jingoistic songs like
"Britannia Rules the Waves" or political posters like that of Marianne
leading the French Revolution. America's icon is a little deceptive.
Although we have rejected the European fathers for an ideal of "moth-
erland," the celebrated statue, with its sentimental verse, seems to
proclaim a Demeter who will feed all comers. She nevertheless is called
Liberty, a distinctly Athenean epithet, and moreover she has her militaristic assistant in Uncle Sam to aid in conscription when needed.

ATHENA, ANCIENT AND MODERN

Human incarnations of the Athena spirit, as in Joan of Arc or Queen Elizabeth, have occurred quite seldom in Western history (see box, "Outstanding Athena Women in History"). Until modern times, it has been easier to find patriotic icons or fictitious heroines, such as Shakespeare's Rosalind or Defoe's Moll Flanders, than actual incarnations of her archetype. Just how extraordinary this is becomes apparent if we reflect that throughout history women have easily come to know some, though not all, of the other goddesses directly in their lives. Most women have experienced the power of Demeter in becoming mothers, just as many know Aphrodite's passion from falling in love. But to experience Athena power has been rare until recently. However much the citizens of Athens owed to her as their supreme culture mother, she was kept firmly in her place on Olympus and in no way offered as a model for actual women. Even in her temple she had priests, not priestesses. As psychologist Philip Slater shows in *The Glory of Hera*, women in Athenian society were either mothers, slaves, or prostitutes, never leaders or intellectuals. The poet Sappho was a significant exception to this rule.[1]

About the only time in Western history when women embodied something like the Athena spirit with full support from their society was in twelfth-century southern France at the time of the so-called Provençal culture of the troubadours. Eleanor of Aquitaine and Marie de Champagne were the inspired leaders of a culture in which women were equal, free, learned, and powerful. Women were idealized, and a number of celebrated aristocratic women troubadours wrote and held court. Here, the Athenean love of learning and the spirit united with Aphrodite's erotic delight in the beauty of the feminine, and Hera ruled as queen. Though it was short-lived, something of that period endures

---

[1] More recent feminist works have confirmed Slater's insightful picture, written in 1968, of the wretchedness of women's life in ancient Greece. Notably, Sarah B. Pomeroy's *Goddesses, Whores, Wives and Slaves* (1975) and Eva Cantarella's *Pandora's Daughters* (1981), in which she concludes, "The true female condition in Homer was this: total exclusion from political power and participation in public life; subordination to the head of the family and submission to his punishment; and finally, ideological separation. Forbidden to think about anything but domestic matters, the woman cannot even talk about male matters. Faithless, weak, fickle, she was regarded with suspicion" (p. 33).

OUTSTANDING ATHENA WOMEN
IN HISTORY

Despite male reluctance to let Athena women with creative intellects and political vision express themselves or hold power, certain remarkable women have made their indelible marks on our history and our consciousness. Here are a few of them, not all widely known.

Hrotsvit of Gandersheim (c. 932–1000) was a nun who wrote prolifically from the library of her convent in Germany, contributing widely to the intellectual and spiritual life of her time. She was the first dramatist since classical times and the earliest known poet in Germany. She wrote verse legends, prose prefaces, historical epics, and no less than six dramas. Her portrayals of women are original and vibrant, never relying upon mere allegorical stereotypes.

Unprotected by the convent or marriage, there was little a woman could do to support herself independently in the late Middle Ages. Yet **Christine de Pisan** (c. 1364–1430) became the first woman in France to live by her writing. Originally Venetian, she left Italy when her father became attached to the French court. There she met and married a Frenchman, who died when she was only twenty-five, leaving her with three children and little inheritance. So she turned to writing all kinds of poetry and prose, producing fifteen major works between 1399 and 1405, including the periodically rediscovered classic *The Book of the City of Ladies*. She was famous for upholding the dignity of women, attacking, for example, the cynical view of women in Jean de Meung's part of the *Roman de la Rose*, an epic of courtly love.

Queen Elizabeth I (1533–1603), the Virgin Queen, combined many Athenian virtues with actual Hera power. She inspired the greatest era of English history by her astute political judgment and her visionary national leadership. Like Athena she loved the companionship of heroes, surrounding herself with famous adventurer-explorers such as Sir Walter Raleigh,

Sir Francis Drake, and the earl of Essex. A whole literary cult grew up around her, fed by Edmund Spenser's *Faerie Queene* and by many patriotic passages in Shakespeare's plays. Erudite and immensely cultivated, she was herself a poet. Her political and cultural achievements in raising England to greatness are inestimable.

The paintings of the artist **Sofonisba Anguissola** (1532–1625) are of such technical accomplishment that they have been mistaken for Titian. Neglected until recently by art historians, she was a highly respected painter of the late Renaissance, having been guided in her youth by Michelangelo. For twenty years she served as portrait painter to King Philip II of Spain, establishing an international reputation with her intimate and original portraiture. When she was ninety-two, the young Anthony Van Dyke came to study her brilliant techniques as an artist.

If there was ever a manifesto by a radical Athena, it is *A Vindication of the Rights of Women* by **Mary Wollstonecraft** (1759–1797). Though she was close to many of the revolutionary leaders in France, she quickly realized that the French Revolution was not bringing about the liberation of women, as she and her circle had hoped. This disillusionment inspired her to publish her famous treatise in 1792, a work rightly called the first great feminist document. In it she wrote, "I have thrown down the gauntlet. It is time to restore women to their lost dignity and make them part of the human species." This great Athenean challenge still stands today.

Called by inner voices to preach the emancipation of slaves and women's rights, **Sojourner Truth** (1797–1883) left her domestic employ to travel all over the American North. Although illiterate, she was a remarkable and fearless orator. She traveled on foot, telling of the abuse and indignities of slavery as she and her relatives knew it. She worked tirelessly to find jobs for slaves freed after the Civil War and in 1850 published her autobiography, which helped support her.

in the spirit of romance—and in modern feminism (see Aphrodite chapter).

But even if women could not emerge in ancient Greece and take their place beside the heroes, as Athena did in the myths, the longing must have been there. The myth of the Amazons, a society of fierce warrior women who lived almost entirely without men, could be seen as an expression of that longing, born of frustrated Athena energy, for true female community and active companionship—something that is finally emerging in the feeling of sisterhood in today's feminism.

Athena longs to be born—not as an innocent girl but as a fully developed adult woman, able to fight and create in a world dominated for so long by the fathers. The political and intellectual emergence of women that has been building during all of this century may well embody this final birth of Athena, so long frustrated, so long a headache to patriarchal Zeus.

It is impossible to estimate whether the patriarchs of the West have been most deeply disturbed by the thought of a takeover by Athena or by Persephone, queen of the underworld and her guardian spirit, Hecate: do they most fear invasion from without by virago Amazons or from within by the supposed dark forces of witchcraft? The unspeakable depths to which men sank during the witch-hunts of the Middle Ages tends to suggest the latter. Yet in some ways the vanity with which men have held themselves the sole possessers and dispensers of godlike reason is even more acutely threatened by the image of the goddess of wisdom incarnate. For what can disturb the male ego more than an intelligent woman who not only sees the flaws in what he has made but refuses to excuse them just because he is a male? Knowledge—and even prior to that, education—is power. So, from Plato's Academy onward, men have kept women ignorant for fear they might answer back and make men's grand designs seem humbug.

ATHENA GROWING UP

Despite our culture's determination to program stereotypical gender roles into young children—dolls for girls, guns for boys—Athena's major traits, and particularly her androgynous capacity, can easily be observed when her archetype is strong in young girls. Intelligent little

Athenas soon master language—and argumentation! Their strong egos make them every bit as contentious and combative as boys. In fact we expect to find Athena, as a young girl, preferring to play with boys, taking their rough-and-tumble both physically and verbally. Like her equally androgynous sister Artemis, she is proud to be a tomboy. More competitive and more argumentative than Artemis, however, her motto might well be, "Anything you can do I can do better."

Competition as well as disputes actually toughen her; she soon overcomes any sense of inferiority around boys, establishing confidence that will stand her in good stead as an adult. And although she likes to win as much as any boy, she doesn't need to dominate for the sake of it; being the leader is the role coveted by her even tougher sister, Hera. Well in control of her feelings, young Athena will hesitate to cry to get her way, and unless she has an equally powerful amount of Aphrodite in her psyche, she will not use seduction to achieve her ends.

Young Athena's exceptional intelligence will often show in her extraordinary ear for language, which will absorb vocabulary well beyond her developmental norm. She loves words, wordplay, and debate. In fact, she loves to have the last word much of the time. Later on she will come to realize that the ability to wield words can be one of her most powerful tools, to be turned into an effective combative weapon in careers like law, journalism, or political advocacy.

Sometimes young Athena's precocity can be quite disarming; the goddess of wisdom can sometimes emerge within the consciousness of a very young child to remarkable effect. There is a delightful memoir entitled *Mister God, This is Anna*, by an Irishman living in London named Fynn, which describes the pronouncements of a young girl he adopted. Anna was a spiritually enlightened "wise child," who had clearly found God at around the age of four. Here is how she reacted to the Bible when introduced to it:

> Reading the Bible wasn't a great success. She tended to regard it as a primer, strictly for infants. The message of the Bible was simple and any half-wit could grasp it in thirty minutes flat! Religion was for doing things, not for reading about doing things. Once you had got the message there wasn't much point in going over the same old ground. Our local parson was taken

aback when he asked her about God. The conversation went
as follows:

"Do you believe in God?"

"Yes."

"Do you know what God is?"

"Yes."

"What is God then?"

"He's God!"

"Do you go to church?"

"No."

"Why not?"

"Because I know it all!"

"What do you know?"

"I know to love Mister God and to love people and cats
and dogs and spiders and flowers and trees—and the catalogue
went on—"with all of me." . . .

Anna had bypassed all the nonessentials and distilled centuries of learning into one sentence: "And God said love men,
love them, and love it, and don't forget to love yourself."
(p. 19)

Growing Athena soon learns to curb her frustration at male stu-
pidity and ineptitude, however. Even as a child, she is quick to learn
that in our society both fathers and teachers usually favor boys over
girls for their mental abilities, so she will use books and whatever
resources she has available to gain equal recognition for her own intellectual prowess. Unless her mother has solid Hera achievements in
the realm of business, or else intellectual pursuits or some creative
expression, she will tend to belittle her daughter, often driving young
Athena to seek her father's approval instead.

Although she might enjoy the cut and thrust of competitive sports
during adolescence, the Athena woman invests in them only as a limited
outlet for her mounting ambition. This is where she differs markedly
from her independent sister Artemis: physical competition interests
her far less than intellectual achievement. Athena is much more likely
to develop musical or artistic skills at around this time. She may discover, too, that she has writing and debating ability; college journalism,
public speaking, and political action groups may draw her. And above

all she will be seen to excel in the more traditional academic pursuits; with her clear mind and talent for logical organization and articulation, she will do equally well in the arts and in the sciences. She may even find a promising career opening up before her in such traditionally male-dominated professions as medicine or law.

LOVE AND MARRIAGE

Adolescence and young womanhood could well be a time of considerable confusion and chaos concerning Athena's sexual identity. Already she is moving toward the fatherworld, in which she will eventually have to survive, so she may be more tuned into her own father and brother's mentalities than to the fripperies of fashion and dating that fascinate Aphrodite. Since she can win a man quite easily on an intellectual level, she will often underestimate more traditional forms of courtship and will be surprised when her date's mental passion suddenly turns physical. She may be quite spontaneous and natural in her sexuality, but she is equally likely to be quite unconscious of her body. For all her ego armoring, masculine sympathy, and liberated ideas, she can be extremely shy until she becomes more experienced. This is the "maidenly" part within her.

Throughout her life there will always be a degree of reserve in the Athena woman's sexuality (remember that so far we are talking about the "pure" Athena type, not a woman who is also comfortable in the world of Aphrodite). Athena is, archetypally speaking, a virgin. For all her worldliness and savoir faire, her sexuality as a woman remains relatively indistinct. She has put so much of her libido into mental and extraverted activity that she has given her body and its deeper needs less than their proper due. She may think that she is doing just fine in bed, but sometimes there is a lack of true orgasmic satisfaction, or there may be troublesome infections, growths, or menstrual problems, which she treats as purely physical problems.

It is obvious to anyone who knows her that the Athena woman seeks success in the world; her fighting spirit has, after all, equipped her to win whenever possible. Very often, therefore, she will place the Demeter world of motherhood on the back burner for as long as she feels is gynecologically safe, if not forever. The Hera world of marriage will attract her only to the extent that it will further her or provide a good base for her worldly operations. In any case, her fierce independence would insist that no mate in any way limit her or demand her primary allegiance to *his* career or personality; if anything, she would demand the reverse, or at best, a carefully worked out agreement in support of her tremendous need for freedom and autonomy.

Marriage for an Athena woman will frequently be stormy until she has figured out what she really wants from life and quits taking her own uncertainty and secret vulnerabilities (the maiden beneath the armor) out on her mate. She will spar with him, compete with him, and often despise him because he is not as tough as she is. It infuriates her that he receives all the traditional laurels and demands her sympathy as well. Faced with the demand to be superheroes during their twenties and thirties, men expect their wives to comfort and cosset their wounded egos in a motherly way. Nothing could be more calculated to drive an aspiring Athena wife to near homicidal rage. She wanted a mate as a companion in arms, a sparring partner to keep herself in fighting shape, just as it used to be with her brothers as a kid. Instead, she gets a whimperer who retreats into therapy, Eastern religions, or extramarital affairs with the complaint that "my wife doesn't understand me."

ATHENA AND THE FATHERWORLD

The Greek myth tells us that Athena was born out of Zeus's head, and Aeschylus has her say, "I am strongly on my father's side." We can hardly speak about Athena in the modern world without looking at her relationship to fathers and the fatherworld. But this is not an easy task, since the Athena woman today prides herself on her independence from structures of patriarchal society and often feels insulted at the very idea that she might have derived anything at all from such a degenerate system. Such is the case with many feminist Athenas.

Nevertheless, when we try to look dispassionately at the archetype of Athena, we are struck by two distinctly masculine sides to her character: a love of the father and a love of heroes, both of which she carries within her as fundamental parts of her psychology. Understood symbolically rather than literally, they tell us a lot about her: "father" stands for her highest strivings for intellectual and spiritual fulfillment, the ideals she seeks in her world, while her "heroic" consciousness stands for the manner of action by which she sets out to achieve such goals.

What Athena seeks to learn from and emulate is not the simple behavior of the biological father, important as his role might be, but rather *the father principle*. It is the archetypal good father that she longs to be born out of, those Zeus qualities that the king of the gods represented when he was on his very best behavior: wisdom, justice, responsible rulership, good counsel, kindness, protection, magnanimity, natural pride and dignity. They are all "higher" and thus spiritual-intellectual qualities, appropriately stemming from the head of the sky god. (The "lower" qualities of Father Zeus, evident in myths of his philanderings, never enter into Athena's relationship with him; but they are displaced elsewhere through another father-daughter relationship, Ouranos and Aphrodite, where the latter is born from her father's genitals. See Aphrodite chapter.)

Once we take Athena's love of the father out of the biological realm, we begin to recognize essential parts of her character type. This is not to deny that Athena may have a very strong admiration for her actual father, only that it will be incidental rather than a simple cause of her idealism. Many an Athena is born with a weak or nonexistent father who cannot fulfill her archetypal expectations, but so great is her longing that as soon as education opens up her intellectual horizons, she fixes upon a cultural father, such as Gandhi, Marx, or Jesus.

Predictably we find the Athena woman most at home in arenas where she can use her active and creative mind to its best advantage and where she can pursue and shape her ideals. Business, government, education, science, medicine, law—all these are fertile ground for her in the modern world now that the patriarchal restrictions are finally dissolving.

It is, of course, no accident that all these professions have traditionally been called *the fatherworld*. Men have been guilty of literalizing the archetype, making it gender specific, insisting that only a man can manifest the father principle—which is to confuse a biological act with a social responsibility. As Athena women all over the world are showing, women are capable of exercising creative leadership and decision making at every level of the old power pyramid established by men. It is a social revolution unparalleled in Western history.

Not surprisingly, men are more than a little threatened by this incursion into what they had grown to think of as their world. No longer can they fall back on the rather stale clichés of privilege, the assumptions of old-boy support, the platitudes of authoritarianism. Athena sees everything with new eyes; she is, after all, entering the boardroom, the courthouse, or the operating room for the first time as practitioner, and with her passionate concern for truth she is not quite so ready as her male peers to accept the discrepancies between the ideals of the textbook and actual practices.

All this derives from the fact that the Athena archetype is essentially *youthful*, and with youth comes idealism. Athena is driven by a sense of commitment to a higher purpose, by an active concern for the well-being of the community she lives in, often for humankind at large. She does not enter medicine the way many of her cynical brothers do, for big money, but because she genuinely cares; for the same reason, she is far less likely to sell out in law or politics.

Well informed and armed with her acute intellect and the determination that goes with a sense of purpose and order, she is a powerful force to be reckoned with in whatever section of the fatherworld she chooses to enter. From the outside, particularly from the perspective of her enemies, Athena may seem strident and often humorless. But from the inside she feels a kind of relentless drumbeat that calls upon her to take up her sword against the injustice and suffering she feels and sees so acutely all around her.

ATHENA THE HEROINE

If the first thing we notice about the myth of Athena's birth is that she is born out of Zeus's head, the second is that she emerges fully armed, ready for action. She is no ivory-tower academic; she wants to be right there in the thick of battle, be it political, social, or intellectual. She would agree with the poet W. H. Auden that "act from thought should quickly follow. What is thinking for?"

Hollywood, TV, and film producers, with their sixth sense for emergent archetypes, have recently been drawn to Athena's powerful and appealing image. In the late seventies Vanessa Redgrave and Jane Fonda, two charismatic actresses with strong political agendas of their own, created a new kind of screen heroine. In *Julia*, which is based upon a Lillian Hellman story, Redgrave plays a politically aware woman who gives up her safe life to fight fascism in Europe in the thirties; Fonda plays the writer who follows her progress. In a more contemporary scenario, *The China Syndrome*, Jane Fonda plays an investigative news reporter who helps expose a cover-up at a nuclear power plant.

Between them, Redgrave and Fonda have helped to establish a contemporary Athenean heroine who is politically committed, passionately concerned to expose corruption and injustice, and prepared to sacrifice her life in the service of the underprivileged and oppressed. More recent variations on this theme have appeared in movie portrayals such as Sally Field in *Norma Rae*, Meryl Streep in *Silkwood*, and Sissy Spacek in *Marie*.

The image of a smart, principled, no-nonsense heroine has filtered down into TV cop series and soap operas, too. Even the heroine of an old-fashioned macho movie like *Raiders of the Lost Ark*, today has an Athena toughness about her, running her own bar in the Himalayas, standing up to roughnecks. Gone are the swooning, helpless Aphrodites of "feminine mystique" whom Betty Friedan so brilliantly described. The new breed of heroine is quite capable of standing up to a male bully or of drinking a male rival under the table if necessary.

Movies with a more psychological bent are also exploring the wounded, vulnerable side of Athena as well as her heroic qualities. Jill Clayburgh's fine portrait of *An Unmarried Woman* stands out, as do several of Meryl Streep's films, notably *Plenty*, an English chronicle of the slow disillusionment of a heroic young Athena as her ideals crumble in postwar Britain.

We quote these Hollywood figures because they are stereotypes we all know. Larger than life, it is true, but valuable because they show Athena's heroic qualities writ large and because they correspond to aspects of the new feminine emerging among the mass audiences who daydream about them. Needless to say, for the vast majority of women who are encountering Athena for the first time, the experience is anything but glamorous. Like the old heroes of mythology, a woman's path to the distant goal, be it toward a degree, a promotion, getting published or elected, or obtaining artistic engagements, is often slow, arduous, and painfully lonely—particularly if she is also trying to live out her duties as Demeter, with young children to raise, and to appear as glamorous as Aphrodite to her latest lover.

The numerous demands that are made upon the Athena woman out there in the often inhospitable and hostile fatherworld really put her on her mettle. Now we can understand the symbolism of the Greek goddess's armor a little better. Athena women today must be tough; they have to take the same falls as men—and a few more. Like any oppressed minority they have to be twice as good as the guardians of the structure against which they must prove themselves, whatever the arena of endeavor.

Armoring is the metaphor that psychologically describes a well-defended ego. It can be applied to a person of either sex who is not easily slighted by criticism or attacks on his or her character or competency. The Athena personality can come back with an answer and always turn a confrontation into an advantage. She is not simply defensive, but rather aggressively self-confident. Men have always received more awards for such a resilient persona, but now, as more and more women find how useful it is for them, too, a new personality structure, uniquely imagined in the warrior goddess, is emerging.

HEROINE'S PROGRESS

Just as an adolescent boy goes through a stage of ridiculing everything his mother says or does, flaunting his coarse male language, refusing to clean up or do anything domestic, so a young woman in whom Athena is beginning to emerge will go through a similar period of disagreeing with practically everything her mother says or does. Mother is seen as stupid, old-fashioned, prudish, and restrictive.

The last thing young Athena ever wants to be is like her mother, who represents mindless domesticity and motherhood. Demeter qualities that pull in the very opposite direction to which her education and financial independence are now impelling her. Of course, later in her life she may have to come back full-circle to the Demeter in herself that she has rejected, but for the time being, her mother's world is the necessary foil against which she defines her movement out into the wider fatherworld of opportunity, independence, and advancement.

Once out in the world, having left home and gone, let us say, to the big city or to college—both Athena realms (Artemis would head for a farm commune or join a trans-Atlantic yacht crew)—she meets the next challenges to her growing sense of self and independence. Finding work, paying rent, managing a car and a bank account, and of course figuring out how to get ahead. Just like young men in the past who traditionally went to the city to seek their fortunes, she, too, learns all kinds of tricks about survival and how the system works.

Today, magazines such as *Working Woman*, *Ms*, and *Cosmopolitan* conspire to help her to dress in ways that blend in best with prevailing corporate decor, to learn just how sexy to be or not to be, to order drinks that are more "assertive," and to help her to manage her new earnings. She is acquiring the persona that adapts to a patriarchal world, in which, as yet, she has very little power but in which, if she plays her cards right, she can rise. She is learning the Athena role of the *dutiful daughter*.

Here we are caricaturing Athena's heroic emergence as that of a young woman leaving home at about the age of twenty, but the same process can take place at any time in her life where a woman leaves the home environment to go out and find financial independence in the world. It may happen suddenly and of necessity, such as when a marriage falls apart and she must support herself, or else it can happen by choice when her children have grown up and left home. Often these are extremely creative and exciting times, but they are also frightening and challenging to an older woman setting out for the first time into Athena country. She should have no fear, because one of the great saving qualities of Athena energy is her youthfulness; biological age proves to be of very little importance once the creative spirit of the goddess is invoked. For Athena is always present once a woman is roused to dare something new; Athena loves courage and resourcefulness and amply rewards those who manifest them. Fortunately in the world around us there are many, many examples of emergent Athena among older women, so no woman who is initiated later in life into her adventurous consciousness need feel alone or uninspired.

According to Jung's psychology, once the aspiring heroic ego has made the break from the mother and from home and can function independently in the fatherworld, a further and more difficult challenge presents itself, a scenario that he calls slaying the father. In a young man's psychology it can often crystallize around a decision to leave a comfortable job with a large organization and start up alone in business, or to make a bid for a higher managerial position as a post comes vacant. Clearly an Athena woman who is also rising steadily in some business or political hierarchy can be faced with a similar choice. Or it may be a challenge in an intellectual sense: publishing a radical book that may cost her academic support but make her name as a voice in her own right. These, and more direct political challenges to an established system, hierarchy, or worldview, are all versions of the symbolic process of slaying the father to become fully herself.

Precisely here, many an Athena woman, just like her male heroic counterpart, may balk at the thought of a huge loss of income, possible business failure, or the risk of losing a carefully established reputation. Respectability and a predictable income suddenly seem much more attractive today than they did ten years ago, when feminist rhetoric was fresh in her ears and she didn't have a young child to support and various other responsibilities. So she may compromise, become settled into her place in the larger hierarchy of things, intellectually still alert and in touch but, in terms of her independence, something of a dutiful daughter, obedient to an organization or system that embodies values she respects and may even have helped to create. She may decide to "settle down," to use an old-fashioned term, and slowly mature into an older Hera figure, a powerful supporter and promoter of the new establishment, her more revolutionary days behind her.

ATHENA, THE DUTIFUL DAUGHTER . . .

To slay the father or to submit to him? In terms of dealing with the established order or status quo, this is the question that inevitably confronts Athena as it does every man. She is forced, sooner or later, to define herself somewhere along that inescapable political abstract scale that stretches from extreme Left to extreme Right. For, like it or not, she is now out in the world; she has power and she has principles, which means she must find her relationship to political reality.

If she comes from a more conservative political background, with a strong, supporter-father, the Athena woman will tend toward being a dutiful daughter. She will put her vigorous energy into upholding and promoting the fatherworld as the status quo. Her business firm, the government, and her favorite media pundits will generally be seen as benevolent and protective. Though she may wish to reform and improve parts of the system, she will do so from within, leaving the foundations of the structure generally unquestioned. After all, the patriarchal fathers she most admires gained wealth and influence from their early heroic efforts, so why should not she? The message she received from them is that whosoever perseveres will be rewarded in the end. And so she becomes a good student, a staunch supporter, an exemplary employee. With her obvious talent for understanding the practicalities of things and thinking the way men do without threatening them, she rises steadily in the hierarchy, be it in banking, in the corporate world, in politics, or in academia—or even Hollywood, as Sherry Lansing showed.

An almost exemplary model of the career of Athena as dutiful daughter is nursing, where obedience to a rigidly authoritarian fatherworld is carried to almost subservient extremes in return for well-earned respect and a high degree of responsibility. Not surprisingly, many nurses come from families where the father was a doctor, just as a recent study, *The Managerial Woman*, by Margaret Hennig and Anne Jardim found that all the successful businesswomen they studied had strong fathers already in executive positions, on whom they later modeled themselves professionally. This study also confirmed that these fathers took an active role in encouraging their daughters to develop what we have called "heroic" Athena qualities, enabling them to feel comfortable and equal in the male world. As the authors say, summarizing their research:

All [women studied] had had extremely close relationships with their fathers and had been involved in an unusually wide range of traditionally masculine activities in the company of their fathers, beginning when they were very young. They believed they had been given unusually strong support by their families in following their own interests regardless of the sex-role attributes of those interests. Finally, they thought they had developed a very early preference for the company of men rather than of women. (p. 76)

Here is part of an interview they quote, which is typical in its emphasis of the part played by the father in the lives of these women who were to grow up to hold positions of considerable power in the world of management:

"As I can think back Father was really something special. As far as I can recall, I was Daddy's special girl. There were always special times set aside for him and me to be alone. When I was very young, he would take me places on Saturday afternoon. He was a very active man and I was always expected to be active with him. In the winter we would go sledding and skating. He taught me to skate when I was four and he used to show me off to all his friends who had sons older than me. 'See,' he would say, 'you may think she is just a girl, but watch her outskate these boys of yours.'" (p. 78)

Already this young girl was learning to be a companion to her father and was expected to be no different than boys, if not better. The whole emphasis of the molding of her sexual identity is androgynous from the beginning, a much more expanded sense of what it could mean to be a girl than the daughter who is drawn only to the motherworld of Demeter. According to the women studied, their fathers "added to their definition of themselves as people," not simply as girls.

With fathers as supportive and encouraging as this, it goes almost without saying that the dutiful Athena's political attitudes and worldview are going to tend toward conservatism. Either she has internalized the professionalism of her own father or has found a collective father she can admire in the larger organization she has chosen. Either way she has a deep respect for authority and institutional power, seeing her superiors, the "fathers," as basically benevolent and protective. Whether she inclines to the extreme Right like the Daughters of the American Revolution or toes a traditionalist party line like a Phyllis Schaffly or an Anita Bryant, or creates a more provocatively hip picture of making it in a man's world—Helen Gurley Brown and *Cosmopolitan*—this obedient Athena never for one moment intends to rock the boat.

The academic world has inevitably attracted many dutiful Athenas who nevertheless incline to the left of center politically. A generation ago the old stereotype of the bluestocking exemplified this type of Athena, as did many independent writers, artists, and other intellectuals (see box, "Athenas of Another Generation").

...OR THE ETERNAL REVOLUTIONARY?

But for all the achievements, sung and unsung, of the legions of dutiful Athenas now infiltrating every corner of patriarchal society, by far the most visible and vocal of all the Athena women in our midst are the members of what is mostly called the women's movement. The last thing feminist Athenas see about corporate structures, government, or academia is that they are run by benevolent and all-protective fathers. Quite the contrary, they see all such institutions, whether church, state, school, or business, as deeply tainted by over two thousand years of accumulated patriarchal tyranny, hypocrisy, and abuse.

Obviously the radical Athena has a very different relationship with the father principle than her dutiful half sister. Did she have a tyrannical father that she rebels against or did she have a weak father who disappointed her? Unfortunately we know of hardly any studies of the family background of radical Athenas comparable to *The Managerial Woman* that show clear patterns of relationship to the father (and even this study selects only *successful* executive women, leaving out women who rejected their father as a model or who went their own way).

There is compelling evidence that women who are drawn to working as social workers with victims of rape and other kinds of violence were themselves victims of abusive fathers. But this by no means accounts for the large proportion of feminists who are hostile to the male establishment. On the contrary, we find in our own practices as psychotherapists that many radical Athenas are just as angry at their fathers for being so passive and for failing to provide precisely the support that the managerial women with strong fathers got so readily.

Sometimes an Athena woman feels a deep sense of betrayal by her father because a brother is highly rewarded for things she is succeeding in equally or better. But more often it is an insecure father's *unconscious* possessiveness of his adolescent daughter that undermines her confidence to be out there in the fatherworld. Much as her natural Athena

ATHENAS OF ANOTHER GENERATION

We knew how those women were. They wore tweed suits, sensible shoes, and were highly respected. We did not use the words *spinster* or *old maid* anymore except in card games, in reference to fairy tales, or to describe the unpopped kernels at the bottom of a bowl of popcorn. Those women lived in isolation in places like Switzerland and New York City where they had rooms, houses, or brownstones of their own, walked on concrete in winter and on pine needles in summer. They didn't have children (we thought), but they wrote books, and their love lives (if they had any) were shrouded with a blue haze that made one think of spiritual conditions. They were forthright, open-minded, clear-eyed, at least until the blue cataract haze clouded their vision late in life. But this only gave the impression that their inner vision was stronger.

They were emissaries of psyche. Vestals who had chosen to stay within the temple. They knew the catacombs, the labyrinth, had walked the Sacra Via, but easily crossed the bridge to the modern world where they taught YWCA courses in the 1930s on such things as "Psychological Mindedness for the Career Girl." They developed lasting friendships with women who shared the same goal of "making the unconscious conscious." We thought at first, in the distinction-eradicating blur of the 1960s, that this goal was like yoga, another discipline for attaining higher consciousness.

But those women (in our imagination) did not have the sort of bodies that practiced yoga. Their sturdiness lent itself rather to trail riding in jodhpurs, carrying heavy tea trays, books, and logs for the fire. The fires they kept burning (and here a bit of red comes into the otherwise pale blue and tweedy picture) were not the fires of frontier women warming water at the hearth to keep a household's hundred needs met, nor the fires of lanterns hung high in the gables by colonial women who watched the black sea each night. Their fires were *inspired*. Intellectual illuminations lit by the flint of making connections. Olive Schreiner (*Dreams, Woman and Labor*) described her mother by this light—candlelight flickering in the room of their South African farmhouse. After the children were asleep she paced the floor with an open book, hungry for words. Driven, as those women were, by the Quest for Meaning. She was disciplined, hearty, heroic: such maidens were to become the matrons of a new psychological order.

—Nor Hall, *Those Women*, pp. 9–10

talents impel her to be out there in the world, she is held back by *his* fears and ambivalence, which she carries inside her. She feels stifled, trapped, and limited by self-doubts that are in the end part of his psychic makeup, not hers, and her frustration at the lack of support breeds great anger and resentment inside her. So, it is not hard for her to project those feelings of oppression, hypocrisy, and arbitrary authoritarianism onto the fatherworld at large—and not without considerable justification.

Nevertheless, such cases will be found to explain the anger of only a small proportion of radical Athenas, by no means all. We are skeptical of reductive explanations that attribute everything to their influence of the biological father alone. Goddess psychology is a sociocultural psychology that doesn't just rest with family influences. We agree with the feminists that patriarchy as a deeply ingrained social institution breeds imbalances and disturbances in women's psyches that are inherited at a much deeper level, the level Jung called the collective unconscious. The anger within women that has been building for many generations now is the energy that serves to fuel the emergence of

radical Athena. It is, we believe, an essential part of the powerful goddess dynamic currently changing our very culture at its archetypal roots.

The fact that a radical incarnation of Athena is now bursting forth
so strongly all over Western society (to say nothing of certain Third
World countries; witness "Las Madres de la Plaza de Mayo" in Argentina) may mean that it is for once the daughter instead of the son who
will overthrow the father principle, thus signaling the end of patriarchy.
What the poet Tennyson said of the dying King Arthur might well
apply to the demise of patriarchal culture: "The old order changeth,
giving place to new. And God fulfills himself in many ways, lest one
good custom should corrupt the world." Radical Athena would only
add that the change is long overdue and that the Goddess has yet to
be allowed her share in fulfilling herself!

It is no accident that the vast majority of women who identify in
one way or another with the women's movement were involved in the
social and political movements of the sixties in America and Europe.
Awareness of the damage to the planet's ecosystem, contact with Marxist thinking, and a recognition of the realities of life in the Third World
shattered once and for all the cozy view of middle-class reality that
most of the "counterculture" generation had grown up with. For the
first time, for example, the paternalism of the large corporations was
seen to hide appalling exploitation and corruption in Third World
countries. It became clear to many, too, that slavery, colonialism, racial
oppression, and the subjugation of women were all part of the broader
picture of Western historical development, in which what was occurring
at the very deepest level was *the suppression of the feminine principle at
the very heart of our culture.* Such is the conclusion of the visionary work
by Susan Griffin, *Woman and Nature,* which evokes horrifying parallels
between man's exploitation of Mother Earth (in Latin, *mater,* or
"*mother,*" is cognate with *materia,* or "*matter,*") and the brutalization of
women's bodies in the name of religion and science.

"Humanity is outraged in me and with me," wrote George Sand
about the tyranny of her day in the last century. "We must not dissi-
mulate nor try to forget this indignation, which is one of the most
passionate forms of love." She was speaking and still speaks for all
radical Athenas who are tormented by the suffering and injustice they
cannot help but see once they turn their gaze away from the narcissistic
concerns of the middle-class worldview. Some of the great political

writers and activists of this century, consumed with similar indignation and a burning passion for justice, have been Athena women driven by this great humanitarian vision: Rosa Luxemburg, Simone de Beauvoir, Dorothy Day, Angela Davis, Simone Weil.

ATHENA'S DILEMMA: CIVILIZATION IS REPRESSION

In many ways the extreme and unusual case of the last of these women, Simone Weil (1909–1943), French intellectual, socialist, and mystic, brings into sharp focus both the intense strengths and the painful weaknesses of a life lived almost entirely through the inspiration of the goddess Athena (see box, "Simone Weil: A Radical Athena of Our Times"). She combined both the radical and the dutiful aspects of Athena in her life, since she not only observed total inner obedience to a transcendent God known in prayer and meditation but also saw it as her duty to attack every manifestation of social injustice wherever it occurred. People who knew Simone Weil reportedly found her aloof, but passionate in her relentless pursuit of intellectual and spiritual truth. She is said to have once outargued Trotsky when the Russian socialist was exiled in Paris. Simone Weil's premature death at thirty-four from tuberculosis came during one of several hunger strikes in sympathy for French prisoners of war in Germany. She had always been frail, deliberately neglecting her body on what were clearly ascetic principles. She also suffered from migraines for much of her life. Her remarkable life and the no less remarkable manner of her death raise a number of crucial questions from the perspective of Athena and the other complementary goddesses. There is no question that Simone Weil's unswerving pursuit of political and spiritual truth, her tireless social activism on the public platform and in the factories, and her willingness to sacrifice her life in the cause of the oppressed are expressions of all that is finest in Athena. But the way in which she died and in which she consistently neglected her body throws into sharp relief a danger that arises whenever we allow one single goddess to dominate our personality: *exclusive unconscious identification with a single goddess archetype to the neglect or denial of other goddess energies can lead to a one-sidedness that has all the features of neurosis.*

SIMONE WEIL:
A RADICAL ATHENA OF OUR TIMES

The French intellectual Simone Weil (1909–1943) lived a life that exemplified many aspects of Athena consciousness to a remarkably evolved degree, though we can also detect a strong Persephone counterpoint. Born in Alsace, of a freethinking, educated Jewish family, her father a doctor, she was early recognized to have an extremely precocious mind, as was her brother André, a mathematical prodigy.

Simone's received bourgeois worldview was shattered once and for all when she was eight years old by the sight of German prisoners of war, apparently starving to death, en route to a prison camp. By adolescence this deeply serious young girl made a resolve that her life was to be one of service to mankind; as part of this she took a private vow of chastity. Passionately caught up in Marxism while studying philosophy at the Sorbonne University in Paris, she became known to her fellow students (who included Simone de Beauvoir) as the Red Virgin. But she was soon to live up to her principles by working in factories and organizing educational programs for workers, at the same time campaigning and writing for the Left. Horrified by what she witnessed of the totalitarianism of Hitler and Franco, she campaigned endlessly for the sanctity of the individual, which she saw as consistently neglected by Marxism, mass movements, and the abstractions of politics. For a time she worked with the Resistance movement during the Nazi occupation of France. Her posthumously published manifesto, *The Need for Roots* (1952), reverses most political thinking by rejecting human rights as the basis of political philosophy and asserting instead that it is "the needs of the soul" that are truly fundamental.

In the last five years of her life she underwent a mystical awakening to Christ, known only to a handful of friends. Her Athenean hunger for spiritual wisdom was now amply filled, as her extraordinary mystical *Notebooks* (1956) testify. A more accessible collection of her spiritual writings, *Waiting for God* (1951), was also published posthumously. She died tragically at thirty-four of an undiagnosed tuberculosis aggravated by her hunger strikes in sympathy for French prisoners of war. She was at the time working for de Gaulle's government in exile in London.

In Athena we encounter over and over again what is probably the most severe of the wounds that our six goddesses have been obliged to bear in order to accommodate the supremacy of the patriarchal spirit. For Athena is condemned to be crucified upon the opposites of mind and body, spirit and matter, culture and nature. Born into the world of the father intellect, all her energy must endlessly revolve in the head. So, in Simone Weil's case, all her intense concentration upon the philosophical and mystical ideas that cram her voluminous note-books and papers, magnificent as they are, led almost certainly to her migraine headaches. At the same time, such an overemphasis on the head was for her also a deep denial of bodily reality; she was deliberately neglectful of both her appearance and her need for food. Curiously her writings abound with the metaphor of the hunger of the spirit. Indeed, her favorite poem "Love," by the mystical poet George Herbert, ends with the line, "So I did sit and eat." She also regarded the Lord's Prayer as "spiritual food."

In this hunger for the spirit and for what Jung has called more generally Logos, that which emanates from the spiritual father, God, we cannot help seeing in Simone Weil a huge compensatory reaction arising from her denial of the body. To deny the body is, in a broader sense, to deny matter, or material reality. Put simply, an overdeveloped Athena consciousness goes along with underdeveloped matter/*mater* consciousness.

SIMONE WEIL'S TESTAMENT TO HIGHER TRUTH

When science, art, literature, and philosophy are simply the manifestation of personality they are on a level where glorious and dazzling achievements are possible, which can make a man's name live for thousands of years. But above this level, far above, separated by an abyss, is the level where the highest things are achieved. These things are essentially anonymous.

It is pure chance whether the names of those who reach this level are preserved or lost: even when they are remembered they have become anonymous. Their personality has vanished.

Truth and beauty dwell on this level of the impersonal and the anonymous. This is the realm of the sacred; on the other level nothing is sacred, except in the sense that we might say this of a touch of colour in a picture if it represented the Eucharist.

What is sacred in science is truth; what is sacred in art is beauty. Truth and beauty are impersonal. All this is too obvious.

If a child is doing a sum and does it wrong, the mistake bears the stamp of his personality. If he does the sum exactly right, his personality does not enter into it at all.

Perfection is impersonal. Our personality is the part of us which belongs to error and sin. The whole effort of the mystic has always been to become such that there is no part left in his soul to say 'I'.

The human being can only escape from the collective by raising himself above the personal and entering into the impersonal. The moment he does this, there is something in him, a small portion of his soul, upon which nothing of the collective can get a hold. If he can root himself in the impersonal good so as to be able to draw energy from it, then he is in a condition, whenever he feels the obligation to do so, to bring to bear without any outside help, against any collectivity, a small but real force.

Every man who has once touched the level of the impersonal is charged with a responsibility towards all human beings: to safeguard, not their persons, but whatever frail potentialities are hidden within them for passing over to the impersonal.

—Extracts from "Human Personality"
in *Selected Essays, 1934–43*, pp. 13–16

ATHENA'S WOUND: THE DENIAL OF THE BODY

Had she lived today, Simone Weil would no doubt have been diagnosed as having anorexia nervosa, a complaint that haunts the lives of so many young women living busy, ambitious lives in the city, as well as teenage girls unable to come to terms with their sexuality and their embodiment. The fatherworld feeds them with admiration, advancement, and intellectual esteem very often, but the body wastes away, as if saying, "I am unimportant, ignore me," yet at the same time, "Feed me, I am starving." Even when such afflicted women are concerned with dress and appearance—Aphrodite matters—it will often turn out, when they are questioned, that their image of their body is purely mental and unsensuous, entirely lacking in substance or corporeality.

What, then, has happened to Athena's connection to her bodily self and to her mother? To Demeter? And to Aphrodite?

The Greek myth of Athena's birth tells us that her true mother was Metis, a Titan who belonged to the pre-Olympian race of deities suppressed by the later patriarchy. The act of swallowing Metis was

Zeus's clever way both of making sure she would not have a son who would overthrow him (a constant patriarchal nightmare) and, at the same time, of incorporating her "wisdom," since the Greek word *metis* means exactly this. If the goddess Metis was a Titan, then she belonged to the matriarchal period described in our introductory chapter; her "wisdom" is therefore no more nor less than the very matriarchal consciousness that proclaims the endless mystical cycle of birth and death, change and transformation. Since the only goddess to survive intact with initiatory knowledge of these mysteries is Demeter, it is fair to say that, as Mother Goddess in our sixfold typology, she is the closest to Metis.

Psychologically speaking, Metis/Demeter represents the mother function in Athena that has been split off. This missing function becomes replaced by *spiritual* nurturing from the father, but a father who is himself psychically at war with the mother principle. What Athena is most out of touch with and most deeply in need of is warm, natural, physical mothering; attention to basic bodily needs; and unconditional love. All these functions are what come most spontaneously to Demeter, and presumably the long-forgotten wisdom of Metis. But is Athena's fate to identify with the father in establishing her sense of self in the world? Her tragedy is that the more she does this, the more she will inevitably incorporate *his* denial of the mother principle as well as suffering her own estrangement from her mother self.

Jung has written vividly of the painful extremes to which the unconscious rejection of the mother can lead the Athena woman. His words are worth quoting for their summary of the many ways in which the suppression of all that is instinctual and bodily can manifest archetypally in the neglected Demeter and/or Aphrodite sides of a woman's nature. He calls this denial "the supreme example of the negative mother complex," writing as follows:

> The motto of this type is anything, so long as it is not like Mother. . . . This kind of daughter knows what she does *not* want, but is usually completely at sea as to what she would choose as her own fate. All her instincts are concentrated on the mother in the negative form of resistance and are therefore of no use to her in building her own life. . . . All instinctive processes meet with unexpected difficulties; either sexuality

does not function properly, or the children are unwanted, or maternal duties are unbearable, or the demands of married life are responded to with impatience and irritation. . . . Resistance to the mother as *uterus* often manifests itself in menstrual disturbances, failure of conception, abhorrence of pregnancy, hemorrhages and excessive vomiting during pregnancy, miscarriages, and so on. The mother as *materia*, "matter," may be at the back of these women's impatience with objects, their clumsy handling of tools and crockery and bad taste in clothes.
—"Psychological Aspects of the Mother Archetype,"
pp. 24–25

In Jung's vivid description we see Athena at her most wounded, deeply and frustratingly cut off from the roots of her feminine being, caught in a vicious circle that her head denies as real. Even though she may find some support in the fatherworld of her career or become an angry intellectual, she finds she cannot function fully in either realm, so all-consuming of her energy is the disturbance. In fact, in the excess of her rage against the mother, she will displace its overflow onto men and the fatherworld generally, perhaps withdrawing bitterly into poverty as a hopeless welfare mother or joining a radical feminist group or lesbian community that readily encourages her to indulge her anger.

No longer merely a radical, this wounded Athena has practically become a nihilist, almost possessed by a death goddess like the Medusa or the Indian Kali. And sadly, however much the group experience or lesbian love provides her with some degree of the much-needed mothering and nurturing, the true pain at the core of the complex is rarely touched. Instead it becomes absorbed into the group's political identity, enabling her to hate men as predators and see pregnancy as "the temporary deformation of the body for the sake of the species," in feminist Shulamith Firestone's words. Whatever the rhetorical intent behind such slogans, they now carry for wounded nihilist Athena all the intensity of her rage. By allying with other rabid man haters she seems to help create a modern version of the legendary communities of the Amazon women of the ancient world. The companionship of the group, which can be such a source of creativity for Athena in happier circumstances, becomes a politically sanctioned way of hiding her vulnerability and of burying it even more deeply.

In such extremes, the nihilist Athena is seized by a terrible and agonizing conflict. In the desperation and frustration of her rage she continues to add to the weapons of her intellectual armory. She has a retaliatory barb for every insult or misunderstanding that threatens her carefully constructed system of beliefs about herself and her world, whether political, social, or psychological. Only to the closest comrades in arms will she open herself in any measure, and even then it is mostly to focus on the enemy "out there" or to sympathize with "his" victims. An ironic vicious circle begins to operate: the more she rages against sexist tyranny and screams for justice on behalf of its victims, the more she drives away even her most liberal-minded sympathizers of either sex. Unconsciously, it is as though she has activated one of the most powerful and puzzling images in the iconography of mythic Athena: the head of the Medusa, the monster whose skin was draped across the breastplate of the goddess, leaving all who came near in awe of her.

THE SHIELD OF THE MEDUSA

The monstrous Medusa is one of a large number of images of the Terrible Mother that occurs in myth and religion all over the world. This figure usually likes to drink blood, dismember bodies, and devour babies. The Indian Kali, the Hebrew Lilith, the Celtic Sheila-na-gig, and the Balinese witch Rangda are some of the better-known variations on this archetypal personification of death. The Terrible Mother is the other pole of the Mother of Life; together they form the all-inclusive Great Mother, who is both life and death.

Greek religion had long since ceased to give power to the Terrible Mother by the time of the ascendency of Athens. So, figures like the Medusa, the Furies, and the Gorgon became deadly enemies of the heroic patriarchal religion that Pallas Athena represented (see box, "Athena and the Terrible Mother"). Having slain the Medusa, the goddess Athena seems to assimilate some of her power, since she wears her terrible face upon her shield.

Psychologically we could say that Athena consciousness, which is aligned more with patriarchy and the spirit, is in conflict with an even deeper layer of the matriarchal psyche than Demeter/Metis, givers of

ATHENA AND THE TERRIBLE MOTHER

In the myth of Perseus and the Medusa, Athena plays the role of guardian and guide, along with the god Hermes. Perseus has been given the job of bringing to his jealous stepfather, King Polydectes, the head of one of the three deadly Gorgon monsters, named Medusa. The king obviously thinks he can be rid of Perseus by sending him on this mission, since every mortal who looks Medusa in the face is turned to stone. Nevertheless, after various adventures Hermes and Athena come to Perseus's aid. Athena helps him primarily by giving him her polished bronze shield, in which he can see the reflection of the Medusa without being petrified (literally "turned to stone") when he slays her. This he does successfully, cutting off the hideous head writhing with serpents.

Both Freudian and Jungian psychoanalytic writers have interpreted this myth as a young man's struggle with the devouring and possessive image of the feminine that the infant child first sees in the mother. As an infant the boy child fears being swallowed by the very womb itself, which is imagined as a "vagina dentata," a vagina with teeth. In its universal form this monstrous image is called by Erich Neumann the archetype of the Terrible Mother, since she exists in the iconography of all matriarchal cultures in one form or another.

Usually a young hero has to slay some such monster as an initiatory trial to separate himself from the regressive pull of the power of the mother in his unconscious. In the Perseus story Athena represents the higher or spiritual mother belonging to the patriarchy that Perseus wins as his guardian spirit.

From the broader historical perspective of the struggle between matriarchy and patriarchy, Perseus, whose name means "destroyer," is acting for the patriarchy to suppress the old matriarchal consciousness. For, as Robert Graves states, the Gorgon Medusa was already a deadly enemy of Athena, which is to say a rival matriarchal religion that had to be suppressed by one of her hero warriors. The hideous face of the Medusa is thought by Graves to have been a prophylactic mask of a moon priestess designed to scare the uninitiated away from secret rites. By wearing it Athena takes over the terrible aspect of the Great Mother without any of the deeper meaning of her cyclical lunar mysteries of life and death (better understood through Demeter and Persephone, using the goddesses we discuss elsewhere in this book).

Another hero whom Athena protects from the Terrible Mother and supports in his desecration of matriarchal power is Orestes. When he murders his mother to uphold the honor of his father, Orestes is pursued by the Erinyes, otherwise known as the Furies. Only by making a sacrifice at the altar of Athena can Orestes be absolved of his matricide. Thereafter, the Erinyes act submissively, as benefactors of the patriarchy, although Graves again asserts that they represent another matriarchal priesthood subjugated by patriarchal Athenian religion. Since there were three Gorgons and three Erinyes, it seems reasonable to assume this triplicity represented the Triple Great Mother herself (see Demeter chapter).

life. Athena consciousness, from the evidence of the Perseus and Orestes stories (see box), is also at war with the Terrible Mother, who, as the goddess of death, carries the opposite but complementary side of Demeter. The tragic irony of the Athena woman's fight against tyranny and victimization is that the more she fights it, the more she manifests the feminine archetype of death and destruction in her own defensive psychic armor. As Jung once remarked, "You always become the thing you fight the most." And by projecting this energy outward through her "persona," or public self, the wounded Athena woman perpetually fails to integrate it inwardly. The images of the victim and persecutor face opposite directions in her psychic makeup: as the hurt victim, her wound is turned inward and kept hidden; but as the angry, righteous persecutor, it is turned outward, obsessively seeking battle, revenge, retribution, on behalf of certain lofty principles.

Because Athena is so identified with the fatherworld, however unconsciously, she tends to inherit the patriarchal fear of the Dark Mother's powers, not seeing them as a part of her own psychic makeup. What is most helpful for her is to go inward into the lower reaches of both her psyche and her body in search of the bleeding victim in herself, who is, more often than not, trapped somewhere in the underworld by an inner tyrant she has inherited from the unconscious of the fatherworld.

What is missing in both the psychology and the myths of Athena is any model for the transformation of the maiden in her. For all the reasons given so far—cultural and personal—Athena consciousness has adapted so well to prevailing patriarchal/intellectual structures in the modern world that she has taken on some of its fixed "either/or," "all-or-nothing" values with her masculine mode of ego structuring. Something of this rigidity has to go before she can move from the unchanging, *eternal* values of the mind to the *cyclic* values of matriarchal consciousness. What is needed is some sort of sacrifice, so that energy so locked into upper realms may flow downward and reconnect with lower and darker energies that have become purely destructive in their isolation from the cyclic flow.

Athena's overuse of her head can so often be her chief defense mechanism. Even if she is seriously inclined to take a deeper look at herself, she will choose groups or therapies that reinforce her intellectual prejudices with more talk, more discussion. A clever Athena can fool even the best psychotherapist for years with an array of seeming insights and apparent progress without ever confronting her bodily self. Sometimes her dreams will yield images of waterskiing or skating or flying, indicating that she is staying on the surface emotionally or is "up in the air," in her head. Occasionally she will even dream of being beheaded, as though the unconscious were trying to tell her even more dramatically to let go of her head. The most valuable thing she can do at this point is to dance, get some massage, or work with a body-oriented therapist.

The Greek image of Athena as a maiden with a sword and armor suggests a huge tension between a tough outer "masculine" persona and an extremely vulnerable inner feminine self that remains undeveloped and hypersensitive, virginal in the sense of untouched. Even the most successful and charismatic Athena women will report in ther-

SIMONE DE BEAUVOIR'S ATHENEAN VISION OF THE FREE WOMAN

The free woman is just being born; when she has won possession of herself perhaps Rimbaud's prophecy will be fulfilled: "There shall be poets! When woman's un-measured bondage shall be broken, when she shall live for and through herself, man—hitherto detestable—having let her go, she, too, will be poet! Woman will find the unknown! Will her ideational worlds be different from ours? She will come upon strange, unfathomable, repellent, delightful things: we shall take them, we shall comprehend them." It is not sure that her "ideational worlds" will be different from those of men, since it will be through attaining the same situation as theirs that she will remain different, in what degree these differences will retain their importance—this would be to hazard bold predictions indeed. What is certain is that hitherto woman's possibilities have been suppressed and lost to humanity, and that it is high time she be permitted to take her chances in her own interest and in the interest of all. . . .

To emancipate woman is to refuse to confine her to the relations she bears to man, not to deny them to her; let her have her independent existence and she will continue none the less to exist for him *also*: mutually recognizing each other as subject, each will yet remain for the other an *other*. The reciprocity of their relations will not do away with the miracles—desire, possession, love, dream, adventure—worked by the division of human beings into two separate categories; and the words that move us—giving, conquering, uniting—will not lose their meaning. On the contrary, when we abolish the slavery of half of humanity, together with the whole system of hypocrisy that it implies, then the "division" of humanity will reveal its genuine significance and the human couple will find its true form.

—*The Second Sex*, pp. 795, 813–14

apy how insecure and anxious they really feel inside, despite all the outer recognition and achievement. In one of our workshops a well-established psychology teacher told of how she had been videotaped leading a group therapy session. The way she remembered the session, she thought she was nervous, lacked incisiveness, and generally came across very poorly in the group. On seeing the videotape she was shocked to find how confident, forceful, and charismatic she appeared to the outer world.

This experience of the split between the fragile inner maiden and the tough outer fighter tends to be taken for granted by women who live strongly in Athena's world. Since they experience themselves inwardly as sensitive and discount their persona, which they *know* is only a front, they tend to be unaware of the effect this outer self is having on those around them. Here is the paradox that leads us to the heart of Athena's wound: the more she covers up her vulnerable maiden, the fiercer her protective shield becomes and the more unconscious she will be of it. The heart of Athena's wound is the wound in Athena's heart, and this is precisely where many of the Greek images show the Medusa's head—over her breastplate. In psychological language, the heaviest layer of the defensive structure will be nearest to the heart of the complex. For, like a wounded animal, the deeply hurt Athena woman will fiercely drive away those who might most help her, because she has no way of letting down her defenses, taking off her armor, and exposing the raw and infinitely sensitive core of her feminine being. In D. H. Lawrence's novel *Women in Love*, where Athena is caricatured as the aristocratic, intellectual Hermione, the hero, Birkin, turns on her in a moment of disgust, accusing her of being heartless and cold. Unable to contain her rage, she seizes a huge glass crystal and smashes it down on his skull. In response to his unfeeling penetration of her armor, so great is the pain of exposure that Hermione retaliates with all the deathly violence of the Medusa.

When her armoring has become rigid and her rage sits on the surface like a trap set to close its jaws on whoever may venture too close, the deeply wounded Athena woman fails to see that her softness and vulnerability are actually the place of entry into the lost parts of her feminine being, the point of contact with the other goddesses she is out of touch with. Linda Leonard, describing the armoring phenomenon in *The Wounded Woman*, says of such women that "insofar as their armor shields them from their own feminine feelings and their soft side, these women tend to become alienated from their own creativity, from healthy relationships with men, and from the spontaneity and vitality of living in the moment" (p. 18).

Deep down Athena is out of touch with the two goddesses of love: the maternal love of Demeter and the sensual love of Aphrodite, both goddesses who dwell in their bodies and who are, in their softness and vulnerability, willing to risk intimate contact in relationships and willing, too, to risk pain and loss.

WOUNDED ATHENA: A MODERN EXAMPLE

When Kate, an attractive young woman of twenty-eight, first came into therapy, she seemed to want to spend all her time attacking the whole institution of therapy as a waste of time and money. Since she continued to come, she was clearly getting something from it, if only the pleasure of ridiculing her therapist. In fact, what she was really doing was testing whether this was a safe place to let out her feelings. She had learned that the best form of defense was attack, so she set out first of all to find chinks in her therapist's armor. Since her therapist didn't respond in kind, the sparring she had anticipated was frustrated; but at least she wasn't thrown out of the office and she was, after all, calling the shots.

Slowly and painfully she began to remove her porcupinelike armor and talk a little about herself: "I'll tell you what I feel but I don't give a damn what you think," she said defiantly. The defiance and anger, it turned out, were all associated with an extremely unloving, cruel mother, whom she was naturally afraid her therapist might turn into. Her mother had frequently locked her up in her bedroom, refused to serve anything but cold food through most of her childhood, and was once found in the garage trying to kick a stray cat to death. Outside of schizophrenic and physically abusive mothers, it was one of the more damaged experiences of the Demeter function we have come across. Kate had, in fact, experienced nothing of real mothering, since her actual mother was sunk in bitterness and a neurotic search for pity and attention from her husband and daughter. Kate eventually admitted, too, that her mother had beaten her frequently.

Kate's psychological condition reminded one of a taut piano wire. One felt that, if touched unexpectedly, she would jump a foot into the air. She talked and smoked incessantly. She was quite thin; her chest especially seemed extremely tight. One time she produced a fantasy of being surrounded by a sheet of glass, another time of being alone on an island and hiding from people who came to it. Her descriptions of her sexual relationships were sentimentally romantic, physical details being glossed over in favor of shared intellectual interests.

Beneath her anger she admitted a deep sensation of "not being there" as she put it. She didn't really have any vivid, immediate feelings other than anger. Often she would retreat into a fantasy world of far-away places, mostly in country settings. One day she found herself walking by a river, similar to one she knew in Colorado, and she met a very fat Indian woman, whom she liked immensely. This figure, the Fat Lady, as we came to call her, proved to be the healing factor in therapy, more powerful than anything the therapist could provide. It was a manifestation, an epiphany, one might say, of the goddess Demeter, bringing with her all the love, warmth, and nurturing Kate had lacked as a child. After painting the Fat Lady frequently and dialoguing with her in her private journal (which she steadfastly refused to show to her therapist) a remarkable transformation began to occur in Kate. It was as though her cold, stiff body language slowly began to soften, and she loosened up, warming inwardly to a new source of energy in herself.

Kate now began to talk of her father, almost for the first time. She had grown to see him as a weak man who had withdrawn from family fights and never took a stand on anything. She began to see how in relationships she had been drawn to older men who always disappointed her, just like her father, and how she always had to do things all alone. Kate began to see how she had adopted her mother's bitter attitude toward weak men by becoming strong herself. And like her mother, she had been left feeling alone and unloved, still stuck in childhood disappointments, unable to grow emotionally. She learned to use her bright, fast mind to get the attention of teachers and, later, older men.

At this point in the therapy a lover appeared in her life, close to her own age for a change, a somewhat shy, gentle, research physicist. His sensitivity mirrored hers in a certain way, since he tended to live a lot in his head and in a strongly delineated fantasy world. There turned out to be sexual difficulties in the relationship, but they tackled them together bravely. He was prepared to go into therapy and benefited a lot from sharing his carefully guarded inner life. It seemed that they both shared the same problem, that they were mirroring each other in a certain way. In their fear of deep feelings and the body, both had learned to retreat into fantasy, which was safe and could be controlled. But slowly, because they both had the courage to share their vulnerabilities with each other and experience genuine and not manipulative love, their sex life began to open up and blossom. Aphrodite had appeared and was bestowing her most precious gifts, gifts that only two lovers who have taken down all their defenses can know, because, in John Donne's words, they now "watch not one another out of fear."

In the background the Fat Lady continued to watch and was a constant companion in Kate's inner reveries. When she came to her final session, she asked what her therapist thought of her getting married to her new lover. The therapist hesitated, saying, "Why are you asking that? You always automatically discount my opinions." "Yes, but tell me what you think anyway," Kate replied. "I think it's a wonderful idea," her therapist said quite spontaneously. "You're right," said Kate, "that's what the Fat Lady said too." So strongly had her inner connection to Demeter in the form of the Fat Lady become that she no longer needed her therapist. A new phase in her life was about to begin. A true inner dialogue between her Athena self and her Demeter and Aphrodite selves had now opened up. No one could say that all would be clear sailing from now on—these goddesses have strong opinions themselves and are known for their disputes—but whole new possibilities and ways of being were now available to Kate. She was no longer trapped by the wounds of one unhappy, isolated goddess, either personally or collectively. She could listen within to the various goddesses' lively dialectic and make her own choices to live a freer and more fulfilled life.

THREE

ARTEMIS: THE HEART OF THE LONELY HUNTRESS

Come with bows bent and with emptying of quivers,
Maiden most perfect, lady of light,
With a noise of winds and many rivers,
With a clamour of waters, and with might;
Bind on thy sandals, O thou most fleet,
Over the splendour and speed of thy feet;
For the faint east quickens, the wan west shivers,
Round the feet of the day and the feet of the night.
—ALGERNON CHARLES SWINBURNE,
CHORUS FROM *ATALANTA IN CALYDON*

ARTEMIS IN THE MODERN WORLD: A DISPLACED GODDESS

Artemis doesn't stand out strongly in the modern world. For one thing, she isn't really at home in the city, with its fast-paced high-tech lifestyles and upwardly mobile values. When we run into her in the city, she'll probably seem rather shy, perhaps reserved. Small talk doesn't seem to interest her, and we have the impression she really wants to be somewhere other than chatting on the street or in a restaurant. It's easy to mistake her for her sister Athena by the vigorous energy she seems to emit. But the energy we're picking up isn't mental; it comes from her lithe, athletic body, which loves to be physically engaged in the project of the moment.

A further clue may be her clothes. She's not dressed in a sophisticated outfit the way most busy Athenas are. In her old jeans and loose shirt she may look as though she's just helped someone move into a new apartment or is on her way to a workout. And should we meet her again, she may be just as casually dressed as before. Clothes, either as emblems of status or as a way of turning heads (Aphrodite's concern), just don't seem important to her.

The reason is simple: the Artemis woman is only superficially related to the "civilized" world. She is not at home in the city, because deep down she belongs in the wilds. To the ancient Greeks, Artemis was goddess of the wild places, most at home hunting in the mountains, following the rhythms of the animals, at one with the cycles of the moon (see box, "To Artemis").

The key word for Artemis, then, is *Nature*. In this respect she is the opposite of her otherwise quite similar sister, Athena, whose gift today is to empower women to be major contributors to the intellectual, political, and creative life of our cities and hence to the quality of our *civilization* (her key word). Athena and Artemis, with their strong energy and their independent spirit, have a lot in common: they are, in our view, the two sisters who are closest to each other on the Goddess Wheel. Since theirs is an extremely important connection for modern women, we will compare and contrast them frequently in this chapter.

To meet the Artemis woman in her own element, it is necessary to get away from the cities and the highways. We may even have to leave our automobile behind. We may find her leading horseback trekking expeditions in the Rockies or homesteading in northern California. We might track her down in a wet suit with a marine biology team or photographing wildlife in Alaska for the Sierra Club's bulletin. She could be a painter or a sculptor, living as the artist Georgia O'Keeffe did on the edge of the desert in New Mexico. Or she might be part of an experimental community, like the famous Farm of Stephen and Ina May Gaskin in Tennessee.

The Artemis woman often likes a rugged life-style and she's eminently well suited for one, physically speaking. There's something intensely youthful and sometimes slightly boyish about the physique of an Artemis woman. Even in later life an Artemis woman will retain a strong, energetic body that she keeps fit and well tuned. It is very rare

TO ARTEMIS

I sing of bright Artemis of the golden arrows;
Goddess of the wild hunt and slayer of many deer;
I bless you, holy Virgin, great sister of Apollo
He with his golden sword.

In the shadows of the hills, across the windy
mountain-tops, I hear her hunting;
there she draws her mighty golden bow,
letting fly her fatal shafts.

The peaks of lofty mountains tremble,
the dark woods echo with the cry of beasts
fleeing in terror. The whole earth shakes;
even the teeming sea,

In and out she darts, her heart undaunted,
killing, killing, killing—
animals of every kind and stature.

Then, when her great appetite is satisfied,
her love of the chase appeased,
she sets aside, unstrung, her mighty bow.

Now she seeks the grassy slopes of Delphi,
her brother, dear Apollo's splendid hall
and there calls up the Graces and the Muses:

Her bow unslung, her arrows put aside,
She dons a lovely dress,
and now she leads a sacred dance
with songs to Leto of the fair ankles—

Leto, who bore such children
as the world has never seen!
Supreme in act, supreme in wisdom.
Eminent of gods.

> Farewell, great children of Zeus and of Leto,
> she with the beautiful hair,
> I will sing of you again.
>
> —from *The Homeric Hymns*
> (authors' translation)

to find an overweight or sedentary Artemis. She likes to walk, jog, play competitive sports when she can, or else tend animals, sail, ride horses—anything to keep her outdoors, on the move. It's physical energy, life energy that drives her, not the mental energy of her sister Athena or the erotic energy of Aphrodite.

With all this physical energy and her strong drive for achievement, men are often a little in awe of her. She may run faster, climb better, or lift heavier weights than many men. She often seems to manage just fine without men. Actually, neither she nor her sister Athena have a consort or known lover in popular Greek myth. Psychologically this is because they both represent types of women who are born with strong "masculine" qualities already in their makeup.[1] Athena could be called tough-minded, while with Artemis it's more that she's tough-bodied. Men who can't keep up with her intensely active, often muscular style had better stay away.

In the last century, in America and in European colonies in Africa and Asia, many women came to live a more or less pure Artemis lifestyle as pioneers or settlers. This was especially true of the women who braved the western frontier of America. Anne LaBastille has collected many of their stories in her fascinating book *Women and Wilderness*. Some of these pioneer wives were reluctant Artemises, loathing their wild environment and endlessly pining for the comforts of the East Coast or Europe they had left behind. But for other women the

---

[1] We know this is a loaded term and that Artemis women are especially sensitive to it (along with the word *feminine*). Briefly we mean by *masculine* those *active, combative,* and *independent* qualities that are stereotypically fostered in boys and played down in girls. We do *not* believe they belong solely to the male psyche, as we shall explain in detail.

wilderness ceased "to be a battlefield and became a place of personal and professional fulfillment," in the words of Anne LaBastille. Here, for example, is what one of the happier settlers, Elinore Pruitt Stewart, had to say about her life on a cattle ranch in a wild part of Wyoming around the turn of the century:

> To me, homesteading is the solution of all poverty's problems, but I realize that temperament has much to do with success in any undertaking and persons afraid of coyotes and work and loneliness had better let ranching alone. At the same time, any woman who can stand her own company, can see the beauty of the sunset, loves growing things, and is willing to put in as much time at careful labor as she does over the washtub, will certainly succeed; will have independence, plenty to eat all the time, and a home of her own in the end. . . .
>
> I have tried every kind of work this ranch affords, and I can do any of it. Of course, I *am* extra strong, but those who try know that strength and knowledge come with doing. I just love to experiment, to work, and to prove out things, so that ranch life and "roughing it" just suit me.
>
> —from *Letters of a Woman Homesteader*,
> quoted by LaBastille, pp. 28–29

In this century, however, the trend has reversed. We've observed that many Artemis women today are more frustrated than they realize, mostly because they are living in the city. The almost cultish trend toward highly disciplined fitness regimes and women's body building speaks of huge reserves of untapped Artemis energy when seen from the goddess perspective. Inside many a super-fit city athlete there is an ancient Amazon longing for an entirely different kind of life-style.

Fortunately a lot of women over the past fifteen to twenty years have recognized and responded to this inner "call of the wild." In *Women and Wilderness*, a book every woman who feels Artemis stirring should read, Anne LaBastille describes the process whereby "women are living, working and playing, by their own free choice, and in increasing numbers, in the wilderness."

We fully agree with LaBastille that this is nothing short of a social phenomenon. Here is how she summarizes this quiet revolution:

Across our continent women are entering the traditionally male bastions of wilderness work and life. They are out-of-doors as forest technicians, park rangers, marine and wildlife biologists, speleologists, ethologists, herpetologists, conservation officers, professional environmentalists, wilderness guides, survival and firearms experts, hunters, fisherwomen, sportswomen, and just plain backwoodswomen. Sometimes alone, sometimes with families, they are proving beyond doubt that women *do* have wilderness in them. (p.1)[2]

Artemis is alive and well in our midst and is in fact changing the consciousness of many women. She's far less obvious than her sisters Athena or Aphrodite or Hera, but she's there nevertheless. And with her deep sympathy for the earth and for all living beings, which in our era are seriously threatened by wanton technological plunder, pollution, and greed, she may prove, of all the goddesses, to have the most important message of all for us (see box, "The Return of Artemis").

CLASSICAL ARTEMIS: FROM GREAT MOTHER TO MAIDEN HUNTRESS

We are all familiar with the image of Artemis (later the Roman Diana) as a slender, maidenly, scantily dressed moon goddess, attended by her hounds, golden bow in hand. In this portrayal, as in many popular versions of the Greek myths, she appears as pure, lovely, but rather colorless. It is as though she's been admitted to the company of the other Olympian gods and goddesses as some sort of token nature lover; clear-skinned and virginal, but naive in the worldly ways of the patriarchy.

One of the sources of this striking but essentially tame image of

---

[2] In this last sentence LaBastille is referring to a rather poignant poem called "Women," lamenting the loss of the Artemesian spirit. Written by Louise Bogan, in the twenties, the first stanza reads:

> Women have no wilderness in them
> They are provident instead.
> Content in the hot cell of their hearts
> To eat dusty bread

THE RETURN OF ARTEMIS

The Virgin Artemis, archetype of a femininity that is pure and primitive, is becoming important once more. For a long time, we have had no representation of absolute femininity, that is, one defined neither by relationship to a lover (Aphrodite), nor to a child (Demeter or Mary, Mother of Jesus), nor with a father (Athena), nor to a husband (Hera).

In fact, femininity is rarely represented in the absolute, but rather in relation to some other reality of the masculine world. Usually, when a woman withdraws into a territory closed to the male, she is perceived as a pariah, a sorceress, or a crazy woman. When depicted in literature, cinema, or television, feminine virginity occurs generally in a tale about a male introducing himself into this realm and transforming the virgin into a "real woman," as if femininity could never be complete in itself. As for the woman who dares persist in retreating, one is left with the understanding that she is too ugly, bad-tempered, or otherwise defective. She is more distrusted than esteemed. In contrast, we admire figures of male hermits, sages, illuminati or simply solitary men; they are not presented as being incomplete because they keep their distance from the opposite sex or remain chaste.

Artemis, who is very beautiful, some say as beautiful as Aphrodite, thus comes to sanctify solitude, natural and primitive living to which we may all return whenever we find it necessary to belong only to ourselves. An Amazon and infallible archer, Artemis guarantees our resistance to a domestication that would be too complete.

Moreover, as protectress of flora and fauna, she is the figure most directly concerned with the contemporary ecological debate and its related social choices.
—Ginette Paris, *Pagan Meditations*, pp. 109–10

the virgin goddess is Homer's epic *The Iliad*. In a famous scene toward the end of the story, the gods are bickering about the outcome of the Trojan War as their various heroic champions, such as Achilles, come to grief. At one juncture, Artemis scolds her brother, Apollo, for withdrawing from the fray. Immediately, like some bossy old stepmother, Hera seizes her by the wrists, boxes her ears, and scatters her arrows on the ground. In tears she retreats to Father Zeus, who takes her in his lap to comfort her. Clearly we are meant to see her as little more than a girl.

Like so many of the Greek myths this scene is a pitiful example of just how much the primordial power of the Mother Goddess had to take a backseat to the later greater glory of the patriarchs and warrior heroes. One would hardly guess from *The Iliad*, or from many of the myths, that Artemis was in fact the most popular of the Greek goddesses, her cult surpassing that of Demeter, Athena, or Aphrodite. Yet Martin Nilsson, the great scholar of Greek religion, tells us:

> Artemis was the most popular goddess of Greece, but the Artemis of popular belief was quite a different person from the proud virgin of mythology, Apollo's sister. Artemis is the goddess of wild Nature, she haunts the woods, the groves, the luscious meadows. There the "rushing Artemis" hunts and dances with her attendant nymphs. She protects and fosters the young of animals and growing human children. In her cult occur orgiastic dances and the sacred bough. . . . A favorite subject of archaic art is the figure formerly called "the Persian Artemis," now the "Mistress of Animals," a woman holding in her hands four-footed animals or birds of different kinds.
> —*A History of Greek Religion*, p. 28

One of the greatest shrines in the Greek world was dedicated to Artemis. This was the famous temple to Diana of Ephesus in Asia Minor (now Turkey). A huge statue of her, which has survived in copies from Roman times, shows her with many breasts, unmistakably the Mother who feeds all. In fact, there is no question that this Artemis was the Great Mother herself, triple in her power as the new, full, and waning moon: Maiden, Mother, and Crone.

But as we have seen again and again, the later Greek patriarchy found it more comfortable to keep these mighty powers separated. So they restricted the role of Mother mostly to Demeter, consigned the Crone's closeness to death and the afterlife to Persephone and Hecate, and sentimentalized the complex nature psychology of Artemis into that of an adolescent Girl Scout playing with bows and arrows in the woods.

Artemis is probably the oldest of all the Greek goddesses. Older than Athena's first cities, older than Aphrodite's first love temples, older even than Demeter, the corn mother who presided over the very beginnings of agriculture. Artemis belongs to the most ancient stratum of human memory.

PRIMORDIAL ARTEMIS: GODDESS OF THE ANIMAL POWERS

Some have traced Artemis's origins to the hunting tribes of Anatolia, where the mythic Amazons were said to have dwelt. Others derive her from the ancient great nature goddess Cybele of Asia Minor, a Lady of Beasts often shown flanked with lions, stags, birds, and other creatures. But it seems possible, according to Walter Burkert's authoritative *Greek Religion*, that Artemis may go back even to Paleolithic times, given the way that Greek hunters would hang the horns and skin of their prey on a tree or special club-shaped pillar in her honor.

Cultures that subsist on hunting wild animals, before agricultural settlement and the domestication of animals, have a very intimate relationship to the quarry they hunt. They must be nomadic, following the migratory seasons of the herds or packs. They must get to know the mating and other habits of the animals they follow, becoming in tune with their rhythms and cycles. But above all, the hunter must learn to enter a primal dance of death with his prey, accepting that he may as easily be killed as kill. This leads to a kind of mystical identification between man and animal, between the hunter and the hunted.

A recent and quite gentle version of this identification is described in Conrad Richter's *The Trees*, a novel of pioneer life and growing up in the thick midwestern forests of America in the early 1800s. (The heroine Sayward is a fine literary example of the Artemis wilderness spirit.) In a striking scene one of Sayward's sisters, Genny, is being chased in the woods by an indentured, or "bound," boy:

> Genny could hear the bound boy calling her now. It came over her she was a deer, too. The bound boy was hunting her like men always hunted women and wild things. Never would they let them be to live their own lives. No, men always came after, smelling and tracking them down. But the bound boy would never find her. She was a young doe. A delicious wildness came up in her. The woods looked different now. The trees and the bushes, even the poison sumac, were friendly. They stood over her and bent down at her and tried to hide her. You had to be a deer to know how the wild things felt when a man was after you. (cited in LaBastille, p. 56)

This kind of consciousness, called by anthropologists *mystical participation*, underlies all the rituals we know in hunting cultures of wearing animal skins and horns. It is a theme we will return to. This unusual attitude of mind also lies behind all animal and human sacrifice in the urge to offer back to the animal powers of life and death what is rightly theirs. For the ancient hunting cultures it was necessary to be *part of* the great cycle of nature, not to try to control it. This is an ecological wisdom that is hard for us to comprehend today.

Yet this mystical participation with the natural world was starting to be lost even to the first urban Greeks of Homer's time (c. 850 B.C.). Theirs was a warrior and later a colonizing culture, for whom hunting had become more a sport than way of life. So Artemis and other hunter figures, such as the great Orion, were by then vestiges, dim memories of a time when men and women lived closer to wild nature, to life and death.

One crucial area, however, where the feral wisdom of Artemis was strongly retained was in all matters pertaining to childbirth and the protection of young sucklings. We can hear echoes of the primordial Bear Goddess (see box, "Artemis and the Bear") and her sympathy for all those who give birth alone and unattended like the animals. To the Greeks, Artemis became *the patroness of midwives*; she would come to all women who called out to her while giving birth. But her presence was an ambivalent one in the sense that she, as Death Mother, might

ARTEMIS AND THE BEAR

Readers of Jean Auel's evocative novel *The Clan of the Cave Bear* will recall how the tribe's shaman or medicine man dons a bearskin so that the great bear spirit can speak through him. In such practices there is a continuity with the later Greek Artemis, whose chief totem animals were the bear and the stag. Even the root of her name, *art-* is cognate with the Indo-European root word for bear.

Many myths about bears surround Artemis. In the very earliest Greek stories she appears as a she-bear with her cubs. Nothing could be more fierce than a mother bear protecting her cubs, but at the same time, nothing seemingly more tender than her carrying them in her abundant fur. No wonder, then, that, in the words of Marija Gimbutas, "the maternal devotion of the female bear made such an impression upon Old European peasants that she was adopted as a symbol of motherhood" (*The Goddesses and Gods of Old Europe*, p. 195).

Artemis as the Bear Mother survived in classical Greece in the cult of Artemis of Brauron. Young Athenian girls, not older than nine years, were dedicated to the goddess *as young bears*, called the *avktoi*. They dressed in bearskins and did bear dances in her temple. Scholars think a rite of initiation into the goddess as both bear and huntress and protectress of women in childbirth was intended. Goats were ritually slaughtered during these ceremonies, so there is little question that the pubescent girls were also being shown the dark side of the Mother and her blood mysteries of death, sacrifice, and renewal.

In a late myth from patriarchal times one of the followers of Artemis, Callisto, is turned into a bear after being seduced by Zeus. But the earliest version no doubt referred to a sacred mating of the goddess herself as a bear. (See also box, "The Myth of Callisto and the Great Bear.")

also claim the newborn unless she was properly invoked and propitiated. According to the classicist Kerényi, women who survived childbirth gave their clothes to the temple of Artemis of Brauron in Athens, but the priestess also inherited those of women who died in giving birth—"dread trophies of the Huntress," as Kerényi comments.

Even though Homer patronized Artemis and hunting had dwindled to the status of sport by classical times, the image of the ferocious Huntress was kept alive in popular religion. Awe-inspiring vestiges of "the way of the animal powers," in Joseph Campbell's phrase, survived in religious cults outside of the cities. Every year, at the temple of Patrae, Pausanias reports, hundreds of animals of every kind were sacrificed to Artemis herself in the flames of a huge holocaust.

Clearly Artemis was still seen in part as a fierce and bloodthirsty goddess, the Death Mother herself, who, like the Indian Kali, must be placated with live offerings. Perhaps this is why the more sophisticated urban Greeks of Athens tended to sentimentalize her; they hardly dared to look this bloody side of Artemis in the face.

Bloodlusting Artemis haunts the Homeric Hymn, too (see box, "To Artemis"). Here we find her delighting in the hunt, "killing, killing, killing." But notice, too, how this takes place in the distant woods, displaced far from the city. Nevertheless, in a remarkable transformation Artemis is somehow able to put away her mighty bow in order to initiate and join a beautiful dance at her brother Apollo's great mansion. Civilized grace and decorum prevail as the Moon Goddess plays in the realm of the Sun God. This hymn is probably the closest that the later Greeks ever came to holding the two sides of the Great Goddess together in their consciousness as harbinger of both life and death. It is a remarkable invocation, containing as it does images of both the civilized and the savage world.

ARTEMIS TODAY: GROWING UP

It is hard for us today to see Artemis except through "civilized" eyes. Except for the few of us who have grown up on farms, hunted, or fished, "nature, red in tooth and claw" remains an abstraction or a neatly packaged story in a National Geographic special.

Yet not so long ago in American culture an Artemesian life in the wilderness was not only possible but fairly common. The American pioneer woman embodied the rugged, close-to-the-earth qualities of the goddess and was schooled, as a result of harsh circumstances, to live with death and often violence. Most frontier women could wield a gun as well as a cooking pot—sometimes better (see box, "Frontier Artemis: Calamity Jane").

Today the frontier life-style is truly marginal and rare. But we believe that many Artemis women, failing to fit into the urban Athena mold, are moving back to the country. So, Artemis consciousness is still very much with us, and to the extent that we *are* all citified and a little squeamish about killing our own dinner, we stand in much the same ambivalent relationship to her wilder nature as did the urban Greeks of Athens.

Spotting the Artemis child in the classroom is easy. Her dislike of long hours at a desk will tend to make her seem backward, bored, or sullen to her teachers. She'd obviously rather be somewhere else. In fact she'd probably learn a lot more doing practical things with some older family member than being in school, but alas things aren't set up that way any longer. Any physical activity or nature walk, however, will get her undivided attention, provided it's not too regimented.

The strong side of young Artemis that might be mistakenly called masculine is in fact her intense love of freedom, independence, and autonomy. It will show up as aggression, too, to the extent that she will always put up a fight to maintain her freedom. So, where young Athena likes to be just as smart as her brothers, Artemis likes to be as tough as them, if not tougher. She'll be the tomboy, out there scrapping and punching with the worst of the boys. She soon learns to swallow her tears and plan revenges for humiliations, giving as good as she gets. Mothers wanting a pretty Aphrodite will quickly despair of her total disregard for clothes or cleanliness. It's as though she'll wear jeans for life. She knows they are the most practical for climbing trees, going on muddy tromps, and participating in ball games.

Before puberty she is quite oblivious to gender differences, feeling fully and confidently a girl because of strong bonding with her mother (the Artemis myth tells of a good and powerful mother, Leto, who bore Artemis painlessly). It's her very confidence in her feminine self that enables her to explore her "masculine," which is to say her free-

FRONTIER ARTEMIS: CALAMITY JANE

Calamity Jane—born Martha Jane Cannary in 1852—had a wilder life than most men, even in the Old West. She had at one time or another been a bartender, scout, gambler, drinker, cowgirl, sharpshooter, prospector, stage driver, and cook, according to Anne LaBastille. She was for a time a stunt woman in Bill Cody's Wild West Show, a prostitute, and later the wife of Wild Bill Hickok. In her letters to her daughter, Janey, we see both the tough and the tender side of her. Here is an extract in her colorful style and wild spelling:

[Writing of the women of Deadwood City who disapproved of her] They came into the salloon with a horse whip & shears to cut off my hair. Well Janey I fixed them in my own way. I jumped off the bar into their midst & before They could say sickem I had them all howling. I cut off one of the bitches old black locks & thrashed the whip over their heads. You see, I wear pants so I can get around while these peticoted females yell for help. You should have seen her when I jumped off the bar. I grabbed her hoop skirt & three petticotes & flung them all up over her head. She couldnt fight back so I had her just where I wanted her. I tore off her long pantalets & left her standing there in her birthday bloomers for the men to get a treat. . . . I'll never live to be very old Janey. I cant stand this awful life very many years. I sometimes think I'll be married again & then the thought of being tied to one man's shirt tail sickens me. I wish things were different & I could live on through the years knowing I would someday have you with me.

—*Let Them Speak for Themselves; Women in the American West, 1849–1900,*
cited in LaBastille, p. 44

dom-loving, side so early and so energetically. She has little time for the trivia of dolls, parties, and dress-up.

Unless she has another Artemis girlfriend with whom to share her outdoor escapades or her latest animal obsession (toads, gerbils, praying mantises, dogs, horses), she may begin to find being a stereotypic "young girl" somewhat problematic. This is because our society begins very early to reward boys for aggression and competitiveness and girls for compliance and charm. Yet her instincts—Artemis is very instinctual—tell her that traditional "feminine" behavior and little girls' games are somehow superficial, if not false. She is fully aware that her "tomboyish" love of fighting and scouting games somehow alienates her from other girls. She is starting to experience "gender-role confusion." (Young Athena has this problem, too, but since she's not so physically energetic as Artemis, she'll find a place hanging out with adults or older kids, impressing them with her precocious view of the world.)

Sometimes the young Artemis will have an older or slightly younger brother who values her Amazonian spirit and makes her his close companion in adventures. He may get her into the boys' clan before it becomes exclusively male. Such brother-sister bonds can be very special and affirming for the shy and rather socially awkward prepubescent Artemis. We can certainly feel the ancient bond between Artemis and her brother, Apollo, at work in such friendships.

But if she finds no admiring brother or similarly rugged girlfriend, a young Artemis may have her first and perhaps bitter taste of loneliness. Introversion is forced upon her, and in the absence of real open spaces she may fantasize a life far away: on a farm with animals; in a distant country; working with tribal peoples; or as a forest ranger, explorer, or traveler. From within she hears the atavistic call of the wild, and a longing awakens, a longing to *return* that may haunt her all her life until she follows it. But for the time being she learns to keep her own counsel. Hard though it is, being alone teaches her that she has self-sufficiency and independence, qualities that will be two of her greatest strengths as a woman.

ADOLESCENT AMAZON

In ways not unlike her sister Athena, Artemis may find puberty and the emergence of her womanhood a deeply confusing time. She must

face outer and inner forces now building beyond her control. Outwardly, whatever equal status she previously had in the boys' clan is
suddenly and mysteriously withdrawn. She is excluded now for not
being one of them, despite all the years of shared adventures.

Inwardly her budding young body is perplexing to her, so she tends
to hide its changes under loose shirts or baggy sweat suits. It's an
acceptable and safe place to hide her deepening role confusion. She
may not know who she is yet, but she certainly knows who she *isn't*;
she wants little or nothing to do with the giggling and titillation of
dating and parties. Her Aphrodite and Hera sisters' obsession with
clothes, makeup, and interesting boys only arouses her scorn.

Fortunately there are temporary escape routes from this gnawing
confusion of identity. Where Athena usually escapes into her head,
becoming academically smart, Artemis escapes into her body. Almost
any type of physical pursuit can successfully provide adolescent Artemis with a healthy, fulfilling, and socially rewarding channel for her
dynamic energy. And though she will not think of it in this way, it
helps to postpone the whole issue of her sexuality.

So we find adolescent Artemis as the athlete, the gymnast, the
dancer, the jogger, the tennis player, the swimmer, the skier, the rider,
and so on, depending on the resources available to her. The need to
be part of a male group is partly if not completely assuaged by being
a member of a women's or mixed team and by going to competitive
events, championships, or other gatherings where male and female
differences are largely sublimated in the group identity or the club
membership of the particular sport or activity.

For adolescent Artemis, to belong to athletic or sports teams and
similarly challenging physical disciplines in many ways resembles the
ancient Greek cult of the "little bears," the avktoi of Artemis (see box,
"Artemis and the Bear"). Young pubescent girls in Athens from nine
onward were able to identify with their wilder natures and the huntress
within them. It was a kind of initiation into Artemis for those not suited
or ready for more domestic feminine roles or sexuality.

Today an athletic identity can often provide a similar initiatory
bridge between girlhood and womanhood. These incredibly strict disciplines, which sometimes lead to international levels of competition,
teach a young woman skills of power, strength, and endurance.

As for the young Artemis who is lucky enough to grow up in or near the country, there still remains one major animal cult comparable to the avktoi of ancient Athens. This is probably the quintessentially Artemesian pursuit: horses. Whether she is lucky enough to own her own horse or pony or merely ride and groom a friend's, this can easily become an all-absorbing passion of her adolescent years, if not her life. A deep, intuitive communion with this most intelligent of beasts, a physical rapport that evokes archaic and erotic fantasies and the thrilling chance to take off into the woods and the fields—these things put the Artemis woman rapturously in touch with the core of the nature goddess within herself.

FINDING HERSELF: IS ARTEMIS THE ETERNAL ADOLESCENT?

The archetypal energy of Artemis bursts through most powerfully in adolescence. Adolescence represents the very peak of Artemis energy in women whom she blesses. It is so powerful, in fact, that women who live almost exclusively through Artemis remain in many ways perpetually youthful. Physically speaking, this is a wonderful gift, but there are pitfalls when Artemis comes to dominate a woman's consciousness to the exclusion of other goddess energies throughout her life.

Just as the bear cult did in ancient Athens for young pubescent girls, athletics and other absorbing physical pursuits can act as useful bridges between girlhood and womanhood. And of course, the modern term *adolescence* was coined to describe such a transitional period. But the danger for the young Artemis woman is that she may never fully cross that bridge, remaining caught in her sports persona or her backpacking or animal preoccupations, substituting these for the development of certain social skills, the risk of relationships, and becoming a fuller member of society.

Not that crossing the bridge into adulthood and womanhood is easy for anyone. That period of adjustment and adaptation can last throughout our twenties and longer. But it is clearly much easier for a young woman with a large dose of Aphrodite's relatedness, or Athena's academic and intellectual aptitudes, or Hera's strongly inculcated sense of social values. It's not so hard for Demeter, either, since marriage and having children soon gives her an immediate and satisfying adult identity as mother.

What makes it so hard for the Artemis woman? Why is she tempted to stay in her adolescent persona longer than most?

We have already glimpsed the seeds of her problem in childhood. First of all, she identifies with *boys'* activities, behavior, and dress. She rejects the culturally prescribed image of little girls as "sugar and spice and everything nice." And for good reason. She rightly knows she is not that kind of female—these are Aphrodite and Demeter roles, ones our society loves to sentimentalize in children.

So young Artemis knows who she is *not*. But this doesn't help, given the freedom-loving nature of her psyche, to know who she *is*. Just becoming a successful sportswoman, explorer, or marine biologist in her twenties won't be enough by itself. There is nothing about any of these and similar professions and careers that will define her as a woman; they are in fact quite neutral roles that could be performed equally by a man or a woman. Moreover, they all tend to be solitary occupations, requiring little of Artemis in the way of relatedness or the expression of that infuriating concept, femininity.

And she's right to be infuriated by it. It's mostly loaded toward male fantasies of what women should be—sweet little wife and mother, gorgeous sex object and admirer of the sacred male ego, or successful career woman.

ARTEMIS'S WOUND: THE PAIN OF ALIENATION

Artemis's wound involves the loneliness of being relegated, both psychologically and sometimes literally, to the fringes of society. She has been denied any true identity as a woman. Her fierce love of freedom and her independent cast of mind often make it especially hard for her to accept the life-styles of mother, wife, or career woman that belong to Demeter, Hera, and Athena. Indeed, she will often feel contempt for the values and forms of conventional society. She is deeply offended that the patriarchy has never been able to contain her fierce spirit or fully recognize her unique gifts as a woman.

Many of the conflicts of contemporary Artemis were present in our client Chris:

Chris was a tall, rather broad-shouldered young woman who had always perceived herself as something of a misfit. She felt different from her more conventional sisters and was teased by her one brother at puberty, leaving her excessively self-conscious about her femininity. Dating was agony for her, so she avoided it.

She had always been a good athlete, winning running, swimming, and downhill skiing awards throughout her adolescence. At home she was somewhat of a handywoman, liking to do odd carpentry and repair jobs, a skill she learned from her father. Later she became good at working on automobiles. But during adolescence she made few close friends, even in her sports teams, so increasingly she tended to hide out by immersing herself in her repair projects.

In college she meandered aimlessly between more sports and various science options, but the frenetic social life depressed her, and she became reclusive and drank excessively for a while. Eventually she dropped out of college to live with a sullen but colorful veteran of the Vietnam War who, it turned out, mainly lived from drug dealing. Chris wasn't particularly happy with him, but she was glad to share a remote cabin outside of town and was quite fascinated by his drug connections. Their sex life wasn't especially good, and after a while they began to have bad fights and drifted apart. She kept a German shepherd dog she was devoted to.

While doing volunteer work in a battered-women's shelter, Chris became friendly with the women's action group who ran it and ended up living in their small lesbian farm commune. In the country again she felt peaceful and, for once in her life, valued by the fiercely independent and individualistic women she lived with. She felt affirmed in her differences and became a useful practical member of their community. She found she had a talent working with the farm animals, becoming quite an expert on the goats they bred and milked. She was introduced to mountain backpacking by one of the community and found special delight in solitary retreats in the nearby national forest.

Finding well-paid work was always a problem for her, since she had so little inclination to get qualifications or be around larger cities. She slowly developed skill as a potter and found herself assisting a woman who had her own kiln and shop. Today they are partners and she is quite well known as a potter in her region. She teaches pottery in a local experimental college and is somewhat active in feminist politics; her ties with her lesbian commune remain, but she lives alone once more. "Essentially," she says, "I'm a loner."

In her therapy Chris worked on restoring her damaged self-confidence in her Athena abilities to get through college and function better in the world on a financial level. She also needed to challenge her shyness and let some Aphrodite energy brighten up her rather serious and stolid social life. Fortunately she met a quiet young carpenter, with whom she is now living, and together they are renovating an old barn as a shared living space. Chris will have to work hard to build her own world on the fringes of conventional society, but she has many valuable qualities and skills to do so, now that she is overcoming some of her isolation.

There are three goddesses on the Goddess Wheel with whom the partriarchy has always had difficulty: Aphrodite, Persephone, and Artemis. Aphrodite for her boundless eros, Persephone for her visionary genius, and Artemis for her untamable energy. Together, under the paranoid male fantasy of the witch, they were scapegoated and persecuted in the Middle Ages and remain deeply alienated to this day.

Artemis has survived well enough in peasant socieres, where she could keep her secrets to herself. Her strength and resourcefulness were valued in pioneer periods. In the last few centuries an upper-class Artemis such as Isak Dinesen (a.k.a. Baroness Karen Blixen) could afford to live independently, but for the most part there has been no place for her true spirit.

Outwardly attractive and "sexy" Aphrodite women seem to get all kinds of male attention. Young Artemis long ago learned to do without such attention, but she still feels resentment because her feelings of exclusion are fueled. If Artemis can come to understand something of Aphrodite's wound (see Aphrodite chapter), she might perceive how they are both living in reaction to patriarchal stereotyping in different ways. In workshops we have found that Aphrodite and Artemis often have a lot to say to each other, however reluctantly.

The psychological fact of the matter is that Artemis is really androgynous, which means that she is both feminine and masculine, something to be proud of. (How many men can comfortably say that?) This is the real secret of her enormously developed inner strength and independence. She already has in her makeup those masculine qualities that all the other goddess types (except Athena) project onto and give away to men.

This is the clue to her "virginal" nature as symbolized, but rarely understood, in the Greek image of the goddess as Maiden. In the ancient world a virgin was simply an unmarried woman. As we noted with Athena, the word had nothing to do with chastity—even Aphrodite was regarded as a virgin goddess in the ancient sense, despite her phony Olympian marriage to Hephaistos.

Psychologically, *virginity* means "self-sufficiency." When a woman is complete and whole in and of herself, she does not really need much, if any, external male energy to complement her. If we can get this psychological fact straight, we may start to look at the Artemis woman's sexuality in a new and different way.

Understanding her separateness, we can sense her sexual coolness, which the later Greeks, we think, misread or perhaps idealized as chastity. The Artemis woman isn't looking for eros in the Aphrodite sense of intimate, feeling relationships. Her true relationship is *with herself*, finding her own inner balance of male and female. That's why, in one of her forms, an Artemis woman can easily live alone, as a mystic, a contemplative, or a reclusive artist. That is the higher meaning of chastity.

Androgyny, as many Jungian writers have pointed out, is a precondition of celibate spirituality. For such women the energy remains inside, being converted into visions, mystical raptures, and a profound sympathy for all of nature and all beings. The lives of the great Christian saints Hildegard of Bingen (c. 1098–1179), Juliana of Norwich

(c. 1342–1413), and many others could be studied in this light.[3] Hildegard, for example, was a great healer, poet, musician, and visionary, while Juliana was known to have penned the famous utterance "God is our Mother."[4]

Women such as these often chose to be total recluses or very solitary. Great visionary experiences, whether those of a medieval Juliana of Norwich or a modern Georgia O'Keeffe, are often nourished by the spirit of the remote wilds or the desert. When "the world is too much with us" as Wordsworth, a very Artemesian poet put it, the contemplative spirit of the goddess cries out to be renewed in solitude and in inner, not outer discourse. The Artemis woman knows this instinctively, even if her contemporary fate has planted her in the city, obliging her to develop some extraverted Athena skills. Sooner or later she will find a way to withdraw to some cabin near Yosemite, a farm in Kentucky, a little-known island in the Caribbean—wherever the wilderness calls her. In solitude she recaptures a deep and wordless dimension of her soul that is mirrored in the silent activity of animals, the soaring of birds, the heave and crash of the ocean, the naked drama of the desert, the majesty of mountain peaks.

The psychologist Ginette Paris talks of her own experience of the movement between the busy city life of Athena and the regenerative power Artemis can bring in solitary retreat:

> When social life absorbs one's energies completely, it is
> time to penetrate the deep forest of Artemis and allow nature
> to replace human relations. It seems to me that there is a very
> evident link between a life rich in relationships and the need
> for solitary retreat in which the ego receives no stimulation.
> In my personal experience, solitude only became important
> during and after five years of intense and nourishing communal

[3] For further examples, see recent revisionist picture of Artemesian (as well as Athenean) spirituality among Christian woman mystics, *Medieval Women's Visionary Literature*, by Elizabeth Alvilda Petroff.

[4] An important recent development within Roman Catholicism is the movement started by the Dominican Matthew Fox, which he calls "creation spirituality." This approach attempts to refocus Christian awareness back toward the earth and created nature as a counterbalance to centuries of Christian denial of the earth and the body. We see this as an important development for Artemis and the other goddesses, so long alienated by Christian asceticism and hatred of the feminine.

life comparable to a group session of thousands of hours! This communal experience so "nourished" me with relationships that, when it ended, I needed a whole year of solitary life, listening to the wind in the trees and the fire in my stove, to digest this experience and re-kindle the desire for human companionship. This same need for solitude reappeared several years later when, my two children having attained a certain independence, I needed to be alone (for more frequent and shorter periods), rejoicing each time at not hearing the sound of my name for several days. . . .

Every woman and every man, saturated with relationships and contacts, finds that the presence of others hinders one's presence to oneself and is attracted by the asceticism, simplicity, and naturalness that characterize Artemis. Then solitude appears as one of the ways of entering into her world.

—*Pagan Meditations*, pp. 134–35

ARTEMIS AND HER SEXUALITY

But what of Artemis's sexuality? It's most certainly not absent. We don't subscribe to the chaste young maiden picture. That was surely Greek patriarchal propaganda to make sure daughters don't get pregnant by the wrong males; it's all a part of the institution of patrilineal succession that we discuss in our chapter on Aphrodite.

The real clue to the sexuality of the Artemis woman is to be found in one of her most potent and central symbols, her role as Lady of Animals. The secret of Artemis's sexuality lies, we believe, in her instinctual connection to her own animal nature. When the Artemis woman is deeply in touch with her true eros, her love play is wild and fierce.

Once we begin to look at how Artemis's consciousness is expressed through her animal manifestations, we can read some of her myths in a different light. One major myth of hers that makes a great deal of sense seen in this way is that of the maiden Callisto.

In the later and best-known version of the Callisto story, the maiden is a nymph, a follower of Artemis, who gets turned first into a bear, then into the Great Bear constellation after being impregnated

THE MYTH OF CALLISTO AND THE GREAT BEAR

The Greeks told the story of the young follower of Artemis called Callisto, whose name meant "the most beautiful." Zeus, in his typical way, seduced her, getting her pregnant. Enraged, Artemis, turned her into a she-bear for violating her pledge of chastity. The goddess was ready with her hounds to hunt the hapless Callisto, but Zeus intervened to save her from death by taking her up to heaven, where he turned her into the Great Bear constellation.

In one version of the story, Zeus becomes a bear to seduce Callisto. In another it was said that Zeus himself turned Callisto into a bear and that jealous Hera set Artemis to hunt her in error. Yet in the very earliest version of Callisto's story she and Zeus both mate as bears, suggesting a sacred wedding union of the animals.

Putting Callisto up in the sky as the Great Bear might seem an honor, but it really turns her into a lifeless abstraction, a name. It smacks of patriarchal guilt and Zeus's failure to fully own his instinctual, animal self. However, animal nature cannot so easily be suppressed, as a continuation of the later myth shows. Before her death Callisto was said to have given birth to twins: one twin was the bear Arkas, who became the first ancestor of Arcadia, and the other was Pan, the famous goat-footed god of that same region of Greece. To this day, Arcadia remains one of the wildest parts of Greece.

by Zeus (see box, "The Myth of Callisto and the Great Bear"). But scholars point out that *kallisto*, meaning "the most beautiful" in Greek, was merely an early epithet for Artemis the Great Mother. So Callisto would be the "maidenly" or unmarried form of Artemis herself. And, insofar as the patriarchal myth claims Artemis as Zeus's daughter, some divine incest starts to creep into the story.

However, incest is not the truly shocking part of the story. Incest has always been a prerogative of the gods and goddesses—how else could the first divine beings procreate? What is much more scandalous about this story is the moral slant. The patriarchal viewpoint of the first Olympian parents, Zeus and Hera, requires that Artemis, the model for all good and obedient daughters, must remain chaste in order to protect patrilineal descent. So, with typical perverted and all-too-familiar logic, the victim Callisto/Artemis is blamed for Zeus's violations![5]

Literal chastity, then, is, in this context, a propaganda weapon with which the patriarchal Greeks attempted to control their daughters and hence the male succession of property. For one thing, making Artemis pure helps to put down Aphrodite, always a threat to Hera's institution, marriage. For another, it helps Zeus and the fathers maintain a double standard with regard to their daughters and their own sexuality.

Yet all the evidence suggests that this kind of chastity does not belong to the original matriarchal Artemis. We feel that her primal lovemaking is much better symbolized by the earliest known version of the myth: the supreme god and goddess as two bears making love.

In support of such a radical-sounding view of the goddess and her sexuality, here is how Merlin Stone vividly describes Spartan followers of Artemis (Sparta, incidentally, is south of Arcadia—Pan country—on the Greek Peloponnesian peninsula):

In the classical age of Sparta, where the veneration of the Goddess as Artemis continued to thrive, women were extremely free and independent. According to both Euripides and Plutarch, young Spartan women were not to be found at home but in the gymnasia where they tossed off their restrictive clothing and wrestled naked with their male contemporaries. Women of Sparta appear to have had total sexual freedom, and though monogamy was said to be the official marriage rule, it was mentioned in several classical accounts that it was not taken very seriously. Plutarch reported that in Sparta the infidelity

[5] This kind of barefaced rationalization of male sexual abuse is still with us today in the common attitude of the police, the courts, and the public that rape victims, and even some abused children, are really to blame for being attacked. "She was asking for it" is the outrageous way this is often put.

of women was even somewhat glorified, while Nicholas of Damascus, perhaps as the result of some personal experience, tells us that a Spartan woman was entitled to have herself made pregnant by the handsomest man she could find, whether native or foreigner.

—*When God Was a Woman*, p. 53

The Spartan women's freedom was not an isolated instance in the ancient world; Stone quotes archaeologist Jacquetta Hawkes regarding the temple of Diana of Ephesus:

At this city [Ephesus] and indeed in Ionia generally, women and girls enjoyed much freedom. While women certainly won influence and responsibility by serving at the temples and great state festivals of the goddesses, there was also the liberation of the ancient cults. Respectable matrons and girls in large companies would spend whole nights on the bare hills in dances which stimulated ecstasy, and in intoxication, perhaps partly alcoholic, but mainly mystical. Husbands disapproved, but, it is said, did not like to interfere in religious matters. (p. 53)

What we learn from classical times, when the cult of Artemis was strong, is that sexuality was free and barely constrained by the social institution of marriage and issues of paternity. Sparta honored the warrior woman for more than just her prowess in the gym or on the track. We feel that today's Artemis women need to know this so they do not feel like outsiders because of our narrow modern views of sexual identity.

VISIONS OF NEW COMMUNITIES

The great strength of the Artemis woman is her independence, her self-reliance, and her will to achieve. And she is right to be proud of these qualities. Only men who can match them are worth bothering with. Why should she waste her time on men who are weak, dependent, and lacking in confidence? Such men will in any case feel deeply threatened by her, and she's unlikely to find them appealing or manly enough.

When it comes to relationships, Artemis is in complete agreement with her sister Athena: at all costs they both want to maintain their full and untrammeled independence. No clinging vines, no mama's boys, no adoring, sonnet-writing Lotharios, thank you! They both want plenty of space, physically and mentally, to do their own thing. Yes, they do want companionship, but of a different sort. Athena wants mental support, someone she can chew over her latest article with or debate the current political crisis. Artemis likes a man around, too, but usually not for his brains. She wants him to hold the fence post, pass her the rope on a rock climb, or be with her sweating and exhausted after an afternoon of cross-country running. She likes to work alongside him, enjoying a sense of shared physical endeavor and achievement. We might call this a kind of *parallel relatedness*, the communion of shared activities.

Artemis's brother, the Greek god Apollo, might well offer a model for this kind of relationship. Their mythic bond speaks of camaraderie and close friendship, where they each retain strong but distinct identities and spheres of activity. They live fairly separate lives, but at the same time share pursuits such as hunting or camping or skiing.

A modern Artemis might be a trainer in an Outward Bound center and her Apollo a consultant and organizer of wilderness trips. Sometimes they work together, more often they are off separately for weeks at a time.

When such pairs are content not to ruin the silence by a lot of superficial chatter, their connection is deep and intuitive. The Apollo mate may complement her wildness with his love of culture. As the Homeric Hymn suggests, when the wild chase is over, she will come to his place and show another, wondrous side of her eros to him: her dancing, her deep love of the rhythms of the earth, and the lovely swaying and leaping of her supple body. And perhaps deep within her the distant wilds still stir as she dreams of ancient goat-footed Pan. This part she may show to no man.

But it's not always that easy for the Artemis woman of today to find an independent, caring male to honor her strong personality and love the wilderness in her. For one thing a wounded sense of self-esteem, from that first early isolation from other girls, then exclusion by the male group, may have left her prickly, defensive, and more than a little shy and withdrawn. Without knowing it, she tends to push many men away when they press for intimacy.

In many ways the shy or fiercely independent Artemis may come to prefer the companionship of women like herself, with whom she can form strong bonds. Women's groups and women's communities will often appeal to the Artemis woman who has despaired of men. Just as men have for centuries excluded women from their groups, for the sake of their own power and self-identity, so today many women's communities are practicing their own kind of exclusivity. Like the fabled Amazon tribes, they often live quite androgynous lives, building, organizing, financing their communal houses or farms with few or no men. It is, for many women, a deeply satisfying and fulfilling existence, a highly creative experiment that our society has yet to appreciate.

Jean Shinoda Bolen, in *Goddesses in Everywoman*, sees Artemis as the archetype behind the feminist movement, with its strong emphasis on "sisterhood." Unquestionably Artemis is a powerful factor in bringing women together in alternative communities, though we feel that the radical Athena's intellectual contribution is of equal importance to feminism. There is no question that together these two goddesses are behind one of the most important social revolutions of our time.

MALE FEARS: THE HUNTER OR THE HUNTED?

For a man, having a relationship with an Artemis woman might be quite a challenge. For one thing she may brusquely reject intimacy (though not sex) and leave him wondering where he stands. But more disturbingly, her self-sufficiency and toughness may stir in him dim apprehensions of the ancient Huntress or some other image of the Terrible Mother. Much psychoanalytic literature on the so-called male "mother complex" is full of discussions of unresolved infantile fears of "the devouring mother," whom Robert Bly has vividly dubbed the Teeth Mother.

The myth of Artemis's encounter with the hunter Actaeon is instructive here from the points of view of both Artemis and Actaeon, who intrudes upon her (see box, "The Myth of Artemis and Actaeon"). It suggests that the open, vulnerable side of Artemis only feels safe

THE MYTH OF ARTEMIS AND ACTAEON

Deep in the forest, overgrown with pine and cypress trees was a valley sacred to Artemis. Here there lay a woodland cave, etched from the rocks by time, with a natural arch and a lovely pool fed by a spring of clear water. Here, when she was wearied by the chase, Artemis would retire with her nymphs to be bathed and refreshed.

One fatal day the young hunter Actaeon happened to stray into this remote and unfamiliar part of the forest. The great goddess herself, her bow and arrows on the ground, stood before the sacred cave surrounded by her nymphs. Standing head and shoulders above her nymphs, she was discovered in all her nakedness by the wide-eyed young hunter. The nymphs shrieked in horror, doing their best to shield their mistress from this unbidden mortal. Surprised, without her sacred weapons at hand, the goddess scooped up a handful of water and threw it in the young man's face. "Now say, if you can, how you saw me when I was unclothed!"

Immediately, from where the drops of spring water fell upon his head, the hunter felt the tips of stag's horns sprouting forth. Then his neck elongated, the tips of his ears became pointed, his arms and legs lengthened into spindly legs with hooves, and dappled hair covered his body. Glimpsing his face in the water, he saw he had become a stag. He tried to let out a howl of despair, but no sound came.

As he hesitated, not knowing what to do, his pack of hounds espied him. In no time at all they raced toward him. Unable to cry out that he was their master, he fled from them in terror. By the time Actaeon's hunting companions caught up with the hungry pack, the hounds had done their bloody work. Their master, torn to pieces, lay dead from countless wounds. Only then, some say, was the goddess's anger at her violated chastity justly appeased.

—Authors' summary from Ovid's *Metamorphoses*, Book III

far from men and civilization; the Virgin Goddess *is* the virgin forest. Artemis echoes the immortal words of Greta Garbo, "I want to be alone." And she must be clear about this need. There is nothing pathological about this withdrawal. It is where Artemis renews herself at the Great Mother's fountain of youth.[6]

But when a man, such as Actaeon, wishes to know the naked truth of the Great Mother, he must be prepared to know both life and death, beauty and cruelty. When he meets her in the cultured world of her brother Apollo, symbol of light, reason, and moderation, she shows the beautiful and exalted side of her nature. But if he seeks her deep in the forest, he meets her as "nature red in tooth and claw."

The fate of Actaeon, the hunter hunted, torn apart by his own hounds, recalls a Greek god very close to Artemis, the god Dionysus. The classicist and philosopher Friedrich Nietzsche was the first to see so clearly that Dionysus is really the dark brother of Apollo. To the Greeks, Dionysus was a god of wine, orgiastic ecstasy, and divine madness, belonging, like Artemis in the forest, as Lord of Animals. Originally a matriarchal god of the year and divine son of the Great Mother, he died each year, sacrificially dismembered. His body and blood were scattered as a sacramental guarantee that life on earth would be renewed. As proof, he was reborn with the spring.

In later revivals of his worship an animal was hunted in his stead by his women followers, the frenzied maenads, who tore it apart, limb from limb. This bloody practice, evoked in Euripides' stunning drama *The Bacchae*, must have been a remnant of a forest animal sacrifice among hunting tribes. Dressed in fawn skins and uttering savage hunting cries, the maenads recall Artemis and her wild followers. In this play a human victim, Pentheus, is torn apart for deserting the religion of Dionysus.

Many modern movies written and directed by men are attempts, however grotesque, to come to terms with the male fear of the Teeth Mother and the dismemberment of Dionysus. This is part of the appeal

[6] Springs or "holy wells" were always sacred to the Earth Mother as sources of healing and blessed visions. Celtic Ireland abounds with them. Lourdes in France is still a healing site, and the oracle at Delphi was once a place of prophecy; both are over sacred springs. The Holy Grail, too, is often associated with water or, when lost, the lack of it, as with the "waste land." For a further discussion of "earth magic," see page 124.

of Alfred Hitchcock's *Psycho* and Brian de Palma's *Dressed to Kill*, in which both murderers are obsessed with the feminine as Death. Both women and men with knives commonly feature. Glenn Close's lurid role in *Fatal Attraction* is of this sort, as is Isabella Rossellini's in *Blue Velvet*. Whether the killer is male or female, we are in the archetypal realm of Artemis and Dionysus, the Hunters who slay. Their Hindu cousins or equivalents are Shiva and Kali, with their dripping knives, corpses, and severed limbs.

For a man to enter the mysteries of Artemis fully would entail what could only be called a Dionysian consciousness, which requires both a kind of androgyny in a man and a willingness to master his terror of the Death Mother. Certain kinds of male shamans, therapists, and healers are equipped for such an apprenticeship with the Dark Mother, but for most, fables such as Actaeon's death and the fate of Pentheus stand as cautionary tales for men to keep their noses out.

By the same token, for a woman to delve deeply into this side of her Artemis nature requires that she own the primitive power of her bloodlust and what effect it may have on a man—the Athena woman has a parallel task with her Medusa.

ARTEMIS AND THE CALL OF THE WILD

We remarked at the beginning of this chapter that many Artemis women are unconsciously quite frustrated with their lives simply because they are living in a city. Some, of course, have chosen to be there for economic reasons, but this is not true for the majority, in our experience.

So, what, we might ask, are so many Artemis women doing in the city?

The answer is a historical one: accident. It is estimated that toward the end of the nineteenth century nearly 80 percent of the American population still lived on the land and only 20 percent were city dwellers. In the last century this figure has completely reversed. Now there are 80 percent in the cities or suburbs. So most women today grow up influenced more by Athena's urban goddess values—career, education, intellectual prowess—than by their great grandmother's experience of the family farm, animals, vast open spaces, and the ever-changing wheel of the seasons. This inevitably means that there are a lot of displaced Artemis women in our midst.

Today, thousands of women, to whom farm or country life would have been natural and fulfilling, grow up in urban or suburban environments that are basically alien to them. This is why they often feel misfits in modern society: they are *physically* out of place. The fundamental Artemesian need to be connected to the earth and the natural world cries out to be honored.

An example is Julie, who came to one of our workshops:

> Julie was a pretty, conservatively dressed woman of twenty-four who had grown up in a comfortably affluent family with a dauntingly authoritative Hera mother and a distant father. Julie had learned early in life that approval would be given only for proper behavior—which included polite manners, clean clothes, and good grades. A natural Artemis who loved sports and horses, she was never permitted to join the family for dinner until after she had showered and changed her clothes. Craving approval from her mother, she learned to conform to the alien social disciplines of Hera by becoming a junior partner in a prestigious law firm. On the surface Julie appeared successful by any standard. But it quickly emerged through the process of the workshop that in fact she was deeply unhappy and felt very insecure in her upward mobility. She felt, she said, "like I've sold my soul; given up my freedom for acceptance and success. Sometimes I just want to throw it all away and go live in the mountains with a dog and a horse."

Fortunately, as Anne LaBastille's *Women and Wilderness* documents, there are lots of signs that Artemis women are beginning to return to their true environment, finding careers and opportunites to live closer to the natural world. Much of their work as conservationists, country midwives, biologists, and so forth, goes quietly unsung, but once in a while some remarkable achievement will catch the public eye. The work of animal ethologist Jane Goodall is an example. From half a lifetime of intimately living with and studying chimpanzees in their natural environment in Kenya she has single-handedly changed our understanding of these complex animals.

The overall movement of return probably began when it was common to talk of the so-called back-to-the-land movement of the sixties. First there were experimental communes and Eastern-style ashrams and the appearance of Stewart Brand's famous *Whole Earth Catalogue*, a survivalist's bible. Stephen and Ina May Gaskin founded the Farm, in Tennessee, a cooperative structure in which all property and produce were held in common. Similar communities sprang up all over the United States.

Despite a strong element of hippie romanticism about the early experiments, a few cold winters sorted out the romantics from the realists. Today there are many thousands of families and communities that have resettled successfully and creatively on the land. Both of the authors lived for many years in Vermont on farms and shared in all kinds of experiments with living on the land, which, as we can attest, are far from romantic.

Other signs of rising Artemesian consciousness are also strongly noticeable. In Europe the Green Movement, an offspring of the anti-nuclear movement, has mobilized awareness of the dangers of nuclear and chemical pollution on a global scale. Critics of industrialism, such as E. F. Schumacher, in his classic *Small Is Beautiful* (1973), have proposed more organic and less wasteful models of community. For the first time we are beginning to hear widespread talk of environmentalism and the necessity for a science that honors the balance of nature; *ecology* has become a household word.

In America the ecological movement is strong, though less well known than it is elsewhere because of a timid press and the power that nuclear and corporate lobbies have over government legislation on environmental issues. But thanks to influential writers such as Dolores LaChapelle, Rachel Carson, Barry Commoner, Murray Bookchin, Wendell Berry, and Kirkpatrick Sale, awareness is changing. In 1988, in the wake of widespread droughts and irregular weather in the United States and the wholesale death of ocean seals in northern Europe, the mainstream media finally woke up to the appalling effects of our negligence. Magazines and television programs were suddenly full of stories of ocean pollution and the dire predictions of the greenhouse effect, which threatens to heat up the entire globe as the ozone layer of the upper atmosphere continues to be depleted by chlorofluoro-carbons.

Perhaps most significant for women are the number of powerful, even visionary feminist works that have appeared. Artemis and Athena have combined their forces to put the crisis into perspective. Land-marks have included Mary Daly's *Gyn/Ecology* (1978), Carolyn Merchant's *The Death of Nature* (1980), and Susan Griffin's passionate Artemesian lament for ruined nature, *Woman and Nature* (1978). Griffin's lovely dedication of her book reads like a prayer to the silent Artemis dwelling within all women and all of nature:

These words are written for those of us
whose language is not heard, whose words
have been stolen or erased, those robbed
of language, who are called voiceless or
mute, even the earthworms, even the shell-
fish and sponges, for those of us who
speak our own language. . . .

In 1980 a new word, *ecofeminism*, entered the language, marking the rising groundswell of conferences and action groups clamoring for the protection of animals, plant life, the ecosphere, and more. In James Lovelock's book, *Gaia: A New Look at Life on Earth*, he speaks of this radical awareness as "the Gaia Hypothesis," an idea he developed with biologist Lynn Margulis. Lovelock and Margulis remind us that the whole earth is a living organism, whose global health is now at risk. Never before has the raising of Artemis consciousness been so urgent.

EARTH MYSTERIES, WICCA, AND THE SHAMANIC REVIVAL

Another landmark event for Artemis in 1980 was the appearance of Robert Bly's startlingly original poetry anthology for the Sierra Club, *News of the Universe*. Very quietly, it inaugurated a whole new vision of the poet and poetess in our society. Bly, whose own goddess research has been a major inspiration to us, sees poet and poetess as no less than the lost shaman and shamaness of the precivilized world. Ever since the reaction of the Romantics to industrialism in the nineteenth century, he maintains, a major poetic impulse has been to return to a prescientific consciousness of our place in nature. As Bly repeatedly puts it, "we have to get out of the house." With Denise Levertov he invites us, in the words of her beautiful poem, to "come into animal presence" (see box, "Come Into Animal Presence").

What poets Bly, Levertov, and Gary Snyder and writers like Charlene Spretnak, Annie Dillard, and Kirkpatrick Sale are today eloquently reminding us is that the return to Artemis and the values of the earth is a profoundly *spiritual* revolution. But not spiritual in the rather pallid sense the word has been reduced to by earth-denying Christianity. Instead we are witnessing a reawakening to *earth spirit energy* and to spirit communion with the animal and plant worlds. This was always the province of the shaman, but has long since been lost to civilized Western consciousness.

Part of the many-sided reawakening of Artemesian earth spirituality has been going on in Europe for some time now. In Britain there was the rediscovery of the ancient Celtic White Goddess, thanks to Robert Graves's famous book. Then came the radical insights of John Michel, in his visionary book *The View Over Atlantis*. Michel realized that ancient stone circles and similar sites were used to regenerate the surrounding earth by the conscious manipulation of the ancient "serpent" or "dragon" forces actively converging beneath them. The serpent was known to the ancients as the major power symbol of the Great Mother.

In both Britain and America a new understanding of witchcraft has been emerging for some time now. Under the name of Wicca (the root from which the word *witchcraft* is said to derive) all kinds of Neo-Pagans, as Margot Adler fondly calls them, have been delving into the sources, real or reconstructed, of European shamanism.[7]

"The craft of the wise," as Wicca is commonly characterized, is thought by many to have been "the old religion" of Diana, practiced all over Europe until well after the arrival of Christianity. The Horned God of the hunters, known to the Greeks as Dionysus and to the Celts

---

[7] Margot Adler's book, *Drawing Down the Moon*, strikes us the most balanced introduction to this tangled subject one could possibly wish for. To capture some of the ritual and communal spirit of the movement, we also recommend Starhawk's *The Spiral Dance: A Rebirth of the Ancient Religion of the Great Goddess*.

COME INTO ANIMAL PRESENCE
by Denise Levertov

Come into animal presence
No man is so guileless as
the serpent. The lonely white
rabbit on the roof is a star
twitching its ears at the rain.
The llama intricately
folding its hind legs to be seated
not disdains but mildly
disregards human approval.
What joy when the insouciant
armadillo glances at us and doesn't
quicken his trotting
across the track into the palm brush.

What is this joy? That no animal
falters, but knows what it must do?
That the snake has no blemish,
that the rabbit inspects his strange surroundings
in white star-silence? The llama
rests in dignity, the armadillo
has some intention to pursue in the palm-forest.
Those who were sacred have remained so,
holiness does not dissolve, it is a presence
of bronze, only the sight that saw it
faltered and turned from it.
An old joy returns in holy presence.

> (from *The Jacob's Ladder*, New York:
> New Directions, 1961.)

as Cernunnos, may have been worshipped as the consort of the Lady of Beasts. Certainly the disappearing Horned God could easily have provided the image of the Devil, who is largely a medieval Christian invention.

The actual followers of the old matriarchal ways of Diana came, tragically, to be identified with the so-called witches. These women (there were men too) so horribly persecuted, were most likely shamanic healers who lingered on in the outlying mountain regions of medieval Europe. The orgiastic sabbats, where the sacrifice of children was darkly rumored, sound like the dim stirrings in folk memory of the old Dionysian and Artemesian festivals in the forests, or their north European equivalents.

Predictably, the male fear of the Teeth Mother surfaced again in the imaginations of a celibate Church dominated by men. The late Middle Ages of Europe, with its unspeakable witch burnings, were a sorry time for the goddesses. For not just Artemis and her way of the animal powers was condemned as belonging to the Devil. Aphrodite's sexuality as well as Persephone's visionary and psychic powers were all lumped together in the fearsome stereotype of the witch. Nevertheless, along with Wicca and similar movements, an important resurrection of the old shamanic and healing traditions of Europe is taking place.

THE BEAUTY WAY OF THE EARTH: ARTEMIS IN NATIVE AMERICA

Under different names the goddess spirit that the ancients of the Old World knew as Artemis has always been present on this continent among all the Native American traditions that revere the "beauty way of the earth." North America's most tragically oppressed peoples have never ceased to practice a holistic, grounded life-style that more than compensates for the one-sidedness of Christian "spirituality." In the native traditions there have always been a Sky Father *and* an Earth Mother living in harmony. With his genius for intuiting the essence of precivilized cultures, D. H. Lawrence wrote this powerful description of a Pueblo dance ceremony in 1928 in his essay "New Mexico." In it he put his finger on what the Western traditions have lost or perverted:

> . . . never shall I forget watching the dancers, the men with the fox-skin swaying down from their buttocks, file out at San Geronimo, and the women with seed rattles following. The long, streaming, glistening black hair of the men. Even in ancient Crete long hair was sacred in a man, as it is still in the Indians. Never shall I forget the utter absorption of the dance, so quiet, so steadily, timelessly rhythmic, and silent, with the ceaseless down-tread, always to the earth's centre, the very reverse of the upflow of Dionysiac or Christian ecstasy. Never shall I forget the deep singing of the men at the drum, swelling and sinking, the deepest sound I have heard in all my life, deeper than thunder, deeper than the sound of the Pacific Ocean, deeper than the roar of a deep waterfall: the wonderful deep sound of men calling to the unspeakable depths.
>
> —From *Phoenix*

What moved Lawrence so profoundly in the twenties is reaching more and more women and men today who, like him, are repulsed by much of the harshness of life in the big cities and the ugliness of urban-industrial sprawl that disfigures so much of the landscape. With the rising swell of enthusiasm for Native American teachers and shamans, a small but growing number of adventurous spirits are going on vision quests into the wilderness or looking into alternative methods of healing and spiritual practice right here on this continent.

A handful of charismatic women from the Native American traditions are currently emerging as extremely powerful and influential teachers all over the country; among the most prominent we could mention Oh Shinnah, Twyla Nitsch, Dhyani Ywahoo, and Brooke Medicine Eagle. In the communities they have founded, in the workshops and in the medicine gatherings where they teach, their quiet but deeply grounded presences are inspiring models for many women of European descent searching today for what we might call the lost Beauty Way of Artemis (see box, "Dhyani Ywahoo's Beauty Path").

Many of the more traditional women elders and teachers naturally

DHYANI YWAHOO'S BEAUTY PATH

In the morning I sing a simple song of thanks, as my grandparents taught me. I am singing for all my relatives, everyone who lives and breathes, even the stones, for the crystals are alive and they grow just as we do. Through our experience with life, through our interactions with one another, we learn to put aside anger, we learn ways of communion, we find ways of resolution. . . .

As a young child, that was a first step upon the Beauty Path. Just learning to sing a morning song of thanks, and sitting quietly and realizing that there truly is light moving through this body, made the words of my grandparents take more meaning in my heart. . . .

Many of us are looking again to simple ways of living, dignified ways that do not enslave us to wage labor in order to pay for things we don't really need, becoming ever more dependent on technology that pollutes the Earth. It is fine to chop our own wood, it is fine to make a cookfire outside. To live simply is to see without attachment. Our status, our position, is determined not by the work we do outside but by the work in our hearts and how we assist others. The effort to recognize and speak the truth is the greatest work that any of us can do. It is to realize the power of our clear mind and to call forth the best from all the people with whom we walk along life's path. This is a gift of giving and receiving. Then one's heart feels it will burst with a sense of love and appreciation, free of confining fears.

—*The Voices of Our Ancestors*, pp. 58–59

wish to remain hidden from the public eye and media exploitation. But even they are slowly, but cautiously allowing their luminous and much needed wisdom to reach those who are so hungry for the spiritual vision of that aspect of the goddess the Greeks called Artemis.

One example of the transmission of this wisdom which we recommend to our readers is a collection of stories by Anne Cameron called *Daughters of Copper Woman* (Vancouver: Press Gang Publishers, 1981). For years, this writer reports, she had been hearing stories from the native people of Vancouver Island in Canada, "stories preserved for generations through an oral tradition that is now threatened". The native women, who eventually gave her permission to retell some of these stories, are from a matriarchal, matrilineal society, according to Cameron. These powerful, wise women are, as she explains, "members of a secret society whose roots go back beyond recorded history to the dawn of Time itself" (from the preface). In this tradition, the Great Mother is called Copper Woman. She is both eternal and takes on many forms, having many daughters and granddaughters who carry different aspects of her teachings. In one of these lovely stories she becomes Old Woman, that aspect of the goddess we call the Crone (see Demeter chapter), she who both gives life to all things—with her loom—and she who takes away—with her broom.

Another fine introduction to how the Americas before Columbus were saturated with the Artemesian mystical sense of the unity of woman, man, and nature is Joan Halifax's "survey of visionary narratives" called *Shamanic Voices* (New York: Dutton, 1979). In one of these verbatim records, Brooke Medicine Eagle describes her ritual training with a Northern Cheyenne medicine woman, which culminates in a vision quest of great power and beauty. The account must, of course, be read in its entirety, but here, as a fitting ending to this chapter, we quote Brooke's deep and urgent understanding of what is needed to rebalance the male and female energies of the whole planet, if it is to be regenerated:

> . . . Down off that mountain in a slow, soft, and gentle step come the old women, Indian women, dancing down. They either *are* light or carry light. They wind down the mountain and then encircle around the hill I am on. And as they dance around in a circle, very quickly, into that circle comes another

circle, this of young women, of my age and time, young women that I know, and they, too, are dancing. Those two circles are dancing and moving, and they begin to weave in and out of each other, sway in and out of each other. And then inside of that circle comes another circle of seven old grandmothers, white-haired women, women who are significant to me, powerful old women. . . .

The circles around me disappear, and I am again alone with the Rainbow Woman. . . . She said to me that the earth is in trouble, that the land is in trouble, and that here on this land, this Turtle Island, this North American land, what needs to happen is a balancing. She said that the thrusting, aggressive, analytic, intellectual, building, making-it-happen energy has very much overbalanced the feminine, receptive, allowing, surrendering energy. She said that what needs to happen is an uplifting and a balancing. And because we are out of balance, we need to put more emphasis on surrendering, being receptive, allowing, nurturing. She was speaking to me as a woman, and I was to carry this message to women specifically. But not only do women need to become strong in this way; we all need to do this, men and women alike. (pp. 88–89)

FOUR

APHRODITE: GOLDEN GODDESS OF LOVE

Age cannot wither her nor custom stale
Her infinite variety . . .
—SHAKESPEARE,
ANTONY AND CLEOPATRA

APHRODITE: THE PEOPLE'S GODDESS

No goddess was ever so well loved as the goddess of love herself, Venus-Aphrodite. And no goddess has been so well represented in all the arts. Ever since she first stepped from the waves on her celebrated scallop shell, artists have painted and sculpted her, poets have extolled her beauty, and lyricists have composed melodies for her (see box, "Sappho's Hymn to Aphrodite.")

The Greeks and Romans adored her for her glorious beauty, her gentleness, and her many amorous adventures. Her equally beautiful divine son, Eros—the Roman Amor or Cupid—was considered by many the embodiment of her greatest gift ever bestowed on mankind. In fact, in a relatively late myth Eros is credited with the creation of

SAPPHO'S HYMN TO APHRODITE

Sappho was an enormously influential Greek poet of the sixth century B.C. She lived on the island of Lesbos (hence the word *lesbian*), where many young women came to be educated by her in the feminine mysteries of menstruation and sexuality and to celebrate the goddess Aphrodite in poetry, dance, and music. Much of her lyric poetry, considered by many some of the finest in the West, has been lost. Copies of her works were publicly burned in Rome and Constantinople in 1073 by order of Pope Gregory VIII. Here is the only one of her poems that survives in its entirety.

> On your dazzling throne, Aphrodite
> sly eternal daughter of Zeus
> I beg you: do not crush me
> with grief
> but come to me now—as once
> you heard my far cry, and yielded,
> slipping from your
> father's house
>
> to yoke the birds to your gold
> chariot, and came. Handsome sparrows
> brought you swiftly to
> the dark earth,
>
> their wings whipping the middle sky.
> Happy, with deathless lips, you smiled:
> "What is wrong, Sappho, why have
> you called me?
>
> What does your mad heart desire?
> Whom shall I make love you.
> Who is turning her back
> on you?

Let her run away, soon she'll chase you;
refuse your gifts, soon she'll give them.
She will love you, though unwillingly."

Then come to me now and free me
from fearful agony. Labor
for my mad heart, and be
my ally.
        —from *Greek Lyric Poetry*, trans. Willis Barnstone,
                        New York: Schocken Books, 1962

the world itself. Like Dante's cosmic "love which moves the sun and all the other stars," the Eros generated by the goddess was seen by the Greeks as the living force behind all things. Aphrodite naturally held a respected place on Mount Olympus, even though Hera, as jealous guardian, bitterly opposed her licentious sexual behavior.

In our times Aphrodite gives every impression of having left Olympus to move to Hollywood. It's as though, for the last few generations, certain great screen beauties—Greta Garbo, Marilyn Monroe, Elizabeth Taylor—have actually incarnated the goddess. Their public lives have even taken on a mythic quality: Garbo's mysterious withdrawal, Monroe's tragic death, Taylor's epic relationship with Richard Burton, are just a few examples.

Yet Aphrodite worship is not just confined to Hollywood. She is celebrated everywhere, *Aphrodite pandemos*, the Greeks called her— the goddess "among all the people." Daily the soap operas, Harlequin romances, and political scandalmongers retell her age-old stories of secret passion, jealousy, and betrayal. Sexologists nationwide compute her multiple orgasms or map out the most arcane secret places of her intimate anatomy. Dr. Ruth channels her down-to-earth wisdom of the body. Tele-evangelists decry her excesses. Fashion magazines dote on her. Centerfolds glorify her nakedness. Pornographers and pimps unscrupulously exploit her.

Never was a goddess so intimate and so public at the same time!
But was this always so? Was it like this in ancient Greece?
Hardly. The Greeks had no media to fan a natural longing almost

to the point of hysteria. They still retained a strong sense that sexuality is a sacred gift and not a commodity to be exploited, which is why they honored Aphrodite. It is only the modern world that is so obsessed with Aphrodite's physical charms that it has almost lost touch with her sacred dimension.

But between us and the Greeks stands Christianity, a religion whose early founders were horrified by Aphrodite's liberal love of the body and of sexual pleasure. So, for nearly two thousand years Western culture has learned to denigrate and suppress every impulse that might belong to the goddess of earthly love. But today, as part of a reaction that has been under way since the last century, we have swung from deprivation to excess. Instead we seem desperately hungry for romance, for sensuality, for erotic imagery, and for pleasure.

Like it or not, our culture has lost all perspective on Aphrodite and her divine gift to us, Eros. We believe the Greeks may help us to get some of it back, though that may not be so easy, given the puritanism we have all inherited. Nevertheless, that culture does offer us some major clues as to why we now have such mixed feelings about letting Aphrodite fully into our consciousness and our world.

In her most radiant form, Aphrodite has many "golden gifts" for us. Women born under her influence possess a natural appreciation of sexuality and beauty as sacred qualities. Aphrodite women have a wonderful flair for that kind of intimate education that can only take place in the boudoir. As the initiator of the salon, Aphrodite has always excelled at civilizing brutish and cloddish male energy.

APHRODITE'S WORLD

Aphrodite was and is, in all things, a *sensuous* presence. To the ancient Greeks she was "the golden goddess." Like a glorious sun, she shone down upon their precocious culture and blessed it with the arts of sculpture, poetry, and music. Nothing delights her more than the gratification of the senses by beautiful means. She loves fine dresses, lustrous flowing hair, jewelry, adornments of all kinds. This is why the very earliest of Greek statues of the goddess show her clad in sumptuous finery. Today she rules the fashion industry, cosmetics, and the richly glamorous world of magazines such as *Vogue*.

A modern Aphrodite's childhood may well be marked by endless dress-up games and fashion parades—she might even become a child model, she's such a natural exhibitionist. With her inborn aesthetic sense, she may later find her way into the worlds of fashion modeling, acting, hostessing, interior design. Or else she may gravitate to the media, where she will be a good reporter or interviewer with her extraverted interest in people. But whatever her job, it will inevitably be around groups of people, be it a busy office, store, or organization, where her natural ability to relate to others, her warmth, and her charm will quickly attract the notice of her bosses.

Carl Jung defined eros in its more generalized human context as *relatedness*, the quality of being connected. This gives us another essential clue to the nature of the Aphrodite woman: important as sexuality is to her, it is always part and parcel of being in relationships, never an end in itself. It's the personal connection with her mate or lover, the *exchange* of pleasure between them, that can make sex so ecstatic for her.

Relatedness, which is to say, the whole issue of relationships, is central to understanding the Aphrodite woman. It doesn't matter whether we know her for only an hour or for a lifetime. She wants us to be fully, feelingly, humanly present—related. This is as important to Aphrodite as mental clarity is to Athena or moral propriety is to Hera. Without it she pines away or loses interest.

Above all, Aphrodite wants relationships to be loving, whether they be amicable, social, physical, or spiritual. Relationships where there is *heart*. A true Aphrodite woman cares little for the social requirements of a "good marriage" that Hera, her rival, would want. And she finds the nurturing mother love of Demeter too one-sided. As for Athena's platonic "marriage of true minds," it's far too mental.

With their instinctive warmth, Aphrodite women get on well with others—especially men, of course—seeming to find their way through life as much through connections and chance meetings as through careful planning. Her sister Athena's career aspirations are somewhat of a bore to her. The chance of a Mediterranean cruise will easily cause her to drop out of school—and probably land her an unusual job to boot! With her easygoing eros, she can be quite an opportunist.

She's not particularly interested in marriage or children as such either. When children come along, she'll be a warm, generous, and often unconventional mother. But she won't make them the center of her life, as Demeter will. Nor will she always get married, much to Hera's outrage.

No, Aphrodite is rarely in favor of settling down. Rather, she is inclined to see life as something of an adventure, and always one with a possible romantic outcome. It's a sexy, active, and untrammeled male she's looking for; preferably sophisticated, educated, and armed with American Express rather than a pistol.

Remember that the Aphrodite woman is essentially civilized and sensual. Backpacking in Colorado or African big game hunting is really not her style, no matter how handsome or tough the male who invites her. Rugged adventures are for Artemis, just as lone political adventures are for Athena. Aphrodite likes to be sure of cocktails and some clean linen on her adventures. You are more likely to find Aphrodite beside an elegant swimming pool than by a wild mountain lake.

APHRODITE GROWS UP—FAST!

To be blessed by Aphrodite generally means that a woman will be very much at ease with her body and have a healthy, uncomplicated relationship with her sexuality. As a little girl she may easily shock her mother with a natural curiosity about her body and her sexual organs. Later, regardless of attempts to instill a minimum of modesty, she may manifest an almost casual attitude toward sex. She is, in the best sense of the word, a natural pagan.

Right from the start there is something highly attractive about her, though not necessarily a conventional kind of beauty. The Goddess, remember, has a thousand ways of bestowing her charms. The Aphrodite child will learn early on to flirt with her father and, provided he is not threatened by this, receive from him her first positive feedback about her attractiveness. Thus reinforced, she may begin to practice her skills on any or all of his friends—much to their embarrassment! For her, it is simply an innocent use of her inborn erotic talent.

When she reaches adolescence, she will have to learn to bring her budding eros under control. In the modern world it can and will get her into all kinds of trouble. Physically she will mature early and be forced, as a result, to mature early socially too. Her good looks and friendly extraversion will inevitably make her a center of libidinous attention for all the young males around her. Naturally she will be flattered. She'll learn very quickly about the dating game and how not to break too many youthful male hearts.

Young Aphrodite's first subtle lessons in relationships are beginning. In fact her busy social calendar may now become the center of her life and fantasies. How different from adolescent Artemis, who is probably off canoeing, or Athena, who is absorbed in books and school, or Hera, who is busy running the student body, for example.

Sometimes the young Aphrodite will mature early into a stunning loveliness far beyond her years. The young Elizabeth Taylor was just such a beauty when, at eighteen she married Mike Todd, twenty-five years her senior. Here's Helen Gurley Brown interviewing her about it:

> HGB: You were only eighteen, but you were ready for love?
> ET: I was ready for love and ready for the experience of love-making.
> HGB: So it's just in your genes?
> ET: I guess it's in my genes. It's something I was born with. Before men, my great love was for animals, which I still have. Then it was men and, of course, children. The list keeps growing.
>
> —from "Girl Talk with Elizabeth the Great"
> in *Cosmopolitan*, (September 1987), p. 239

Another young Aphrodite we all know is Brooke Shields, who portrayed the awakening of adolescent sexuality in *The Blue Lagoon* and a child prostitute in *Pretty Baby*.

Quite apart from the predators of the media jungle, precocious beauty may be a blessing or a curse to the young Aphrodite still in high school. Young men her age will be in awe of her, whereas she may well find them immature and boorish. Before long she will be courted by male admirers quite a bit older than she is, and soon she may find herself quite socially isolated from her peers.

It is a pattern an Aphrodite woman will repeat in different ways throughout her life. Her exceptional looks can be an instant passport to other, more glamorous worlds, but with this comes a distinct alienation. She may come to know a certain inner loneliness, a feeling that she is out of her depth, and she will put all the more energy into her outer persona, her lovely mask, to compensate. Because so many men want her just for her looks, as a conquest or as a status symbol, she will often come to doubt her own self-worth. "A sex symbol is a thing, and I'm not a thing," Marilyn Monroe reportedly said. Like poor Marilyn, many an Aphrodite woman may come to feel very insecure about her other very real talents. So strong is outer pressure that she has forgotten that no woman should be forced to be just one goddess exclusively. Here we are beginning to glimpse Aphrodite's wound, which we will return to later.

Young Aphrodite's attractiveness and her free and easy rapport with the opposite sex have, then, set her apart from her peers from the very beginning. Many of her women contemporaries will be a little jealous of her, which, in her good-hearted way she will find hard to understand. And though the Aphrodite woman may have a handful of very close women friends over the years, she remains essentially drawn to men for the majority of her intimate relationships.

If the young Aphrodite woman can accept that her special gifts are destined to set her apart in this way, she may find she has a golden passport to a larger world than the one she grew up in. Sometimes it will be in the form of job offers she would be foolish to turn down. Big companies, exotic locales, new people may suddenly appear on her horizon. Or else, feeling boxed in and bored in her small-town office routine, she may simply take off for the big city, adventurously prepared to wing it on her charm and a few phone numbers.

Aphrodite is so mysterious and fascinatingly exotic to men that she tends to be a disturbing presence in the workplaces of the fatherworld. Regardless of which goddess is strongest in them, most women working today have learned to wear more modest, often neutral work clothes, trying not to look too alluring at work. Magazines such as *Cosmopolitan* and *Working Woman* wisely offer advice on just how much or how little, depending on the job.

If a young Aphrodite woman finds the trim, conservative business clothes Athena wears too confining, she may need to question whether or not she's in the right job. It's no good for her to dress provocatively and then complain about male advances or being disliked by women co-workers. There is such instinct for sexual display in Aphrodite's makeup that she will probably do much better in a modeling or acting career.

The world of modeling, PR work, acting, or hostessing will find plenty of use for her talents if she can hustle, but she may soon find she's quite an expendable commodity in a highly competitive market. She will need all that charm and every bit of Athena savvy at this stage if she's going to survive on the basis of her looks alone.

If she escapes the misfortune of being sexually exploited by unscrupulous men, she may discover something—that she has her *own* capacity for exploitation: as a seductress. Here is our first glimpse of the power side of Aphrodite's psychology: *the siren*. She may find that her greatest asset in the superficial world of show business, promotion, or modeling is her sexual freedom.

The old cliché about aspiring young actresses finding their way into their first roles via the casting couch contains more than a grain of truth. In our sex-hungry society the Aphrodite woman's looks are a sought-after commodity, and she can easily learn how to bargain with them. Of course, she risks becoming hardened sexually and emotionally. But she can also choose her influential lovers shrewdly and selectively. If she does, these important experiences will be her course work in what the French would call *l'éducation sentimentale*—the education of the feelings.

As young Aphrodite becomes more confident in her choice of men, all kinds of possibilities open up. Somewhere in her twenties the Aphrodite woman may well have an affair with a relatively older man that will be a turning point in her life. He will be worldly, sophisticated, and well established in his career. He will be her mentor or her coach in her new ventures. And he will probably be married. Here is the not untypical story of Marian, one of our clients:

Marian was an exceptionally lovely teenager and found that modeling jobs offered her quick, immediate incomes that made finishing college unnecessary. The men in the modeling agencies wined and dined her, and she found that her favors won her better jobs on occasion. In her early twenties she had a well-appointed apartment of her own, an expensive car, and a lot of contacts in the magazine world.

But after a while the fast life-style began to pall. Few of

the men she dated wanted very long romances. They were greedy for the other new and exciting young bodies that were in plentiful supply in the world she inhabited. So she pitched her sights a little higher, going after an older boss who claimed a very "open" marriage. She was convinced he would leave his wife for her.

Their affair, though a good relationship in itself, led nowhere. After eight years he dropped her abruptly and went back to his wife. She had been working less and less, living in an apartment he kept for both of them. Suddenly she was out on the street, with little to show for her eight years but some fond memories and a wardrobe of clothes.

In therapy a great deal of bitterness toward her boss's wife emerged. This woman represented the stability, constancy, respectability, that Marian wanted for herself—which she seemed to sell herself short of. Many of the qualities of her boss's wife began, on probing, to remind Marian very strongly of her own mother. The two had always been at loggerheads; her mother having always disapproved of Marian's precocious sexuality and Marian having always thought of her mother as prudish about sex.

In therapy Marian began to see how she was playing out the time-honored dispute between Aphrodite and Hera, over passion versus marriage—a dispute where the married incumbent is most often the winner. She realized she needed some of the acquired social power that belongs to Hera and the whole institution of marriage if she was not to keep repeating the same abandonment scenario. Eventually she began to let go of some of her negative stereotypes of marriage and her sentimentally glamorous clichés of being the cherished mistress.

One of Aphrodite's hardest lessons then is that in the modern world she will often be "the other woman" to many men. It is part of an ancient archetypal triangle peculiar to her, in which the values of eros are pitted against the values of fidelity and marriage, and one she may find herself in many times during her life. (We shall return to this complex dynamic later in this chapter.)

Nevertheless, the Aphrodite woman should never have to feel

ashamed of her secret affairs, whatever righteous Hera has to say about them, for they are intensely valuable and beautiful in and of themselves. When she is deeply committed to such a relationship, to which the word *affair* does scant justice, she will prove an exceptional confidante, a spiritual as well as sexual friend. What men are attracted to in her is not just her physical loveliness but her spontaneous feminine wisdom in matters of the heart. She understands people well, and above all she understands her man.

In the ancient world a woman who could be both a sexual and a spiritual confidante to a man was called by the Greeks a *hetaera*, literally a "companion." (The Japanese geishas resemble them in many respects.) Among the Greeks, since a hetaera had no marital status, she was by definition an upper-class prostitute, but as such she was often highly educated in the arts and philosophy.[1] Then as now she acted as what the French (who seem to have a monopoly on Venusian terminology) call a *femme inspiratrice*—a woman who inspires a man, often creatively.[2]

In her talent for working closely with both a man's feelings and his creative projects, the Aphrodite woman is bringing out what Carl Jung called a man's *anima*. The anima is the feminine part of every man, which relates to his undeveloped capacity for feeling and relationships. Toni Wolff writes of how the Aphrodite woman as hetaera stimulates this side of a man:

> The function of the Hetaira is to awaken the individual psychic
> life in the male and lead him through and beyond his male
> responsibilities towards the formation of a total personality.
> Usually this development becomes the task of the second half
> of life, i.e. after the social position has been established.
>   —"Structural Forms of the Feminine Psyche," p. 6

[1] Thornton Wilder has a moving short novel about a Greek hetaera called *The Woman of Andros*.

[2] The first modern psychologist to identify the hetaera (and Aphrodite) as a psychological type among women was Toni Wolff, Carl Jung's close associate and, in some respects, his hetaera. For a description of Wolff's four female types, see appendix B. By far the best discussion of Aphrodite we know of is Ginette Paris's *Pagan Meditations: Aphrodite, Hestia, Artemis*.

When an Aphrodite woman is in love with a creative or publicly active man, she will greatly expand his sense of himself and his capacity for intimacy. As Toni Wolff adds, her "instinctive interest is directed towards the individual contents of a relationship in all its potentialities and nuances in herself as well as in the man" (p. 6).

On the positive side this can obviously have enormous benefits for the development of a man's creative eros. On the negative side, however, too much eros may distract a man from his public tasks. He may totally lose his sense of outer direction, like the Greek hero Ulysses who is at first pleasantly delayed on his travels by the nymph Calypso but then nearly loses himself entirely to the dangerous enchantress Circe. Wolff writes of this danger:

> For the man, relationship in all its potentialities and nuances is usually less conscious and less important, for it distracts him from his tasks. For the Hetaira, it is decisive. Everything else— social security, position, etc.—is unimportant. In this lies the significance and the danger of the Hetaira, [who . . .] may bring the man to a point where he himself loses his clear vision of outer reality: he may for instance give up his profession to become a "creative artist"; he may divorce, feeling that the Hetaira understands him better than his wife, etc. She insists on an illusion or some nonsense and thus becomes a temptress; she is Circe instead of Calypso. (p. 6)

Clearly Calypso, the nymph, and Circe, the sorceress, represent the positive and negative sides of Aphrodite's influence on a man.

When a man begins to be in touch with his anima, she becomes like his muse, helping him with new ideas and creative work. Yet he rarely experiences his anima directly. More often she is projected or *seen in* the woman he idealizes. Not every man's anima corresponds to Aphrodite, but if she does, this anima brings him closest to his creative and passionate self. This also explains the need in many male artists, poets, and musicians for a particular kind of companion. The writer H. G. Wells, for instance, was known to have admitted that he couldn't write a book unless he had a consuming love affair concurrent with his writing.

THE POWER OF ATTRACTION OR THE ATTRACTION OF POWER?

While young Aphrodite's older lover is busy rhapsodizing over the image of his anima in the mirror of her Venusian personality, she is also seeing some of her own unrecognized masculine in him. Projection is never a one-way event. What she encounters in the powerful fantasies she may have about him is the aspect in a woman that Jung called the *animus*. She may also be experiencing, in addition, the image of her father she always adored. So the relationship may bring out the heightened excitement of incestuous feelings and, if she is fortunate, resolve them once and for all.

After a good experience with an older lover the young Aphrodite woman attains her full maturity and genuine confidence in herself. From now on the power and authority, the wiles and deviousness, of the male world will hold no fear for her. She has seen, in more ways than one, to its very heart. And she is now a privileged witness of some of its more hidden goings-on.

Powerful, influential, and sometimes eminent men in public life often feature quite prominently in a mature Aphrodite woman's life; she is drawn to executives, tycoons, and politicians. She is as attracted to them as they are to her. She can make such a man feel more powerful, and in return he gives her status, security, and an entrée into glamorous places where she can shine. Late-night dinners, discreet weekends, and the behind-the-scenes intrigues of important men excite and fascinate her. If her Athena side is stimulated, she may make a good confidante and potential business partner. But mostly her warmth and easy sexuality provide the man with whom she is intimately allied a release from the pressures and mental intensity of a largely male world, where he must always emanate success.

It has often been observed that politicians have a powerful sex drive. Not surprisingly, then, Aphrodite may play an important part in their private lives. In 1977 Dr. Sam Janus and his wife, Dr. Barbara Bess, a psychologist-psychiatrist team, published their book, *A Sexual Profile of Men in Power*. The majority of their informants were high-class call girls and madams in New York, Los Angeles, Washington, San Francisco, and Las Vegas. Their somewhat shocking finding was that nearly 60 percent of the call girls' clients were politicians or men in public office of some sort.

In a *People* magazine interview Janus and Bess were quoted as saying, "We are reluctant to quote an exact figure, but a safe bet would be nearly half of the members of Congress were customers of the women we interviewed." We are familiar with scandals that broke around figures like Wilbur Mills, Wayne Hays, and Senator Gary Hart, and we know that J. F. Kennedy and his brother Robert had secret liaisons. Anthony Summers, in his book *Goddess; the Secret Lives of Marilyn Monroe* documents how the ill-fated star had affairs with both Kennedy brothers at different times. But stories like these that become public seem to be only the tip of a substantial iceberg. In most cases the politicians who sought out illicit relationships in one of Aphrodite's sub-rosa worlds were married. Politicians who are not married inspire little public confidence, of course. But Janus and Bess noted an important psychological dynamic in these men. They needed to see their wives at home as "good," or worthy of Hera, in goddess language, and their girlfriends, the Aphrodite women, as "dirty." Their statement speaks volumes about one of the deepest wounds in the feminine in our society: a split in *masculine* psychology imposed upon women.

One thing is clear: the power drive and the sex drive are reflections of each other. These men have what Wilhelm Reich called *phallic-narcissistic characters*. Driven by a need for approval as males, they choose tough, extraverted, achievement-oriented roles, but beneath this powerful outer drive they are emotionally quite immature. Politics is an endlessly frustrating game, where tangible success and immediate approval are rarely earned. But the phallic drive can most easily be satisfied through sexual conquest.

The Greek myths about Aphrodite offer further clues to her involvement with phallic, power-driven males. One such clue is her liaison with Ares, the war god, who with his sword and fierce aggression is unmistakably phallic. Mars and Venus feature similarly in a rather idealized allegory of the union of war and peace created by the warmongering Romans. Janus and Bess actually describe the typical politician of their research as "a man who is a combatant [but] doesn't feel satisfied just battling men in elections. He has to balance his life by battling with women."

Aphrodite's involvement with warriors runs through Western culture. In myth, literature, and legend we all know Paris and Helen of Troy, Antony and Cleopatra, Siegfried and Brunhilde, Lancelot and Guinevere, Othello and Desdemona, Napoleon and Josephine. Since war is pivotal to much of Western history from the Peloponnesian War of the Athenians onwards, many of our major epics are war stories. So, wherever we find Mars/Ares and his arts of war, Aphrodite won't be far away with her arts of love. Perhaps this harks back to the times of tribal warfare when women were often the spoils of war, but it remains an undying motif from Homer's *Iliad* to the present. *War and Peace*, *Dr. Zhivago*, and *Gone With the Wind*, all feature major love and war themes.

APHRODITE'S BIRTH

There is another and in some ways deeper mythic background to Aphrodite's involvement with phallic males. This is the fascinating Greek myth of her birth. The story that has come down to us from Hesiod (see box, "The Birth of Aphrodite") actually derives from patriarchal times. This is important because it mirrors precisely the kind of collective psychological problem we are still struggling with today.

Hesiod's account of the birth of the gods tells how Aphrodite was born from the severed genitals of the Sky Father, Ouranos. Here is an inescapable connection to male sexuality that could account for Aphrodite's attraction to everything phallic. We could also say that she carries something of the excess or overabundance of her father's sexual energy.

In the myth we are told that Earth Mother Gaia's son, Kronos, threw the severed genitals into the ocean. Time (Kronos) has come to render the tyranny of the sky, which is the mental realm, impotent. Kronos was a god of agriculture, so his wisdom and power belong to the earth, along with his mother, Gaia. But he actually helps bring his tyrannical father not just down to earth, but *down to water*. There is a cosmic drama of the elements going on here: earth, air, and water.[3] The outcome of the suppression of earth by air is a new birth out of

[3] The missing element, fire, will later be supplied by the war god Ares (the Roman Mars) and by Aphrodite's smith husband, Hephaistos.

THE BIRTH OF APHRODITE

The best-known Greek myth of Aphrodite's birth inevitably has a patriarchal bias. It shows the goddess born from the severed genitals of Ouranos, the sky god. The event has lost none of its splendor and poetry, as the following summary demonstrates:

At the time of the creation of the early gods, Gaia, the Earth Mother and Ouranos, the Sky Father, had given birth to many divine children. Among the later births came the Titans, monstrous sons who hated their father. So Ouranos just pushed them back into poor Gaia each time a new one emerged.

Finally one of the youngest sons, Kronos, who also hated his father, turned upon Ouranos and castrated him with a stone sickle that Gaia made especially to punish her cruel mate. Casually he threw the severed member over his shoulder, and it fell to earth. From the bloody drops came forth the Furies and the Giants, but the member itself fell into the stormy sea, where it was carried by the waves.

From the foam that formed around the severed member there grew a girl. First she was washed to Kythera and then to Cyprus, encircled by the waves. There the lovely goddess stepped forth, with her two companions, Eros, whose name means Love, and Himeros, whose name means Desire. And as her feet touched the earth, grass grew up beneath her. Her name, to mortals, was Aphrodite, which means, "born of the foam."

Aphrodite is also known as *philommedes*, "laughter-loving," as *urania*, the "heavenly one," and as *pandemos*, "belonging to all the people." She delights, it is said, in the whispering between young girls, the smiles and deceptions, and all the sweet delights and charms of love.

On Olympus she was welcomed by all the other gods and goddesses, where she rules all acts of pro-creation and every aspect of the arts of love and beauty.
—Retold from Hesiod's *Theogony*, 176–206

water—Aphrodite. Water often represents feeling and connection in the language of myth and dream.

Like most tyrannical fathers, Ouranos comes to fear that his sons will want their piece of the action, so he tries to suppress their birth. In doing so he becomes completely out of touch with Mother Gaia, earth consciousness, and the mystery of procreation. His punishment is to lose his own phallic-centeredness, his power to generate anything new. Sky consciousness becomes impotent.

But notice what happens to his lost genitals. They turn into the very opposite of him. Out of old, crusty, masculine tyranny comes young, innocent, feminine beauty. A miracle has occurred. A miracle of the reversal of psychic opposites. When such a radical reversal occurs, it means that, psychologically, there is a huge need for compensation. *Aphrodite's overflowing sexuality today, as in ancient Greece, appears in reaction to excessive mental control from above by the masculine.*

It also means that patriarchy cannot hope to control the essentially expansive nature of feminine energy. Suppress the fecundity of the earth (Gaia) and it will spring up again in time (Kronos) as joyful erotic energy (Aphrodite).

To their everlasting credit, the Greeks were never inclined to throw out their female deities in favor of a single Father God as did the early Jews and Christians. Aphrodite was allowed to stay along with the other goddesses. And she continued to be greatly loved, although she came to occupy a somewhat ambiguous place on the fringes of urban Greek society.

In Greece, the more socially approved goddess was Hera, who ruled marriage. However, the myths betray that her Olympian marriage with Zeus was by no means a happy one (see Hera chapter). Nevertheless, as the wife of the supreme patriarch, Hera stood symbolically closest to the center of power.

Perhaps some might consider it a dubious honor, but Aphrodite came to rule *extra*marital relationships for the Greeks. At least she was recognized and celebrated, not denigrated and exiled, like the Lilith of Jewish myth. Possibly the Greeks recognized that a warlike society such as theirs needs a place for erotic release and were prepared to be frank about it—puritanism had not been invented yet. But it was equally possible that they wisely recognized in Aphrodite the remnants of a much more ancient strain in human social behavior, a strain both matriarchal and polygamous.

APHRODITE'S ANCIENT LOVE TEMPLES

Where, then, did Aphrodite originally come from?

She certainly wasn't Greek to begin with. Most scholars now see her as a descendant of the Sumerian goddess Ishtar (later the Babylonian Astarte), who was both a love goddess and the supreme queen of heaven. Between 3000 and 1800 B.C., Ishtar had her temples of love where she was served by her priestesses, the *qadishtu*, who were known as the holy women.

The qadishtu have been misleadingly called sacred prostitutes. This term is a misunderstanding of their true function, which was the *sanctification* of eros and procreation. If a man who came to the temple pleased a qadishtu, she would sleep with him as a ritual offering to Ishtar. A child born of such a union would belong to the temple of the goddess.

For centuries such temples were widespread in the Near East, forming an essential aspect of a matrifocal society we can scarcely imagine today. The exiled tribes of Israel had difficulty reconciling with this side of goddess worship when they encountered it. Their patriarchs and prophets rarely missed a chance to inveigh against "the great Whore of Babylon"—Astarte-Ishtar herself.[4]

Derivatives of such practices that found their way to Greece from the Near East over the centuries may have formed the basis for what became the worship of Aphrodite. According to Merlin Stone, in *When God Was a Woman*, as late as A.D. 150 women celebrated the feast of Adonis at the temple of Aphrodite in Corinth by sleeping with a stranger of their choice.[5] A much more common secular derivative of sacred sexual worship in Greece was the widespread presence of the hetaeras. These often sophisticated high-class courtesans were much favored throughout classical times.

Yet socially the status of the hetaera had already greatly degenerated by the time of the Golden Age of Athens. Under the sway of a largely male-dominated culture, hetaeras were kept on the fringe of respectable life. The essentially patriarchal and monogamous values of Hera, goddess of marriage, presumably saw to that. No matter how high the regard Greek men had for individual hetaeras, according to classical scholar Sarah B. Pomeroy in her book *Goddesses, Whores, Wives and Slaves*, there are no records of any married women ever becoming hetaeras. On the other hand, many hetaeras got married!

WHY APHRODITE SO THREATENS PATRIARCHAL SOCIETY

If an anthropologist were to study the cultural taboos surrounding contemporary network television, one of the striking things he or she would observe is how differently we treat violence and sex. Hundreds of times a day our programs show gunfights, killings, beatings, and thuggery of every kind. While there is some control of violence on TV, it is much less evident than the conscientious control of sexual scenes. Bare breasts are unthinkable on American television, and cop-

---

[4] Goddess worship was much more prevalent among the early Jews than is generally known. Latter-day Jewish historians have done a very effective retroactive cleanup of the record. According to Raphael Patai's book, *The Hebrew Goddess*, all biblical accounts are "relatively late reworks." He shows in this study—called "revolutionary" by the *Saturday Review*—how important the Goddess Asherah was in primitive Jewish culture.

[5] See especially chapter 7, "The Sacred Sexual Customs."

ulation, though occasionally hinted at, is never depicted. It is as though this culture has an insatiable hunger for violence and a terror of sexual pleasure.

What is so dangerous about Aphrodite's sexuality? Why is she so often depicted as a seductress, a witch, a femme fatale? To the Greeks there was the sorceress Circe luring the men of Ulysses, turning them into swine. To the Christian fathers a seductive woman was the very epitome of sin. In the Middle Ages there were dangerous nixies or water nymphs who would entice wandering knights to their doom. In modern times it is Anna Karenina dragging her lover, Vronski, into social disgrace and exile or Hester Prynne branded with the scarlet letter. Today television has many a soap opera siren ruining reputations through her gold-digging machinations.

And always the bait is sexual fascination, which men seem utterly powerless to resist. The Greeks rationalized their paranoia by giving Aphrodite a magic girdle, which could disarm all men and gods who threatened her.

Yet there's something highly suspicious about these examples— the men in them are all depicted as *victims*. Victims of their own un-acknowledged feelings maybe, but surely not actual victims of women. It smacks too much of displaced guilt. For if any social group has been victimized in the patriarchal West, it is women.

There seem to us to be two factors at work: *male fear of loss of power* and *a horror of the body*. The power issue goes back to the great shift that occurred from the matrilineal to the patrilineal family long, long ago. The body issue is more recent, originating with the ascetic strain in Christianity.

MATRILINEAL FREEDOM VERSUS PATRIARCHAL CONTROL

When early societies were ignorant or uncertain of a child's father, it was naturally easier for descent to pass from mother to child. This was the *matrilineal* solution to the problem of paternity. In this arrangement it was commonly the mother's brother (the child's uncle) who was the authority figure and the source of wealth and power. The father might have a bond of affection with the child, but little more. In such a social setup, women could be as free as men sexually, any children conceived being theirs by matrilineal descent. And most important of all, *all property passed from mother to child.*

In patriarchal societies, as we know only too well, property and lineal descent passes primarily from father to son: this is *patrilineal* inheritance. Legitimate paternity is absolutely crucial in this arrangement because it guarantees not just the inheritance of property and title but the *spiritual* continuity whereby the fathers may be immortalized through their sons. In such a situation a wife's *fidelity* is all important as a guarantee of men's continuing material and spiritual power.

It therefore goes without saying that Aphrodite's sexual openness cannot be tolerated in a wife; *it threatens the very fabric of patriarchal society.* It can be tolerated to a degree in a mistress or a prostitute, because she has no legal status regarding children. This is why Anna Karenina, Camille, and Madame Butterfly all die tragically in the great nineteenth-century romances. They are sacrificial victims to the continuance of the great imperial patriarchies. Viewed this way, the institution of mistresses or prostitution is really a mutilated remnant of the ancient matrilineal societies that once worshipped the Great Mother.

The original way of Aphrodite can, by its very nature, occupy only an ambiguous and powerless place on the fringe of the patriarchal world. Here the very most she has been permitted to do is to provide a source of guilty pleasure for the fathers. The fathers are collectively, not individually, guilty, to be sure, but they are guilty nevertheless, because the system they inherit has essentially dispossessed and subjugated women for several millennia.

The saddest consequence of the alienation and dispossession of Aphrodite from earliest times to the present lies in the devaluation of her greatest gift to us: relationship. Bertrand Russell, in his iconoclastic *Marriage and Morals*, summed it up neatly in 1929:

> Love as a relationship between men and woman was ruined by the desire to make sure of the legitimacy of children. And not only love, but the whole contribution that women can make to civilization, has been stunted for the same reason. (p. 27)

Russell maintains that women have been kept deliberately uneducated and ignorant by their husbands for fear that they may betray them.

As far back as Plato the illusion has been fostered that true friendship and spiritual communion can exist only between men and that the love of women is inferior. The Greeks, the Romans, the Renaissance, the British Empire, and of course, the Roman Catholic church all based their political power on tightly knit male elites of one sort or another bound together by homosexual loyalty.[6] With the exception of those in the Church, the men of these societies all had wives. But their wives were mostly denied access to the male world, being valued chiefly for their dynastic connections and procreative functions, chief among which has always been the production of a male heir. Demeter and Aphrodite were not allowed to mingle in the patriarchal order.

CHRISTIANITY'S FEAR AND LOATHING OF EROS

The other major factor behind the patriarchal fear of Aphrodite is the horror of the body inculcated by Christianity. The Greeks and Romans, for all their homosexual preferences, had a healthy pagan love of both male and female bodies, as their statues show.[7]

There is no evidence that Jesus either looked down on women or abominated sex. If anything, he was sympathetic to the inferior status of women and had very close women followers.[8] The first culprit, by common consent, is Saint Paul. Paul was obsessed with preventing fornication. This was the chief value of marriage in his eyes. Though it was preferable by far to remain sublimely celibate like him, wherever the flesh is weak it is, in his immortal words, "better to marry than to burn" (I Corinthians 7:9)—the "burning" referred, of course, to lust!

Paul and that other spiritual giant and misogynist Saint Augustine succeeded in stamping Christianity and the West with a loathing of sex

---

[6] A fascinating study is John Boswell's eye-opening work of scholarship, *Christianity, Social Tolerance and Homosexuality.*

[7] An important recent study describes their essentially healthy attitude toward sexuality: Aline Rouselle, *Porneia: On Desire and the Body in Antiquity.*

[8] For the radical view that Jesus' closest disciple was Mary Magdalene, we recommend Elaine Pagels' revisionist study, *The Gnostic Gospels.*

and the body from which we have never fully recovered. ("To Carthage I came, where there sang all around my ears a cauldron of unholy loves," wrote Augustine describing the years of his temptations.) Soon, following their lead, and in pious reaction to the excesses of Roman decadence, hundreds of men and women took to the North African and other deserts to become ascetic hermits of unbelievable strictness. (One, for example, Saint Abraham, claimed never to have washed in fifty years.)[9]

By the end of the third century, the debate over celibacy for priests had begun. It was to last nearly a thousand years, until papal authority settled it on the side of Saint Paul. A major argument was that sexual contact with a woman might defile the holy sacraments.

Over the centuries a series of dire equations were established in the minds of Christians: *Woman = Earth = Dirt = Sex = Sin*. The fall of man was due to Eve, so the Church never ceased to warn men that it is woman who will lead them down the primrose path to hell—interestingly, Aphrodite is the chief goddess of flowers.

THE SPIRIT OF ROMANCE

Consequently, the suppression and loss of Aphrodite during the early Middle Ages meant a coarsening of the quality of life in general. For women, the Dark Ages were especially gloomy. Fortunately the old northern tribes, with their Celtic matriarchal roots, kept Aphrodite's spirit alive. By the twelfth century a remarkable renaissance of the Goddess occurred. Part of it stemmed from the Celtic revival of the great bardic stories of Arthur, Guinevere, Lancelot, and the Grail. Part of it came from the Crusaders' contact with the East, where a chivalric and mystical love poetry about women flourished. The new bards were the troubadours, who, in the words of C. S. Lewis, "effected a change which has left no corner of our ethics, our imagination, or our daily life untouched." The surviving lyrics of the women troubadours show an extraordinary sophistication about matters of the heart in many ways more subtle than those of male troubadours.

---

[9] As our book went to press, a major new work appeared confirming this grim perspective on Christianity: Elaine Pagels, *Adam, Eve and the Serpent*.

An entirely new form of Aphrodite's religion had been born: romance and the spirit of courtly love. Its first patroness was Eleanor of Aquitaine (who was also strongly blessed by Hera and Athena). It flourished briefly in the South of France—Provence, Languedoc, Aquitaine—where it stimulated the most glorious stories and poetry of sublime love, tragic love, eternal love. One of the great prototypes of all romantic literature, *Tristan and Iseult* was penned (see box, "Forbidden Love"). Legendary "courts of love" were said to have existed where lovers publicly disputed their quarrels and grievances before a panel of ladies learned in the Codes of Love.

During this brief but luminous interlude, women were accorded a dignity and status unknown either before or since in Western civilization. The possibility of full Venusian consciousness reopened and, in a fashion unheard of in patriarchal Christianity, woman and all the values of the feminine were placed *higher* than man.

It did not, nor could it, last. A terrible war, the Albigensian Crusade, was fought against the colorful and cultured courts of the south, many of whose nobles were heretics. How the so-called Catharist heresy combined with the sensual worship of the idealized, but nevertheless flesh-and-blood lady of the troubadours we shall probably never know. Several of the most important of the documents of the heresy were only recently shown to be a late forgery by the Church.[10] From that time forward the troubadours dared, on pain of death, sing of only one lady, the Virgin, a heavenly queen, not an earthly woman. Attainment of the Holy Grail became increasingly Christianized, for the quest had to be undertaken only by "chaste," that is, ascetic figures such as Sir Galahad. Aphrodite had been betrayed once more by the pleasure-hating puritans of the Church. The Grail symbolism of the sacred vessel of blood, the cosmic uterus of the eternal great Mother, was entirely lost.

FALLEN APHRODITE

The psychological consequences of denying Aphrodite any real place in the culture of the later Middle Ages were twofold: widespread sexual

---

[10] See Peter Marin, *Provence and Pound*.

FORBIDDEN LOVE:
TRISTAN AND ISEULT

At the heart of all Western romance, as it derived from the troubadours and courtly Celtic bards of the twelfth century, is the love of a noble lady and a heroic young knight who is her vassal. Betraying her husband, the lady consummates their exalted passion in secret, though she and her lover both know that ultimately it is doomed. Lancelot's love for Arthur's Queen Guinevere haunted the medieval imagination, as did the love of Tristan for Iseult. Scholars, critics, and moralists have argued endlessly about whether this type of love really belongs in Western society. Is it a remnant of Celtic matriarchal practices or even Oriental love rites, as Denis de Rougement's classic work *Love in the Western World* argues? For us it most certainly reflects Aphrodite's tragic alienation in the patriarchal world.

Here is the crucial, unforgettable moment (which inspired Wagner's famous *Liebestod*, or love-death passage) when Tristan and Iseult realize for the first time the fuller implications of their love. They are on board ship with Iseult's servant, Brangien. The plot to renew King Mark's failing love for Iseult with a love potion has misfired, as we learn.

> On the third day, as Tristan neared the tent on deck where Iseult sat, she saw him coming and she said to him, very humbly, "Come, my lord."
>
> "Queen," said Tristan, "why do you call me lord? Am I not your liege and vassal, to revere and serve and cherish you as my lady and Queen?"
>
> But Iseult answered, "No, you know that you are my lord and master, and I your slave. Ah, why did I not sharpen those wounds of the wounded singer, or let die that dragon-slayer in the grasses of the marsh? . . . But then I did not know what now I know!"
>
> "And what is it that you know, Iseult? What is it that torments you?"

She laid her arm upon Tristan's shoulder, the light of her eyes was drowned and her lips trembled. . . .

"The love of you," she said. Whereat he put his lips to hers.

But as they thus tasted their first joy, Brangien, that watched them, stretched her arms and cried at their feet in tears:

"Stay and return if you can. . . . But oh! that path has no returning. For already Love and his strength drag you on and now henceforth never shall you know joy without pain again. The wine possesses you, the draught the King alone should have drunk with you: but that old Enemy has tricked us, all us three; it is you who have drained the goblet. Friend Tristan, Iseult my friend, for that bad ward I kept take here my body and my life for through me and in that cup, you have drunk not love alone, but love and death together."

The lovers held each other; life and desire trembled through their youth, and Tristan said, "Well then, come Death."

And as evening fell, upon the bark that heeled and ran to King Mark's land, they gave themselves up utterly to love.

—*The Romance of Tristan and Iseult*, pp. 38–40

---

neurosis and the emergence of paranoia about witches. Gordon Rattray Taylor puts it bluntly in *Sex in Society*: "It is hardly too much to say that medieval Europe came to resemble a vast insane asylum."

Carl Jung has described how the loss of the troubadour's love service—Aphrodite's true priests—led directly to the witch-hunts (see box, "Jung on the Virgin Mary and the Medieval Witch Persecution"). In a word, by substituting the worship of the Virgin Mary, Aphrodite was driven underground and her vilified image kept obsessively alive in the sadistic imaginings of the Inquisitors. For, once they had mas-

JUNG ON THE VIRGIN MARY AND THE MEDIEVAL WITCH PERSECUTION

It is not generally known that the cult of the Virgin Mary was directly derived from the troubadours of the twelfth century. The Church feared that the troubadours' liberated view of women would undermine its priestly, and all male, authority. So, in the aftermath of the Albigensian Crusade (1209–1220) it took the opportunity to tar the troubadours with the same brush as the heretics. At the same time, it assimilated the worship of the individual lady of the troubadour cult to the worship of Our Lady, the Virgin. Carl Jung commented as follows:

> This assimilation into the general Christian symbol dealt a death blow to the service of woman, which was really a swelling bud in the process of soul-culture for man. His soul, which expressed itself in the image of the chosen mistress, lost its individual expression in this translation into the general symbol.
>   —*Psychological Types*, p. 292

Replacing real women with the worship of Mary is seen by Jung as a major setback for men's psychological development, especially in the area of relationships. It also distracts attention from the virtues of real women. But there is an even grimmer consequence of this repression: the awakening in men's unconscious of the *witch archetype*. Jung put it this way:

> The relative depreciation of the real woman is . . . compensated by demonic impulses [from the unconscious, which reappear] projected upon the object. In a certain sense man loves woman less as a result of this relative depreciation—hence she appears as a persecutor, i.e. a witch. Thus the delusion about witches, that ineradicable blot upon the Later Middle Ages, developed along with, and indeed as a result of, the intensified worship of the Virgin.
>   —*Psychological Types*, p. 293

sacred the heretics, they set about unearthing the secret followers of the Goddess, allegedly the witches.

As everyone knows, witches were believed to take part in orgies with the Devil, with whom they performed every imaginable sexual act. Less well known is that these stories were all derived from "confessions" wrung from innocent women under appalling torture supervised by the celibate male priesthood of the time. Clearly, in psychological terms, the priests projected all their repressed and lurid sexual fantasies onto the women and then punished them for it—often with humiliating sexual torture.[11] Not even the racial crimes of the Nazis quite equal the depths of sexual hatred to which the so-called spiritual leaders of the late Middle Ages sank.[12]

APHRODITE'S LITERARY ROLES: ETERNAL FEMININE TO FEMME FATALE

But the spirit of romance did not die even if the courts of love disappeared and the Church became ever more obsessed with what it tried to obliterate. Despite each new wave of puritanism, generations of writers, poets, and artists would periodically revive the great romantic themes of the eternal feminine and redemption through love; Dante's Beatrice, Goethe's search for the realm of the Mothers in *Faust*, Wagner's *Tristan and Isolde*. Renaissance painters loved to represent Venus.

Shakespeare explores love, of course, but in a vein more realistic than romantic. The way he portrays his hapless heroines—Juliet, Ophelia, Desdemona, Cleopatra—often shows him struggling with deep male ambivalence about the beautiful beloved. One part of him is the passionate Romeo, ecstatic Othello; the other, the cynical, foul-minded Iago or prurient Angelo in *Measure for Measure*. One of his sonnets sums up the accumulated sexual self-disgust of generations:

[11] We agree with Norman Cohn's *Europe's Inner Demons* on this.
[12] We speak further about the witch and scapegoating in the Artemis and Persephone chapters. Sexuality, blood sacrifice, and psychic power became quite fused in the paranoid unconscious of the Middle Ages, which means that we are often talking about Aphrodite, Artemis, and Persephone when it comes to witchcraft.

The expense of spirit in a waste of shame
Is lust in action; and till action, lust
Is perjur'd, murderous, bloody, full of blame,
Savage, extreme, rude, cruel, not to trust,
Enjoy'd no sooner but despis'd straight; . . . (Sonnet 129)

Jealousy and guilt about the victimization of the loved one inevitably figure in plays like *Othello* and *The Winter's Tale*. Shakespeare's solutions are often tragic, even though his comedies explore happier unions. Oscar Wilde was to sum up the same male ambivalence about Aphrodite over two centuries later, writing in prison about an actual man who murdered his wife out of jealousy: "For each man kills the thing he loves."

The Romantics were often to return to Aphrodite in reworkings of the Tristan myth. The fictional love affairs of Emma Bovary, Anna Karenina, and Camille cannot be contained by the societies in which they live and inevitably lead, as with Isolde, to alienation and death.

The femme fatale side of Aphrodite also becomes a fixation among painters, poets, and dramatists in the late nineteenth century. We find images of seductive Eve figures enveloped in huge serpents in the paintings of Franz Von Stuck. Salome with the severed head of John the Baptist haunts the imaginations of Oscar Wilde, Gustav Klimt, and Richard Strauss. Such men succeeded in making conscious that dark fusion of Aphrodite and Persephone that had so obsessed the Middle Ages, but now it is contained as art rather than projected. The stage was set in Vienna for the entry of the tireless Dr. Freud, who dedicated himself to befriending among his many patients deeply neurotic manifestations of the alienated goddess Aphrodite.

In our own century, novels and movies continue to play with the great Tristan theme of doom-laden love, of rejected Aphrodite. Somerset Maugham recounts, in *Of Human Bondage*, the life of a young prostitute; the hero of D. H. Lawrence's *Sons and Lovers* falls in love with a married woman (Lawrence himself eloped with one); John Fowles's *The French Lieutenant's Woman* is seemingly about a rejected mistress. The theme is far from being exhausted.

APHRODITE'S ETERNAL TRIANGLES

This rather depressing historical detour helps us understand why Aphrodite so often plays the outsider, the "other woman," the tragic outcast, or the femme fatale. She represents for the majority of our culture a somewhat dangerous form of relationship: the way of passion (see box, "George Sand"). Her disregard for patriarchal standards, particularly monogamy, upsets our deeply ingrained sense of morality and propriety—that dose of Hera we all got from our mothers at one time or another.

For most of us, it is safer to allow Aphrodite to live solely in our imaginations, through books, movies, TV, and gossip. No wonder we lavish billions upon Hollywood. It is a form of insurance policy. If the stars live out her wayward adventures sufficiently, either on film or in the bedrooms of Beverly Hills, the goddess, we hope, will leave us in peace.

It is by no means so easy, of course. A woman may be born endowed with the goddess's gifts of loveliness and liberality. In this case her life will follow many of the patterns we described earlier; the entanglements of passion may run her life. But suppose, whether you are a man or woman, the goddess has remained dormant in you for most of the first half of your life. Or suppose you are blessed by Hera with a contented, but not passionate marriage. Or suppose Athena has you in a good career with little in the way of serious relationships, or that Artemis has you thoroughly independent and self-sufficient. Should Aphrodite appear now, all chaos can break loose.

First she will send that playful young herald, her son Eros. He will probably arrive during one of the drier sexual periods in your life or your marriage. Now suddenly, out of the blue—he always strikes from behind—you are head over heels in love with the new tennis instructor at the gym, your neighbor's teenage baby-sitter, or your husband's new young partner in the firm. And it is frequently the most awkward or socially inappropriate of circumstances. (Naturally, Aphrodite doesn't give a fig—her favorite fruit—about *that*.)

So, first it's all those snatched, dyspeptic lunchtime meetings. Then, if you are married, it's guilty weekends away disguised as business trips. Or if you are not, the utterly intoxicated disruption of all your plans,

GEORGE SAND: A ROMANTIC WRITER'S HOPELESS LOVE

George Sand (1804–1876) was one of the great radical writers and spokeswomen of the early Romantic movement in France. Undoubtedly she was one of the great Athenas of her age, her male companions sounding like a *Who's Who* of Romantic art, music, and literature (Chopin, Delacroix, and Heine, for example). But when she was thirty, Aphrodite entered her life in full force. Having long since abandoned a wretched marriage of convenience, George Sand fell in love with the poet Alfred de Musset. Though he was frequently unfaithful to her during their liaison, on the one occasion when she betrayed him, he dropped her mercilessly. Her intimate diaries reveal the agonies of her unrequited and all-consuming passion:

> Sometimes I am tempted to go to his house and pull on his door bell until the cord breaks. Sometimes I imagine myself lying down outside his door waiting for him to come out. I would like to fall at his feet— no not at his feet, that would be madness—but I would like to throw myself into his arms and cry out, "Why do you deny your love for me?". . .
>
> Alfred, you know that I love you, that I cannot love anyone else but you. Kiss me, do not argue, say sweet things to me, caress me, because you do find me attractive, in spite of my short hair [she had cut it off and sent it to him], in spite of the wrinkles that have come on my cheeks during these last few days. And then, when you are exhausted with emotion and feel irritation returning, treat me badly, send me away, but not with those dreadful words, *the last time.*
>
> I will suffer as much as you wish, but let me go to you sometimes, if only once a week, for the sake of the tears, the kisses, which bring me back to life. . . .

He is wrong. Is he not wrong, my God, wrong to
leave me now that my soul is purified and, for the first
time, my strong will has lost its power? Is it my will
that is broken? I do not know and I am content to
remain ignorant. What do I care about their theories
and social principles! I feel, that is all. I love. The force
of my love would carry me to the ends of the earth.
—*Revelations: Diaries of Women*, ed. Maryjane Moffat
and Charlotte Painter, pp. 80–81

schedules, creative endeavors—everything. All the daffiest clichés start
to vibrate with rapturous meaning. You walk around trying to hide
that glazed look. Even your pets look at you strangely. You are, of
course, suffering from a madness Plato long ago diagnosed as a form
of possession—possession by Aphrodite's emissary, Eros. Your closest
friends can only humor you, hoping it will pass or at least not get you
run over.

In its most benign form this madness involves only two people and
can lead to a wonderful, fulfilling relationship, even to an exceptional
marriage. But more often than not Aphrodite seems to want three to
play with her, so you find yourself as either the unfaithful spouse or
the lover outside the established relationship.

It is, we think, no accident that one of the most popular of the
myths about Aphrodite involves a marital triangle. Not surprisingly
the Greeks couldn't quite make up their minds to whom Aphrodite
should be married (for the fact is, she shouldn't be married at all). In
one version it's Ares, the war god, in another it's Hephaistos, the divine
smith. In fact, at one of her shrines, at Dodona, Aphrodite was even
worshipped as the wife of Zeus.

At any rate, in the most famous story, she has a steamy affair with
Ares, even though her father, Zeus, has married her off to Hephaistos,
the ugly, lame smith (see box, "The Myth of Aphrodite's Affair with
Ares"). In Homer's story, Hephaistos is something of a figure of fun,
the archetypal cuckolded husband, and our sympathies, like those of
the gods, tend to be with Aphrodite and her lover.

THE MYTH OF APHRODITE'S AFFAIR WITH ARES

Ares and Aphrodite had fallen passionately in love and were meeting clandestinely. He had given her many gifts, and their passion was at its height when they planned to meet at her husband Hephaistos's palace one day when he was away. But the Sun was acting as a spy and told the lame smith of the deception. Consumed with fury, he went straight to his anvil and began fashioning a mighty chain net of gold to catch them and hold them firm.

Cunningly he attached the chain to the bedposts with fine gossamer and made a show of leaving town. Ares, who had been waiting for this opportunity, soon arrived to find Aphrodite waiting for him. Full of desire for each other, they made straight for the bedchamber and lay down. But, just as the crafty old smith had devised, the golden net fell upon them so that they could neither escape nor move.

Still acting as a spy, the Sun told Hephaistos of his catch, and the smith in his rage called loudly on the gods of Olympus to come witness his betrayal.

"My cunning net is going to keep them fast until Father Zeus returns every one of the gifts I made him to win her. She may be his daughter and a lovely creature, but she's the slave of her passions."

Roused by his angry cries, the gods of Olympus all came to see what was afoot. The goddesses, however, stayed at home out of modesty. When Poseidon, Apollo, and Hermes all saw the sorry couple, they burst into uncontrollable laughter. When the laughter subsided, they agreed that Ares should pay the adulterer's fine—all except for Hermes, that is, who would himself have risked anything for a tumble with the golden goddess.

Finally, with Poseidon agreeing to cover Ares' fine, should

he wriggle out of it, Hephaistos set them free and they fled, Ares to northern Greece and Aphrodite to her favorite shrine at Paphos on Cyprus, where she was bathed and oiled by her attendants, the Graces.

—Adapted from Homer's *Odyssey*, Book 8

But why does Hephaistos get ridiculed? Partly, it seems, because his marriage to lovely Aphrodite is rather absurd to start with. Any older man who marries a ravishing younger woman is surely taking his chances, particularly if, like the smith, he isn't good-looking. The classicist Jane Harrison put her finger on the discrepancy when she wrote that "once admitted to Olympus, a regulation husband had to be found for [Aphrodite], the craftsman Hephaistos, but the link is clearly artificial."

There's nothing new in the discovery that arranged marriages usually don't work on the emotional level. When the gods are summoned to observe Hephaistos's captive couple, caught in his net *in flagrante delicto* (literally "in the flames of delight"), they find the sight so ludicrous, they burst into Homeric laughter. As though the goddess of love could be satisfied with one husband!

The fact seems to be that Aphrodite speaks to a part of all of us that is basically "intolerant of patriarchal monogamy," in Jane Harrison's words. For whatever the many blessings of marriage as an institution and a civilizing factor, we have something of that powerful residual longing for the old matriarchal way of eros that Aphrodite once ruled.

Undeniably not every woman—or man—feels it that strongly, since the goddesses influence each of us to differing degrees. But for the woman in particular in whom Aphrodite is strong, the clash between the personal claims of love and the collective roles and values required by marriage can be an agonizing one.

The Greeks and the Romans were openly tolerant of all kinds of sexual behavior. The gods themselves are so promiscuous that righteous indignation would be absurd for them. Certainly men in the ancient world wished to guard the fidelity of their wives to ensure the legitimacy of their heirs but they were quite open about their double standard regarding Hera's and Aphrodite's values. It is only much later that the puritanical side of Christianity becomes so cruel in its righteous punishment of adultery and "the scarlet woman."

We may think ourselves more liberal today, but the double standard hasn't changed. When a man sleeps around, we might tut-tut a little, but when a woman makes one false move, her whole reputation can be ruined in the community.

More often than not, a woman who incautiously allows her Aphrodite nature to lead her into a serious affair with a married man may often be courting heartbreak and anguish. She may have the inestimable power of access to his innermost feelings, but his wife has the greater weight of society, the law, and "decent" opinion on her side. In the power struggle between Aphrodite and Hera, Aphrodite is most often the loser. It is often the source of one of her deepest wounds, as we shall show.

But we must never forget the good side of Aphrodite's affairs, which has a value and a quality all its own. When a woman totally gives herself up to the great passions of Aphrodite, she learns to live wholly in and for the moment. There is a kind of Zen quality to this. No yesterday, no tomorrow, only the incandescent present, in which a look is an eternity, a touch a moment of grace.

This timeless quality is felt because an affair has so little place in the regular routines of daily life. The lover and the beloved become each other's universe. There is a wonderful sense of this compressed time in the comedy *Same Time Next Year*, in which a couple have an affair outside of their own marriages, in a remote motel once a year. The story scans a selection of their meetings over a period of nearly twenty years. But although they age and change, they seem to be living in an eternal present. This captures something of the unreal nature of Aphrodite's world when we are secretly in love.

Sometimes it happens that when her lover is married and she is not, Aphrodite spends a lot of time alone. She may suffer from her loneliness but eventually may learn to live with it. It is a hard lesson for one who longs to be close, to be companionate. But it tends to reinforce her ability to live existentially, for the moment, and to bring grace and beauty to a world where most people barely pause to be really present except in a most perfunctory way.

APHRODITE'S SALONS: THE INSPIRING WOMAN

In her healthiest manifestation, an Aphrodite woman may become the inspiring wife or mistress of a powerful and creative man and at the same time able to explore her own power and creativity. Usually she will have some broader or more radical vision of society as a whole that allows her to detach comfortably from the conventional mainstream. Such a vision suggests a strong amount of Athena supporting her. Lou Andreas-Salomé (1861–1937) is a good example of this. This brilliant and remarkable woman, blessed with well-integrated Aphrodite and Athena in her nature, was at one time the mistress of the poet Rilke, an inspirer of Nietzsche, and a confidante of Freud's; she herself contributed important papers to early psychoanalysis.

Sometimes an Aphrodite woman in the full flow of her creativity will also attract to her younger writers, poets, artists, or performers, creating a kind of salon around herself. Such salons were fashionable in Europe in the late eighteenth and nineteenth centuries. Madame de Staël (1766–1817) gathered French poets and intellectuals around her and introduced them to German Romantic writers, thus inspiring the French Romantic awakening.

A century later in Dublin, Lady Gregory (1852–1932) generously supported the young poet W. B. Yeats and the playwrights John Synge, Sean O'Casey, and George Bernard Shaw; she was at the very center of the celebrated Irish revival. In Paris, also at the beginning of this century, the writer Gertrude Stein (1874–1946) became a patroness of avant-garde painters and writers. Her then famous apartment in the rue de Fleurus became a noted literary salon and art gallery, welcoming the painters Pablo Picasso, Juan Gris, and Henri Matisse; the writers Ernest Hemingway and Ford Madox Ford; and the poet Apollinaire.

In England, Lady Ottoline Morrell (1873–1938), another literary hetaera with a strong Athena side, attracted to her country house, Garsington Manor near Oxford, many intellectuals and writers during World War I and after. Writers D. H. Lawrence, Aldous Huxley, and

Katherine Mansfield, philosopher Bertrand Russell, and economist
Maynard Keynes all visited and stayed at this lively intellectual haven—
and several of them had affairs with their hostess.

In and around all of the salons and cultural centers we describe
here, most of the men and women had unconventional relationships
with either sex. They lived far outside of middle-class conventionality
and Hera's monogamous morality for the most part. Yet complex and
entangled as many of their erotic involvements were, the freedom that
an Aphrodisiac life-style gave them inspired works of great beauty and
vision that were to affect many generations that followed.

APHRODITE'S WOUNDS

And yet, despite these relatively rare examples of how Aphrodite can
shine and inspire with her eros and creativity, she has, like each of the
goddesses, been wounded to a greater or lesser degree in our culture.
Patriarchal rule has forced the goddesses into submission or silence at
every phase of Western society, from the Greeks onward. As we show
in this and other chapters, their greatest gifts and ancient wisdom have
over and over again been betrayed, abused, and distorted.

But possibly none of them have suffered so or been so abused as
Aphrodite. Hera and Athena have learned to accommodate themselves
to the fatherworld, even if at considerable cost. Demeter, as mother,
has always been indispensable. Artemis and Persephone, deeply misunderstood and alienated, have retreated almost beyond the fringes of
consciousness, one physically, the other psychically. But at least in
retreat there is safety and the creation of alternative life-styles.

Not so for Aphrodite. The patriarchy can't live without her and
they can't live with her either, as the old cliché goes. Since the time
when men first wrested patrilineal control from women, they have
mistrusted Aphrodite's liberal polygamous spirit. So they have done
everything possible to confine and restrict her, by making her either
a concubine, a prostitute, a courtesan, or a mistress. But in their longing
for her ecstatic, almost mystical gifts of love and pleasure, men have
never been able to banish her entirely. As Saint Augustine prayed,
"give me chastity and continency, but do not give it yet!"

On rare occasions Aphrodite has wielded what little power she has socially. Once in a while a very wounded Aphrodite will resort to blackmail or murder. Occasionally, as femme fatale, she may even bring down a government, as the call girl Christine Keeler did in a scandal that rocked Britain in 1963. One wonders at the depths of contempt for men that led Mata Hari to cause countless deaths in World War I by her betrayal of French secrets to the Germans.

Yet, as a rule, Aphrodite is not vindictive. She is far more inclined to nurse her wounds in silence, faithful to the memory of her lover, no matter how cruelly he has abandoned her. For at heart, something men rarely realize, Aphrodite is profoundly and eternally generous and forgiving.

Much of Aphrodite's woundedness stems from her alienation from the other goddesses. In a society that often treats her with hostility, disapproval, and manipulativeness, she sorely needs their strengths and perspectives. With her predominantly *feeling* nature, she could, for example, benefit from some of Athena's powerful thinking ability and her career pragmatism. And if she could overcome her age-old distaste for Hera's values of settling down, stability, and fidelity, Aphrodite might ask Hera to help her win social respect and a more comfortable and secure place in the modern world. (All of the founders of salons we've just described had strongly developed Athena or strong Hera qualities.)

Tracy was one of our clients who got into trouble because she thought very little of marriage and Hera's values. Here is her story: Tracy was a very attractive, bubbly young woman who, after graduating from her state college, moved to the city to work for a brokers' firm. She met lots of men in the course of her work and soon found she could charm any she wanted into bed. Settling down was far from her mind. She loved to party, pick up a new man, and enjoy "blowing his mind" with her imaginativeness in bed. Drugs, especially cocaine, enhanced her fun.

When Tracy realized she had a drug problem, she sought help, but in the withdrawal process she suffered severe depression. She couldn't bear evenings alone in her apartment, so she would habitually pick up a man simply for physical companionship. She wanted a more permanent relationship by now, but her neediness and moods drove away all the men she liked. A vicious circle of neediness, rejection, and depression drove her into alcohol abuse. She longed for a relationship it seemed she could not have.

Tracy was clearly a pleasure addict in more ways then one—sex, drugs, partying. She was letting her life be totally run by Aphrodite. She needed some of the energy of the independent goddesses, Athena or Artemis, to help her cool off a bit. Either of them might help her get out of her excessive narcissism and her need to be gratified by others. Athena could teach her how to strengthen her ego by staying focused on specific goals and gaining social rather than sexual approval all the time. Artemis could teach her how to be alone and self-sufficient, particularly how to be less dependent on men. Only when these goddesses became stronger in her would she be ready for Demeter and children and Hera's responsibilities.

In the case of Marian, the client we described earlier in this chapter, we saw how this young woman took a certain superior pride in being "the other woman," seeing more deeply into her lover than his wife did, understanding him better, so she thought. When this happens, a woman is becoming a little addicted to Aphrodite's intimate psychology and her glamor and is losing her perspective. Children and family responsibilities (Demeter and Hera) would soon deflate the glamor and spread some of that overconcentrated eros around a bit. So Marian had to do some important dialogue work with those two goddesses in herself in order to discover why she put them down.

Our last story, that of Melanie, is much more tragic:

Melanie came from a poor country family. Her father and older brother abused her sexually from the time she was five onward. Her mother, if she knew, pretended not to. At puberty her precocious sexual development only inflamed her father more, and he forced her into regular oral sex with him. She was sleeping with other boys by thirteen and had had an abortion by sixteen.

At seventeen she simply packed a small bag, stole money from her father's billfold, and took a bus to a big city. She found that being a hooker on the streets near the truck stops easily got her more money to supplement her waitressing jobs. Soon she ended up as a topless dancer and small-time hooker. Sex came easily to her, since she had become so hardened to men's needs over the years. A born survivor, Melanie learned to stash away some of her earnings.

One day she got on another bus and went back to the state she had left, but to a different small town. She met and married a local farm salesman who was solid and devoted to her, but she could never bring herself to reveal her past to him. Kind as he was, she had been so emotionally numbed by brutal and casual sex over the years that her marriage was not easy. She never enjoyed sex and was deeply troubled by her own hardness and self-disgust. This was when she sought out therapy.

Melanie's early experiences of abuse led her to falsify her Aphrodite behavior and responses and become a hardened sexual performer rather than a sensitive lover. She had learned to parody Aphrodite, reducing all her tenderness to fakery and manipulation. Probably having a child would awaken some of Melanie's own lost tenderness so the Demeter love could reopen the channel to her deeply wounded Aphrodite self.

PASSION AND COMPASSION

We would like very much to be able to conclude with hopeful signs that Aphrodite is regaining her former dignity and power. But alas, when we look at the larger world, we see only more and more media exploitation of her sacred image. And when we look at our clients, we find the habitual denial of pleasure, alienation from the body, and a fear of deep intimacy.

To live fully and honestly with Aphrodite and her wound is a difficult and often painful task for modern women, one that may go back countless generations. It is in many ways safer to live confident and well armored in Athena, safer to retreat and be alone with Artemis, safer to become everyone's mother as Demeter or the wife of a businessman as Hera than to face the heartrending wounds of the love goddess.

Earlier we quoted Jung's opinion that the feminine was deeply devalued in the Middle Ages. In trying to suppress the lovely Venusian culture of Eleanor of Aquitaine and her contemporaries, the Church forbade men to worship a flesh-and-blood woman, as the troubadours had taught. In place of a real woman and the possibilities of real relationship they substituted instead an ideal woman, the Virgin Mary.

Could it be that all of us, women and men alike, are held ransom to a similarly impossible ideal today by the media instead of by the Church? Is it possible that our puritanism runs so deep that as women we are still unable to enjoy being fully and sensually embodied and loved as we are?

How many women feel deeply inadequate every time they open a fashion magazine or watch a shampoo ad? How many men feel as though they can never be happy until they find that perfect pair of breasts, that haunting smile, those heavenly thighs?

Even if it is no longer the Virgin who is deliberately cast up into the sky, aren't we doing exactly the same thing with Aphrodite in the media? Haven't we turned the goddess, yet again, into a fleshless, bloodless, totally unattainable ideal of the Perfectly Beautiful Woman?

The first thing that must happen if Aphrodite is to regain her self-respect is *to be given back her body*. And this means that every woman in search of lost Aphrodite consciousness must start to fully love and cherish her own body, exactly as it is, not in terms of some ideal of what it ought to be. And men must stop comparing every desirable woman to some impossible inner picture they carry around.

One step is to explore the lost or forbidden realm of *touch*. Often it is our practice as therapists to send both our women and our men clients off to get regular massage sessions as a basic part of their therapy. We believe passionately that we all need to explore our sensual nature, otherwise our eros is, in D. H. Lawrence's words, nothing but "sex in the head" (see box, "D. H. Lawrence on The Greater Power of Aphrodite").

Remember, then, that Aphrodite is a completely unabashed sensualist. She loves things that arouse *all* the senses: she loves perfumes, especially flowers; she wants her clothes to feel good on her skin; she loves finely blended colors, sentimental music, fine food. All these

D. H. LAWRENCE ON THE GREATER
POWER OF APHRODITE

She caught him passionately to her, pressed his head down on her breast with her hand. She could not bear the suffering in his voice. . . . She wanted to soothe him into forgetfulness. And soon the struggle went down in his soul, and he forgot. But then Clara was not there for him, only a woman, warm, something he loved and almost worshipped, there in the dark. . . .

All the while the peewits were screaming in the field. When he came to, he wondered what was near his eyes, curving and strong with life in the dark, and what voice it was speaking. Then he realised it was the grass, and the peewit was calling. The warmth was Clara's breathing heaving. . . . What was she? A strong, strange, wild life, that breathed with his in the darkness through this hour. It was all so much bigger than themselves that he was hushed. They had met, and included in their meeting the thrust of the manifold grass stems, the cry of the peewit, the wheel of the stars. . . .

And after such an evening they both were very still, having known the immensity of passion. They felt small, half-afraid, childish and wondering, like Adam and Eve when they lost their innocence and realised the magnificence of the power which drove them out of Paradise and across the great night and the great day of humanity. It was for each of them an initiation and a satisfaction. To know their own nothingness, to know the tremendous living flood which carried them always, gave them rest within themselves. . . . They could let themselves be carried by life, and they felt a sort of peace each in the other. There was a verification which they had had together. Nothing could nullify it, nothing could take it away; it was almost their belief in life.

—*Sons and Lovers*, pp. 353–54

things are part of the awakening of eros for her. These are the ways in which we can create the sacred space into which she can gently enter.

Once we are fully in our bodies, another miracle may happen. We may start to really *feel*. Not just sexual arousal, although that will be there, but more a kind of melting, an opening up of our vulnerable places, a sensitivity to subtle moods and atmospheres. The Greeks said that Aphrodite wore a magic girdle with which she could enchant the most aggressive of males and render him vulnerable to seduction. (Even Hera brought herself to borrow it on one occasion.) It means that when she is present in any loving relationship, she will melt down all our armoring, all our defenses, leaving us totally disarmed and open.

Such moments may bring deep sadness, fear, irritation at being exposed. When our shell is gone, only our tender parts show. We are tempted to close up again, go back into our heads, gossip, run away, control things, complain. These are all reactions to the clumsy emergence of our long-buried feelings. If we are able to just sit with them a while, Aphrodite will teach us to be tolerant and patient.

For Aphrodite is a goddess not just of passion but of *compassion* too. In the Orient she has a very close equivalent in Kuan Yin or Kwannon, the goddess who embodies the greatest virtue of the Buddha, which is compassion. More than any of the other goddesses, it seems to us, Aphrodite has, like the Buddha, accumulated wisdom through suffering and forbearance. She has been rejected, abandoned, degraded, and had her heart broken so many times that it has grown to mighty proportions in its capacity to love.

A Jewish saying runs, "God wants the heart." Nothing could be more true of Aphrodite; we should also say of her, "The Goddess wants the heart." For the heart symbolizes all that is authentic and true of our deepest, least-defended selves. And when two hearts are open to each other, then the magic of eros can flow between them. This is Aphrodite's greatest gift, the commingling of two hearts in harmony with the great sensual commingling of our physical beings. When both channels are open, the goddess is truly present to us.

FIVE

HERA:
QUEEN AND PARTNER
IN POWER

I sing of Hera on her golden throne:
immortal queen, daughter of Rhea,
eminent indeed:
she was the sister and the wife
of great Zeus, the thunderer.
glorious is she, honored on Olympus,
revered of all the gods,
the equal of Zeus, wielder of lightning
—*THE HOMERIC HYMN TO HERA*

RECOGNIZING HERA

Hera will always stand out in a crowd. She is confident, in command of herself, and, more often than not, in command of others. Hera consciousness is most noticeable in an older woman, where the full impact of her natural authority and dignity can be felt. She is one who seems born to rule, regardless of actual social class. In the second half of her life her natural affinity for power will emerge, sometimes as elitism, often as snobbery, and occasionally as pure *realpolitik* when she is the ruthless head of some organization or even state. Queenly, somewhat arrogant, often intemperate, Hera in her full bloom emanates self-assurance and unwavering rectitude. Hera is, in the words of Rider Haggard, "She who must be obeyed."

Hera thrives within the partnership of marriage. A lone or single Hera woman—divorce or bereavement excepted—is a rarity. As the wife of Zeus, the ancient Greek goddess Hera was coruler on Olympus, where officially she shared power with the ruler of the gods. She was also the goddess of marriage, even if, as we shall see, her own was far from happy.

When we meet Hera today, on the surface she will have a successful marriage, grown children she is proud of, and frequently the weight of a family tradition behind her. In appearance she will be well but conservatively dressed, manifesting a "large" presence, which isn't necessarily reflected in her actual physical size. We may meet her on planning boards, at receptions, or in country clubs. She is clearly someone of stature and status, someone who immediately demands our respect.

In the modern world she is often incarnated most prominently as the wife of "the great man," married, for example, to some highly successful businessman, the chairman of this or that board or possibly a college president. In the most coveted of all Hera roles in America, she would of course be married, as the First Lady, to the president.

It goes without saying that when in power, Hera is a formidable opponent in any debate or clash of will, whether in the family or in the political sphere. Executive energy, a strong will, and resolutely fixed ideas characterize the mature Hera. In her authoritarianism she is easily lampooned, easily remembered by her imperious one-liners: the apocryphal "We are not amused" of Queen Victoria; the famous "Off with their heads!" of the Queen of Hearts in *Alice in Wonderland*.

When high up in an organization or institution, she can be as ruthless as any mogul or tycoon. Members of the British government in the Thatcher years have been more than a little startled by such imperiousness in their prime minister. In the United States the behind-the-scenes manipulations of Nancy Reagan have had a similar absolutism to them. Even a seasoned executive like Donald Regan admitted, in his memoirs, to being shocked at how the First Lady was all set to fire the ailing CIA director, William Casey, on Christmas Eve, despite reports that he lay close to death.

With or without a powerful mate, the modern Hera is invariably the matriarch, the queen bee in her immediate circle be it large or small. If she is not felt in the political arena, she will certainly stand out in her family environment. Often she will rule her extended family, in which, respected or reviled, unacknowledged or feared, she is a force to be reckoned with. Contemporary television soap operas about large wealthy Texan or Californian families always have a Hera figure—Jane Wyman's portrait of the *Falcon Crest* matriarch used to typify the breed, though others have since succeeded her.

HERA'S SOCIAL AWARENESS

More than any of the other goddess types, the Hera woman is extremely conscious of her position in society. She not only upholds all the most conservative values of her social caste, she will often be the arbiter of new standards and tastes. In fact she will seem to others who stand in her way quite arbitrary and opinionated. She loves to hold forth, when surrounded by loyal followers, even if it is only at the level of gossip, at which she is an expert.

Because of her evident social aspirations Hera is most at home in those gatherings or institutions that celebrate and reinforce her status and dignity. She loves all family occasions when she can be surrounded and revered by her children and grandchildren. Their love is often secondary; it is far more important that they respect and honor her as the center of things in matters of family and social decorum.

Nothing shows Hera in all her pride and glory so much as a traditional wedding when one of her daughters is getting married. After months of eager and frantic preparation in which she has overseen everything right down to the very last canape, the big day arrives and she can be there, in the front pew of the church to preside *ex officio* over the nuptials. She is dressed in her most tastefully chosen finery, subtly offset by the neutrality of her husband's suit. Her family and closest friends are all around her, properly awed by the solemnity and dignity of the occasion. Much as everyone's eyes will be on her daughter as bride and the young groom, it is, as she well knows, really her day, for she has in effect brought together all the components—religious as well as social—for this great ceremonial. In this sense she is the true patroness of the occasion, just as the Greek goddess Hera presided over the very institution of marriage, celebrating the *hieros gamos*, or "sacred marriage," of the supreme god and goddess.

All family gatherings and social occasions, not just weddings, will bring out the very best in the Hera woman. She loves to feel around her the throbbing of a community brought together by shared values and traditions. On a larger scale a Hera woman will often be found running charity organizations, banquets, receptions, balls, and fund-raisers. There is no question that she likes the work entailed in the actual business of organization, making all the calls and contacts and checking out names, credentials, backgrounds, and pedigrees.

Because of her exactingly high standards, she will appear to those less inclined overly critical, opinionated, even dictatorial. While she may sit on many committees, she really has little patience for them as instruments of democratic decision making. She usually knows exactly what she wants and will move anything or anyone—politely, of course—to get it.

Regardless of her social origins, Hera will almost always aspire to prominence in any group she belongs to. In a working-class family she will make her presence strongly felt as the chief authority on what "our family" does or does not approve of. She cannot help being something of a snob, for she always feels bound to uphold her vision of family and social "respectability"—one of her favorite words. Always seeing her mate, her family, and her children as that much better than others, she will usually have all kinds of expressed or fantasied aspirations for them.

Naturally she will stand out even more prominently in middle- and upper-class milieus, since money and leisure have always allowed the cultivation of her favorite kind of social display. "Society" will often mean for her the place to which one should aspire in her scale of values, which is unashamedly hierarchical and aristocratic. When Hera was married to Zeus high up on Olympus, we can imagine her "looking down" on the world from her lofty position. But the Hera woman does not need to be born into nobility or WASP elites to feel aristocratic; her impulse to rule seems innately given wherever she finds herself.

Because respectability and social position are so important to her, Hera will take the business of finding a mate for herself or her offspring with the utmost seriousness. In Oscar Wilde's hilarious comedy of manners about the British upper class of the last century, *The Importance of Being Earnest*, we meet a formidable Hera in the character of Lady Bracknell. While interviewing Jack Worthing, an independently wealthy and therefore eligible suitor for her daughter, Gwendolen, the following exchange takes place:

> Lady Bracknell: Are your parents living?
> Jack: I have lost both my parents.
> Lady Bracknell (shocked): To lose one parent, Mr. Worthing, may be regarded as a misfortune; to lose both looks like carelessness.

As an orphaned child, Jack receives the full force of Lady Bracknell's contempt. People without parents, in her view, have no place in "society." Marriage to her daughter is therefore, for the moment, utterly out of the question.

HERA AND ZEUS: A STORMY OLYMPIAN MARRIAGE

To the ancient Greeks Hera was the queen of the gods who, with her husband, Zeus, ruled on Mount Olympus. Yet even today, in places like Argos, Samos, and preclassical Mycenae, there remain temples to her ancient cult, in which she was worshipped with a secondary consort as the Great Mother Goddess and specifically the goddess of marriage. Nevertheless, what little we know about her comes mostly from Homer's *Iliad*, where she is portrayed as the jealous and interfering wife. The scholar Walter Burkert has written that "in comparison with the high esteem of her cult, Hera almost seems to suffer something of a loss of status in Homer and to become almost a comic figure. As wedded wife of Zeus, she is more a model of jealousy and marital strife than of connubial affection."

What Burkert hits upon is undoubtedly the need that male-dominated cultures have to lampoon powerful women, a need still felt today and certainly present, though affectionately, in Oscar Wilde. It is a way of alleviating not only fear but a large measure of the guilt men feel for denying women power. When the Greeks preferred to subscribe to Homer's caricatures of the jealous wife and the philandering husband, they probably did so to the neglect of the more solemn respect owed to Hera as goddess of marriage.

As far as the evidence of myth goes, Hera had good reason to be angry and jealous of her husband, Zeus. As "father of gods and men," he seemed to have taken his role quite literally, busily begetting both— yet hardly any of his offspring were conceived within the confines of his official marriage. Among the gods he is said to have fathered Artemis and Apollo by the goddess Leto, Hermes by the goddess Maia, Persephone by the goddess Demeter, Dionysus by the goddess Semele, and Athena (in somewhat unorthodox fashion) by the goddess Metis (see Athena chapter). But the only god that was born from actual wedlock of Zeus and Hera themselves was Ares, the god of war and the least popular of all the Greek gods.

In addition to his dalliance with the various goddesses he had numerous amorous adventures with mortals, often in animal form. Disguised as a swan, the story goes that he seduced Leda and sired both Helen of Troy and the twin Dioskouroi. Disguised as a bull, he seduced Europa, fathering Minos and Rhadamanthys. He also fathered Herakles after seducing Alcmene. And perhaps we should mention his famous homosexual love for the beautiful Trojan youth Ganymede, whom he seduced in the guise of an eagle.

In many ways Zeus and his unbounded promiscuity are an assertion of the ultimate power of the fatherworld and hence of patriarchy for the Greeks. As the supreme ultimate phallic male his virility is portrayed as inexhaustible. But there may have been a political motive in these stories, as classical scholars Jane E. Harrison and Robert Graves have long asserted (see box, "Hera: A Conquered and Coerced Goddess"). According to their readings, Zeus's promiscuous entanglements with other goddesses most likely reflect the period of Greek history when the northern warrior tribes invaded and coopted the old cults of the Great Mother. For many generations early Greece was something of a cultural melting pot, made up of a polytheistic mixture of various forms of worship. Unlike the history of the early Israelites, where the supreme god Yahweh forbids all other gods and especially goddesses before him, Zeus unites with many of them and in doing so produces new religious forms and cults.

So, when we look at Hera's miserable marriage with Zeus, we can read it on two levels: first, as a portrait of the uneasy merging of the religion of the patriarchal warrior tribes who invaded from the north with existing matriarchal cults of the Mother Goddess, and second as

HERA: A CONQUERED AND
COERCED GODDESS

Few writers on Greek religion and culture have been so respected as Jane Ellen Harrison (1850–1928), the Cambridge classical scholar. Harrison used both the ethnographical discoveries of Sir James Frazer's *The Golden Bough* and pioneering anthropological studies of matriarchy and patriarchy to arrive at a persuasive picture of the evolution and social context of early Greek religion. Her conclusions, unpopular among the academic patriarchs of her day, are now accepted, radical revisionings of Greek history though they are. Here is how she saw Hera and Zeus:

If then we would understand religion, we must get behind theology, behind, for the Greeks, the figures of the Olympians, and even the shadowy shapes of the daimones, and penetrate to the social conscience, and first and foremost to its earliest and perhaps most permanent expression, to social structure—the organized system of relationships.

This brings us back to the Olympians. Of what social structure are they the projection?

Undoubtedly they represent that form of society with which we are ourselves most familiar, the patriarchal family. Zeus is the father and head: though Hera and he are in constant unseemly conflict, there is no doubt about his ultimate supremacy. Hera is jealous, Zeus in frequent exasperation, but none the less finally dominant. The picture is intensely modern, down to the ill-assorted, incongruous aggregate of grown-up sons and daughters living idly at ease at home and constantly quarrelling. The family comes before us as the last forlorn hope of collectivism. . . .

Olympos is in Northern Thessaly. We are so obsessed by the literary Homeric Olympos that we are apt to forget that Olympos was, to begin with, an actual northern mountain. Zeus, father of gods and men, Zeus the sky god, with all the heavy fatherhood of Wotan, is a Northerner, or has at least been heavily modified by Northern racial influence. As the Father, though perhaps not wholly as the Sky-God, he is the projection of Northern fatherhood. He, or rather his fatherhood, came down from the north with some tribe or tribes, whose social system was patrilinear. Hera was indigenous and represents a matrilinear system; she reigned alone at Argos, at Samos, her temple at Olympia is distinct from and earlier than that of Zeus. Her first husband, or rather consort, was Herakles. The conquering Northerners pass from Dodona to Thessaly. Zeus drops off his real shadow-wife, Dione, at Dodona, in passing from Thessaly to Olympia, and at Olympia, after the fashion of a conquering chieftain, married Hera, a daughter of the land. In Olympos Hera seems merely the jealous and quarrelsome wife. In reality she reflects the turbulent native princess, coerced, but never really subdued, by an alien conqueror.

—*Themis: A Study of the Social Origins of Greek Religion.* pp. 490–91

an actual mirror of the huge tensions within the marital relationships of the early Greeks.

Robert Graves, in *The Greek Myths*, believes that the myth of the marriage of Zeus and Hera goes back to the time of the Dorian invasion. The Dorians, a barbarous northern hunter tribe who invaded Greece at the end of the second millennium B.C., brought with them their hunting and sky gods Zeus and Apollo. The indigenous peoples of early Greece, particularly those around Mycenae, are thought to have followed cults of the Great Mother similar to those of the Cretans and the Celts. Still honoring the Mother Goddess, these peoples allowed women a greatly revered status and saw them as carriers of magical power.

Graves believes that during a period of the uneasy occupation of matriarchal Greece by the warrior kings, the old priesthood of Hera staged a revolt, which was crushed and the priestesses humiliated. The sacred marriage of Zeus and Hera thus refers to the forced amalgamation of the old mother cults into the Olympian or sky religion, ruled by the Thunderer, Zeus the All-Powerful. We follow Graves in thinking it highly probable that the conqueror massacred most of the men and offered the women, including their priestesses, the grim choice between slaughter and submission to the new order.

The unhappy state of Greek marriage, then, was already quite an ancient compromise by the time of Homer's *Iliad*. The status of the mother religions was already fragmented and divided, as we have seen with all the other goddesses, and while marriage remained a crucial part of the social fabric, as it is in all human societies, it had come to reflect the power structure of a patriarchy for whom descent through the son was primary. Sad to say, marriage as an institution had little to do with love or passion—these concerns belonged, but peripherally, to Aphrodite, the patroness of hetaeras, prostitutes, and all kinds of erotic alliances. As Robert Briffault sums up the situation in ancient Athens in his classic work *The Mothers*, "we have not a single instance of a man having loved a free-born woman and marrying her from affection" (p. 112).

Perhaps, then, it is no accident symbolically that the only child born to Zeus and Hera is Ares, god of war. Certainly Zeus and Hera are constantly at war on Olympus. Moreover, one of the causes of stress in the Athenian and Spartan family was that the man was constantly expected to live in readiness for military service.

Seduced by our rather romantic images of the splendor of ancient Athens, with its democracy, its peripatetic philosophers, and its wondrous drama, we tend to forget today that war played a huge part in the everyday life and consciousness of the Greeks. So it is not altogether surprising that, for all Homer's eulogizing of warrior heroes in his epic, *The Iliad*, war over the centuries had many harsh social consequences for the Greeks at the level of family life. Wife beating, drunkenness, prostitution, prisoner-of-war concubines, and homosexuality could all be directly attributable to the failure of the warrior caste to integrate themselves fully into civilian life.

Strikingly similar problems exist today in America. Thousands of families of Vietnam War veterans still suffer the violent and destructive aftereffects of that war. Add to this the terrible effects of alcohol in provoking family violence throughout our culture and we get a very grim picture. For the fact is that we have barely begun to look at how the violence implicit in imperialistic cultures such as ours has seeped into everyday masculine consciousness and lies behind the huge rate of marital failure and divorce. Zeus remains with us as the archetypal wife beater, as does Hera in her wretched role as the archetypally battered wife (see box, "Zeus Threatens Hera With Violence").

HERA AND MODERN MARRIAGE

Although most women in modern Western society have considerably more freedom than the women of ancient Greece, the basic structures of marriage have not changed that much. True, Christianity has made marriage a sacrament, but except in the more liberal shades of Protestant thinking, marriage is still regarded as primarily an institution for the procreation of children. It remains more or less patrilineal. Neither the sexual happiness of wives nor their individual rights get much attention from conservative Catholics or fundamentalists, thanks to centuries of puritanism and the Christian attitude that still regards women as innately inferior to men.

The romantic idea of marrying for love and the expectation of sexual fulfillment derives exclusively from the troubadours of the Middle Ages and from the cult of courtly love, not from Christianity; the Church fervently opposed such developments, consistently trying to impose restrictions on the expression of eros (see Aphrodite chapter). Most certainly we have a powerful romantic image of marriage today, but it is largely a literary and media creation, albeit an extremely influential one.

A contemporary wife is still mostly expected to be there *to support her husband* and *his* aims and goals, not the other way around. Many men, it is true, have in recent years become seriously involved in raising

ZEUS THREATENS HERA WITH VIOLENCE

The Father of men and gods . . . turned on Hera with a black look and his voice was terrible as he called her to account. "Hera," he said, "you are incorrigible: I am sure this is your doing. It is through your wicked wiles that Prince Hector has been stopped from fighting and his people have been routed. I have a mind to strike you with my bolt and let you be the first to reap the fruits of your unconscionable tricks. Have you forgotten the time when I strung you aloft with a couple of anvils hanging from your feet and your hands lashed together with a golden chain you could not break? There you dangled, up in the air and in among the clouds; and the gods on high Olympus, though they rallied round you in their indignation, found it impossible to set you free. For I seized anyone I caught in the attempt; I hurled him from my threshold, and when he reached the ground he was too weak to stir. But even that did not relieve the heartache I still felt for the godlike Heracles, whom you, after suborning the Winds to abet you in your evil schemes, had sent scudding over the barren sea before a northerly gale. You swept him off in the end to the peopled Isle of Cos; but I rescued him from Cos and brought him back to Argos where the horses graze, safe after all he had been through. I am reminding you of this to put a stop to your intrigues and teach you how little you can rely on the loving embraces you enjoyed when you came here from Olympus and cajoled me into your arms."

The ox-eyed Lady Hera shuddered as she listened to this, and hastened to reassure him: "Now let my witnesses be Earth, and the wide Heavens above, and the falling waters of Styx (the greatest and most solemn oath the blessed gods can take), and your sacred head, and our own bridal couch, by which I would never dare to forswear myself—that it is due to no prompting of mine that Poseidon the Earthshaker is doing Hec-

tor and the Trojans harm, and helping the other side. I can
only suppose that he was sorry for the Achaeans when he saw
them hard-pressed beside the ships, and acted of his own free
will. Indeed, I am quite ready to remonstrate with him and
pack him off. You have only to say where he shall go, Lord of
the Black Cloud."
                          —Homer, *The Iliad*, Book 15, pp. 271–12

their children, and they at least fully appreciate how much time, labor,
and dedication this involves. But to date no man has seriously suggested
that women be paid for their labors or that this in any way constitutes
an economically estimable contribution to society. When women become pregnant, they almost always suffer financially in their ongoing
jobs. While Europe has made great strides in maternity benefits, the
United States lags disgracefully behind. Becoming a mother inevitably
means being economically penalized.

In other words marriage still exists primarily to perpetuate patriarchal supremacy and only secondarily for the benefit of women. The
high divorce rate and the decision of so many women today to follow
the lone path of Athena, as single career women, or to juggle a job
and single motherhood speak loudly of the inadequacy of marriage as
a place of growth and fulfillment for the majority of women as they
are evolving today.

Yet, for all its limitations, humiliations, and shortcomings, the Hera
woman is deeply attracted to marriage. She doesn't want to live and
work alone. The price of that freedom is too great. Fundamentally Hera
embodies the instinct to become mated, to *partner* a man. In this and
many other respects, the role of wife has deep meaning for her. However romantically, she deeply longs to share in the venture of raising
her children, creating the unique unit called a family, and seeing her
husband achieve a solid and respected status for them all in the eyes
of the world. She believes, in short, in the fundamental value and
necessity of the traditional family and is courageously prepared to sacrifice many things to ensure its continuance.

To Athena and Artemis, Hera as wife might seem to be giving away all her power to her mate. But to Hera this is in fact experienced as gaining power. She becomes more than she was as a single woman when she enters the marriage partnership. In her new identity as wife and helpmate she becomes the embodiment of all that will make her husband complete, and she in return becomes the embodiment of his completion. In many respects this is what marriage is really about; self-completion through the other, though how this happens is essentially a mystery in the deepest sense of that word. This, to be sure, is why Christianity has deemed matrimony a sacrament. (We will return to this theme later.)

HERA'S AMBITIONS

And yet, there are considerable pitfalls in Hera's search for self-completion through her mate, particularly when she is younger. Because the Hera archetype only fully manifests in a woman in the second half of life, all the power eventually due to a budding Hera will lie dormant in her during her years as a younger woman. In her deep admiration for strong and ambitious males and with such a natural longing for partnership, she will all too readily put her own ambitions on the back burner, sinking her considerable energies into her young marriage and, before long, her growing family. In this sense her skeptical Athena sisters are right, she *is* giving her power away, but in young Hera's eyes it is more of a long-term investment she intuitively expects to pay off later.

On the surface a young Hera will actually bear a strong resemblance to a young Athena. They are both bright, self-confident, and energetic. Both value education and are anxious to understand and function successfully within the male-dominated society they see around them. But their ambitions are very different. Observe them in their graduating year at college, for instance. The young Athena will be busily checking out all the graduate schools she can, academic or professional training being front and center. The young Hera woman, however, will be far less interested in graduate school as such than in keeping her eye carefully trained for the men most likely to succeed and ensuring that she can date them. In short, young Hera looks for a husband while young Athena looks for a career.

Essentially the difference between the two goddess types is that Athena uses her power and drive for perfection in the service of her career, whereas Hera, particularly when she is younger, prefers to stay at home, using these qualities instead to command the ideal marriage and the ideal family. Athena's development of her masculine qualities, despite the cost to her feminine self, is nevertheless of great use in the cut and thrust of the fatherworld, where achievement is so important.

It is not that the young Hera does not have ambitions like Athena, but rather that hers include husband, children, and family. In that respect we could say that she is much more ambitious than her sister; she wants it all. She wants a comfortable home, security, a dependable husband, wonderful children, a respected place in the community, and, very often, a job. She is usually realistic enough to realize that she cannot have the home and the job all at once. So she will happily, even obsessively devote herself to her family for as long as it takes. She will dutifully stay at home and find local volunteer jobs in the community or work associated with her children's school in order to keep her organizational hand in.

Unlike Athena, with her deep ambivalence about marriage and children, young Hera gives all the appearances of taking motherhood in her stride and of making quite a serious business of it. But she is by no means a soft, tolerant, permissive mother in the way Demeter would be. The ruler and organizer will very soon emerge in young Hera with her children. She has exacting standards, usually inherited from her own mother. She expects good behavior, tidy rooms, obedience, and politeness from her children. To this end she is fully prepared to train and discipline them, quite strictly, if necessary.

With her deep concern for status and social respectability, the Hera wife and mother is a disciplinarian, because she wants her children to reflect her values as completely as possible. Her sons are expected to be successful like their father and her daughters to marry well into families of which she would fully approve. It is the familiar pattern we see with so many women and their families.

Nevertheless, it is hard to escape the impression of considerable narcissism in all this; when Hera wants herself to be so well represented by her children, one must suspect that deep down she is not at ease with who *she* is at the core. We will return to this crucial aspect of her psychology, which borders on her woundedness, later in this chapter. For the moment, let us consider the chief focus of her marriage: her husband.

HERA AND HER HUSBAND: THE POLITICS OF PARTNERSHIP

Basically, a Hera woman wants two things from her husband—partnership and equality. In the end this means that she wants every bit as much power as he has. But unless for some reason she cannot have children, it is rarely possible in her twenties and thirties for her to share fully in his business partnership or career. She sacrifices her drive to rule in the outer world for running the home and attending to her children, tasks she will tackle with the utmost seriousness.

To justify this, she will often make much of the concept of duty in her marriage. The young Eleanor Roosevelt said of herself that at the time of her marriage to Franklin she "had painfully high ideals and a tremendous sense of duty at that time, entirely unrelieved by any sense of humor or any appreciation of the weakness of human nature."

Since for much of the early part of her adult life Hera is obliged to live at a remove from the very thing she wants most to be part of, she will become deeply interested in her husband's career. This is completely in contrast to the Demeter wife during this period, who is simply exultant at all the babies and young children she can now indulge. For young Demeter it barely matters whether her husband is a bank manager or a bus driver, so long as the bills get paid.

But not so Hera. She avidly follows every step, every promotion, every piece of recognition in her husband's progress, taking each new emblem of success as a feather in her own cap as much as his. It is in this period that she may begin to develop her very considerable skills as a hostess and social entertainer for her husband's close friends and work associates. This kind of gathering is extremely satisfying to her, since she can comfortably show her husband off and bask in his reflected glory. With her keen instincts and acumen in the assessment of people she will in fact be an immense asset to her husband in sizing up potential colleagues, partners, and rivals in his world. As she meets other wives of aspiring businessmen or executives or professionals, she will, of course, find herself taking mental notes and indulging her inborn taste for gossip. In her imagination she is beginning to project herself more and more into the world of power.

As the years pass and her husband achieves greater prestige and position, she, too, will grow in her self-assurance as the wife and partner who has truly trodden every step of the way with her husband. She is an extravert, which means that she will enjoy interacting with and manipulating people. She has an intuitive understanding of the most complex and Byzantine of power structures and enjoys sizing up the various players in any power game and charting each rise and fall.

Intrigue and gossip fascinate her, but she can usually be counted upon to be discreet; in fact she can be a superlative diplomat. Frequently, because she has become her husband's chief confidante and advisor, she will exercise considerable influence over him. When this is the case, as it is with Nancy and Ronald Reagan, she can become very possessive and fiercely protective of the great man she has helped create.

Sometimes, as in the case of Livia, the wife of the Roman emperor Augustus, she may become a highly accomplished politician behind the throne, a kind of female éminence grise. It is reported by Suetonius that Augustus was careful to put all his conversations with her in writing! And writer Gary Wills cites Suetonius further that her son, Tiberius, "avoided frequent meeting with her, or any prolonged conversations in private, not wanting to acknowledge the guidance he occasionally submitted to" (New York Review of Books: Review of Donald Regan's For the Record, Sept. 24, 1988 p. 38).

HERA IN POWER

Throughout her life Hera will instinctively gravitate toward power and powerful men, especially those in politics, business, and the more patrician levels of society. She is truly fascinated and impressed with public figures and the way they operate. Nothing, as we remarked earlier, makes her feel more important than to give her mate input on the current meeting, deal, or crisis that he is negotiating.

It came as a surprise to Donald Regan, serving as White House chief of staff during the Reagan presidency, to realize just how closely Nancy monitored Ronald Reagan's activities and how much she assumed it was her right to do so. As he commented ironically, "Mrs. Reagan regarded herself as the President's alter ego not only in the conjugal but also in the political and official dimensions, as if the office that had been bestowed upon her husband somehow fell into the category of worldly goods covered by the marriage vows" (*For the Record*, p. 123). Yet we wonder whether Regan was simply being disingenuous or genuinely naive, to think that the First Lady should have no input in presidential decision making. Surely he had hardly forgotten Rosalyn Carter and Ladybird Johnson, both powerful presences in the White House. Perhaps, in Donald Regan, what we hear is the voice of Zeus at his most patriarchal, indignant in this case that his thunder had been stolen.

Yet is is rarely easy for rulers and leaders to share great power with their wives, their queens, or their empresses, for a simple reason: it is always easier for one person to make a decision or a decree than two. Because of this most monarchies have given the spouse subsidiary power as consort of the monarch.

The dilemma of power sharing is amusingly illustrated by the following apocryphal story about the marriage of Beatrice and Sidney Webb, two powerful political figures in the development of British socialism early in this century (the two were closely associated with George Bernard Shaw).

The story goes that shortly before Beatrice and Sidney, who both had behind them considerable political careers, were to be married, a friend asked Beatrice, "You and Sidney are both extremely strong personalities. How are you going to make the decisions in your marriage?"

To this question, Beatrice replied without any hesitation: "Oh, that is simple: Sidney will make all the big decisions, but I shall decide which *are* the big decisions!"

Hera women who are fulfilled in their desire to command and influence as ruler, leader, or queen and yet remain partners are quite rare. Byzantine empress Theodora managed this with Justinian, as did Britain's Queen Victoria and Prince Albert (see box, "Powerful Heras in History"). More often than not there are marital and dynastic strug-

POWERFUL HERAS IN HISTORY

If we look back through history, the great Heras who ruled peacefully and amicably with their husbands are few and far between. Most of them attained power in patriarchal eras through dynastic succession rather than political maneuvering, so their positions did not always reflect their ambition for power.

Boadicea (1st century A.D.) was a Celtic warrior queen who led a revolt against the Romans who occupied Britain. When her husband died, the Romans unjustly appropriated her people's land and brutally flogged her and raped her daughters before her eyes. Courageously she called all the neighboring tribes together and led a revolt against the Romans. Though successful at first, the revolt was eventually crushed. She represents the finest of Hera qualities in a society where matriarchal power was fully respected and women were equally honored with men as leaders.

One of the most inspiring of Hera stories in history is the life of the **Empress Theodora** (508–548). Born the daughter of a circus bear-tamer, later an actress and prostitute, according to legend, she rose to become the wife of the Emperor Justinian. As empress of Byzantium she was responsible for several notable political and religious victories on behalf of her husband, whom historians see as the weaker of the two. She has rightly been praised for instituting major legal reforms to punish enforced prostitution, which was then rampant in Constantinople, for improving the status of marriage, for making divorce easier, for making rape a capital crime, for enabling women to inherit property, and for generally raising the status of the women of her time.

The formidable **Eleanor of Aquitaine** (1122–1204) lived at a time when women could inherit titles and land no differently than men. She came to grief, however, with her husband Henry II when her ambitions to rule over the united French and English kingdoms cost her sixteen years in prison. Her earlier marriage to Louis VII of France had fared little better. Even though she had insisted on following him to the Crusades, he deeply resented her insistence on the independence and authority of women, eventually divorcing her.

The marriage of **Catherine the Great** (1729–1796), famous as the czarina of Russia, fared little better than Eleanor's. Bored by her political marriage to Czar Peter III, an eccentric and dissolute man, she took a lover named Grigori Orlov. Orlov and a group of conspirators had Peter first deposed and then, it is conjectured, murdered. There is no doubt that she was in many respects a truly enlightened autocrat, bringing many admirable reforms to a quite backward nation, but she in no way embodied the Hera ideal of partnership.

Nearer to our time, we find another inspiring Hera in full possession of her powers in the person of **Abigail Adams** (1744–1818), wife of President John Adams and mother of President John Quincy Adams. In the words of Judy Chicago, she was "a patriot, revolutionary, abolitionist, writer and feminist. She managed all the business and farm affairs for her family, advised her husband, John, and was one of the great letter writers of her time. She spoke out against slavery eighty-five years before the abolitionist movement" (*The Dinner Party*, p. 167).

Queen Victoria (1819–1901), who succeeded to the throne of Great Britain and Ireland when barely eighteen, proved a devoted and popular ruler during her long reign. She married her first cousin, Prince Albert, whom she deeply loved, and bore him nine children. He was a dominant influence in her life, so much so that after his death she grieved for three years, refusing to appear in public during her mourning. Despite her conscientious record of public service, recent biographers suggest that, left to herself, she would have preferred to devote her energies to her children. She represents, therefore, an unusual integration of both Hera and Demeter styles and values.

gles or just plain conflicts of authority: this was certainly the case with Eleanor of Aquitaine's stormy marriage to Henry II of England.

More typically, as in the tragic case of the Puritan wife Anne Hutchinson (1591–1643), an early American colonial settler, Hera's ambitions are seen as a threat to patriarchal supremacy and are curtailed, often brutally. Anne Hutchinson had educated herself in the theology of her church, that of John Calvin, and had begun to challenge certain dogmas, encouraging women to discuss divine matters among themselves. For her pains she was driven from the Massachusetts Bay Colony after being tried for heresy—a charge never proven. She was to die shortly afterwards, murdered by hostile Indians near New York. The words of her condemnation by the Calvinist church fathers reveal how deeply women's power was feared and resented then: she was accused of being a "husband rather than a wife, a preacher rather than a hearer, and a magistrate rather than a subject."

How can Hera be fully herself *without* in one way or another threatening the assumed supremacy of male power? This is a question still essentially unresolved to this day. It is true that certain women do, when their families have grown up, rise to considerable heights in politics or management, often running their own corporations or businesses. One thinks of a Golda Meir, a Margaret Thatcher, or an Elizabeth Arden. But as in these examples, more frequently they do this alone, without the help of a mate. They have, in fact, careers that parallel their husbands', not shared ones.

So the challenge of sharing power is not really faced. Centuries of inequality in the home cannot be rectified so quickly in the public arena. When the Greeks portrayed the squabbling between Zeus and Hera on Olympus, they may have been honestly, but despairingly representing the impossible tensions that always arise not just between the sexes within a marriage, but also from the inevitable disproportion between public and private power.

A man who is a tiger in the boardroom may, as we well know, be a pussycat at home. And his Hera mate, if she is stuck at home with no outlet for her power drive, may easily turn on him; after all, she wishes to keep her own claws sharp. A great deal of the jealousy that Hera had for Zeus in the Olympian soap opera was as much about his intrigues as about his philandering.

UNHAPPY HERA MARRIAGES: LADY MACBETH OR THE UNTAMED SHREW?

What if Hera's husband turns out to be far less powerful than she? What if she doesn't marry a heroic, phallic male who is prepared to go forth and do battle with the world, winning wealth and position for her? It is bad enough when the Hera wife feels excluded from the excitement of a successful mate's public life, but what is Hera to do with a mate who totally fails to measure up to the demands of position and authority?

So far we have more or less assumed that when a Hera woman marries her modern equivalent of a Zeus, he will be a man who embodies power, charisma, and ambition, as well as an upholder of all the spiritual and moral virtues we described above. This is certainly what she was on the lookout for in college or in her early twenties at all those parties and graduation balls. She knew exactly what she wanted, even if she could not articulate it directly: someone to match her own fantasies of being strong, forthright, and hard-driven, the type of man the psychoanalysts call a phallic male and the clinical psychologists a Type A personality.

Sometimes—and it is a story we all know—a budding young Hera woman will misjudge her choice of life partner, marrying a man who seems to her full of promise but who, for one reason or another, falls by the wayside in the early years of climbing the corporate ladder or establishing political influence. She may mistake affability and boasting for authentic personal power, finding herself stuck with a man who is prepared to take second place or to philosophically let life pass him by. She has, it seems, projected her power drive onto the wrong budding Zeus, and now, too late, her error of judgment boomerangs back on her as she labors with a growing family and few prospects of her husband rising further in his once-promising career.

There are two common reactions that young Hera will have to this unfortunate predicament. One is to become like Lady Macbeth, to manipulate her flagging husband from behind the scenes, scripting his every move, plotting every advance, until he becomes virtually a mouthpiece for her own overweening ambitions. Like Lady Macbeth, such a woman will obviously be the stronger of the two, countering his nicer, conscientious persona from behind with steely calculation and quite ruthless plots to further him in the world she wishes them both to rise in.

Until her husband fully lives out such a Hera woman's desires and fantasies of his potential, she can be in private a relentless nag, a bully, even a petty tyrant to both her husband and his associates. And when she does get her way, it will often feed her hunger for even more power through him. Something of this ruthlessness was exhibited in the much publicized marriage of Leona and Harry Helmsley, the New York hotel tycoons. Marriages like this are soulless because such a woman has totally sold out her feminine self for masculine power. Sadly these marriages more often than not degenerate into alcoholism, emotional alienation, and sometimes violence.

A more extreme reaction occurs if it turns out that the ambitious Hera woman's mate is completely ineffectual and resists her attempts at manipulation. When her husband thus deprives her of any larger arena for her power drive, Hera's appetite for influence and intrigue tend to be played out among the members and generations of her own family. Her husband is henpecked, her children dragooned, and her friends regaled with endless complaints. In her bid to become the family matriarch, she is ridiculed behind her back as "the wife who wears the pants," the scold, the harridan, the butt of every old-fashioned mother-in-law joke. No longer a Lady Macbeth who gains the whole world at the price of her own and her husband's soul, she has now become an untamed shrew.

HERA'S PHALLIC PROTEST

Underneath these extreme tensions, it is not hard to see at work the same marital dynamics that belong to Zeus and Hera. It is an example of psychoanalyst Alfred Adler's idea of "masculine protest" in women, a protest above all directed at the husband's once again denying the wife any real power except in the home.

Pistol-packing women and knife-wielding women, from Hic-Mulier and Lady Macbeth (see box, "Shrewish Women in Shakespeare's Time") through Lizzie Borden and Ibsen's Hedda Gabler, have haunted our society and the male imagination for several hundred years. Some psychoanalysts have gone so far as to term them *phallic women*, by

SHREWISH WOMEN
IN SHAKESPEARE'S TIME

It is no accident that many of the terms for unhappy Hera wives—*hag, nag, shrew, virago, vixen, termagant, fishwife*—have a distinctly archaic character to them. The caricature of the shrewish wife that Shakespeare gives us in Kate (and also, potentially, in Beatrice, who marries Benedict—"my Lady Tongue," he calls her) had begun to reach epic proportions by the late Renaissance. According to Carroll Camden's book *The Elizabethan Woman*, it is in 1617 that we first see a printed reference to the "woman of masculine gender." King James was scandalized, apparently, by "the insolencie of our women, and their wearing of brode brimmed hats, pointed doublets, their hayre cut short or shorne, or some of them stilettoes or poniards and such trinkets of like moment."

We know, too, that Shakespeare experimented in several plays—*Twelfth Night* and *As You Like It*, for example—with role reversal, in which the woman characters Viola and Rosalind dressed like and pretended to be men. Possibly he was commenting on the same trend that disturbed King James.

An anonymous literary attempt to satirize the movement came in James's reign under the witty title of *Hic-Mulier*, which means "the he-woman." Its subtitle describes it as "a medicine to cure the coltish Disease of the Staggers in the Masculine-Feminines of our Times." In the form of a dialogue, the author upbraids Hic-Mulier for wearing manly attire, "a Leadenhall dagger, a High-Way pistol" and for "a mind and behavior suitable or exceeding every repeated deformitie." What is interesting is Hic-Mulier's reply. She says, anticipating Simone de Beauvoir by several centuries, that the meanings of *male* and *female* are bound to change through the ages.

Cultural historians such as Marshall McLuhan have commented that the Renaissance represents a huge shift in consciousness, to which we are still reacting today. Society was

moving away from the collective and unself-conscious values
of feudalism, where every person had a fixed role in a preor-
dained hierarchy. In its place the Renaissance ushered in a fast-
moving and opportunistic world characterized by what
McLuhan calls "the new shrill and expansive individualism." In
the medieval world each person had the confidence of knowing
exactly who he or she was in the fixed pyramid of power, a
position, role, or function commonly reinforced by a distinctive
uniform or livery. But as the Renaissance spirit swept Europe,
men and women felt more and more cut adrift. The result was
that "each man had to become his own Phoenix" as the poet
John Donne was to put it. Men and women, in short, had to
re-create their own identities.

One's self-identity is, of course, deeply bound up with the
clothes one wears, so that certain women, as well as men, were
obliged to experiment with all kinds of different dress forms.
In such a deeply insecure world it is not altogether surprising,
further, that certain of the more ambitious women should want
to adopt the swashbuckling attire of the male heroes of the
day, such as Raleigh, Essex, Drake, and so on.

On the surface there are many similarities between the
heroic piracy of the early Greeks and that of the Elizabethans.
Possibly the exaggerated phallic drive in the men, coupled with
the continued subservience required of wives, brought about
a deep double reaction among certain women. At home they
vented their frustrations in outbursts of shrewishness while in
public they mimicked, not without a certain mockery, the
cocky, phallic posturing and display of the court peacocks.

obvious analogy with phallic males of Freudian jargon. The Jungian
writer Toni Wolff was also trying to pin down this particular feminine
personality structure when she sketched the psychology of the Amazon
woman as one of her four types. The other types—Mother, Hetaera,
and Medial Woman—correspond closely to our depictions of Demeter,

Aphrodite, and Persephone (see also our introduction), but we experienced some difficulty with her description of the Amazon woman, who could be Athena, Artemis, or Hera, as we see them.

Toni Wolff herself thought the term "Amazon" somewhat misleading, and this has also been the reaction of many contemporary women who have encountered it. This, as we explained earlier, is why we find it more useful to subdivide her Amazon type into Athena, Artemis, and Hera types. Once we do this, we can see that all three have distinct phallic qualities—Athena is intellectually agressive, Artemis rugged and independent, Hera is forthright and strong-willed—but they clearly exercise their phallicism differently and in distinct spheres.

Neither Artemis nor Athena in their purer forms are primarily drawn to relationships, which means that their masculine phallicism can be strongly transformed or sublimated in highly creative ways: it provides Artemis with the enormous physical energy she has for her practical and adventurous activities; to Athena it gives a certain focused power to achieve her intellectual goals.

But with Hera, whose chief concerns are with partnership and power, her phallicism can easily present her with grave problems in her relationships. Since her phallic drive is all too often frustrated by an unequal partnership, she can become seriously unbalanced psychically and intensely driven by the very thing she wants to be in control of. Jungians have termed this difficult and distressing state animus possession, when the frustrated masculine side of a woman takes over in a destructive and critical fashion in most aspects of intimate life. Lady Macbeth's drivenness is of this nature. The playwright William Congreve had in mind this state, too, when he wrote, "Heaven has no rage like love to hatred turned, / Nor hell a fury like a woman scorned."

Some of Toni Wolff's more pointed comments on the negative aspects of the Amazon woman are worth quoting, since they seem to belong very definitely to Hera. For example:

> Her negative aspect is that of a sister who, driven by "masculine protest," wants to be the equal of her brother, who will not recognize any authority or superiority . . . who fights by using exclusively male arms and is a Megaera [one of the Furies or Erinyes] at home. . . . Personal complications are dealt with in a "masculine" way or are repressed. Patience or compre-

hension of anything still undeveloped or in the process of developing or gone astray is lacking, both in respect to herself and to others ("I am looking forward to the time when my children are grown up.") Marriage and relationship are viewed under the aspect of achievement, primarily her own achievements; success and efficiency are her watchwords. The Amazon is also in danger of misusing human relationships as a means of "business" or for the sake of her career.

—"Structural Forms of the Feminine Psyche," p. 8

HERA'S WOUND:
THE PAIN OF POWERLESSNESS

Hera's dynamic is that she wants to be out there where the action is, and the source of her protest is that she hates her husband—hers and everyone else's—for excluding her from it. If she shares equally with her husband in the home, she feels fully entitled to do the same in the outer world. Such is the essential theme of Zeus and Hera's quarrel in the opening book of Homer's *Iliad*: Zeus has been consulting with Metis, a former paramour, on how to aid Achilles in the Trojan War, and Hera immediately turns upon him for not consulting her. It is not just his sexual, but even more his *political promiscuity* she is really jealous of, his ability to have his finger in so many different pies, his freedom to move and share his thoughts with so many advisors, male or female.

In other words, Hera is jealous of *the freedom her husband has to be a moving force in the world*. Deep down she wants to live and behave exactly like a man in a man's world. When the male world in the form of her closest companion rejects her, it is experienced as a deep narcissistic wound to her self-esteem, a wound around which hurt, resentment, and jealousy almost inevitably accumulate (see box, "Zeus and Hera Quarrel on Olympus").

Hera, when she is obliged to stay in the home, has little opportunity to develop her social, political, and executive skills. In reaction, the first thing she does is possessively cling to her husband, making him the source of her own vicarious politicking, demanding to be his sole

ZEUS AND HERA QUARREL
ON OLYMPUS

Zeus sat down on his throne; and Hera, looking at him, knew at once that he and Thetis of the Silver Feet, the Daughter of the Old Man of the Sea, had hatched a plot between them. She rounded instantly on Zeus. "What goddess," she asked, "has been scheming with you now, you arch-deceiver? How like you it is, when my back is turned, to settle things in your own furtive way. You never of your own accord confide in me."

"Hera," the Father of men and gods replied, "do not expect to learn all my decisions. You would find the knowledge hard to bear, although you are my Consort. What it is right for you to hear, no god or man shall know before you. But when I choose to take a step without referring to the gods, you are not to cross-examine me about it."

"Dread Son of Cronos," said the ox-eyed Queen, "what are you suggesting now? Surely it never was my way to pester you with questions. I have always let you make your own decisions in perfect peace. But now I have a shrewd idea that you have been talked round by Thetis of the Silver Feet, the Daughter of the Old Man of the Sea. She sat with you this morning and clasped your knees. This makes me think that you have pledged your word to her to support Achilles and let the Achaeans be slaughtered at the ships."

"Madam," replied the Cloud-compeller, "you think too much, and I can keep no secrets from you. But there is nothing you can *do*, except to turn my heart even more against you, which will be all the worse for yourself. If things are as you say, you may take it that my will is being done. Sit there in silence and be ruled by me, or all the gods in Olympus will not be strong enough to keep me off and save you from my unconquerable hands."

This made the ox-eyed Queen of Heaven tremble, and curbing herself with an effort she sat still. Zeus had daunted all the other Heavenly Ones as well, and there was silence in his palace.

—Homer, *The Iliad*, Book 1, pp. 37–38

confidante, unrealistic as this may often be. But if her ambitions are really strong, she will never be satisfied with this. Her demands for information and opinions about his colleagues and work decisions will be a constant source of friction between the two of them, however sympathetic and generous he may try to be.

Inevitably the ambitious homebound Hera wife who tries to live through her husband in this way feels closed out. Her phallic side has been thwarted and rejected. In her need to be so close to her husband she unconsciously demands an almost symbiotic closeness; she wants to be inside his very skin, as it were. For most men, such psychic penetration by a woman's energy is intolerable. It starts to summon up deep infantile fears of the overwhelming power that psychoanalysts call "the devouring mother," like the hungry witch of fairy tales who wants to eat young babies. Such a fear surfaces in Shakespeare's *Macbeth* in the form of the witches, who form a psychic counterpart or shadow to Lady Macbeth's overweening ambitions. The only reaction most men have to such penetrating power is to retreat from the intimacy demanded and seek out male companionship—or indeed other women, Zeus's stratagem.

Spurned and frustrated by her husband in this way, the Hera woman will usually fall back on her family. Here, at least, she seems to have absolute power. But sadly for all, except in certain rare family structures that have retained a traditional role for the matriarch, Hera tends to be most unhappy making the family arena the sole focus of her sovereign ambitions. More marriages come to grief and more families are tyrannized by unfulfilled and wounded Heras than by any other goddess type. And more alcoholic, abusive, and psychotic mothers are to be found among such deeply frustrated Hera women.

For a Hera woman is simply not able to sit back and enjoy her babies and growing children the way a Demeter or Artemis or Aphrodite woman can. Hera's form of mothering can be quite harsh, and if she received little or no Demeter or Artemis or Aphrodite indulgence from her own mother, she will raise her children to feel dragooned and criticized, that they are somehow never good enough. When a woman acts as mother through the archetype of Hera alone, without support from the other goddess energies, there will be trouble.

The Greek image of the goddess Hera hardly helps. Classical scholars know of no single representation of Hera as a mother with her child. Motherhood simply wasn't one of the attributes that the Greeks imagined in Olympian Hera. It is even reported that when the temple of Hera was open in Athens, the temple of Demeter, the goddess of fertility and motherhood, was closed. One could hardly imagine a more graphic expression of Hera's fundamental incompatibility with motherhood.

The Amazon woman that Toni Wolff describes fits exactly the style of the contemporary reluctant Hera mother. She will, as Wolff says, run her family in terms of achievement and success. She'll have all kinds of plans and projects for them from the moment they can crawl. Whole childhoods tend to be sacrificed to the restless ambitions of these frustrated Hera mothers, whose relentless energy is largely misspent and inappropriately directed into careers for her offspring that she herself should really be following. She is impatient for them to grow up and secretly intolerant of childish behavior, as Toni Wolff also remarks. In fixing rigidly controlled standards of perfection and attainment for her children, she may unconsciously be setting them up to feel the kind of failure that inwardly she is perpetually tormented by.

FRUSTRATED HERAS: A BETRAYED GENERATION

Many people know this kind of mother from the receiving end. In fact we have observed a pattern among a whole generation of women born in the twenties and thirties. These mothers display an overly disciplined mothering style that belongs, we believe, to frustrated Hera consciousness, deeply lacking in the confident and loving nurturing that belongs to Demeter as mother. At one level this may have been due to the disruptions wrought by World War II. While their husbands were away on military service, many women, both with and without children, took active roles in the war effort. They got a strong taste of power and independence, which was immediately taken away from them again when their husbands returned from the war.

During the forties and fifties, in both America and Europe, huge emphasis was naturally put on rebuilding society and making an emotional center of the home and family. It was the era of endless new

labor-saving gadgets and fancy technology—dishwashers, washing ma-
chines, televisions, and more. Domesticity and the loving wife were
heavily projected in the media: *Leave It to Beaver, Father Knows Best,*
and so on all caricatured the happy wife at home, content with children,
doting husbands, and an immaculate *Better Homes and Gardens* house.
What the men who dreamed up these images clearly wanted was good,
consoling Demeter for them at home, now that the war was over. And
the advertisers on TV wanted lots of active consumers. At some level
they had felt threatened by women in the workplace during the war
and now wanted them back home.

Naturally this generation wasn't only comprised of Demeters, however much men wanted it that way. The generation who came to maturity during the war also contained frustrated Athenas, Artemises, and,
above all, frustrated Heras, and every one of them felt trapped by their
marriage. But it was those mothers who were basically Heras who
seemed to suffer most from their confinement within the fur-lined
prison the fifties created for dutiful wives. Athena mothers of this
generation had the aptitude and ambition, very often, to go back to
school and start new careers after their children were gone; Artemis
stayed single; Aphrodite went her own way. Hera women, by contrast,
more frequently felt ill educated and ill equipped to catch up with their
successful and independent daughters.

It is a sad fact that Hera women generally do not seek out therapy
or go to workshops. By and large this is because their extraversion
disinclines them to look inward and because they usually prefer to
tackle problems with their well-honed common sense and willpower.
An exception to this general pattern was one of our clients, Janet.

Janet came into therapy at the age of fifty-four following the
death of her husband of thirty years. Dan had been an executive
in a large corporation before a massive heart attack killed him
on the tennis court. An intelligent and sophisticated woman,
Janet was surprisingly unprepared for the task of sorting out
the complex financial and emotional problems that arose in the
wake of Dan's death. Janet's three children, aged twenty, sixteen, and twelve were shattered by a loss they felt as abandonment and were "acting out" in various ways. Janet, herself,
felt dazed, bewildered, and confused by the sudden changes.

The first part of Janet's work in therapy had to do with the journey through Persephone's underworld. Frightening dreams and a nagging feeling of depression pulled her inward, where she began to look at some of the unfinished business of her marriage, especially their sex life. The first obvious benefit in opening up to Persephone became evident in her children. Their schoolwork began to improve and their relationships with friends returned to normal. It was as though Janet's inner work was freeing them up to get on with their own lives.

The second part of Janet's work was to find a meaningful life-style now that her old familiar one had ended. Like many women her age, she had married soon after graduating college and had settled down to comfortable domesticity almost immediately. The family lived in a large, tree-shaded house in a community that included the benefits of a country club and good schools. It was agreed early in the marriage that Dan would be the breadwinner and Janet would look after the family and social matters. Over the years they had done a great deal of social entertaining on behalf of Dan's rising career, and Janet was known as an expert at giving dinner parties. But aside from these duties and involvement in several local charitable groups, Janet had done very little else. Her Athena identity was very weak but much needed. She began to research the possibilities of what she might do with her time.

After much thought Janet decided to start a catering service out of her home. The idea allowed her to capitalize both on her contacts in the community and on her experience as a hostess. With her knowledge of social forms and graces, she would be able to offer experienced counsel to her clients as well as providing them with food and flowers. The idea proved a brilliant one. Today Janet is president of a very successful enterprise.

HERA AND HER DAUGHTERS

If there is a strong generational theme that we see among women who are now in their thirties and forties, it is one of deep alienation from their mothers. Many of these women were daughters who developed their Athenean and Artemesian independent life-styles as a result of the women's liberation movement of the sixties. Almost all of them had mothers who would qualify as frustrated Heras. Most grew up with their mothers' frustrated Hera ambitions as well as unfulfilled Athena and Artemis impulses nagging constantly in their ears or seeping into their unconscious minds. Because these ambitions were quite unconscious in the mothers they were absorbed by the daughters as a mixture of simmering resentment and jealousy. Never in our recent history have these three powerful goddess energies been so close to the surface yet so held down as in the forties and fifties. No wonder books like Doris Lessing's *Golden Notebook* make such painful reading.

Inevitably much of what these daughters have to report about their mothers comes heavily filtered through a good deal of anger. But it nevertheless tells us a great deal about both them and the psychology of their Hera mothers. For in many ways, these daughters were and are struggling to break free from the very restricted patterns of womanhood their mothers were sold. And they must still pay a heavy price for their freedom. As daughters they seem fated to carry within them the residue of their mother's frustrations, frustrations that have now turned to resentment, sickness, and often barely concealed envy.

Many of the women who come into therapy today in their thirties and forties have surprisingly similar complaints about their mothers. They speak about how their mothers' needs and fears dominated them, or how they could never really be themselves because their mother demanded quite crippling standards or narrow life-styles of them. Or else they complain of how horribly trapped they felt, unable to break free of their mothers' constant interference in their lives.

The Jungian analyst Marion Woodman, in her important book *Addiction to Perfection* (see also box, "Hera's Addiction to Perfection"), has made a psychological study of such destructive mother-daughter relationships, particularly as they manifest themselves as anorexia nervosa and obesity. The diseases of over- and under-weight she rightly sees as symptomatic of a deep woundedness with regard to authentic mothering—what we would here call a lack of Demeter mothering. Largely written from the point of view of the daughters of Hera mothers, it is extremely valuable in helping to understand how so many

HERA'S ADDICTION TO PERFECTION

Here is how Jungian analyst Marion Woodman summarizes the deep and pervasive alienation from their Hera mothers that so many daughters feel today:

> Most of our mothers "loved" us and did the very best they could to give us a good foundation for a good life. Most of their mothers from generation to generation did the same, but the fact remains that most people in this generation, male and female, do not have a strong maternal matrix out of which to go forward into life. Many of our mothers and grandmothers were the daughters of suffragettes who were already on the way to a new role for women. Some of them longed to be men; some related to their masculine side and dominated their household with masculine values so the atmosphere was geared to order, to goal-oriented ideas, to success in life, success that they themselves felt they had missed. The gall of their disappointment their children drank with their mother's milk. Unrelated to their own feminine principle, these mothers could not pass on their joy in living, their faith in being, their trust in life as it is. Geared to doing things efficiently, they could not surrender to allowing life to happen. They dared not allow themselves to react spontaneously to the unexpected. And since their children were sometimes the unexpected, these infants had three strikes against them before they were put into their cradles, unexpected not only in their persons, but in their temperament since they had feelings and thoughts that were not in accordance with their parent's projections of what their children should be. Within that attitude there is no room for life to be lived as it is, no room for either parent or child to relax into "I am"; conse-

quently, the child lives with an elusive sense of guilt, the personification of the mother's disappointment less in her child than in herself. The child grows up attempting to justify its very existence which in psychic reality it has never been granted.

Addiction to Perfection, pp. 16–17

Woodman's book, which should be read in full by any woman for whom the preceding passage resonates, points sharply to the root of what we must call Hera's woundedness: that she is out of touch with the ground of her feminine being and has instead substituted masculine values of power, perfection, and success, which she herself may have inherited from her mother.

women's lives are driven, almost to possession, by the wounded mother image within them.

The problem, as Woodman sees it, following certain insights of Jung's, is that the mothers we are here calling frustrated Heras were themselves inadequately mothered, *as were their own mothers* for a number of generations back. What this means is that the problem has been compounded for generation after generation—possibly as far back as the Industrial Revolution, which so alienated women from the land and the cycles of the earth. Thus, more recently, instead of authentic mothering, these mothers have unconsciously transmitted to their daughters a set of perfectionist rules and unreal expectations regarding goals and success, which have very little to do with discovering their individual feminine nature—which could be any one of our goddess archetypes. More tragically still, their daughters are left to struggle with the deep, unacknowledged pain that derives from being cut off from their own feminine ground of being. This is Emma's tragedy in *Terms of Endearment* (see box, "Hera in the Movies").

Both Hera and Athena in their mythic biographies suffer painfully from their alienation from the mother principle. Athena is robbed of

HERA IN THE MOVIES

In the well-known film *Terms of Endearment* we watch Aurora Greenway, a classic middle-class Hera mother, endlessly trying to run the life of her daughter, Emma, a devoted Demeter, whose marriage she strongly disapproves of. Aurora fails to save Emma from what she sees as her daughter's gradual decline into the mediocrity she has chosen in her nice, but spineless husband, a small-town college professor. But Aurora's interference is plainly a substitute for getting on with her life. (She has a long-overdue sexual fling with a raunchy neighbor, but it barely softens her crustiness.) Despite endless phone calls in which Emma patiently mothers her mother, no real dialogue ever takes place between them.

Tragically, Persephone intervenes in the form of a cancer that Emma contracts; it brings mother and daughter briefly closer together, and we begin to feel Aurora's agony at losing the daughter on whom she pinned so much. But we are left suspecting that all kinds of dark, unexpressed feelings of rage lurked within Emma's cancer.

In many ways the ending is psychologically unsatisfying. Emma never lets out her anger at her interfering mother, and Aurora can only belatedly begin to show her true feelings when Emma is on her deathbed. Hera and Demeter remain essentially alienated. The unvented feelings therefore fester in the background, only to be claimed silently by Persephone, with whom the daughter has now become unconsciously identified. The dying daughter is in many ways a martyr to the Demeter love that probably neither woman ever received directly. The cancer is the embodiment of the feelings of lovelessness, disappointment, and rage the daughter, too busy being everyone's long-suffering Demeter, could never express.

her true mother, Metis, when Zeus appropriates the pregnancy (see Athena chapter). Hera, although she has Rhea as her mother, is too possessed by her power drive to develop the gentler qualities necessary for nurturing and child rearing. As we remarked earlier, nowhere in Greek art is Hera represented as a mother with her child.

To compensate for this void, both goddesses are seen to turn to the father principle as a surrogate for real mothering. In Zeus they find loftier nourishment in his ideals of the spirit and the mind: morality, law, justice, duty, fidelity, and tradition. These bywords of Zeus, the father of the gods, now become the ruling principles for both Hera and Athena. Worthy as they are, they have quite different psychological connotations from the earthy, spontaneous, life-affirming nurturance, warmth, and love that we associate in goddess psychology with Demeter, with Rhea, and with grandmother Gaia, the first Earth Mother of the Greeks.

"Spirit," the Fourteenth Dalai Lama once wrote, "is at home in high places." He could well have been talking of sacred mountains such as Olympus and Ida just as much as the Himalayas. This is the spiritual topography where Hera and Athena came to live. But the Dalai Lama also noted that "soul is at home in the deep shaded valleys," the places we would associate more with the Earth Mother. The price Athena and Hera pay for their intimate communion with spirit is in many ways, therefore, a loss of soul. Both of them need to reconnect with the qualities that belong to Demeter, and for this a certain rigidity of principle needs to be sacrificed; a degree of softness needs to be recovered. It is the work of considerable inner reconciliation.

HERA AND HER SONS

When a Hera woman has sons, the problem of her masculine imbalance is even more pronounced than with her daughters. All the excess of phallic energy that can find no full expression in her outer world or through her husband will be deflected onto the sons instead. They quickly become the displaced expression and living embodiment of the unsettled energy in her masculine self. Many a young adolescent son goes out into the world with all kinds of ambitions that he never questions as his own but that are really his mother's. Often, because of the deep, unresolved tensions between wife and husband, his youthful ambitions will run sharply counter to his father's wishes for him. The son is being used as an unconscious pawn in the parents' unresolved power struggles.

Freud claimed to detect this triangle of mother and son versus father that appears in early childhood—the famed Oedipus complex— and he emphasized its sexual and incestuous component. Certainly it can be seen in a frustrated Hera mother during her son's childhood, but it returns much more strongly in late adolescence when the son begins to manifest all of his mother's secret fantasies, acting out her young hero. D. H. Lawrence felt and deplored this terrible seductiveness in his own unhappy mother and saw it around him in other mother-son relationships:

> If you want to see the real desirable wife-spirit, look at a mother with her boy of eighteen. How she serves him, how she stimulates him, how her true female self is his, is wife-submissive to him as never, never it could be to a husband. This is the quiescent, flowering love of a mature woman. It is the very flower of a woman's love: sexuality asking nothing, asking nothing of the beloved, save that he shall be himself . . . The woman now feels for the first time as a true wife might feel. And her feeling is towards her son. . . .
>
> And thus, the great love-experience that should lie in the future is forestalled. Within the family, the love-bond forms quickly, without the shocks and ruptures inevitable between strangers. And so, it is easiest, intensest—and seems the best. It seems the highest. You will not easily get a man to believe that his carnal love for the woman he has made his wife is as high as the love that he felt for his mother or sister.
>
> The cream is licked off from life before the boy . . . is twenty. Afterwards—repetition, disillusion, and barrenness.
>
> —*Fantasia of the Unconscious*, pp. 127–28

One can hardly miss Lawrence's simmering anger in this passage. In many respects he had championed his own mother's anger and frustration at being trapped in a violent marriage in the industrial squalor of a small English mining community. Throughout his life his own attitude toward women remained deeply ambivalent, as his poems and novels and those who knew him attest; he both worshipped them and hated them.

Anger and the inability of a man to submit easily to a wife or lover are, more often than not, the major fruits of a Hera mother's possessiveness of her son. But so is intense creativity. As Lawrence remarked in the same context, "No wonder they say geniuses mostly have great mothers," but then he adds woefully, "they mostly have sad fates."

The twin psychic factors that Lawrence seems to have inherited from his mother—anger and frustrated creativity—have, it turns out, very exact parallels in Greek myth, personified as the two primary male offspring of Zeus and Hera's marriage: Ares, the fiery and hated god of war, and Hephaistos, the crippled and ugly smith. And as with all children, the characters and behavior of these gods are very precise mirrors of the unresolved issues of their parents' relationships. But more particularly, because of Hera's frustrated need for power, they reflect back the two extremes of her unexpressed masculine side, her animus, in Jungian terms.

In Ares we see Hera's disputatious, bullying, violent tendency, the part of her that likes the outlet of fighting for its own sake and that makes her almost as disagreeable as Ares much of the time. Though he is technically Zeus's son, Zeus will have almost nothing to do with him, implying that he is really Hera's child. Inevitably sons of unhappy marriages find themselves being drawn into the acrimonious disputes of their parents, either by bitterly taking sides—the way of Ares—or attempting to be the peaceable mediator—the way of his brother, Hephaistos. In the Trojan War, Ares supports Aphrodite, champion of the Trojans, thus succeeding in alienating both his mother and his father, who support the Greeks. But most of all, Ares symbolizes the never-ending marital war between Zeus and Hera.

Ares never marries. He has many affairs—chief among them with Aphrodite—and sires countless children outside of wedlock, but he never truly mates. As an expression of Hera's rage, he seems to hold the whole institution of marriage in contempt. However, it might be more correct to see this rejection of patriarchal marriage more as a crude revival, with Aphrodite especially, of the old matrilineal custom where paternity and strict fidelity were irrelevant. Even so, when Christine Downing, in her fine commentary in *The Goddess*, describes his character as "a self-defeating hypermasculinity," she puts her finger on the unbound and essentially destructive rage that he inherits from Hera's frustrated phallic self.

Hephaistos represents the other pole of Hera's rage and jealousy at Zeus. Here is how a Homeric hymn has her tell the unhappy story to the gods:

> Hear me all of you, gods and goddesses, how Zeus undertakes
> to bring shame upon me—how he is the first to do so, after
> having taken me to wife. Without me he has born Athena, who
> is glorious among all the immortals, whilst my own son, whom
> I bore, Hephaistos, is the least of us all. I myself threw him
> into the sea.
> —Carl Kerényi, *The Gods of the Greeks*, p. 151

It is as though she were saying to Zeus, "I'll show you!" and, like many a vengeful act, her resentment backfires in the form of the misbegotten, crippled child. In Downing's words again, Hephaistos is "her crippled animus, an expression of her own thwarted masculine energies." When Hera casts him out of heaven, according to one version of the myth, he lands on Lemnos, an island once famous for its bloodthirsty women. Here we get hints once more of the primitive side of Hera as Death Mother who is denied blood sacrifice except vicariously (see box, "Hera's Creative and Destructive Sons: Hephaistos and Ares").

But Hephaistos eventually becomes the smith and shieldmaker to the gods, trying endlessly to intercede for his mother in her disputes with Zeus. In Homer's *Iliad* we hear him talk of Hera as his "beloved mother," despite the fact that she consistently rejects him quite brutally. In fact his talent with metalworking as a smith, as well as his deformity, relates him to the ancient, magical arts of the underworld, of the early alchemical transformation of metals. Early metalworkers were shaman-magicians, usually mutilated in some way as part of their initiation rite. In their specific mythology the smiths were traditionally dwarves, who dwelt in the depths of the earth as servants of the Earth Mother.

Hephaistos, then, represents Hera's rejected but enormous potential for creativity and, in addition, her alienation from the mysteries

HERA'S CREATIVE AND DESTRUCTIVE SONS: HEPHAISTOS AND ARES

Many men who are born to domineering Hera mothers will frequently sublimate her overwhelming psychic presence into some intense creative endeavor. Often, though by no means always, such men will also become homosexual as well as artistic. In terms of goddess psychology we could say that they have chosen to live out more of the Hephaistos side of their mother's phallic energy than the Ares side, which they tend to deny or split off. As a rule, however, the Ares aspect is bound to appear somewhere in their fantasy life, their creative work, or, more tragically in their personal life. Tennessee Williams, Oscar Wilde, and D. H. Lawrence illustrate these patterns.

Tennessee Williams clearly lived with the creative inner tension of both Hephaistos and Ares. His plays are full of domineering and frustrated Hera figures, no doubt modeled on aspects of his mother, yet he deals creatively with the split-off violence of Ares in several of his plays, such as *Sweet Bird of Youth*.

In *Suddenly Last Summer* he confronts the dark energy of a Hera mother in no uncertain terms. The main male protagonist is an effete and unproductive poet, Sebastian, who lives entirely with and for his aging mother. Despite an attempt to marry a young woman and escape from his mother, Sebastian is horribly cannibalized by a horde of young boys—most likely homosexual—while visiting the Galápagos Islands. The manner of his death symbolizes the "devouring" side of the Great Mother that lies behind his personal mother's possessiveness and the destructive power of her Ares animus.

Another well-known creative homosexual genius who had a domineering Hera mother he nevertheless adored was **Oscar Wilde**. Lady Bracknell in *The Importance of Being Earnest* is a witty and affectionate caricature of her. Here, too, Wilde, like Tennessee Williams, lived out his mother's unexpressed Hephaistos creativity. But unlike Williams he was less able to express his Ares destructiveness in his literary work. Some of it is directed at the seductive mother figure in *Salome*, but essentially it remains split off, as in *The Picture of Dorian Grey*, which is prophetic of his downfall. Self-destructively he drew Ares' wrath upon himself in the form of social condemnation and punishment. Public trial and humiliation for his homosexuality led to his imprisonment and premature death at the age of forty-six.

In **D. H. Lawrence**, we see the same psychic polarities at work. What is remarkable in his case is that he had the genius to be able to live with both Hephaistos's creativity and Ares' rage. He was enormously creative and not afraid of his passionate anger, qualities that are very clearly personified as the two male protagonists of his masterpiece, *Women in Love*.

In *Women in Love*, Birkin is the restless creative spirit who marries the gentler of two sisters. Gerald Critch, tormented in a darker way, is the violent side, who seeks out prostitutes, never marries, and eventually kills himself after an abortive affair with the other, more intense of the sisters. Interestingly Lawrence did not adopt a homosexual life-style (though there are hints of it in *Women in Love*) but married a passionate and quite earthy woman who was frequently unfaithful to him. If anything, his wife, Frieda, embodied the qualities of both Demeter and Aphrodite.

Williams, Wilde, and Lawrence were drawn to the deeply unresolved aspect of Hera's conflict with patriarchal values and her inability to assert the old matriarchal consciousness. It is left to sons like these three creative men to attempt to complete the cycle of reversion to the lost matriarchal consciousness, even if, as in the case of Wilde and Lawrence, they must pay the price of total alienation and exile from the patriarchal culture of their time. Oscar Wilde was forced to leave England in disgrace after his imprisonment, and Lawrence, a generation later, suffered the ignominy of seeing several of his books banned and publicly burned in his native England. The return to matriarchal consciousness requires of certain men emotional and spiritual sacrifices that their contemporaries rarely understand.

of the earth. The ugly smith challenges the spiritual beauty of the gods with his magical power to create objects of great beauty out of the hidden riches of the earth. He challenges Hera's rage with his clowning—he is the buffoon on Olympus, again a shamanic survival—as well as with his gentle and long-suffering devotion. He embodies a cheerful willingness to find creative solutions to Hera's abiding inner consternation at her own powerlessness in the face of Zeus.

HERA VERSUS APHRODITE: PATRIARCHAL OR MATRIARCHAL PATTERNS OF LOVE?

Both Ares and Hephaistos have a significant relationship to the feminine. Hephaistos generally remains close to women and marries the most "feminine" of the goddesses, Aphrodite herself. He lives on the fringe of Olympian, patriarchal society because he is really connected with more ancient matriarchal consciousness. Working deep within the earth with the inner fires and metals, he is, in Jungian writer Murray Stein's words, "a split-off animus of the Great Mother who 'mimics' the creative processes in the depths of the Mother and brings to birth through his transforming mimicry his works of art" (Hephaistos: A Pattern of Introversion" in *Spring*, Zurich, 1973, p. 39).

Ares has an equally creative relationship to the feminine, but his is sexual and generative. Among his many children the most important are those he sired from his famous affair with Aphrodite (see Aphrodite chapter). From their highly passionate union sprang forth four children, two fearful and two loving: Phobos and Deimos (Fear and Panic) and Eros and Harmonia. They might be seen as a creative attempt to re-balance the ancient conflict between matriarchal-patriarchal tensions within Hera by Ares' instinctual association with her most despised enemy, Aphrodite.

Seen in terms of Jung's idea that every psychic quality, complex, or personality has its opposite or shadow, the marriage of Aphrodite and Hephaistos is very intriguing. Aphrodite, the free and easy, sensuous goddess of love with her fundamentally polygamous consciousness, is clearly Hera's shadow.

Perhaps, too, it is no accident that Ares and Hephaistos, as Hera's two sons, are therefore *brothers*. Seen as a dynamic extension of Hera's own archetypal psychology, they represent an attempt, in mythic terms, to dream the complex on into another generation. Opposite as they are in so many ways—extravert versus introvert, aggressive versus conciliatory, destructive versus creative—they cannot but belong together. Their tension of opposites is nevertheless highly creative and converges, even if it is not fully reconciled, in the figure of Aphrodite, giving them not just a common mother but also a common lover/wife. Thus convergence sets up a second huge tension of opposites, that between the two goddesses themselves. The dynamic could be represented like this, where the broken lines suggest the tension of opposites:

Patriarchal
Values

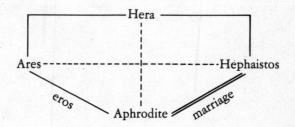

Matriarchal
Values

Aphrodite, in her liberality, represents the very principle of promiscuity that Hera so hates in Zeus. And in Aphrodite it was surely harder to bear, since it is displayed in another female, indeed, in a goddess. What could provoke Hera to righteous rage more than Aphrodite's contempt for fidelity, her disrespect for monogamous marriage and "social propriety"? Yet, as the Greek philosopher Heraclitus once said, "the opposite is what is good for us!" Aphrodite, and her very different attitude toward love and marriage, is the opposite that

Hera needs to quell her phallic imbalance; this is precisely the opposing force to which Hera's two sons lead her.

We are not saying simply that Hera needs a good affair or two, but more that she needs to question whether her high ideals of marriage really serve her. Every indication is that they benefit her husband more than herself, in terms of both freedom, security, and sexual dependence. In a patrilineal marriage a Hera wife is never free so long as she is tied to her husband economically; nor is she secure, since he can always leave her; nor is she sexually independent to choose between the fathers of her children if she wants to.

The long-forgotten matrilineal system, which Aphrodite stands for, made the woman the economic and spiritual center of both the family and the community, meaning that men had little or no claim over children except as rule-giving uncles and indulgent fathers. Such a form of marriage still exists today among certain West African tribes, such as the Ashanti. Such a system gives the women tremendous dignity and personal power, of a kind rarely seen in Europe and the West. In that world Hera's petty jealousies and sexual prudery would be seen as laughable.

Sadly the patriarchal marriage modeled by the Olympian royal couple leads, for the most part, to misery, spiritual emptiness, and an unfulfilled yearning for love. As long as the outer and official values of our society are monogamous, designed to serve mostly men, Aphrodite will continue to cast doubt on them. The polygamous libido that Aphrodite keeps constantly simmering in the background of Hera's respectable model of marriage will always entice men into secret affairs or the underworld of prostitution. The liberal divorce laws that exist in most Western nations today are actually a realistic acknowledgment of this tension between the opposing ways of the two goddesses. In fact frequent divorce may be the only way many men and women can legitimately pursue Aphrodite's polymorphous erotic impulses. Perhaps serial monogamy is just a form of nonsimultaneous polygamy, psychologically speaking!

HERA'S UNLIVED LIFE

Gloria Steinem, speaking no doubt for all Athenas, once said, "The surest way to be alone is to get married." She put her finger on one

of the greatest contributing factors to Hera's woundedness: her isolation from the greater world. Because she is so identified with marriage, family, and supporting her husband's career in the first half of
her life, she will often get trapped in the narrow confines of her home
and her immediate family and friends. The Demeter woman tends to
suffer this way, too, but less so because she is so fulfilled by raising
children. What both Hera and Demeter often lack is the experience
of rubbing shoulders with people out in the world, something that
comes naturally to Athena and Aphrodite women in the courses of
their lives.

A socially isolated life unfortunately tends to reinforce Hera's already strong views on how the world should be run and how people
should behave. Hera is, after all, the eternal moralist among the goddess
types. But when her life experience is limited, she is obliged to rely
on secondhand information—the media, family gossip, her husband.
In this way she becomes more and more opinionated and prone to the
psychological projection of all those parts of herself she has neither
lived nor owned, namely the other goddesses. She may think she knows
a great deal about what is going on in the world, but much of it is
distorted and saturated with fantasies and ruminations that have much
more to do with her own unlived life.

When a Hera woman seeks out psychotherapy because her husband
is having an affair with another woman, she will naturally have much
pain and justifiable rage to work through. What will often emerge when
she is questioned about "the other woman" is that she seems to know
a huge amount about her, even when she has the flimsiest of actual
information to go on. In her extraverted and righteous assurance that
her opinion is objectively justifed, she will actually be betraying a great
deal of her own fantasies about Aphrodite's character, projected onto
her rival.

Even though it is often hard for her, she can benefit from accepting
that this is indeed the Aphrodite side of herself, which she may be
meeting for the first time. Such an encounter between a hurt Hera
wife and her profligate Aphrodite shadow has been elaborately and
wittily portrayed in Federico Fellini's film masterpiece, *Juliet of the
Spirits*. Juliet is a proper, virtuous housewife and a good Catholic who
is shocked to discover that her adored husband is having a well-
concealed secret affair. When Juliet chances to meet her next-door

neighbor, Suzie, for the first time, Suzie invites her to one of her sumptuous parties. It is obvious that Suzie is a well-to-do professional hostess and mistress who surrounds herself with outrageous luxury and adoring lovers of all shapes, sizes, and ages.

In this dreamlike environment deliberately created by Fellini (who well understands dream symbolism and archetypal characters), Juliet meets a series of highly attractive men who, along with Suzie, challenge her to look at her own isolation, her naive view of marriage, and the cold, rigid, puritan values she has inherited from her mother. Fellini commented that the film "expresses the problems of the Catholic woman that are universal." In the same interview he went on to make the following remarks that are deeply sympathetic to Hera's modern plight:

> I want to help Italian women become free of a certain kind of conditioning produced by the middle-class marriage. They are so full of fear. They are so full of idealism. I want them to try to understand that they are alone, and that this is not a bad thing. To be alone is to be all of yourself. Italian women have this myth of the husband. I want to show that it is sentimental this myth. . . .
>
> I believe that husbands should not oppress their wives, consider them private property, place them in slavery without real love . . . The intention of the film is to restore woman to her true independence, her indisputable and inalienable dignity . . . The wife must not be the Madonna, nor an instrument of pleasure, and least of all a servant.
>
> —*Fellini on Fellini*, p. 83

To actually take a lover is irrelevant to Juliet's awakening in Fellini's remarkable film; what really helps her is allowing into her consciousness something of Aphrodite's forbidden realm that she has hitherto seen as so shocking and threatening. It is not that she needs to become polygamous like Aphrodite, but she does need to let go of some of the moralism that separates her from life as actually lived, usually quite harmlessly, by other people.

By temperament the Hera woman is and will always remain monogamous, just as Aphrodite is temperamentally always polygamous and

Athena by nature always single. These are in fact fundamental structures of their consciousness that are in no way affected by the actual act of marriage. Because of these differences each goddess has lessons to learn from the other about relationships: Aphrodite may need to stay longer with her lover once in a while, taking a leaf of faithfulness from Hera's book, for instance. Eros that is kept over time within a single vessel can go through extraordinary alchemical transformations, as many a long marriage has proven.

THE SACRED MEANING OF MARRIAGE

Are we hopelessly stuck with the depressing picture of fractured marriage we get from the later Greek myths of Hera and Zeus, particularly from Homer?

Not entirely, as our researches have found, if we are prepared to dig once more further back into the matriarchal era of Greek religious history. Remnants of a ritual cult of Hera's marriage to Zeus still exist; they speak to a far more profound conception of marriage, one that every Hera woman of today fervently longs for. Yet it is not the eros aspect nor the childbearing aspect of marriage that these older cults hinted at, but more a union of masculine and feminine powers in their fullness and maturity. Such a union is not just one of lovers or procreators, but of representatives of greater powers that ultimately move the universe, powers that can only be symbolized by the highest form of marriage, that of a king and a queen.

Despite all the bickering scenes in Homer's *Iliad*, we do get a glimpse of these older cults during a transcendent moment in the marriage of Zeus and Hera, when they go to the top of Mount Ida to celebrate the mystery of their union. Even the perfection of Aphrodite's matriarchal consciousness is hinted at in this scene, for Hera has earlier borrowed the love goddess's magic girdle, which makes any female utterly irresistible:

[Zeus] the son of Kronos took his Wife in his arms; and the gracious earth sent up fresh grass beneath them, dewy lotus and crocuses, and a soft and crowded bed of hyacinths, to lift them off the ground. In this they lay, covered by a beautiful

golden cloud, from which a rain of glistening dewdrops fell.
(Book 14)

There is little doubt that this scene harkens back to the holiest ceremonies of the Sacred Marriage, the *hieros gamos*, celebrated in many
early cultures, where the Earth Goddess and the Sky God regenerate
the cosmos with their lovemaking. In ancient Sumer the high priest
and high priestess were said to have performed ritual copulation in the
persona of the divine pair on the top of the ziggurats on holy days. In
ancient Greece we know of one such cult of Zeus and Hera's nuptials
on the island of Samos, where their wedding night was said to last three
hundred years.

It seems that when she was celebrated as the Great Goddess in
Arcadia, in pre-Homeric times, Hera was known by three names: Hera
Parthenos (virgin), Hera *Teleia* (perfect or fulfilled), and Hera *Chela*
(widow). Clearly these titles speak of her identity with the entire life
cycle of a woman, much as Demeter's cult does (see Demeter chapter).
In her triple nature the goddess is complete. But unlike Demeter's
cult, Hera as ancient triple goddess does not have a child. So it is not
the mysteries of motherhood that are symbolized, but instead the
mystery of the phases of woman's life *before* marriage, at the *fulfillment*
of marriage, and in the years *after* her husband's death.

The Hera ideal that the Greeks celebrated in earlier matriarchal
times was a complete, whole woman, not the bonded possession of her
patriarchal master that Greek wives later became. The classicist M. I.
Finley says that Hera then was a "complete female whom the Greeks
feared a little and did not like at all" (cited by Downing in *The Goddess*,
p. 73). Clearly her power and her completeness came from the strength
she drew from a matriarchal culture and the honor paid to the feminine
principle.

Jung meditated a great deal on completeness. We cannot be complete or whole as individuals, he believed, unless we are prepared to
acknowledge and live out both the masculine and the feminine aspects
of our nature. Ultimately every woman must "marry"—in a psychological sense—all the aspects of the masculine in her own nature (her
animus), and every man must marry all his inner feminine parts (his
anima). This means, of course, that the members of the opposite sex
we are attracted to will inevitably mirror our *inner* opposite sexual

characteristics. To embark, therefore, on the outer marriage, is to have chosen in one's partner the most longed for and most important image of our inner, unknown self. It is a great act of faith, but if our initial intuitions are accurate, it can be the basis of the major psychological work of a lifetime.

Any Hera woman wants to be honored and loved as a complete woman. Instinctively she knows that marriage is the path by which she must arrive at wholeness. And she dimly knows, too, that the male, the other she loves, must be the mirror of her self-completion. So, for their union to come anywhere near succeeding, she knows she should be able to demand that it start with his full respect for her as a mature adult in full possession of all her power and dignity *as a woman*—not as a child, not as a love object, not as a female clone of his masculine ideals. Few men are strong enough in their own masculinity to complement and balance demands such as these in a woman. The fear of not being equal to women's mature power lies behind all patriarchal domination and subjection of women, back to the Greeks and beyond.

But what is remarkable about this ancient image of the Sacred Marriage is that it does not require that the feminine archetype be superior to or dominate the male—remarkable because there are indeed many images of the male consort as a mere adolescent who was sacrificed to the greater power of the Mother Goddess in the matriarchal era. In the more ancient cult of the Zeus-Hera marriage we find an image of true equality and true mutuality in the exchange and fusion of the masculine and feminine cosmic energies that they symbolize. And from such an image we may also draw a model for human marriage.

When a Hera woman does not succumb to jealousy and destructiveness and feels confidently whole in herself, she is ready to challenge and meet a man on her own power terms. If he is able to meet her with similar confidence in his maleness, the true Zeus-Hera union in its original, not its corrupt, form may take place. The sharing of power in a marriage relationship of such strong equals is never easy or smooth, given the large egos of the couple involved. But we believe that this is still possible today, despite patriarchal distortion of the marriage archetype, as women are able more and more to assume their true dignity and equality. To give a sense of what this may entail, we end with part of a poem by William Carlos Williams that speaks of the fruits

of a long marriage relationship in metaphors that do not shy away from
its harsh realities:

> Romance has no part in it.
> The business of love is
> cruelty which,
> by our wills
> we transform
> to live together.
> It has its seasons
> for and against,
> whatever the heart
> fumbles in the dark
> to assert
> toward the end of May.
> Just as the nature of briars
> is to tear flesh,
> I have proceeded
> through them.
> Keep the briars out,
> they say.
> You cannot live
> and keep free of
> briars. . . .
> Sure
> love is cruel
> and selfish
> and totally obtuse—
> at least, blinded by the light
> young love is.
> But we are older,
> I to love
> and you to be loved,
> we have
> no matter how
> by our wills survived
> to keep
> the jewelled prize

always at our fingertips.
We will it so
and so it is
past all accident.
    —from "The Ivy Crown"

SIX

PERSEPHONE: MEDIUM, MYSTIC, AND MISTRESS OF THE DEAD

Reach me a gentian, give me a torch!
let me guide myself with the blue, forked torch of this flower
down the darker and darker stairs, where the blue is darkened on
blueness
even where Persephone goes, just now, from the frosted September
to the sightless realm where darkness is awake upon the dark
and Persephone herself is but a voice
or a darkness invisible enfolded in the deeper dark
of the arms Plutonic, and pierced with the passion of dense gloom
among the splendour of torches of darkness, shedding darkness on the
lost bride and her groom.
—D. H. LAWRENCE, *"BAVARIAN GENTIANS"*

WHO IS PERSEPHONE?
AN ELUSIVE GODDESS

We may not be particularly struck by the Persephone woman on first encounter. It's not that she's lacking in presence or shy, but more that she's rather self-effacing. Yes, there is an attractive, smiling, often very young-looking face and manner, appealing and seemingly eager to please. More often than not there is a distinctive charm about her, but it is not the glowing allure of an Aphrodite woman nor the natural warmth of a Demeter.

Somehow the Persephone woman seems disinclined to assert herself too strongly. She has none of Artemis's solidity of purpose, that wiry sprung readiness to head off somewhere else. Nor does she have the sure ground of Hera's imperiousness or Athena's intellectual forth-rightness.

There's a peculiar quality of insubstantiality about her that has nothing to do with her body. A part of her, we might even sense, is somewhere else. Yet at the same time, she is so intuitively tuned in, she almost seems to be present in our very thoughts.

In some Persephone women there is an almost transparent quality to them, a kind of spiritual vulnerability. Yet for all this, Persephone women have no common body type. One Persephone woman may be fairly thin, even frail, but another might just as often be overweight and neglectful of her body. We cannot help suspecting that she is more than a little ill at ease with her body and possibly her sexuality. And yet, she hasn't chosen Athena's independent way of intellect or Artemis's way of action as a compensation. In her frailty we sense a yearning for warmth and deep intimacy, though it is often hard to tell whether it is intimacy of the spirit or of the body she really wants.

Already we are beginning to sense the aura of mystery that surrounds the Persephone woman, a hidden connection to spirit and a deep ambivalence toward a world that may willfully misunderstand her. Perhaps, if we look more closely, her charming exterior is no more than that, an exterior subtly designed to protect and conceal an intense inwardness.

The poet e. e. cummings wrote a beautiful poem that evokes the elusive mystery of the Persephone woman beneath the mask:

> somewhere i have never travelled, gladly beyond
> any experience, your eyes have their silence:
> in your most frail gesture are things which enclose me,
> or which i cannot touch because they are too near
> your slightest look easily will unclose me
> though i have closed myself as fingers,
> you open always petal by petal myself as Spring opens
> (touching skillfully, mysteriously) her first rose . . .
> nothing which we are to perceive in this world equals
> the power of your intense fragility . . .

Whether cummings was describing an actual Persephone woman or seeing his own inner Persephone in a certain woman's face is not important (both may coincide in such moments). What his marvelously delicate poem brings out is the subtle dissolution of self and other in a quasi-mystical state of fusion. It is precisely this trancelike loss of self that is so suggestive of Persephone's secret, that uncanny ability of hers to stand at the threshold and cross over into other realms of psychic consciousness.

The Persephone woman, then, finds that she must truly live at the very borders of the known, close to those areas that we describe with Greek and Latin prefixes such as *para-*, *meta-*, and *super-*, which mean "beyond" or "transcending." Her world is *para*normal and the structure of her consciousness is the subject of *para*psychology, a science that studies those fringe areas "beyond" conventional or normal psychology. Equally, because her world is *super*natural, or "beyond" the physical world of the senses, she will be drawn to the teachings of *meta*physics, rather than those of the conventional natural sciences.

It is precisely because Persephone lives at the borders of that which is scientifically known that she feels alienated and uncertain of herself. So powerful is the authority of scientific materialism in our colleges, our research institutions, and the media that such subjects as parapsychology and metaphysics are treated as crankish, belonging to the lunatic fringe. When actress Shirley MacLaine recounts her psychic awakening, magazines like *Newsweek* and *People* patronizingly treat her as some amiable "flake" who is slowly losing her mind. And always lurking in the background of collective consciousness is the Christian fundamentalist bogey of "black magic" and the Devil.

PERSEPHONE, THE MEDIAL WOMAN

To the Greeks, Persephone was the distant Queen of the Underworld, who watched over the souls of the departed, the shades. But she was also known as the maiden, or Kore, who was abducted from her mother, Demeter. How Hades took her into the underworld is one of the best-known stories in all of Greek myth (see box, "The Rape of the Maiden Persephone").

In our chapter on Demeter, we focus on Demeter's agonizing experience when she loses her adolescent daughter. There we look at the myth essentially *from Demeter's point of view and in terms of her*

THE RAPE OF THE MAIDEN PERSEPHONE

The most complete version of the story of how the maiden Persephone was abducted and taken into the underworld comes from the *Homeric Hymns*, one of the earliest sources of Greek myths that we have. (Hades, who is "Kronos's son of many names" is also called Aidoneus here):

> I begin my song of the holy goddess, fair-haired Demeter, and of her slim-ankled daughter, whom Aidoneus snatched away; and Zeus the loud-crashing, the wide-voiced one, granted it. She was playing with the deep-bosomed daughters of Ocean, away from Demeter of the golden weapon and glorious fruit, and she was gathering flowers throughout the luxuriant meadow—roses, saffron, violets, iris, hyacinth, and a narcissus which was a trap planted for the blossoming maiden by Earth (Gaia) in accord with Zeus's plans, a favor to Hades the receiver of many guests; it was radiantly wonderful, inspiring awe in all who saw it, whether immortal god or mortal man; a hundred stems grew from its root; and the whole wide heaven above, the whole earth, and the salt surge of the sea smiled for joy at its fragrance. The girl was charmed by it, and reached out both hands to pluck the pretty plaything—suddenly, the earth split open wide along the plain and from it the lord host of many, Kronos's son of many names, darted out on his immortal horses. He grabbed her, resisting and screaming, and took her away in his golden chariot. She lifted her voice in a cry, calling upon father Zeus, the almighty and good. But no one, god or mortal, heard her voice, not even the glorious-fruited olive trees, except the childish daughter of Perses, Hecate of the glistening veil, who—from her

cave—heard, and so did Lord Helios the glorious son
of Hyperion, as the maiden calling upon father Zeus,
though he was sitting, removed from the other gods,
in his much-besought temple, receiving fine sacrifices
from mortal men.

Her, all unwilling, with the approval of Zeus, he
took away on his immortal horses, Kronos's son of
many names, brother of her father, designator of many,
host of many. As long as the goddess could see the
earth and the starry sky, the flowing, fish-filled sea and
the rays of the sun, she still had hope that her holy
mother and the race of the immortal gods would see
her, and there was still much hope in her heart in spite
of her distress.

—*The Homeric Hymn to Demeter*, trans. Rice and
Stambaugh from *The Ancient Mysteries*, ed. Meyer,
pp. 21–22

relationship to Persephone as a daughter. But here we will talk about the
part of the myth that has received far less attention among mythog-
raphers and psychologists: Persephone, the mature goddess, who eventually became the full-fledged Queen of the Underworld, ruling over
the spirits of the dead with her husband, Hades, the Dark Lord of
Death.

As we have already seen, the character of the Persephone woman
is not at all easy to grasp. Many Persephone women are themselves
highly secretive and often reclusive. The psychic strain of being around
people and the bustle of the marketplace often causes them to retreat
and to eke out a meager existence on the edge of society. Persephone
women need time to be alone a great deal, to pursue their secret
projects, their musings, their communions with the unseen world. This
is what it means to live much of her life in the underworld, among the
spirits.

Today, more and more latent Persephones are finding their way to esoteric writings, alternative forms of healing, and what are loosely called the teachings of the New Age. So now, more than ever, it is timely to penetrate further into the veiled story of Persephone as queen and coruler of the netherworld. We believe her myth has much to say to many modern women who are struggling to understand all kinds of perplexing experiences that are "psychic" in nature or who are, in one way or another, drawn to work with death or who experience much personal tragedy in their lives.

Many things point to the fact that the Persephone woman is endowed with what Toni Wolff, Jung's close collaborator, perceptively identified in 1951 as "the mediumistic or medial personality." Here is how Wolff described her:

> The medial woman is immersed in the psychic atmosphere of her environment and the spirit of her period, but above all in the collective (impersonal) unconscious. The unconscious, once it is constellated [i.e., when a form starts to appear] and can become conscious, exerts an effect. The medial woman is overcome by the effect, she is absorbed and molded by it and sometimes she represents it herself. She must for instance express or act what "is in the air," what the environment cannot or will not admit, but what is nevertheless a part of it. It is mostly the dark aspect of the situation or of a predominant idea, and she thus activates what is negative and dangerous. In this way she becomes the carrier of evil, but that she does is nevertheless exclusively her personal problem.
> —"Structural Forms of the Feminine Psyche," p. 9

As the medial woman, Persephone's major difficulty is that she typically has a weak ego structure—quite the opposite of Athena, Artemis, and Hera, whom Wolff would call "Amazon" types. She is therefore easily susceptible to being overwhelmed when contents, which traditionally would be called "spirits," flood her from "the other side" (i.e., her unconscious mind):

> As the contents involved are unconscious, she lacks the necessary faculty of discrimination to perceive and the language to express them adequately. The overwhelming force of the

collective unconscious sweeps through the ego of the medial
woman and weakens it. (Ibid.)

When she has more of Athena or Hera's ego strength and ability to
discriminate, she can properly formulate or transmit these contents.
Then, as Wolff observes, she has an important and creative role to play
in society:

> In that case she consecrates herself to the service of a new,
> maybe yet concealed, spirit of her age, like the early Christian
> martyrs [or] the female mystics of the Middle Ages. . . . In-
> stead of identifying herself with collective unconscious con-
> tents—quite unrelated to reality—she ought to appreciate her
> medial faculty as an instrument and receptacle for the reception
> of these contents. But to achieve this she will have to find an
> adequate language. Medial women had a social function as
> seers, sybils, medicine women or shamans in previous cul-
> tures—and still have nowadays with primitive peoples. (pp. 9–
> 10)

Little has been added to the literature of Persephone psychology since
Toni Wolff wrote in 1951, but as our understanding of goddess consciousness continues to grow, it is surely time to look more deeply into
her unique vision of things.

DEATH AND THE MAIDEN

The myth describes vividly how the innocent maiden Persephone was
playing one day with all the daughters of Oceanus, including Athena
and Artemis. Suddenly the earth opened up and the great Lord of
Death, Hades, appeared in his chariot and dragged her off, screaming,
to the underworld to make her his bride.

What is the underworld? In the language of modern psychology it
would be called the unconscious. So, Persephone is one who is sucked
not only into the unconscious, the unknown, all that is repressed and
dark (Freud) but also deeper, into the collective unconscious, the world
of archetypal principalities and powers (Jung).

A young girl or woman may experience this in various ways. Some childhood tragedy may plunge her into a state of depression, of brooding withdrawal where she may become inwardly preoccupied with thoughts of a lost parent or sibling. Secretly she may entertain fantasies of finding that dead person by visiting a graveyard that leads her down to some subterranean spirit world (see box, "Descent to Hades: A Modern Woman's Story").

This is what happened to a twelve-year-old girl who came into therapy after her father died of cancer. Her mother was disturbed by her withdrawn behavior and her inability to mourn. Alone in her room she had started to draw ghoulish pictures of skeletons and graveyards. When she was finally able to talk about the pictures, it became apparent that she had visited many of the graves in the family graveyard and had had all kinds of private conversations with the dead, particularly about the manner of their death. Remarkably, she had conversed with spirits of her family going back seven generations. It was a profound encounter with that aspect of the collective unconscious Jung called the *ancestral psyche*; many so-called primitive peoples worship and call upon ancestor spirits, as is well known.

For a while, she admitted, she had indeed been contemplating suicide to join her dearly missed father, but through exchanges with both her departed father and other ancestral spirits she was advised not to take her own life. After finding that sharing her fantasies did not lead to either shame, ridicule, or punishment, she gradually came back from her morbid but enlightening meditations. She soon was able to let out some of the grief that had been frozen up during her sojourn in the land of the dead.

Depression and withdrawal, with or without attendant suicidal fantasies, can accompany loss, separation, or violent trauma at any age in fact. So the descent to the underworld is not limited to childhood. We may find ourselves sucked into Persephone's gray realm after a painful divorce, an unwanted move to a distant part of the country, an abortion, losing a job, being the only survivor of a car crash, or any severe trauma. Always there is some kind of psychic if not physical death. This, after all, is what most loss is: the wrenching away of energy from the image of some loved person, place, or way of life into some huge, empty emotional void. Freud characterized all depression as a kind of mourning for a lost love object.

DESCENT TO HADES:
A MODERN WOMAN'S STORY

Here is a shortened version of a vision experienced by a woman
in her late twenties whom we will call Jane. As a part of her
therapy she used the technique of active imagination, which
entails learning to follow wherever one's inner images take one.
As a child Jane had had a number of tunnel dreams and had
always hunted for trapdoors in her parents' house. This is what
happened when she finally opened the trapdoor:

> I enter the large hall closet where, as child I hid in
> the darkness from my family and cried. Little Jane (me)
> is in there. She is about twelve years old. She is re-
> peating to herself over and over: "I'm so sorry. I'm so
> sorry." I say: "Jane, can I talk to you? I have to know
> why you're so sad."
>
> She starts digging on the closet floor, throwing
> shoes over her shoulder. Suddenly she reveals a trap-
> door. "I'll follow you," I say. It's very dark, a tunnel
> or a cave, I can't tell. Jane has a lantern, but its weak
> light only exposes a small space. She holds it up to the
> face of what looks like a dead woman or a man with
> shoulder-length black hair. The face is waxy and the
> features coarse, almost ugly. Suddenly it moves—not
> dead? or was it just the moving light? Jane moves the
> lantern again to reveal a man's face—handsome in an
> artificial, mannequin type of way. He begins to move,
> very purposefully. We follow. He bends down by a
> kind of stream or underground pool and picks up
> something, which he hands to us. It is an apple with a
> bite taken out of it.
>
> More darkness, the lantern no help. We come to
> a room, as in a cave. Jane shines a light and illuminates
> the faces of the inhabitants: a man with the face of a

coyote; then a man with a steer's skull for a head; then one with his face painted black and white. There are others, all arranged in a circle.

We come to a heavy door. After some hesitation I go through. On the other side I am alone. Blackest black. Intense fear pervades everything. I realize I must calm down, so I do a relaxation exercise. As I get calmer, it becomes not so black—a comfortable darkness. I find I have a lantern again. I continue to walk. An old woman comes toward me in a motorized wheelchair (my grandmother?) Wordlessly she zips me onto her chair and into a high magnificent hall. There is a high thronelike chair, and the person on it I think is a judge. It seems to be part ancient man, part beautiful woman with a face as drawn as a skull and a huge crown upon her head.

She leans over to look at me and gouges out her eyes. They are splendid, gleaming, all-seeing—not kindly, but like a wolf's eyes. Dead as a sword is, without emotion. Gleaming. I receive them, thinking, "What a precious gift!" Hands take my eyes out and put hers in. I see my body turn the color and texture of mud, leather, or a mummy's skin. My face now has the appearance of a witch's, with a truncated nose like a pig. I walk and seem to pass through many images of many people—girls, men, women—and in between each my body pauses, corpselike.

I walk to the door again. I remove the eyes and place them in a pocketbook. Jane is on the other side. We retrace our steps to the trapdoor in the closet. I turn to hug her, but there is a young bearded man, very sad, sitting there. I feel he is also me. I tousle his hair.

The disappearance of a lost love object into an empty void is couched in vivid symbolic language as the descent into the underworld. What is comforting about the Persephone myth is that there is some guardian figure who presides over such terrible periods of energy withdrawal and protects us, as it were, until we are ready to return to normal, daily reality. All the life energy that we lose during depression and grief of one kind or another has metaphorically "gone into the underworld." As we sometimes say to a grieving client, *a part of us always accompanies the lost person or beloved attachment into the underworld.* And when this happens, that part of us is not fully available for normal life, and we need to honor this process, not seek to falsely cheer ourselves up.

Of course such a descent becomes pathological if a large part of us remains perpetually in the underworld; when this occurs, we are bordering on what is clinically called chronic depression. But temporary depression is a natural and quite healthy accompaniment to any kind of loss, in our view. These are natural Persephone happenings that anyone may experience, men or women, young or old alike.

But the woman whose whole life becomes completely identified with Persephone has usually undergone a particularly severe trauma, often in early childhood, which indelibly colors her psychic outlook on life. Inordinate tragedy coupled with excessive sensitivity and a fragile ego create the pattern of the young maiden who is so powerfully and frequently dragged into the underworld that she feels forced, it seems, to spend half of her life there. The mythic structure speaks now not about a temporary depression but a chronic pattern of dual or divided consciousness.

To begin with, such a young girl or woman is clearly going to be a highly reluctant initiate into the dark realms of the psyche. It all comes too suddenly, unbidden, out of nowhere. Utterly powerless in the matter, she finds that she must learn to live in two radically different worlds: the world of life and light represented by her mother, Demeter, and the world of the shades and death, represented by Hades. And so she is divided in her loyalties, her rulership, and her vision of things. She sees both sides: what can be revealed and what must be kept secret. She must be loyal to both the living and the dead. It is an enormous burden, a momentous responsibility that is hers and hers alone.

For the Persephone woman there is always some early element of tragedy in her life that jolts her out of the innocent healthy play with her Athena and Artemis sisters. It could be the early loss of a parent, child abuse, some severe illness, an alcoholic or schizophrenic parent, or even an exceptionally difficult birth. These are never simply causes but rather precipitating events for that early descent into the realm of the dead that young Persephone seems, sooner or later, fated to make.

Jon Klimo's recent book, *Channeling*, notes that the data we have about channels or mediums shows a certain correlation between unhappy childhood experience and the development of this faculty. While this is by no means universal, it does suggest that childhood may often be the time of an early "rite of passage" into the underworld.

If the young Persephone fails to acknowledge the profound effect of that early encounter with the netherworld of death and the spirits, it will come again to her in adolescence or early womanhood. She will find herself prone to accidents or attracting to her people with severe problems, diseases, or violent behavior. She may find herself brutally mugged, even raped. Drugs may suddenly loom large in her life. Or else she is involved in near-fatal accidents or loses a number of friends in such accidents. It may seem that suddenly she is cursed, but in fact it is the return of Hades into her life to reclaim the bride he first beckoned much earlier.

If she is fortunate, the suffering Persephone will find her way to a good therapist who understands the descent and does not make it frighteningly concrete with drugs or hospitalization. She may meet an older woman who is a psychic and who helps her understand that her overwhelming fate is an initiation into the death realm and the vocation of healing or channeling or psychic work of some sort.

Strangely old before her time, a Crone before she is fully a Maiden, Persephone is often wise beyond her years. Outwardly she still retains the innocent looks of the Maiden, a kind of frozen adaptation to the image of her loss, but inwardly she feels burdened by knowledge she can scarcely bear.

THE TWILIGHT OF THE GODS?

Understanding the meaning of Persephone's descent and her connection to the spirit realm is especially urgent today. Thousands of women (and indeed more than a few men) are currently discovering a mediumistic talent for so-called channeling. In addition to this, no one could fail to notice the minor epidemic of enthusiasm for metaphysics, Tarot, astrology, healing, and meditation—all loosely gathered under the banner of the New Age. A part of this, too, is the widely reported resurgence of charismatic movements among various Christian communities and the extraordinary spread of Eastern practices such as Buddhism, Hinduism, and Sufism all over the West.

Could it be, as the late Joseph Campbell, the unparalleled authority on myth and religion observed, that the emergence everywhere of Persephone consciousness that we are currently seeing is actually part of a "twilight of the gods"? In one of his last essays, written shortly before his death, Campbell raised the possibility that the old gods are dying and new ones are breaking forth from the collective unconscious to take their place as humanity approaches a whole new era.

If this is so, from a Jungian standpoint this would mean that the very structures and energies of the deep unconscious, which symbolically we perceive as "gods" and "goddesses," are undergoing a profound shift. So, the type of person who is most sensitive to such shifts, the seer or mediumistic type we are calling the Persephone woman, is going to be right at the center of this momentous eruption of new psychic and spiritual powers.

But important and timely as this emergence of Persephone consciousness may be, it is fraught with difficulties and pitfalls. In common with the other goddess types, when the modern Persephone woman lives out *only* her Persephone nature without experiencing and integrating other goddess energies into her psyche, she may expose herself to considerable suffering.

To live for much of one's waking life "among the dead" can put enormous psychic strain upon any woman (or man) with a mediumistic temperament, especially when her experiences are misunderstood or feared, as is frequently the case. More than any of the other goddess types the Persephone woman can experience deep alienation, sometimes bordering on breakdown, if her true nature and vocation are not recognized. It is especially important that she can call upon the other goddesses to balance and nourish her. From Demeter she may need a sense of body and earth to ground her; from Athena, some objectivity about the disruptive nature of her gifts; and so on.

For the fact is that the underworld is essentially a place of spirits. Which means that it is, alas, singularly lacking in warmth, substance, or what most of us would call reality. How the Persephone or mediumistic woman relates to this realm, with its threats of dissociation, madness, and despair, therefore poses a unique challenge to our psychological understanding.

PERSEPHONE'S DOUBLE LIFE: GROWING UP ABSURD

Unfortunately, most Persephone women grow up with little or no perspective on their chaotic inner experiences and feel them more a curse than a gift. To be psychically attuned to realities that are feared and denied by most people can easily cast her into a living hell. Often young Persephone is raised in an environment that is profoundly intolerant of her strange quirks. So to survive, she learns to withdraw into herself and her secret psychic encounters. And tragically, the more she does so, the more her family sees her behavior as suspect and threatening. Eventually, if she cannot conform sufficiently to family norms, she becomes the source of projection for everything that is dark and alien in her family. She becomes a "problem child" who is weird *because* she will not conform. So, the more her parents and siblings nag her, the more she withdraws; and the more she withdraws, the more it confirms their worst fears.

The psychiatrist R. D. Laing once described the case of a young adolescent girl who would sit in her room for long hours staring at a blank wall. Her parents managed to get her committed to a mental institution for this antisocial behavior ("normal" teenagers would be watching television or dating, of course). There she was obligingly labeled schizophrenic by psychiatrists, to whom she could not explain what she was doing. Laing remarked that in a different culture staring for hours at a blank wall would be considered a form of meditation; this is precisely how Zen monks meditate, as it happens.

What radical psychiatrists R. D. Laing and David Cooper demonstrated two decades ago, is that conventional psychiatry often colludes with a disturbed family in scapegoating the withdrawn, oddball child. The underworld that this and other young Persephones are sucked into is often the residue of some old family secret—incest, madness, prostitution, or illegitimacy, for instance—a cesspool whose lid has been kept firmly closed for generations.

Deeply disturbed by all the "forbidden" thoughts in her family— "we mustn't talk about Great-aunt Hedda"—Persephone cannot turn off her sensitive unconscious scanner. These forbidden thoughts create a silent hell of unbidden nightmares she can barely articulate. What she may actually be picking up quite psychically are chaotic fragments of these closely kept secrets buried in what Jung called the ancestral unconscious. She suffers like the princess Cassandra in Homer's *Iliad*, whose prophecy of the infamous Trojan horse nobody would believe.

The harsh and inescapable facts of life for many a modern Persephone are that she must live and move in two equally inhospitable worlds: the cold and unpredictable world of the unconscious and the unsympathetic and alienating real world. Correspondingly, her personality structure is dual; she possesses an innocent and well-adapted outer mask and a rich, intense other life of which few may ever know and whose meaning will be a lifelong torment to her until she herself comes to terms with it.

For, whether she shows it or not, the Persephone woman has an intense inner life, one that, self-protectively, she rarely reveals to anyone. When left to herself—which is what she most desires—she may write secret journals, paint, compose fantasy fiction, or secretly indulge in her own visions and forms of meditation. Almost in despair of the loathsomeness of suffering humanity around her, she may stumble upon the clear and pure world accessible to astral travel, which is a form of leaving the body in meditation.

Perhaps, when she is growing up, the young Persephone may find her way to occultism or spiritualism via a trusted "oddball" friend or the local library. Her studies will naturally be a closely guarded secret. Yet here, finally, she will be reassured in knowing that she is not weird or abnormal but simply "different" in a more positive sense.

Basic information about the nature of psychism may help her recognize that when, in her inner reveries, she picks up all kinds of information on the inner airwaves, she is in fact being highly telepathic. By experimenting with a Ouija board or automatic writing or keeping a dream journal she may quickly realize she has all the makings of a medium or channel. In a world where her extreme sensitivity and the porousness of her ego often lead her to fear she is losing her very sense of who she is, these practices may seem to offer her a more solid sense of identity.

But by itself, recognizing one's psychic nature is rarely enough to survive in the world. Most Persephone women slide imperceptibly into the real world, with the help of a small amount of Athena or Demeter or Aphrodite in their makeup. They get jobs, become wives and mothers, or find themselves in some service-oriented work, such as nursing. They are sympathetic, highly tuned in to people's needs and feelings. The archetypal child they still carry in them radiates beauty and optimism, so they are often most appealing in their public selves.

Some young Persephones who develop a sufficient handle on their inner worlds will gravitate toward careers as counselors or therapists. They may begin training as healers. Those more confident in their gifts may set themselves up quite successfully as astrologers or Tarot readers, or even teachers of metaphysics. Still others will establish themselves as visionary artists or craftswomen of some kind.

On the surface all these occupations may seem ideal ways of *containing* young Persephone's mediumistic connections to spirit and the unconscious. On one level they give her gift a socially sanctioned form and structure, in which she feels supported and secure.

Yet unless the perspective of her training is both broad and deep, it will not work. All that young Persephone may really end up adopting is a new and appealing persona, yet another adaptation to the needs of being in the world that still leaves her deepest inner woundedness fundamentally untouched. She has still not fully made the descent, which is to say she has not finished with her grief or the hurt of her trauma or fully owned all her death fantasies. Consequently no amount of psychological expertise or metaphysics can make up for this fact. The ailing victim in her still cries out.

One of the telltale signs that the Persephone woman has not really completed her descent is that she seems to remain ever-youthful. She will often continue to wear her hair long and loose well into her forties, sporting flowing, flowery skirts and blouses. At New Age growth centers this is the norm, of course, so it goes unremarked. But the real clue is that her facial mask will often show few if any ageing or stress lines as she enters middle life. She tends to keep a youthful bloom that makes it hard to guess her actual age.

In its extreme manifestation psychoanalysts have termed this split between the outer mask and the almost unreachable inner life *schizoid*, which simply means "split." The origins of this fundamental split have been debated for decades now, but some analysts would even trace it back to birth itself, which suggests a fundamental lack of bonding with the mother.

This corresponds precisely with the archetypal language of the Greek myth, for Persephone is the daughter who has lost her mother and whose real life is lived elsewhere. But when the full implications of this agonizing and abysmal separation are not accepted, the Maiden in her remains frozen, fixated at that horrendous moment of cleavage from the Mother, her own dark depths still unplumbed, her own darkness unredeemed.

PERSEPHONE UNDESCENDED I: THE SEDUCTIONS OF THE SPIRIT

In her darkness and dividedness, the young Persephone woman yearns for the spirit to rescue her and deliver her from her inner confusion. So when she learns of metaphysics and occult practices, she will frequently seek solace in the *higher* authorities of spirit guides, ascended masters, astrology, karma, and so forth. This is part of the motivation that leads her to become a healer or channeler herself.

However, there is often a huge element of compensation in the way of the spirit, of channeled guides and masters, since it is all upward, into the *light* (the favorite metaphor of the New Age). Unless she fully honors her dual nature, one that mediates between both the light and the darkness, the living and the dead, she can become unaccountably arrested in her development. Using the safe persona of the loving New Age teacher, she may cling tenaciously to the archetypal purity of the Maiden. Ever wanting good Daddy Zeus to save her, she evades her terror of the deeper darkness by talking only of her luminous and loving guides and of soul evolution forever onward and upward.

Yet her true savior is not Zeus, but paradoxically, his dark brother Hades. The wisdom of this extraordinary myth is that the source of Persephone's transformation comes *from beneath, from the lower depths of soul, not from the higher reaches of spirit*. If anything, the countless wise male figures being channeled by mediumistic women almost wholesale today from Los Angeles to Kalamazoo are no more than variations on the archetype of Zeus, the longed-for, all-wise father. This is not in any way to cast aspersions on the wisdom of much of this revealed teaching—much of it is profound—*but to emphasize that the spirit in its Olympian form cannot initiate Persephone.*

PERSEPHONE UNDESCENDED II: THE ALL-LOVING MOTHER

Persephone's other chief defense against the descent is to become the very thing she has lost; the all-loving Mother. Here she will take her very real aptitude for a career as a therapist, a healer, or a social worker and unconsciously mold it into the role of professional rescuer. By playing out the role of long-suffering and loving Demeter to all her most needy clients, she of course receives love in return. But in no time at all she will have an overflowing practice of young Persephones, more needy than she and clingingly dependent.

One of the most painful aspects of this defense is that Persephone the therapist will often find her clients invading her life and making havoc of it with their insatiable demands for her love and attention. Once the motherless child herself, she is now spiritual mother to every wounded soul in the neighborhood. Yet she feels as invaded as ever, psychically.

It is still the golden rule of all the helping professions that you cannot take anyone further than you have gone yourself. So, all that the motherly Persephone can do is model to all her dependent clients her own defenses against the descent. Many a social worker falls into this, "the messiah trap," as Carmen Renee Berry calls it in her recent book, *When Helping You Is Hurting Me.*

To be fully effective as a therapist or healer, Persephone must first, like all healers, heal herself. But for Persephone this is not so easy. Ironically her very capacity for empathy and psychic understanding is her greatest obstacle to the process. Unless she finds outside help or undergoes training to develop some Athenean objectivity to help her see how she is in fact dominated by the missing Mother, all she will do is attract to her mirrors of her own unresolved victimization.

Why? Because she does not know how to remain detached and separate from those whose suffering she feels so acutely; *she lacks ego boundaries*. In her openness to the unconscious in herself and others, she is constantly fusing with the personalities and sufferings of those who are drawn to her. Without the objectivity of a strong ego, provided by Hera's worldliness or Artemis's unsentimental practicality, she gets hopelessly bogged down in the morass of her patients' sufferings.

Even if she does not become a therapist or healer, the same pitfalls and temptations apply. In her longing to help others she will often quietly insinuate herself into relationships and households, genuinely believing she is helping lovingly, when in fact it is her own needy self trying to manipulate the situation to get the Demeter love she so deeply craves.

When Persephone herself seeks out help from a therapist, she will again tend to be subtly manipulative. Often she will arrive with all kinds of agendas, eager to share psychic readings or armed with some profound synchronistic knowledge about why she must do this special work with Ms. X or Dr. Y (who must, of course, feel deeply flattered that he or she has been chosen for this great honor). She will selectively reveal parts of herself, the destiny her guides have revealed to her, a glimpse of her victim self, a portentous dream. And if sufficient sympathy is not forthcoming, she will abandon therapy like a frightened rabbit.

Failure in therapy once more confirms her sense that everyone betrays her, uses her, is out to victimize her. She may play money games with her therapist, requesting special treatment, reductions, trades. It is a cry for help once more to the all-powerful Olympian parents, a refusal to follow her path fully into the darkness.

PERSEPHONE UNDESCENDED III: THE BRINK OF THE ABYSS

The reality is that since she has never truly given in to the movement of the descent, she will not let go of the last shreds of her ego, the maidenly innocence that must be sacrificed. And these last shreds of attachment speak volumes about her rage at unjust fate. Yet to hold onto the edge of the abyss with only one finger is in the end no different from holding on firmly with both hands—as long as one does not fall!

Few women ever hung so close and so tenaciously to the brink and yet were able to record Persephone's ambivalence about letting go more vividly than the poet Sylvia Plath. Depressed and sliding inexorably toward her eventual suicide, Plath left behind the records of her struggle with both the Death Lord and the Death Lady in the poems posthumously collected as *Ariel* (see box, "Sylvia Plath's Encounter With Hades").

In her poem "Getting There," Hades is imagined as a Death train; Sylvia voices something of what holds her back:

> How far is it?
> It is so small
> The place I am getting to, why are there these obstacles?

What are these obstacles, then? Plath answers her own question:

> The body of this woman
> Charred skirts and deathmask
> Mourned by religious figures, by garlanded children.

Then comes the longing for the spirit (possibly echoing T. S. Eliot or W. B. Yeats):

> Is there no still place
> Turning and turning in the middle air,
> Untouched and untouchable

But it still is the bodies of the dead and wounded that obsess her in the poem. *It is as though she cannot get on with her own death process because of the horrors she sees all around:*

> I shall bury the wounded like pupas,
> I shall count and bury the dead.
> Let their souls writhe in a dew
> Incense in my track.
> The carriages rock, they are cradles.

SYLVIA PLATH'S ENCOUNTER
WITH HADES

Sylvia Plath's images of the underworld and her suffering are
drawn from the Nazi concentration camps. (Her father was
German and had emigrated from Germany but loathed the
Nazis.)

> Grey birds obsess my heart
> Mouth-ash, ash of eye.
> They settle. On the high
>
> Precipice
> That emptied one man into space
> The ovens glowed like heavens, incandescent.
>
> It is a heart,
> This holocaust I walk in,
> O golden child the world will kill and eat.
>   —from "Mary's Song"

In her poems her father, who died when she was ten,
becomes a Nazi Hades to whom she is drawn in some deep
identification with the suffering of the victims of the Holocaust.
"At twenty I tried to die / And get back, back, back to you,"
she writes, referring to her first suicide attempt—there were
several. She flirts with dark Persephone in these attempts, even
finding in one of her poems the persona of "Lady Lazarus" for
her underworld journeys:

> Dying
> Is an art, like anything else.
> I do it exceptionally well
> I do it so it feels like hell
> I do it so it feels real.
> I guess you could say I've a call
>   —from "Lady Lazarus"

No doubt her attempts to leave were in deadly earnest, yet she survived three, as if a part of her still clung tenaciously to life, to the image of the golden baby that recurs again and again in her poems. Depth psychologist James Hillman, who has written so brilliantly about suicide and the underworld, would say that her mistake was to literalize, to physicalize her descent as actual suicides. Her soul was desperately seeking a rebirth from her descent and may have achieved it, had she not acted it out so tragically. All the archetypal imagery was there in her poems.

And I, stepping from this skin
Of old bandages, boredoms, old faces
Step to you from the black car of Lethe
Pure as a baby.

The last line is the giveaway: she still wants to be pure, Demeter's baby. All her darkness and rage is split off and projected into the dead bodies whom she still mourns. They are images of old, dead, painful parts of self she cannot fully discard. One is reminded of Jesus' injunction: "Let the dead bury their dead."

PERSEPHONE'S WOUND: THE ETERNAL SACRIFICIAL VICTIM

Sylvia Plath was deeply and irrevocably identified with the plight of the victim. She had no way of detaching herself from it at all and eventually became the bride of death. So many Persephone women are powerfully drawn to this role; like the poet Keats, who died at twenty-five, they are "half in love with easeful death." They flirt with death in different periods of their lives. And since they have grown up either as victims themselves or else taking care of one or other of their victimized parents, this pattern is hard for them to escape. Behind the ancient myth of Persephone's descent, some scholars agree, there lies the practice of human sacrifice for the greater good of the community.

When a woman is overidentified with Persephone to the exclusion of all the other goddesses, she will invariably be attracted to situations in which she or others get hurt. She may have accidents or strange illnesses that render her dependent upon welfare. She may find herself unavoidably taking care of ailing or dying parents. She may attract to her charming but ultimately brutal and intimidating men she cannot escape from. None of these events are her doing. They appear out of the blue; relentless, crushing, unexplained.

When we look at these distressing stories more closely, we find one common pattern: she is powerless and usually passive. These things happen to her. Yet she seems, on examination, strangely drawn to them, as if they were indeed her fate. We are led to suspect that the Persephone woman has a secret attachment to a deeply human and intractable theme: *the wretchedness of the innocent victim*!

She seems to have what Freud called a repetition compulsion. Always she is driven to return to her equivalent of that crucial abduction scene in our myth where the maiden stands frozen on the brink of the abyss. Like a stuck needle in a phonograph record, she replays the agony and the pathos over and over again, but never brings it fully to a conclusion.

Jung once pointed out that there are two major forms of spiritual pride or inflation. We are all familiar with the first, the inflation of the hero, the guru, or the world savior, for instance; we all know and distrust their puffed-up rhetoric. But less easy to see through is the pride of the sufferer, the martyr, the victim. Just as the hero endlessly demands (and gets) praise and support from unreflecting bystanders, so the victim draws upon natural wells of sympathy and pity by his or her plight. But what could be more manipulative and in the end more self-serving? It is what a colleague of ours once dubbed the tyranny of the cripple.

Yet, it is a rash person who challenges the victim. For the moment he does so, that challenger becomes the new persecutor and the victim can once more bleed, drawing yet more pity and support.

Only Hades can claim the victim. Only a genuine encounter that brings the death of all ego, all attachment to innocence, can put to rest the misplaced pride of the victim once and for all. This is Persephone's challenge, her moment of truth. James Hillman puts it this way in his extraordinary commentary *The Dream and the Underworld*: "The intervention of Hades turns the world upside down. The point of view of life ceases. Now phenomena are seen not only through the eyes of Eros and human life and love, but also through Thanatos [Freud's name, from the Greek, for the death instinct], their cold unmoving depths unconnected to life" (p. 48).

Here is how D. H. Lawrence, actually contemplating his own imminent death, put it:

Are you willing to be sponged out, erased, cancelled,
made nothing?
Are you willing to be made nothing?
If not, you will never really change . . .

—from "Phoenix"

And what must die in the maiden Persephone? Why, precisely her maidenly innocence, her lovely gentle persona composed of lofty spiritual ideals and New Age sweetness and light. Too much light only casts a very dark shadow, as Jung was constantly reminding us.

What, then, is the shadow of the maiden Persephone? Bluntly stated: enormous rage and a longing for pure, all-encompassing power. Not for nothing was one of the later titles for Persephone in an Orphic hymn, "Mother of the Furies" (see box "Persephone: Mother of the Furies, Queen of the Netherworld").

How is Persephone's dark side recognized? First, in the shape of all those women around her who seem malevolent and arbitrary in their power. Her actual mother is usually the first candidate, but on reflection she will know many from school days and the workaday world. Sometimes she will experience the invasion of various "enemies" on a psychic level. Books like Dion Fortune's *Psychic Self-Defense* will be her bedside reading. If she is immersed in such things, she may feel beset by rivals who are practicing "psychic invasion" via her dreams. Or she will clairvoyantly "know" of black-magic plots that involve her. Or else her guides will reveal to her the evil and corrupt past lives of other women with whom she feels in competition.

When she is actually regressed to remember her past lives, they

PERSEPHONE: MOTHER OF THE FURIES, QUEEN OF THE NETHERWORLD

The very early Homeric hymn that focuses primarily on Demeter (see earlier box, "The Rape of the Maiden Persephone") says very little about the transformation of the maiden Persephone into a mature and powerful queen. Fortunately, a much later hymn, from the so-called Orphic cult, fills out the picture for us. In the following it is clear that she was in many ways seen as an even greater goddess figure than Demeter. Here she can be clearly recognized as uniting the forces of life, death, and transformation in herself.

HYMN TO PERSEPHONE

Persephone, blessed daughter of great Zeus, sole offspring
of Demeter, come and accept this gracious sacrifice.
Much honored spouse of Plouton, discreet and life-giving.
you command the gates of Hades in the bowels of the earth,
lovely-tressed Praxidike, pure bloom of Deo,
mother of the Furies, queen of the netherworld,
whom Zeus sired in clandestine union.
Mother of loud-roaring and many shaped Eubouleus,
[= Dionysus]
radiant and luminous playmate of the Seasons,
august, almighty, maiden rich in fruits,
brilliant and horned, you alone are beloved of mortals.
In spring you rejoice in the meadow breezes
and you show your holy figure in shoots and green fruits.
You were made a kidnapper's bride in the fall,

and you alone are life and death to toiling mortals,
O Persephone, for you always nourish and kill them
too.
Hearken, O blessed goddess, and send forth the
earth's fruits.
You who blossom in peace, in soft-handed health,
and in a life of plenty that ferries old age in comfort
to your realm, O queen, and to that of mighty
Plouton.
— *The Orphic Hymns*, trans. Athanassakis
From *The Ancient Mysteries*, ed. Meyer, p. 105

will often be around themes of priestesses and power struggles.[1] Once more we will meet cold, dark, power-ridden rival priests, priestesses, and queens. Almost always in these scenarios she will be the victim of some power struggle, cursed for eternity. Whatever the historical truth of these stories—and taking them literally could be a good way of keeping them split off—they are all to be understood archetypally as her fear of Hades and the Dark Mother, who is none other than the powerful queen of the underworld she will not own in herself.

In a nutshell, Persephone's real issue is *power*, power that she refuses to own, power that she endlessly gives away, projecting it onto successful women or witchy women, prestigious men or alcoholic bullies. She seeks a savior in powerful people, but her deep attachment to helplessness, innocence, and unconscious rage only makes her feel cut off as if by some ever-widening gulf.

And what is that gulf but the descent to Hades she will not take? In all these defenses she is still crying out for all-powerful Daddy Zeus to deliver her, to longed-for Mother Demeter to restore the comfort and innocence of her lost and utterly wretched childhood.

---

[1] See Roger J. Woolger, *Other Lives, Other Selves*, (New York: Doubleday, 1987) for an account of past-life regression experiences.

THE DARK NIGHT OF THE SOUL

What Persephone has failed to understand is that the victim in her truly needs to be sacrificed and married to the dark powers. The word *sacrifice* doesn't just mean renouncing or giving up, in the sense of losing, but literally "making sacred." All the pain and rage and grief need to be offered up to forces beyond her. Hers is indeed a sacred calling, a life that belongs not to her, but to the goddess and her underworld consort.

Persephone's early tribulations are a potential initiation, and as in all initiations there has to be a death to the profane, everyday world (see box: "James Hillman on the Persephone Experience"). Yes, she is set apart, she is different, but this is no cause for wretchedness or spiritual pride. She is set apart to be a member of what Sir Laurens van der Post once called the priesthood of the suffering. Sir Laurens was recalling Saint Paul, who said that those who are called must learn to "rejoice with them that rejoice and suffer with them that suffer."

How can Persephone as healer or therapist comfort those in despair or close to death if she has never been there herself? No seminar on metaphysics or spirit guides can teach her that. Such things she must learn within herself in the school of her own suffering. As the old alchemist Morienus once said, "The gateway to peace is exceedingly narrow, and no one may enter except through the agony of his own soul."

In the true life of the spirit there is both light and dark, joy and woe, and the unconscious has both a higher and a lower aspect to it. To fulfill her greater destiny, Persephone cannot have intercourse with one without embracing the other. Persephone's deepest challenge is *to unite the dark and the light sides of the goddess in herself.*

This is mysteriously hinted at in the myth by the presence of the goddess Hecate. Hecate is the only witness to Persephone's rape and abduction. She hears Persephone's cries but does nothing at all to come to her aid or fetch help. Could she be in collusion with Hades?

The goddess Hecate was strongly associated with the dark side of the moon and with witchcraft by the Greeks. It was she to whom the murderess Medea paid homage. We cannot escape the fact that Hecate is somehow the patroness of Persephone's descent into Hades; if Persephone's initiation into the depths is to be completed in all its

JAMES HILLMAN ON
THE PERSEPHONE EXPERIENCE

In his book *The Dream and the Underworld*, archetypal psychologist James Hillman writes provocatively about the equivalence of the underworld of the Greeks and the unconscious as described by modern depth psychology. Freud's death instinct, or Thanatos, is, for instance, another version of Hades, according to Hillman. Here is how he views the underworld Persephone:

> The Persephone experience occurs to us each in sudden depressions, when we feel ourselves caught in hatefulness, cold, numbed, and drawn out of life by a force we cannot see, against which we would flee, distractedly thrashing about for naturalistic explanations and comforts for what is happening so darkly. We feel invaded from below, assaulted, and we think of death.
>
> To be raped into the underworld is not the only mode of experiencing it. There are many other modes of descent. But when it comes in this radical fashion, then we may know which mytheme has encased us. We are dragged into Hades' chariot only if we are out in Demeter's green fields, seductively innocent with playmates among flowers. That world has to open up. When the bottom falls out of it, we feel only the black abyss of despair, but this is not the only way to experience even this mytheme.
>
> For instance, Hekate was supposedly standing by the whole time, listening or watching. There is evidently a perspective that can witness the soul's struggles without the flap of Persephone or the disaster of Demeter. In us is also a dark angel (Hekate was also called *angelos*), a consciousness (she was also called *phosphoros*) that shines in the dark and that witnesses

such events because it is already aware of them a priori. This part has an a priori connection with the underworld through sniffing dogs and bitchery, dark moons, ghosts, garbage, and poisons. Part of us is not dragged down but always lives there, as Hekate is partly an underworld Goddess. From this vantage point we may observe our own catastrophes with a dark wisdom that expects little else.

—*The Dream and the Underworld*, pp. 49–50

aspects, it is Hecate who must be honored. Which means that every Persephone woman must recognize and come to terms with the witch and the killer in herself. For these figures, though only indirectly and darkly hinted at, are an essential element of the makeup of the mature queen of the night. Her name in Greek means "she who brings destruction," according to scholars.

When the Persephone woman ignores the patronage of Hecate and projects her witchiness onto others, and when she fails to complete the downward movement toward her true bridegroom, Hades, she may risk serious physical illness, or else she will attract mates or associates with extremely destructive, even perverse tendencies.

At the heart of the great myth lies Hades, who is none other than Death personified. When Persephone the maiden marries Hades, it is tantamount to saying that the maiden in her dies. It is a figurative death, required by the greater wisdom of the psyche, a sacrifice that is also, as we have seen, an initiation.

Willingly or unwillingly, the Persephone woman has been called to renounce her innocent maidenly self and spend a large portion of her life going in and out of the underworld. Most often she will do this in the role of a helper or guide to others. Because she has been there herself, looked at the most terrible sides of human suffering, and survived, she is now a beacon. The work of Elisabeth Kübler-Ross with terminal clients is of this nature. With the dark torch that led her downward Persephone can also lead others back to reunite them with life, with Demeter, or else help them cross over to "the other side."

It is a vocation of mystical proportions, and as in the classic journey of the Christian mystics, the woman or man who is called to this path learns to pass through a "dark night of the soul."

T. S. Eliot was deeply familiar with the process of Persephone's descent and with the dark night of the soul, both from his own spiritual life and presumably from the agonies of his first wife, a Persephone woman who suffered acutely from bouts of madness.

Here is how he describes the process in the voice of a psychiatrist speaking to a young woman in his play *The Cocktail Party*:

[This way] is unknown, and so requires faith—
The kind of faith that issues from despair
The destination cannot be described:
You will know very little until you get there
You will journey blind. But the way leads towards possession
Of what you have sought for in the wrong place

It is no coincidence that all the accounts we have of the abduction of Persephone pass over in silence what happens to her immediately after Hades drags her into the darkness. It is indeed a "mystery," a word that means "something that cannot be spoken," from the Greek *myein*, which means "to keep silent."

Yet we know that death and loss were central to the mystical transformation that every initiate into the way of Persephone had to undergo. The initiate at Eleusis was vividly reminded of her own death, to be sure, when she (or he) was obliged to sacrificially slaughter a pig, whose body was then thrown into a huge noisome pit with scores of others. Anyone who has ever bred pigs will appreciate not only their uncanny, almost human intelligence but also the horrendous shrieks they let out when they sense impending death. The sacrificial pig stood as a chilling ritual substitute for the human initiate who would, of course, die one day herself. Doubtless it was intended as part of a ritual meditation on the attendant terrors of death, but perhaps, too, it contained an inescapable reminder of the transformational mysteries of the Earth Mother. The great Renaissance physician and alchemist Paracelsus, who understood the power of nature (which he called the *lumen naturae*, or the "light of nature") may help us understand this mystery in the following extraordinary passage:

Decay is the beginning of all birth. . . . It transforms shape and essence, the forces and virtues of nature. . . . Decay is the mid-wife of very great things! It causes many things to rot, that a noble fruit may be born; for it is the reversal, the death and destruction of the original essence of all natural things. It brings about the birth and rebirth of forms a thousand times improved . . . . And this is the highest and greatest *mysterium* of God, the deepest mystery that He has revealed to mortal man. (*Para-celsus: Selected Writings*. Ed. Jacobi. Princeton: Princeton University Press, 1951, pp. 143–44.)

AN ANCIENT SUMERIAN PARALLEL: THE DESCENT OF INANNA

Further hints of the great process of the mystical descent can be found if we go back to another great myth of the journey to the underworld, the Sumerian descent of Inanna, which many believe to inform the Persephone story. Inanna is the bright queen of heaven, clearly a moon goddess, who descends of her own accord to the Great Below, which is ruled by Ereshkigal. She descends through seven gates (seven is frequently the number of stages in an initiation), being stripped of her finery piece by piece. Finally, at the last gate, naked, she is judged by seven judges, killed by Ereshkigal, and her corpse hung upon a stake, a kind of crucifixion. There she is left to rot. Eventually Enki, the god of the waters and wisdom, rescues Inanna by commiserating with the groans of Ereshkigal and arranging a substitute. Inanna is restored to life and reascends through the seven gates, her clothes restored at each.

This powerful myth has been analyzed with great insight by Jungian therapist Sylvia Brinton Perera in her book *Descent to the Goddess*, an essential handbook for every woman called to Persephone's descent. Whether or not the Persephone story in any way derives from the much earlier Sumerian myth, it certainly strongly illuminates it. Coming from a matriarchal era, when the Goddess was worshipped more completely, the whole movement of the descent of Inanna is much less passive, and there is no Hadean rapist. Inanna descends of her own will, and she has a male consort, Dumuzi, but it is he who is more passive. In later versions, as Tammuz, it is her consort who becomes the sacrificial victim.

The cultural differences between the two myths suggest that by Greek times, as we well know, the Goddess has largely lost her power. This might explain why the mythic Persephone is more passive and it is Hades who initiates the descent. But if anything, the decline in Goddess power makes it all the more necessary for women, both in Greek times and in our own, to descend to reclaim their deepest power.

Interestingly there is an element of the Greek myth missing in the Sumerian myth that is profoundly important: the *marriage* of Hades and Persephone. We cannot escape the very *phallic* quality of Hades/Pluto, who is sometimes identified by the Greeks with the even more sexualized figure of Dionysus (see Artemis chapter). A major element in Persephone's initiation and awakening is therefore sexual; it has to do with the uniting of the male and female energies deep within the underworld, which could also mean *deep within the body*.

Again and again with our Persephone clients we have seen a deep alienation from their bodies and their sexuality in favor of the non-physical solaces of the spirit. Often this is derived from child abuse and sexual brutality. But this is the very energy they must reown and why the descent is so necessary for them. In cutting themselves off from their pain and distress held in the lower parts of their bodies, they are also alienated from the deepest earth energy that belongs to the Goddess, that energy symbolized by the phallic lord.

To get a full sense of the union of these energies, we must look to India, a culture that has always remained firmly rooted in matriarchal traditions. The equivalent of the phallic lord and consort in India is of course Shiva, and the Dark Mother there is Kali (see box, "Rama-krishna's Vision of Kali"). In some representations they are shown in sexual congress, symbolizing the cosmic union of male and female energies that regenerate the universe. In others a bloody Kali stands upon the corpse of her consort, emphasizing her power as destroyer. This dimension of the sacred marriage of the god and goddess had been largely lost to the Greeks, though some writers, like Ezra Pound, spec-ulate that it may have been revealed to the initiates of the mysteries of Eleusis.

The cult of the so-called Eleusinian Mysteries that developed around Demeter and her lost daughter take their name from Eleusis,

RAMAKRISHNA'S VISION OF KALI, THE INDIAN WORLD MOTHER

The following is taken from the celebrated *Gospel of Sri Ramakrishna*, the most revered spiritual master of India in the nineteenth century. Ramakrishna devoted his life to the goddess Kali and was granted all kinds of visions and ecstasies (*samadhi*) by her. Here, in this summary of his amanuensis, Swami Nikhilananda, is how the sage described attributes of the goddess that the Greeks were unable to fully envision in Persephone or in any other Greek goddess (bracketed material is authors' paraphrase):

[In the divine trinity of Kali, the Nature Mother; Shiva, the Absolute; and Rhadakanta, Love], Kali is the pivot, the sovereign Mistress. She is Prakriti [substance], the Procreatrix, Nature, the Destroyer, the Creator. Nay, she is something greater and deeper still for those who have eyes to see. She is the Universal Mother, "my Mother," as Ramakrishna would say, the All-Powerful, who reveals Herself to Her children under different aspects and Divine Incarnations, the Visible God, who leads the elect to the Invisible Reality; and if it so pleases Her, She takes away the last trace of ego from created beings and merges it in the consciousness of the Absolute, the undifferentiated God.

To the ignorant She is, to be sure, the image of destruction; but [Ramakrishna] found in Her the benign, all-loving Mother. Her neck is encircled with a garland of heads, and Her waist with a girdle of human arms, and two of Her hands hold weapons of death, and Her eyes dart a glance of fire, but, strangely enough, Ramakrishna felt in her breath the soothing touch of tender love and saw in Her the Seed of Immortality. She stands on the bosom of Her Consort Shiva; it is because She is the Shakti, the Power, inseparable from the Absolute. She is surrounded by jackals and other unholy creatures, the denizens of the cremation ground. But is not the Ultimate reality above holiness and unholiness? She appears to be reeling under the spell of wine. But who would create this mad world unless under the influence of a divine drunkenness? [Is not disorder the very foundation of our seemingly ordered universe? The cosmos has evolved out of the primeval chaos.] She (Kali) is the highest symbol of all the forces of nature, the synthesis of their antinomies, the Ultimate Divine in the form of woman.

—*The Gospel of Sri Ramakrishna*, pp. 9–10, 12–13

a small town just outside Athens. These were the Mysteries, which, as we learned earlier, were events that "could not be spoken of." Everyone who was initiated into the secret and most holy ceremony, which took place in the near darkness of an underground chamber, apparently emerged with a wholly new understanding of the continuity of life and death. Persephone's sacrificial death, her union with the Lord of the Netherworld, and her return—reborn—to her mother, proclaimed, for all who partook in it, unshakable confidence in a world beyond death where the soul is renewed for all eternity. (For a fuller account, see Demeter chapter.)

THE TWIN GODDESSES OF LIFE AND DEATH

When Persephone is in the underworld, she makes a bargain with Hades so that she can return to be with her mother, Demeter, for part of the year. She must remain with Hades for a number of months based on the number of pomegranate seeds she swallows, traditionally four, which is one third of the year. Given the blood-and-seed imagery of the fruit, it seems highly likely that this transaction also symbolizes the menstrual cycle, that part of the month when a woman's body must suffer the death of a potential life within her. Which is another way of saying that during the death phase of her cycle every woman must live with her inner Hades. When it is not made conscious in a woman's life, this inner encounter with the necessity of death can produce all kinds of menstrual and premenstrual difficulties. To honor Persephone is to honor the perpetual cycle of life and death. This has been the main contention of a little-known but brilliant book, *The Wise Wound*, by Penelope Shuttle and Peter Redgrove (see also Demeter chapter).

The return to the Mother, to Demeter, however, is no longer the return of a maiden, but of a mature goddess, who now knows sexuality, death, and separation. The return is a reminder that the two goddesses are in fact one, that together they represent the wholeness of being of the Great Mother, who can endlessly be separated from herself, endlessly die, and endlessly be reborn, as woman, as earth, as cosmos (see box, "Persephone: Mother of The Furies, Queen of the Netherworld").

This is an awe-inspiring aspect of the primordial figure of the Great Mother that we have mostly lost today: namely that she contains within her all opposites. She is both youth and age, both maiden and mother, both warrior and tender of the hearth, and, most significantly for this chapter, both life and death.

Greek culture has been justly celebrated for its quality of brilliance and light, its establishment of the supremacy of reason, logic, and philosophy, its pellucid vision of the outer, physical world. If there is a god who epitomizes this consciousness, it is Apollo, sublime god of light, reason, and harmony.

Yet so much emphasis upon the light could not exist without a particularly dark shadow being cast. So, among the gods, as with the goddesses, there are splits and polarities. The darker brother of Apollo is thus Dionysus, lord of ecstasy, madness, divine drunkenness, and sacrificial death, the very antithesis of Apollonian clarity. Likewise, Zeus, imperiously sitting high up on his heavenly Olympian throne, must have a dark brother to oversee the lower depths—the mysterious and barely mentioned Hades. (Hades was occasionally called in Greek *Zeus cthonios*, which means "underworld or subterranean Zeus.")

How these polarities might look can be shown graphically as follows:

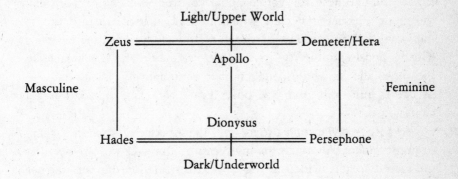

Once we realize this, we can begin to see that Persephone and her mother, Demeter, represent the two major opposite aspects of the primordial Great Mother that the Greek psyche was struggling to maintain. Their myth represents, among other things, an attempt to see the whole momentous relationship of the higher and the lower, the light and the dark worlds, as part of a *dynamic* relationship, a cycle of life and death in which all beings participate.

If it were left to the male gods alone, there would be no such cycle, for masculine consciousness, lacking the inner mysteries of the body, of the menstrual cycle, of pregnancy and birth, has no cyclical awareness built into it. Which is another way of saying that masculine consciousness knows nothing of *the mystery of the life force.*

Masculine, Apollonian consciousness, symbolized by the sun, always tends toward mutually exclusive polarities: something is either this *or* that, it is either day *or* night but not both. This is the whole basis of Aristotle's logic, one of the supreme achievements of Greek culture—at least, according to the official patriarchal view of Western history.[2]

Feminine or matriarchal consciousness, symbolized by the moon, lacks the extremes of mutually exclusive polarities—dark versus light, night versus day, good versus evil—those dualities Western culture, especially Christianity, has grown so fond of. Instead there is the model of the far subtler light of the moon in her infinite variations of light, shade, and darkness, forever changing, forever renewing herself. And the moon's light is reflected, which means that it dwells in darkness but nevertheless partakes of the sun. It includes and encompasses with its gentle luminosity; its shadows are subtle and not harsh like the sun's, and its whole connection to time and periodicity and the psyche is quite different (see box, "Erich Neumann on Matriarchal Consciousness").

As Greek civilization progressed, the Apollonian tendency came to predominate. Although the mysteries of Demeter were retained at the sacred center of Eleusis, the Greeks retreated farther and farther away from speculation or mythmaking about the underworld and life after death. The awesome side of Persephone as queen of death eventually became more frightening the more it was suppressed. And it is, of course, in its suppressed form that it returns to torment the imagination of medieval Christendom in its paranoid fear of witches.

PERSEPHONE AS CRONE: THE WISE OLD WOMAN

Recent research into the origins of the Anglo-Saxon word *witch* suggests that it may be derived from the old word *wicca*, which refers to a practitioner of the craft of wisdom. When the Church persecuted the witches, it also suppressed the ancient wisdom of the Goddess. What was lost was the mature Persephone's secret, the wisdom of one who knows the workings of life and death, the energies that inform the

[2] The view of history that everything worthwhile in the West began with the Greeks has been seriously questioned recently. Most importantly by Martin Bernal's massive scholarly work, *Black Athena: The Afroasiatic Roots of Classical Civilization* (3 vols.), as well as by historian William Irwin Thompson's *The Time Falling Bodies Take to Light*.

ERICH NEUMANN ON MATRIARCHAL CONSCIOUSNESS

Erich Neumann was one of Jung's early associates who devoted many writings to the huge subject of the implications of the mother religions for modern consciousness. His famous book *The Great Mother* is an indispensable analysis of the archetype. Here, in a lesser-known essay, he discusses the cyclical influence of the moon:

> The periodicity of the moon, with its nocturnal background, is the symbol of a spirit that waxes and wanes, conforming to the dark processes of the unconscious. Moon-consciousness, as matriarchal consciousness might be called, is never divorced from the unconscious, for it is a phase, a spiritual phase, of the unconscious itself. The ego of matriarchal consciousness possesses no free, independent activity of its own; it waits passively, attuned to the spirit-impulse carried toward it by the unconscious.
>
> A time is "favorable" or "unfavorable" according to whether the spiritual activity determined by the unconscious turns toward the ego and reveals itself, or turns away, darkens, and disappears. At this stage of matriarchal consciousness, the ego's task is to wait and watch for the favorable or unfavorable time, to put itself in harmony with the changing moon, to bring about a consonance, a unison with the rhythm of its emanations. . . .
>
> The way in which an idea, an inspiration, or an intoxication arising from the unconscious seizes a personality as if by a sudden, violent assault, driving it to ecstasy, insanity, poetry, or prophecy, represents one part of the spirit's working. The corresponding trait of matriarchal consciousness is its dependence for every

intuition and inspiration upon what emerges from the
unconscious, mysteriously and almost beyond influence, when, where, and how it will. From this point of
view, all shamanism, including prophecy, is a passive
sufferance; its activity is more that of "conceiving"
than of a willed act; and the essential contribution of
the ego consists in a readiness to accept the emerging
unconscious content and come into harmony with it.
      —From "On the Moon and Matriarchal
Consciousness," in *Fathers and Mothers*, ed. Patricia
                                      Berry, pp. 40–45

seasons, sexuality, and birth, one who understands the gap between
the two worlds and who honors the ever-present guardianship of the
ancestors. This wisdom she shares with her guardian overseer, Hecate,
goddess of witchcraft and magic.

The mature Persephone who has returned from her journey lives
somehow beyond the ordinary world, but she remains nevertheless
intimately familiar with it. She has become the wise woman who has
"seen it all" and who is therefore always cheerful and good-humored,
if not wryly bemused by human folly. In her completed form she unites
the beginning and the end of the life cycle, birth and death in herself;
so, as an old woman she still retains her youthfulness, and as a young
initiate she cheerfully carries the wisdom of years.

Jean Bolen has recently suggested that this sense of spiritual completeness or wholeness in the returned Persephone may be accounted
for by a certain mysterious phrase about Hecate in *The Hymn to Demeter*
that recounts the mysteries of the Triple Mother Goddess. For when
the mature Persephone has returned to her mother, it was said that
"from that day the lady [Hecate] precedes and follows Persephone."
Hecate, as Bolen puts it, could be seen here as the feminine Holy
Spirit who completes and binds the matriarchal trinity of Maiden,
Mother, and Crone (see also Demeter chapter).

Many women with a strong Persephone element in them confess

when young how much they want to be old, so as to be free of all the constraints of conforming to society. Actually what emerges in this fantasy is closely related to the archetype of the clown, another who stands outside of society and who mocks all our masks and our absurd tragic melodramas. The actress Ruth Gordon often played this kind of Persephone role in movies, her most celebrated being *Harold and Maude*. In this film Maude is a highly eccentric old lady approaching the age of eighty who has absolutely no respect for patriarchal law— she steals a policeman's motorcycle, for example—but who believes in living life to the fullest. At the same time she has decided quite cheerfully that she will kill herself at eighty and visits funerals to get used to the idea!

Another example of this liberated side of aged Persephone is to be found in this delightful poem entitled "Warning" written by Jenny Joseph:

When I am an old woman I shall wear purple
With a red hat which doesn't go, and doesn't suit me.
And I shall spend my pension on brandy and summer gloves
And satin sandals, and say we've no money for butter.
I shall sit down on the pavement when I'm tired
And gobble up samples in shops and press alarm bells
And run my stick along the public railings
And make up for the sobriety of my youth.
I shall go out in my slippers in the rain
And pick the flowers in other people's gardens
And learn to spit.

You can wear terrible shirts and grow more fat
And eat three pounds of sausages at a go
Or only bread and pickle for a week
And hoard pens and pencils and beermats and things in boxes.

But now we must have clothes that keep us dry
And pay our rent and not swear in the street
And set a good example for the children.
We must have friends to dinner and read the papers.

But maybe I ought to practise a little now?
So people who know me are not too shocked and surprised
When suddenly I am old, and start to wear purple.

Frequently, mature Persephone women will find themselves drawn
to the very experience of death and transition as their major life work.
In the last century the selfless work of Florence Nightingale was justly
celebrated. Today nearly everyone is familiar with the remarkable
achievements of Mother Teresa among the derelict street people in
Calcutta and the pioneering work with death and dying of Elisabeth
Kübler-Ross. Such women are the living embodiment of the supreme
wisdom of Persephone as mediatrix between life and death.

A MATURE PERSEPHONE: EILEEN GARRETT

We end this chapter with an example of a Persephone woman who
went through an early initiation into the realm of the shades and eventually emerged to embody all that is finest in the mature Persephone.
This was the life of Eileen Garrett, perhaps the most widely investigated
and respected medium of this century. She tells her story in her autobiography, *Many Voices*, upon which the following is based.
    Eileen's early years in her native Ireland were fraught with tragedy.
When Eileen was barely two weeks old, her mother drowned herself,
and a few weeks later her father also committed suicide. Her mother
had been the daughter of strict Protestants, and her secret marriage to
a young Basque, a Catholic, seemed doomed from the outset. Eileen
came to be brought up by an uncle, who died during her teens. She
was later sent to various schools. She was a difficult and often sickly
child.
    Nourished by the still prevalent faith of the country people of
County Meath in "the fairy world," Eileen would spend long hours
wandering in the hills and fields, not far from the Hill of Tara, the
ancient capital of Ireland. She felt "a deep sympathy with all living
beings" on the farms around her and forged a mystical connection with
nature that was to be a source of profound healing and renewal throughout her life.

During one of her illnesses she seems to have learned to go out of the body:

> I became aware that distance was not important—the rapport between myself and the well-remembered scenes renewed themselves miraculously. I was again able to remain passive and project myself to the countryside; something was taking place between me and the outside world—a new intimacy, independent of the distance between. . . . I had by some conscious means found my way from "here to there." I had discovered a place within the cosmic scheme—a world of feeling into which I had very early stepped unknowingly. Now it revealed itself again to establish the reality of a nonmaterial unification toward which I have often turned instinctively and which has made communication on many levels possible. (p. 23)

Eileen grew up to be exceedingly sensitive on many levels. Once she had a vision of her dead uncle, that seemed to point her life in a new direction. On another occasion a simple wedding ceremony evoked in her what we would now call a past-life flashback:

> A curious relic of irrational superstition overcame me at the marriage ceremony, charging it with a deep mystery that enveloped me. The wedding breakfast feast in earlier times held deep implications. Such thoughts, arising from the depths of myself, brought also intangible fears. In these moments, my untutored mind dramatized my apprehensions. Deeply moved, I had become another person with memories of other beliefs and other ceremonies in a long primitive past. (p. 41)

Death haunted her young womanhood as it had her infancy and childhood. Three boys she bore her first husband died at a very young age, though fortunately a daughter survived. Her psychic sensitivity seemed to be growing, so that living "a dual life," as she described it, eventually led to the breakup of her first marriage.

Around this time, while running a small tea shop in London during World War I, she met many young soldiers on their way to the trenches.

Frequently she was overwhelmed with clairvoyant visions of their impending deaths. Compassion for one young man about whom she had one such premonition led to a short-lived marriage. After only a brief time in the trenches he was claimed by a fatal explosion. Eileen was able to describe clairvoyantly exactly where and how he died.

The liberal circles in which Eileen moved in postwar London eventually led her to attend spiritualist meetings. Here she first heard of the phenomenon of trance. She realized she had possessed this capacity from an early age, "to sleep away from it" as she put it. Another comment in her autobiography is especially telling: "Had I then, at an early age, discovered, all unconsciously, a way of disappearing from pain, boredom, and all disagreeable things?" (p. 43).

Eileen's encounter with the London spiritualist group was to be a turning point in her life, for here were others who shared her experience of channeling and clairvoyance and who struggled daily, like herself, with "a dual life." She received much guidance, training, and support for her abilities and went on to become a much-sought-after medium and psychic counselor. Her writings, too, have brought insight and comfort to thousands.

By integrating the suffering of her childhood and youth, Eileen Garrett clearly came to have deep compassion for those who sought her out in their own pain and distress. Able to live with dignity with the jarring opposites of dark and light within her, she came to earn the authentic titles of both medium and mystic.

SEVEN

DEMETER:
MOTHER OF US ALL

I am not yet born; provide me
With water to dandle me, grass to grow for me, trees to talk
to me, sky to sing to me, birds and a white light
In the back of my mind to guide me . . .
—LOUIS MACNEICE, *"PRAYER BEFORE BIRTH."*

MODERN DEMETER

Hard to mistake Demeter. She's the one surrounded by kids; the one whom babies seem to hang on as from a sturdy tree; the one dishing out the peanut butter and jelly sandwiches; the one who *does* know where the diapers are; the one tending the bruised knees; the one happily cooking for the extra six her husband casually brought home from baseball; the one up all night tending that fever; the one with the seemingly inexhaustible reserves of energy.

The Demeter woman is, in short, the mother among the goddess types. Demeter is more than just a biological mother, though. It's not just having children that makes a true mother, it's an attitude, an instinctive way of caring for all that is young, tiny, needy, and helpless.

Demeter love is a totally dedicated and selfless form of giving and nurturing that we all recognize, however dimly, in the word *mothering*.

Of course, we might not have had such mothering as children; we might only know it through the archetype Erma Bombeck calls Everybody Else's Mother. But the longing is still there even if we didn't experience it, a deep, unshakable fantasy of that warm, enveloping, and utterly satisfying embrace.

It is important to understand what is unique about Demeter's mothering. We are not saying that the other goddesses cannot be mothers, but that to be a mother is the primary guiding principle in Demeter's life. All the goddess types can and do have children and mother them in their different ways. Aphrodite mothers in her indulgent, sensuous way, loving to dress her children up, spoil them with treats, and take them out to the movies. Artemis mothers in a rather fiercely tender, feral way, treating her offspring more like whelps than anything. Athena can't wait till hers are fully articulate so that she can talk to them and nurture their education and mental growth. Persephone, too, is deeply caught up in her children, but in a more psychic and intuitive way than in terms of their physical well-being. Hera's mothering is so full of rules, strictures, and expectations that there is little tenderness in her nurturing.

Yet it is only Demeter who is fully identified with the very activity of mothering, almost to the exclusion of most other concerns. That inexhaustible energy we noted is derived from her total dedication of purpose. She lives almost entirely for her children; she is literally on call twenty-four hours a day, seven days a week.

The Demeter woman is so caught up in being a mother that she neither has nor makes time to worry about getting a new dress or her hair done (Aphrodite concerns). She has not the slightest wish to go off alone (Artemis) and mostly hates the thought of leaving home at all. She has little or no interest in reading books or newspapers or catching the news on TV (Athena obsessions), nor the slightest concern about her children's horoscope or their past lives (Persephone fundamentals). Being on the board of the local planning commission (Hera priorities) excites her about as much as her husband's humdrum job.

Naturally the Demeter woman could find time for all or any of these activities and interests that are so dear to the other goddesses—she knows about baby-sitters—but the fact is, she really doesn't want to. She is happy and deeply fulfilled doing exactly what she is doing, being a mother.

Nothing illustrates Jung's idea that archetypes are impersonal sources of energy better than the Demeter woman. Even though she is constantly giving out to children, husband, and every stray friend in the vicinity, she never seems to tire or to think of herself. It is truly instinctive and unself-conscious, without any ego on her part. There is an open mouth—she fills it; a child is crying—she comforts it; a hand is bleeding—she puts a bandage on it. She is no more an individual personality when she gives out in this way than a mother bird or a mother cat is to her young; she is simply *mother*.

DEMETER, THE NURTURER

Other goddess types are sometimes in awe of Demeter's prodigious nurturing energy and her seemingly selfless devotion to her children and family. "Can she be faking it?" an Athena might ask. "Is she really so unflappable in the face of all that infant mess, noise, and chaos?" Hera might wonder. "How does she always have meals, clothing, lunch boxes, and pills there at the ready?" Persephone might ask in amazement.

Actually some degree of cynicism might be in order around the slightly saintly aura of certain Demeter women. America in the fifties developed a stereotype of the flawless mother in sitcoms like *Ozzie and Harriet* and *Leave It to Beaver*, which may have been a sentimental model for many mothers but an irritation to those who fell short of it. And yet, like all media stereotypes, these shows hit upon a fundamental aspect of the archetype, the selfless devotion of the Madonna.

What the other goddess types may not comprehend, if they have never experienced within themselves the incredible power of the mother archetype, is the deep, natural, instinctual fulfillment in everything that Demeter does. It is not ego fulfillment as Athena and Hera might understand it, nor even spiritual satisfaction, as in Persephone's book, but something quite unknown to any of them.

Closest in temperament to Aphrodite, her opposite on the Goddess Wheel, Demeter is ruled by love—not independence like Athena and Artemis, or power like Hera and Persephone. Like Aphrodite she lives for the other, gives herself for the other, loses herself in the other; it is the other that is the source of all her fulfillment, not herself. The only difference between Demeter and Aphrodite in regard to love is that for Aphrodite the other is the adult beloved, whereas for Demeter the other is the child.

Symbolically Demeter stands for everything to do with earth and vegatative nature; for the Greeks she was a goddess of grains and the mystery of planting the seed that will grow into new life and food. Later, when we examine her mythic background, we will see how multi-layered the Greek understanding of this mystery was. But for the moment let us note how deep her connection is to every aspect of the *life force*, particularly as it affects young, growing, and needy beings.

A healthy Demeter woman is always in touch with physical reality, which is to say the realities of the body and its needs, be they food, warm clothing, getting enough sleep, illness or injury, and—in little babies—needs to eliminate. She seems to understand all the basic instincts that belong to our animal and bodily nature. In this respect she is very different from Athena, whose awareness is very mental and often quite alienated from the body.

DEMETER GROWING UP

The Demeter instinct to nurture can easily be spotted in young girls playing with their dolls. It will be there in those elder sisters who derive pleasure from helping mother with the new baby. Not so much in Artemis, off playing with the boys, or Athena, with her nose in a book, or Hera, organizing some club that she will head. When Demeter is strong in a growing girl, she will be sweet, with a loving temperament appealing to all who know her.

Because the young Demeter is so identified with her mother, there will be an almost symbiotic relationship between them. Mother's values are totally her values, mother's dreams are unquestionably hers too. Whatever her mother's goddess style, the Demeter girl will model herself upon this. If mother loves to cook, daughter Demeter will excel at cooking; if mother raises pedigree puppies, she will too. But most of all she will idealize the style of mother's home and how she raises them all as children, longing for the day when she can replicate such a home and children for herself. (When, as will happen, a mother does not provide any role modeling for young Demeter, she will be obliged to become her own mother's mother. She will "carry" her mother emotionally, becoming rather old and serious before her time. Since she has experienced some of Persephone's "mother loss" very early in life, she may well compensate this loss by marrying and having children while still quite young. This pattern is evident in the burgeoning population of pregnant and mothering teenagers.)

In the healthy young Demeter, however, her worldly horizons will be quite limited by her fixed idea about home and family. During adolescence she will seem to be a sweet, but rather dull homebody to her other, more ambitious goddess sisters. While her Aphrodite sister is absorbed in teenage fashion magazines and the dating game, Athena is out campaigning for human rights, and Artemis is away at national athletic meets, budding Demeter is still mostly at home swapping neighborhood stories with mother.

Adolescent Demeter is not averse to the opposite sex. Her sexuality, as it blooms, is usually quite natural and uncomplicated, even earthy, though she sometimes risks being overly attendant to her partner's needs at the expense of her own. It is simply the nurturer in her that always puts the other first. She will often be as attractive as her Aphrodite sisters but in a quite unself-conscious way; hours in front of the bedroom mirror is not her style. "Be yourself" is her motto.

By her late teens young Demeter may already have a sweetheart she's going steady with, one she will eventually marry. He is likely to be a solid, dependable young man who intends to work in a local sales business that won't take him far from the hometown. Unless she herself has some idea about nursing or wants to work in a day care center, college will rarely figure in her plans. Occasionally she develops some practical skill, such as baking, catering, dressmaking, or pottery, that she can use close to or in her home, but just as often she will have no vocational ambitions at this stage in her life. In her dreams she mostly envisions a cozy home not too far from mother and, of course, those adorable babies that, it seems, she was born to raise.

Unlike young Hera, Demeter doesn't marry for position and prestige in the community; the "young man most likely to succeed" doesn't necessarily attract her. Basically she is looking for a worthy and reliable father for her children who will provide for them all. She may in fact be very naive about work and income for herself, hoping to leave that entirely to her mate. It is simply not in her consciousness to think about being independent and having a career the way Athena, Artemis, and Hera do so naturally.

Many a young Demeter mother whose marriage collapses finds herself in serious trouble as a single mother. She is unable to fit into an economic system that she is in no way trained for and that basically favors men. These are issues her feminist Athena sisters may have thought about theoretically, but there is a huge and unacknowledged gulf between the Demeter and Athena worlds. The busy single career woman in the city and the housewife in the suburbs, ferrying kids around, have little or no common ground in modern society. So, Athena's insights, brilliant and accurate as they are, come too late to divorced Demeter as she encounters the harsh realities of a social system that effectively punishes mothers who are not part of a marriage unit.

Part of modern Demeter's woundedness is that there is no place for single mothers and indeed for women with their children *in the world*; they have both been effectively banished from the world in order to maintain for men a sentimental abstraction called "the home and the family." Historically this is a relatively recent happening, but it is essentially an unhealthy state of affairs, one that we will return to later in this chapter.

DEMETER AND MATRIARCHAL CONSCIOUSNESS

In ancient Greece, Demeter was the preeminent Mother Goddess and had the specialized function of presiding over all forms of reproduction and renewal of life, especially that of plant life. An evolved and complex figure, she stands historically midway between the ancient Neolithic cults of the Great Mother, which flourished in Sumer, Asia Minor, Egypt, and Crete from approximately 4000 B.C. to 1000 B.C., and the Christian era in the West. She retains many of the characteristics of these early cults: she is a goddess of fecundity, fertility, and regeneration; she has a mystical identity with her dark underworld sister, the Queen of the Dead; she gives birth to a Divine Son, who remains her youthful consort rather than becoming a husband or mature equal.

Demeter's central symbol was the sheaf of wheat and, in her mysteries at Eleusis, a single ear of corn. We shall have much to say about the symbolism of flower, fruit, and seed, which makes her very much our Lady of Plants. Her sacred land animal was the pig—frequently a fertility sacrifice all over the world because of its multiple uterus. Her sacred animal at sea was the dolphin.

Demeter's cult is thought to have arrived in Greece from Crete via the early Mycenaean culture of the Peloponnesian peninsula. If this is true, then she is a direct descendant of the Cretan Mother Goddess, who flourished with her attendant maidens, snake-bearing priestesses, and bull cult during the third and second millennia B.C. In other words, Demeter represents the survival of matriarchal religion and its values well into the patriarchal warrior culture of the classical Greeks. The miracle is that the tolerant religious pluralism of the times did not suppress it. Instead, as historian of religion Mircea Eliade describes it, Demeter's religion came very much to complement the ruling patriarchal spirit of Zeus's Olympian cult.

The sanctuary of Demeter at Eleusis, where her Mysteries were celebrated, was in active use for nearly two thousand years. In A.D. 396 this, "the oldest and the most important religious center in Europe," as Eliade calls it, was destroyed by Alaric the Goth. In his wake came "men in black," the Christian monks. A certain local uncanonized "Saint Demetra" survived the Christian suppression, however, and is still known today. Eliade speculates that the spirit of the Mysteries did not entirely disappear, while Ezra Pound was convinced that the troubadours' spring celebrations of *kalenda maia* and their courtly worship of "the lady" drew upon remnants of Eleusinian worship that survived among country peoples of Europe (see box, "The Mysteries of Eleusis").

Another vestige of the old matriarchal consciousness of the Mother Goddess was transmitted in the popular Catholic devotion to the Virgin Mary among Mediterranean people. Almost certainly there is a psychic if not a cultural continuity between Mary, the Mother of God, and the ancient Great Mother goddesses of the Mediterranean and Near East and the goddess Demeter. But even though we know of many medieval representations of Mary with corn and flowers, she lacks the emotional power of the ancient Earth Mothers and their daughters.

Like everything else Christian, the Blessed Virgin suffered a severe

THE MYSTERIES OF ELEUSIS

The following is a very clear summary of the present state of scholarly knowledge about the Eleusinian Mysteries, from *The Road to Eleusis*, by R. Gordon Wasson, Carl A. P. Ruck, and Albert Hofmann, who speculate that the great vision of the initiates may have involved a psychotropic drug. This extract was written by Ruck.

[Every new initiate] walked the Sacred Road, crossing the narrow bridge that still today can be seen, now submerged in the brackish swamp that once divided Athens from the territory of its neighboring village, some fourteen miles distant, a region sacred for its special affinity with the realm of the departed spirits, who were thought to insure the fertility of the adjacent plain of grain. The procession of pilgrims symbolically passed the frontier between worlds, a momentous journey characterized by its difficulty. . . .

Each year new candidates for initiation would walk the Sacred Road, people of all classes, emperors and prostitutes, slaves and freemen, an annual celebration that was to last for upwards of a millennium and a half, until the pagan religion finally succumbed to the intense hatred and rivalry of a newer sect, the recently legitimized Christians in the fourth century of our era. The only requirement, beyond a knowledge of the Greek language, was the price of the sacrificial pig and the fees of the various priests and guides, and a little more than a month's wages, plus the expense of the stay in Athens.

Every step of the way recalled some aspect of an ancient myth that told how the Earth Mother, the goddess Demeter, had lost her only daughter, the maiden Persephone, abducted as she gathered flowers by her bridegroom, who was Hades, or the lord of death. The pilgrims called upon Iakchos as they walked. It was he who was thought to lead them on their way: through him they would summon back Persephone into the realm of the living. When at last they arrived at Eleusis, they danced far into the night beside the well where originally the mother had mourned for her lost Persephone. As they danced in honor of those sacred two goddesses and of their mysterious consort Dionysus, the god of inebriants, the stars and the moon and the daughters of Ocean would seem to join in their exultation. Then they passed through the gates of the fortress walls, beyond which, shielded from profane view, was enacted the great Mystery of Eleusis.

It was called a mystery because no one, under pain of death could reveal what happened within the sanctuary. . . . Ancient writers unanimously indicate that something was seen in the great *telesterion* or initiation hall within the sanctuary. To say so much was not prohibited. The experience was a vision whereby the pilgrim became someone who saw, an *epoptes*. . . .

[Demeter] was the Great Mother and the entire world was her Child. The essential event in these [agrarian] religions was the Sacred Marriage, in which the priestess periodically communed with the realm of the spirits within the earth to renew the agricultural year and the civilized life that grew upon the earth. Her male consort was a vegetative spirit, both her son who grew from the earth and the mate who would abduct her to the fecundating other realm as he possessed her upon his death. . . .

The final solution [to Demeter's loss] is to heal the universe into which death has now intruded by admitting also the possibility of return into life. Rebirth from death was the secret of Eleusis. In Hades, Per-

> sephone, like the earth itself, takes seed into her body
> and thereby eternally comes back to her ecstatic
> mother with her new son, only to die eternally in his
> fecundating embrace. The sign of the redemption was
> an ear of barley, the risen grain, that following the Mys-
> tery would be committed once again to the cold earth
> in the sowing of the sacred plain adjacent to Eleusis.
> —*The Road to Eleusis*, pp. 35–44

dislocation from the very earth itself; her honorific title, Queen of
Heaven, indicates that her divine nature was thought of as spiritual in
a "higher" rather than in a cthonic or earthy sense.[1] Even then, strictly
speaking, her status remains that of a divinely chosen woman, not a goddess. Whatever earth connections she once had have long since disappeared.

It is hard for us today to imagine what it must have been like to
have a goddess and her earth mysteries at the center of cultural and
spiritual life. More than two thousand years of Judeo-Christian culture
have accustomed us to thinking of everything divine as masculine and
somehow belonging "up there" in the heavens. As a result we have
almost forgotten what it is to regard the earth we walk upon as sacred,
as truly our mother, and as the dwelling place of both goddesses and
gods.

Outside of the cities, with their supposedly superior, "civilized"
consciousness, certain places—caves, springs, groves, mountains—
have always been felt to be sacred by virtue of the spiritual energy that
emanates from them. They were often sites of great and awe-inspiring
natural beauty. Delphi, where Apollo was worshipped, is one such place
that has survived virtually unspoiled to this day. All over Ireland, originally a matriarchal culture, there are many "holy wells" that, though
later benignly Christianized, were seen originally as the genitals of the

---

[1] Several Greek gods and goddesses are given the attribute *cthonios*, which means
"subterranean" or "dwelling beneath the earth." Some, like the spring-born Persephone
are thus "autochthonous," which means "born from the earth."

Earth Mother, from which the life force, the *woivre*, or "serpent power," flowed. The sanctuary of Demeter at Eleusis was also built up over a sacred well, where doubtless telluric or geomagnetic earth energy welled up and was felt by the more sensitive of the initiates into the mysteries.

Although Demeter is not strictly an Earth Mother—this title belongs to her grandmother, Gaia or Ge, whose name means "earth"—her myth and her cult belong very much to what happens in and beneath the earth. She and her daughter symbolize the dynamic cycles of nature that occur within the body of the earth and, by virtue of the mystical principle of correspondence, *within the body of every woman*.

Representations of Demeter are actually not of a huge, rotund, pregnant figure like many ancient Earth Mother goddess icons that have come down to us from the Neolithic Age. In all her stories and vase paintings Demeter is represented as approachably human and even modern in her iconography. According to *The Homeric Hymn to Demeter*, the goddess is tall, radiantly beautiful, "slim-ankled," and "golden haired" (like the corn). As a goddess she is awesome when fully revealed, but there is nothing primitive in this image of her. Like all of the classical Greek goddesses, hers is a highly evolved and many-sided psychological and symbolic portrait.

ETERNAL MOTHER AND DAUGHTER

When we talk about Demeter as she was imagined by the Greeks, we must really talk about two goddesses, not one. The heart of both Demeter's myth and her cult—the so-called Mysteries of Eleusis—revolved around her loss, mourning, and reunion with her beloved daughter, Kore (pronounced *kore-eh*), whose name simply means "maiden" in Greek. Nearly all the stone steles and vase paintings that survive show two mature women: Demeter and Kore together. They hold either sheaves or ears of wheat, flowers or torches, or combinations of both—and sometimes serpents (see box, "Robert Bly Speaks of Demeter").

This closeness of mother and daughter emphasizes how profoundly feminine this religious and mythological constellation is. It must harken back to those Neolithic times when, in matriarchal consciousness, the

ROBERT BLY SPEAKS OF DEMETER

The well-known poet and translator Robert Bly has done much to further goddess awareness in the United States. For many years he has sponsored a conference entitled "The Great Mother and the New Father" in rural settings all over the country. Here is part of an early, but widely read interview on the Greek goddesses as what he calls "transformers" of a woman's consciousness:

Let's take Demeter then first. A girl in ancient Greece found perhaps that her mother acted as her first transformer, taking her girlish energy and concentrating it in the feeling area, and also teaching her how to make babies and cooking pots, bringing her energy out into the full circle of the whole community, which may be only an extended family. Play energy is private energy, and that was lifted to a higher intensity. But the energy is still inside the house. It's possible her father acted also as a transformer, but I sense that with Demeter women the main power remains her mother. Her second transformer, still human, might have been a wise old woman, perhaps a grandmother, a sort of woman like Meridel Le Seuer, those old women in the tribe who know things, and help the young woman to ground herself. The second intensification leads directly to Demeter. If the woman is taking this path, Demeter comes along. Her statues show her as a strong woman with a powerful calm alert face. She has near her shoulders wheat stalks and snakes. The snakes are coming up from the grounding area; she isn't holding them, but they're near her, and there's no fear in the nearness at all, because the work has been done. Demeter is not a wife exactly, she's not concerned with the institution of marriage (as Hera is); she carries the cave energy in

undiluted form. The Demeter story was also connected
in a strong way (that no one entirely understands) with
the ability to stop being a girl. . . . Demeter was evidently useful in that area. Demeter lost her daughter.
Her daughter went underground, *not up*. Women spent
three days in the Demeter festivals weeping for the girl
lost when they became adult. Evidently it meant that
if you accepted transformation through Demeter you
had to leave your daughterhood behind, and that is a
terrible grief. Part of you went under the earth. She
taught women to weep about it. As soon as you weep
you're under the earth, and a part of all created things
that grow by loss, and at the same time you exchange
energy with snakes and wheat and pigs.

—"The Great Mother and the New Father,"
(*East West Journal*, August 1978, p. 27)

male was totally other and secondary. As Erich Neumann puts it in his
book *The Great Mother*,

> The close connection between mother and daughter, who form
> the nucleus of the female group, is reflected in the "primordial
> relationship" between them. In the eyes of the female group,
> the male is the alien, who comes from without and takes the
> daughter from the mother. (pp. 305–6)

Kore, the daughter, later came to be known as Persephone. Contemporary scholars cannot agree as to whether this Persephone, who
was queen of the underworld, was originally a separate goddess, whose
worship became assimilated into that of Demeter, or whether she is
merely another aspect of Demeter herself. We treat Persephone as a
separate goddess in this book only in the sense that when, in her mature
form, she became queen of the underworld, she acquired particular
powers and atributions that are unique to her. Psychologically we view

it as artificial and indeed dangerous for any individual woman to treat the goddess of death separately from the goddess of life. In fact, as our chapter on Persephone shows, when a women overidentifies with Persephone's closeness to the spirits of the departed and the death realm to the exclusion of the other goddesses, especially Demeter, psychic disturbance is a predictable outcome. For the moment, when speaking of Demeter, we shall refer to her daughter simply as Kore, the maiden, so as to distinguish the different perspectives.

What, then, was the story of Demeter and her daughter upon which the celebrated Mysteries of Eleusis were based? It is one of the most elaborate core stories of any of the Greek myths and one that we shall only summarize for its main themes and psychological dynamic. As for the Mysteries themselves, though much has been written about them, we have found most scholarly commentaries to be speculative and inconclusive (see box "The Mysteries of Eleusis") though at times richly suggestive.

The myth, as most fully treated in *The Homeric Hymn to Demeter*, runs as follows:

While gathering flowers with the daughters of Ocean, her other maiden sisters, Kore, Demeter's daughter, is abducted by Hades, god of the underworld, and carried off to his realm. For nine days, grieving inconsolably, Demeter wanders the earth, but neither gods nor men dare tell her of her daughter's true fate. Finally Helios, who sees all, tells her it was Zeus who had plotted with his brother Hades to let the Dark Lord marry the maiden.

Her grief now swelled to anger at Zeus, Demeter deserts Olympus and hides herself among mortals disguised as an old woman. She comes to Eleusis and sits by the Well of the Maidens. When the king's daughters question her, she tells them she has just escaped from pirates who have forcibly carried her from Crete. When she offers her services as a nursemaid, the daughters of King Keleos arrange for her to help raise the infant Demophon, son of the queen, Metaneira.

But Demeter does not nurse the infant Demophon. Instead, she rubs him with ambrosia and at night secretly hides him in a fire, for the purpose of making him immortal and eternally young. Before the ritual is completed, the horrified Metaneira discovers her son in the fire. Demeter berates Metaneira for her shortsightedness, saying that her son is now denied immortality. The goddess now sloughs off her disguise of old woman and reveals herself in full grandeur and beauty, so that the house is filled with dazzling light. She demands that the people build her a temple with an altar below it and promises to teach her rites to human beings henceforth.

Once her temple is completed, Demeter retires inside it and stays "far from the blessed gods, wasting with grief for her daughter." And now she sends a terrible drought upon the earth, which threatens to destroy the human race. She spurns all messengers from Zeus, refusing to set foot on Olympus or to let any fruit grow on the earth until she sees her daughter once more.

Finally, persuaded by Zeus, Hades relents, but not before giving Kore a sweet pomegranate seed, which she eats. By this it is agreed by Zeus that she will spend one-third of the year with her husband, Hades, in the underworld and the rest with her mother, Demeter, and other immortals. Mother and daughter are joyously reunited at Demeter's temple at Eleusis, and Demeter miraculously sends up fruit and foliage all over the earth. Finally, before returning to Olympus, Demeter instructs the inhabitants of Eleusis in her sacred and secret rites.

"Blessed is he among mortals who witnesses these things," concludes *The Hymn to Demeter*, "but whoever is not initiated into them or dies without them descends unblessed into the gloomy darkness. . . . And greatly blessed on earth is he whom the gods love for they send Ploutos with his abundant wealth to this man's great house."

THE TRIPLE GODDESS AND THE PSYCHOLOGY OF LOSS

According to ancient tradition the Great Goddess was always triple. Her triplicity is to be seen in the waxing moon, the full moon, and the waning moon, and in how she ruled the upper world, the earth, and the underworld. In human terms she was Maiden, Mother, and Crone. It is these major phases of a woman's life, and the other triplicities by analogy, that are encompassed by Demeter's story. For Demeter sees herself as innocent and untouched *Maiden* in her daughter, Kore. She is *Mother* of that daughter and of all that grows. And when she loses

Kore, she plays the old woman, the *Crone*, whose childbearing years are gone and who stands close to the end of the cycle, to death.

Corresponding to each traditional phase of the cycle are three great losses for every woman who bears children, especially a woman who bears daughters. All of these losses are hinted at in highly condensed form in this extraordinary myth:

First, as a young woman enters puberty, she must undergo the loss of childhood innocence; this is the inner "death of the maiden" that every woman to some extent experiences (and which every mother may be reminded of when she sees it happen in her daughter). This phase is symbolized by the *flower*.

Second, there is the loss a mother undergoes when her daughter (or son) is taken in marriage or leaves home permanently. The marriage of a loved first daughter is always a painfully wrenching experience, as every mother knows. Finally, when all the children, of either sex, have left home, she may experience an "empty nest" depression. This phase is symbolized by the ripe *fruit*.

Third, there is the biological loss each mother undergoes at menopause when she can no longer bear children. Depression often occurs in women at this time, whether or not they have been mothers. The fruitful phase in life has passed, whether or not it was made manifest, and a certain mourning is in order. Yet when successfully traversed, this loss can become a rite of passage into the mature wisdom of the older woman, whom the ancients called the Crone. This phase is symbolized by the *seed*.

Poignant as these three losses and their variations are, the myth also shows us that each of them is an opportunity for an awakening to a new form of consciousness; in fact, each of them is an initiation into the next phase of life. When the maiden dies, she becomes a nubile young woman and before long a mother herself, blessed with her own children. Many of the stone steles from Eleusis show the joyous reunion of Kore with her mother, Demeter. But she is no longer a girl; she is now a full-grown woman and with her is a young son. The flower maiden has now become a fruitful mother.

When the mother comes to the end of her own childbearing, she passes the torch of motherhood to her daughter, ceding the full power of fruitfulness. In dying to the mother in her, the aging woman now has the potential to enter the spiritual community of the elder women, the guardians of the mystery of death.

These phases are rarely completed successfully in the lives of many women today, partly because there remains so little consciousness of these issues in a predominantly masculine and aggressive culture. Nowhere do we find a vision of motherhood and the feminine cycle that is both spiritual *and* grounded in the body which feeds, nourishes, and inspires women as it did in the period when Eleusis flourished.

Demeter today is wounded to the same extent that our whole culture is alienated from the greater cycles of the earth and the lesser cycles of individual women. We have succeeded in reducing a mother to a convenient, if unpredictable biological reproduction machine that either helps or hinders (as in Third World countries) our relentless greed for power and wealth. We have taken the mother out of the community and workplace at large and confined her to a sentimental abstraction called the family. There has been little or no room for Demeter consciousness in our religious and cultural practices until relatively recently, and even today mothers and children are usually the very lowest priorities in any social or economic planning.

Nevertheless, signs such as the struggle for natural childbirth methods, family therapy, a new awareness of nutrition, and the awakening of "Gaia" consciousness of the earth as an organic whole (which Demeter shares with Artemis) may herald the slow, if painful reemergence of Demeter in our world. We may be a long way from the vision of the Greeks at Eleusis, which nourished the classical world for nearly two thousand years, but we hope that the commentary that follows, on the three phases of the Demeter cycle, will help modern mothers understand a little more deeply the sacred dignity of their calling.

THE FIRST DEMETER CYCLE: MAIDEN AND FLOWER

The opening of the *Homeric Hymn*, the earliest record of Demeter's myth, does not waste time with images of Demeter's domestic intimacy with her daughters. This is emphatically not a myth about mother-at-home; it speaks more of motherhood mirrored and enjoyed in the abundance of nature. For a modern suburban mother we grant that this may seem rather alien. Yet the emotional content is not hard to relate to. We cannot help but be struck by the intensity of the love and devotion between Demeter and her daughter as the narrative unfolds. Grief of such magnitude that it envisages an end to all life on earth can only arise from a great and surpassing love.

The love between Demeter and Kore is a lovely, unspoken secret that only a mother and her daughter can really share; men are not a part of it, they are in fact totally alien to it. No matter how much a doting father adores and is adored by his daughter, he is still far from a mother's love of her little girl. He did not bear her in his body; he cannot experience that great mystery.

Part of the secret is the sameness, the mirroring, the fact that when a mother gives birth to a daughter (as opposed to a son, who is other), she sees herself in the innocence, purity, and beauty of this little feminine being. Jung would say that the beauty and wonder a mother can see in her daughter is an awareness of her own transcendent feminine Self, the perfection of feminine being. Much-loved little girls inevitably grow up with all kinds of "princess" fantasies showered upon them whenever this archetype is able to outflow naturally from mother to daughter. The inhabitants of the island of Bali in Indonesia seem to understand something of this mystery. They insist that prepubertal girls are best suited to play the young goddesses in the sacred enactments of their myths.

Much of the antagonism that exists, alas, between so many contemporary mothers and their daughters happens when a mother sees in her daughter everything she never had as a child—her own lack of warm mothering—and her love turns to bitterness and envy. We write of this fractured relationship in our chapter on Hera, who is so strongly identified with patriarchal values through her marriage with Zeus that she becomes painfully alienated from her true feminine nature. The Hera mother's wound arises partly because she has lost touch with the mysteries of Demeter and Kore. What these mysteries once spoke to was the primordial unity and love between mother and daughter and a solidarity among women that reached back into the fullness and timelessness of matriarchal consciousness (see box, "Always Maiden and Always Mother").

The myth actually opens with an idyllic image of this primordial unity: the mother and her daughters are playing delightfully in a

ALWAYS MAIDEN AND ALWAYS MOTHER

The following is the complete statement of a noble Abyssinian woman recorded by the German ethnologist Leo Frobenius and cited by Carl Kerényi in his famous essay, "Kore."

How can a man know what a woman's life is? A woman's life is quite different from a man's. God has ordered it so. A man is the same from the time of his circumcision to the time of his withering. He is the same before he has sought out a woman for the first time, and afterwards. But the day when a woman enjoys her first love cuts her in two. She becomes another woman on that day. The man is the same after his first love as he was before. The woman is from the day of her first love another. That continues so all through life. The man spends a night by a woman and goes away. His life and body are always the same. The woman conceives. As a mother she is another person than the woman without child. She carries the fruit of the night for nine months in her body. Something grows. Something grows into her life that never again departs from it. She is a mother. She is and remains a mother even though her child dies, though all her children die. For at one time she carried the child under her heart. And it does not go out of her heart ever again. Not even when it is dead. All this the man does not know; he knows nothing. He does not know the difference before love and after love, before motherhood and after motherhood. He can know nothing. Only a woman can know that and speak of that. That is why we won't be told what to do by our husbands. A woman can only do one thing. She can respect herself. She can keep herself decent. She must always be as her nature is.

She must always be maiden and always be mother. Before every love she is a maiden, after every love she
is a mother. In this you can see whether she is a good
woman or not.
                    —*Essays on a Science of Mythology*, p. 101

meadow among an abundance of flowers. But like the paradisiacal Garden of Eden, this unity is soon to be shattered by the arrival of the
Lord of Death. This is the first loss, the loss of blissful, almost symbiotic
oneness of mother and daughter, a oneness that begins in the womb
itself, where both are, from the beginning of time, united at the very
source of life itself.

Carl Kerényi comments in his fine essay, "Kore," on how flowerlike
the very existence of these girls is, how, in their beauty and innocence,
they are doomed, like blossoms, soon to fall and fade. He quotes
D. H. Lawrence's poem "Fidelity":

O flowers they fade because they are moving swiftly; a little
    torrent of life
leaps to the summit of the stem, gleams, turns over round
    the bend
of the parabola of curved light
sinks, and is gone, like a comet curving into the invisible

How often do mothers find themselves quietly lamenting the all-
too-swift growth of their children? How soon we lose the priceless
moments of early infancy and childhood: those heartrending angelic
glances, those fleeting words, expressions, gestures, gifts. We try desperately to immortalize them in photographs, home movies, locks of
hair, mementos, reiterated stories. In this respect we are like the Demeter who tries to immortalize the boy, Demophon, in the fire. But
it does not work on the human plane, whatever the motivation. To be
a mother is thus to live constantly with a certain kind of loss, of learning
again and again to sacrifice the moment as the flow of life moves on.

KORE'S AWAKENING: THE DARK
MESSENGER FROM BENEATH

What happens to the Kore herself at this moment of separation? The blossom falls from the tree, to be sure. No longer attached fully to the mother, girlhood is at an end and a deep awakening begins. Pursuing our flower motif, we could attribute everything to the arrival of the male figure, Hades. A deflowering would certainly be an apt metaphor on the outer and social level, and indeed this will eventually be part of a young woman's initiation into marriage and sexuality.

Yet something else happens before the loss of virginity, something that practically all the commentators on Demeter's story have passed over in near silence. Something indeed happens that will change a young woman's consciousness of herself far more profoundly than any male ever can: she begins to menstruate.

Of course, we are not told this fact in so many words in the *Homeric Hymn* or anywhere else; most mysteries concerning the genitals are displaced or expressed symbolically. But to say that Kore becomes aware of the earth opening up beneath her is in effect to say that deep movements are starting to occur *within her own body*. The function of Hades is therefore to carry her downward into a new consciousness of the inner movements of her body as a woman, as a vessel of creation; the great life-death cycle that hitherto dimly and distantly belonged only to the outer world now dramatically announces itself from within her uterus in the form of her first bleeding.

A little-known fantasy film produced in Czechoslovakia called *Valerie's Week of Wonders* captures this momentous subjective experience. The film opens with Valerie, a pubescent girl, walking along a path in the country and suddenly noticing spots of blood dropping from between her legs onto the grass beneath. This startling sight initiates a series of semi-Gothic, fairy tale fantasies, which include a vampire who is pursuing her for her blood and witches who try to inveigle her into their practices.

Clearly Valerie's vampire is a version of Hades. Sinister as he may seem to Valerie, he is, from our point of view, a very helpful figure who illuminates the hidden part of the Greek myth: that Hades is the herald of the blood mysteries. Whether or not a young girl at puberty has been prepared for her first bleeding, her first reaction is frequently one of shock, especially if she has not been instructed to expect a large flow of blood. A quite understandable fear can easily arise that she has been wounded and may bleed to death. It is this that the unconscious picks up and personifies in the form of dark, threatening figures often bearing weapons, always lusting for blood in some sinister way. Another classic fairy tale version of this motif is Little Red Riding Hood, where the Hades figure is the wolf, Demeter is grandmother, and the Kore is dressed in the color that reveals the menstrual meaning of the story.

Our women clients recall over and over again horrified reactions to their first menstruation. "I woke up in bed with blood all over the sheets and thought I was dying," one might say. In hindsight we may laugh at ourselves, but that first realization strikes deep chords within every woman's psyche, however much she later rationalizes and sanitizes them. Unfortunately these primitive and intensely meaningful responses can also become extremely confused and distorted by the complex attitudes of the mother. It may be that our mother did little or nothing to prepare us because she herself received no guidance at this age. Or it may be that she reacted with that deeply ingrained bodily self-disgust that is so typical of our puritan culture. If we were lucky, the event may have been greeted by an embarrassed silence, or perhaps some mumbled pseudoclinical jargon somehow meant to explain "being a woman now."

Unfortunately for most women, the rich stream of feminine meaning that flows with the first menstruation is left unexplained and unhallowed, allowed at best to sink confusedly back into the unconscious. What should have been the first major initiation into the timeless mysteries of motherhood—a mystical identification with the body of the Great Mother who is life, death, earth, and cosmos—is instead an event of self-alienation and shame.

No matter how well-intentioned her mother, it is hard for most adolescent women to avoid some of the collective fear and loathing of the feminine function that has characterized thousands of years of Western patriarchal consciousness. The mysteries of Demeter and her daughter would most certainly put these matters in a quite different light had they survived, but alas, we have no equivalent of them today. Instead we must live with, in Jung's words, that "lack of psychic hygiene [that] characterizes our culture."

LISTENING TO THE WISE WOUND

It is our view, in line with Jung and many of the writers he has inspired, that most menstrual and gynecological dysfunctions can ultimately be traced back to the deeply negative attitudes with which so many women have learned to regard their bodies in general and their menstrual function in particular; what in short we might call the denigration of the feminine blood mysteries. Whatever the precise origins of calling menstruation "the curse," this and the many other derogatory phrases for the menstrual period reveal an attitude to the female body that would be regarded as profoundly pathological in any other culture but our own.

It was therefore an event of considerable importance when the first book to grow out of the *inner*, which is to say, the *psychic* experience of menstruation appeared in England in 1978. This was *The Wise Wound*, by the English writers Penelope Shuttle and Peter Redgrove. In the early seventies Shuttle had consulted the late John Layard, a Jungian analyst, for help with her chronic and severe premenstrual depressions. After carefully recording and analyzing her dreams with him daily over a period of several months, she found that their imagery closely reflected the actual movements in her menstrual cycle. She had rediscovered in the monthly lunar cycle of her dream life the recurring appearance of that inner figure who is, from puberty onward, the herald of menstruation, the figure we believe to have been enshrined in Demeter's myth and known to Greek women as Hades.

What is remarkable is that Penelope Shuttle's premenstrual symptoms slowly disappeared as the practice of listening to and following the inner motifs of her dreams spontaneously brought her into harmony with her monthly lunar cycle, what Erich Neumann sees as fundamental to "matriarchal consciousness" (see box in chapter 6, "Erich Neumann on Matriarchal Consciousness"). Inspired by these insights, she and her husband subsequently wrote their own unique psychology of menstruation, *The Wise Wound*. They found, among other things, that an inner masculine figure (identified with Jung's "animus") has a specific relationship to the menstrual period and to a mature woman's identity as a whole. The authors themselves attempt to describe this difficult and somewhat alien idea:

the energy that seizes the woman in certain circumstances, [is]
often personified in her dreams as a man, dark, mysterious,
criminal, or in her feelings appearing as a masculine-tinged
energy. We have shown that such an energy often appears during the woman's paramenstruum, and represents "the other
dimension" of female sexuality. . . . You could say that because
nature polarizes the sexes into male and female, the unknown
quality in a woman will be represented, likely as not, by a male
figure. You could put this another way by following Bettel-
heim, and saying that as infants we were "deuter," both male
and female in one, and at puberty in women, the male component went underground, as it were. If this last model approaches the truth, we can say that as each menstruation recalls
the circumstances of the first one, the menarche, the occasion
of one's other self going underground is recalled. (p. 119)

What Penelope Shuttle seems to have found is that by cooperating
with the downward movement in her menstrual periods, accepting the
death energy implicit in the shedding of monthly blood, she transformed what has so often been called a curse into a blessing. For one
thing, the authors found that the generative libido that might have gone
into a pregnancy became available for erotic and creative uses.

At some level the Greek women who pledged themselves to Demeter and her daughter at Eleusis must have understood the menstrual
level of the Kore going underground, for it was common to sacrifice
a pig while purifying oneself for the great festivals at Eleusis. The sow
with its multiple uteruses and the shedding of its blood into the earth—
there was a great sacrificial pit at Eleusis—doubtless enabled the
woman both to honor her own bleeding and, by ritual analogy, to
partake in the sacred bleeding of the Earth Mother herself.

Our myth tells us that Kore eventually returns to her mother and
that the earth is once more fruitful. Mankind and, especially, womankind are offered a great lesson in the suspension of the great cycle
of the seasons. They are taught that both death, in the form of Hades,
and Demeter, in her anger and grief, must be propitiated if the great
cycle is to continue. What is true of the greater cycle of the seasons
is also true of the lesser cycle of a woman's menstruation.

For in fact there is not just an annual but a monthly loss. The great
solar cycle of the birth and death of the seasons is replicated in a more

intimate dimension with the twenty-eight-day cycle of the moon, which grows, becomes full, and slowly dies. The last moon phase corresponds both symbolically and physiologically to a woman's menstrual cycle. A woman doctor we heard of described menstruation to her students in a woman's health class as "the weeping of a disappointed uterus." She hits exactly upon the most helpful attitude toward what is in effect a miniature death each month.

One of Demeter's teachings is that each woman, whether she bears children or not, must honor the monthly death and renewal that takes place in her body. It is an integral part of her cyclical nature as woman, as earth being bound mysteriously to the moon. Each month an ovum is released inside her and, except on a very small number of occasions in her life if at all, it will be shed, given back to the earth. Here is the meaning of the pomegranate for Kore; when she goes underground, she discovers the rich red fruit with its clusters of bloodlike grapes, a perfect image of ripe ovulation. It is a blood sacrament with the earth, no more, no less.

THE SECOND DEMETER CYCLE: MOTHER AND FRUIT

The beauty of the myth lies in the never-ending movement of return. Kore returns to her mother; the seasons always return; the inner cycle, with its potential for fruitfulness, returns every month with ovulation and the preparedness of the womb.

And when, one day, the mysterious inner union of male seed and female egg occurs, a woman's personal earth will begin to signal to her the second great initiation into Demeter: pregnancy. Later variants of the myth as well as accounts of the Mysteries tell us that Kore on her return from the underworld brings a child, a young boy. Maiden now becomes mother; the union with Hades as inner herald of menstruation and outer herald of sexuality is complete, and the next phase of Demeter consciousness begins. In a passage quoted in Jung and Kerényi's commentaries on the Kore in *Essays on a Science of Mythology*, (see also box, "Always Maiden and Always Mother") a noblewoman from an Abyssinian tribe describes this awakening with a dignity rarely found in the writing of European women:

The woman conceives. As a mother she is another person than the woman without child. She carries the fruit of the night for nine months in her body. Something grows into her life that never again departs from it. She is a mother. She is and remains a mother even though her child die, though all her children die. For at one time she carried her child under her heart. And it does not go out of her heart ever again. Not even when it is dead. All this a man does not know; he knows nothing.

The noble Abyssinian woman states for us two fundamental facts about this stage of Demeter consciousness that all too easily become lost among all the technicalities of modern scientific gynecology. First, pregnancy totally reorients and reorganizes an expectant mother's sense of her body. Second, a feeling relationship begins with a tiny being who is as yet invisible but who is, with growing degrees, literally and figuratively felt "beneath her heart."

Since it is not in any way our purpose to look into the ways and means of gynecology and obstetrics, there is no need for us to dwell on the organic changes of pregnancy and childbearing as such, except, that is, where they evoke subjective images for the mother herself. Inwardly she will discover ever-expanding sensations of containment, of being a vessel, of hitherto unimaginable hugeness. If ever there was earth as mother, she is it. A riot of physical upheavals seems to have overtaken her body too: she feels overflowing with milk, brimming with newly flowing fluids and juices, possessed by strange appetites, overcome by debilitating nausea; skin, hair, complexion, everything is different. It is all part of the great awakening of Demeter consciousness as fruit-bearing mother.

For many women their first pregnancy is as much of a shock as menarche was. Suddenly one's well-tempered and well-disciplined body is answering to wholly other laws of growth and aesthetics. When Jennifer, the coauthor, became pregnant with our daughter in an Athenean period of her life, she dreamed one night that she was up in the attic trying on clothes when she came across an old and once-comfortable suit of armor. When she tried it on, she found that *it didn't fit any longer*!

Nothing fits anymore with the advent of pregnancy: not clothes, nor food, nor ambitions, nor one's carefully cultivated self-image. Let us cite the memoirs of Isadora Duncan, the celebrated dancer, whom the goddess Demeter removed temporarily from an existence ruled mostly by Artemis and Aphrodite. For all her radical views about having children outside of marriage, actually bearing an illegitimate child brought on considerable ambivalence, not least about her physical self-image:

> August waned. September came. My burden had become very heavy. . . . More and more my lovely body bulged under my astonished gaze. My hard little breasts grew large and soft and fell. My nimble feet grew slower, my ankles swelled, my hips were painful. Where was my lovely, youthful Naiad form? Where my ambition?

After a painful forceps delivery Isadora gave birth. She describes her reactions on becoming a mother as follows:

> Well, I did not die because of it. No, I didn't die—nor does the poor victim taken timely from the rack. And then, you may say, when I saw my baby I was repaid. . . .
> During the first weeks, I used to lie long hours with the baby in my arms, watching her asleep; sometimes catching a gaze from her eyes; feeling very near the edge, the mystery, perhaps the knowledge of Life. . . .
>
> Little by little my strength came back. Often I stood before the wonderful Amazon, our votive statue, with sympathetic understanding, for she, too, was never to be so gloriously fit for the battle again.
> —cited in *Ever Since Eve*, by Nancy Caldwell Sorel, p. 82

DEMETER'S INNER HELPERS

The other great awakening of Demeter consciousness during the nine-month cycle is a psychic one. Potentially this is a great opportunity for introversion, the turning inward of psychic energy. This may manifest in quiet, reflective periods of time spent knitting clothes, preparing the baby's room, gardening, listening to music. It is a time when fantasies of the coming child may emerge quite spontaneously. They should be encouraged, since they contain much rich material for what is termed psychic nurturing—nurturing that is the prelude to the physical and emotional bonding that will take place soon after birth.

Little has been written or studied until recently of the interaction between the mother's and the fetus's consciousness, partly because the fetus was not supposed to be conscious. Yet the remarkable experimental work summarized in Dr. Thomas Verney's book, *The Secret Life of the Unborn Child*, makes it quite evident that the child overhears and absorbs all kinds of messages and feelings from the mother quite early on. A mother therefore needs to be very open with her thoughts at this period if she can; uncertainties and fears will of course surface, but they can still be faced and accepted as fantasies of the unknown, not as literal predictions.

It is helpful to realize, from the perspective of depth psychology and the unconscious mind, that it is virtually impossible for a mother to meditate on an approaching birth without images of its archetypal opposite, death, also appearing. For one thing, the collective unconscious of womankind, which an expectant mother taps into in her reveries, is full of the tragedies of lost children (see the closing of our Artemis chapter). Images of dead children, of monstrous births, fears of deformity, and more surface unbidden in states of reverie, but they are best understood as ghosts from Persephone's underworld realm, the accumulated residues of millennia of feminine experience rather than as individual precognitions.

Balancing these darker forebodings are dreams and fantasies of angelic guardians, of spirit guides, of benign ancestors, especially grandmothers and great-grandmothers, long since dead, who nevertheless appear as if watching over the great happening. Judy Chicago's extraordinary collective work *The Birth Project* is filled with imagery of the felt sense of the inner movements of pregnancy and the guardian forces at work before and at the time of birth.

As an example of the helpful nature of this introverted phase of Demeter consciousness during pregnancy we may cite Barbara, one of our clients who had a lot of anxiety during her third pregnancy. Encouraging her to record her dreams brought up many images of thieves breaking into her house, rearranging the furniture, and stealing things, such as clothes. This was easy to interpret; they were images of the inner physiological changes that disrupted her bodily equilibrium and prevented her from wearing certain dresses.

Then, near the end of her second trimester, Barbara decided to go roller-skating with a friend. She fell and badly bruised her coccyx, but in no way hurt the fetus. Suspecting that her accident had some unconscious prompting behind it, we encouraged her to explore her feelings about it: "I felt completely out of control for a moment or two," she said. "Now I'm afraid I'll lose control of my body completely." The symbolic message to her therapists was clear; she was out of touch with both her inner and her outer earth, which she exaggerated with her roller-skating accident.

On being asked to explore feelings of falling and going downward, Barbara spontaneously produced the following remarkable waking fantasy:

I fall through a hole in our driveway and suddenly find myself underground, where it's dark. When my eyes become accustomed to the dim light I see an old, old woman, a bit like a witch. She's been waiting for me to come, she says, for a long time. Although she's repulsive, I'm strangely attracted to her. She now shows me a huge caldron bubbling away. She says she's brewing babies and that she's the one who has power over life and death, which has been stolen from her. She's plotting revenge. She wants me to stir the caldron, which I'm rather disgusted by; it smells bad and has pieces of bodies in it.

The old lady is planning to get her power back, but she needs my help. I have to take a little brass potful of the potion and bury it in the public gardens near the herbs, under a full moon. The mixture casts a sort of magic spell all around, and I find my usual fear of being attacked by men in this park is completely gone.

When I return to the witch, she seems more subdued and friendly. She's glad I've done the burying. I'm now strangely aware of something being alive in the earth, as though emanations are coming from it. She says I've neglected to pay my dues, and when I ask her, "What dues?" she shows me a tree at the back of the house I lived in when I was eight. I used to believe fairies lived in a crack in the tree.

The witch tells me to climb in through the crack in the tree, and now I find myself underground again, though I have to climb on my belly to go all the way down. At the bottom there's a crowd of little folks who have me take off all my clothes and who bathe me in a huge tub of smooth, brasslike material. I feel like Snow White, since they are all little men. I feel wonderfully looked after and cared for, a lot like a baby.

Next the dwarves send me off, saying I must find something that was lost, something in a golden casket guarded by a terrible dragon. Now I find myself near another tree, an enchanted one from my childhood, where I once buried a bracelet and a silver dime. I realize this tree is one near some bushes where I would go hide as a little girl and defecate, unknown to my mother. Eventually she found out and punished me severely. I realize that mother was the dragon and that somehow I lost my "natural" connections to the outside "magic" world when she punished me and forced me to defecate inside.

Finally, the witch reminds me of the birth of my sister when I was six. "The knowledge of the mysteries was denied you when you were six," she says. (I realize I was deeply disappointed because my mother refused to explain her maternity top to me then.) "But now you must meditate on the process of knitting together in the womb. Enter into your own womb and observe the mysteries going on there. I will speak to you again."

Unquestionably this fantasy gave Barbara a whole new feeling about her pregnancy and her connection to her body. The inner witch, probably an image from the underworld of Demeter-Persephone as life and death combined, had in effect initiated her, by reminding her of her old earthy connections when as child she defecated to the Goddess and talked to tree spirits and when her lowest energy center was fully open, connected by the image of the tree. The underworld dwarves actually resemble a very ancient Greek cult of the Great Mother Goddess, associated distantly with Demeter, where she is assisted by grotesque little servants called the Kabiroi. The underworld mysteries of the womb retain their ambivalent quality, but Barbara is now connected to them through her creative imagination.

As a postscript, we may say that Barbara had her baby, a little girl, without complications and later wrote to us to say how very connected she felt to her daughter as a result of her fantasy work and how differently she now felt about pregnancy and about herself.

DEMETER'S FULFILLMENT AS FRUITFUL MOTHER

Whether or not an expectant mother finds the time or the inclination to go inward during her pregnancy to fantasize about her coming child and "to meditate on the process of knitting together in the womb" like Barbara will depend on many factors. Economic security is of course a major one; if she must work up until near the due date, there will be little opportunity for introversion, even though certain menial and repetitive jobs may actually be quite congenial to such an attitude. An Athenean or an Artemesian woman who is expecting will be so caught up in her extraverted life patterns that this possibility will usually be ignored or deemed unnecessary.

But regardless of the style of pregnancy, the birthing and the actual arrival of a child will mark an abrupt end to a period of either rumination or bustling unconsciousness. The pain of giving birth will often be a kind of initiatory transition out of the idylls of pregnancy into the exacting demands of real motherhood.

From the moment that she finds herself with her new baby, the timeless archetypal power of Demeter consciousness is fully awakened. The pains of labor fade like a restless night, and a rising sunburst of Demeter's all-embracing mother love beams warmly over the helpless and needy little being she has carried unseen beneath her heart for these long months. Many women have been known to change radically with the birth of a first child, despite all their prior fears and insecurities. Others, natural Demeters, awaken to motherhood quietly and confidently, as though everything in their whole lives had been leading up to this moment.

When Demeter consciousness emerges at this major turning point

SOME CONTEMPORARY
BIRTHING EXPERIENCES

Eunice Brinkley, Plainfield, New Jersey:

Shortly after I arrived in the hospital room, the doctor entered. He said, "Let's get this over with before your husband comes in." I said, "What are you doing?" He said, "I'm breaking the bag of waters. This will improve the quality of the contractions."

The contractions tripled and quadrupled. I was shaking in the bed. It was the kind of pain that shoots through and vibrates in your body.

At about a quarter to six, I began to push. I was absolutely thrilled. It felt so good to push—almost orgasmic. I was having such a wonderful time pushing; then they announced that I was going to have a Caesarean.

I started hollering that I was *not* going to have a Caesarean. What could possibly be wrong? They said, "Mrs. Brinkley, your baby's heart rate is slightly affected. We classify him as distressed."

I said, "But I'm pushing! I'm having this baby now!"

No one responded to me. They just started carrying on in a big rush and taking off all the monitoring wires and instruments and taking off all my clothes and shaving my stomach, and the whole time I was protesting.

I protested all the way as they rolled me through the hall—naked on the table—into the operating room. I protested up until the very moment they put me out with anesthesia.

—Quoted in *Mother Jones*, July 1980

Helen Bagshaw, English author and childbirth educator:

My first daughter and I were both abused physically and emotionally at her birth in an English hospital. Fear reduced my pain threshold to such an extent that technology eventually intervened, and my baby was yanked from my body. . . .

My second daughter was born at home . . . in my own bed, welcomed by a gentle midwife and a few loving friends.
—Quoted in Judy Chicago, *The Birth Project*, p. 195

Caterine Milinaire, singer:
The miraculous moment was when I started singing as a continuation of the breathing. I sing to earn my living, and I sang to bring about this baby like I have never sung before. Imagine a labor room with singing women, what a chorus it would be! Singing was a great outlet for my emotions during pregnancy and at birth. It took the place of self-pity. So, when you are in doubt, keep on singing.
—Ibid., p. 197

in her life, a woman's energy will switch, as it were, to an instinctive pattern of selfless extraversion; all her thoughts, feelings, and reflexes now become entirely adapted to the needs of her child rather than herself or anyone else. Her sleep and dream patterns now follow her baby's cycles too, just as her ears will become hyperattuned to every squeak and gurgle. Entertainment, reading novels, fixing the back porch (unless it is to be a play area), helping plan her husband's next sales campaign—*all* of these go by the board.

From the moment Demeter's energy fully takes over her mind—or rather her instincts—a mother will learn a whole new way of being conscious. She will develop a Zen-like capacity to be "in the now," dropping a ladle to catch a falling infant, for instance, or becoming an adept at juggling baby, bottle, telephone, and lunch box all at once in the appropriate way. She learns to "multi-track," as an expert mother and friend of ours once put it, learning to be blithely unattached to the completion of almost anything, be it pancakes, writing checks, telephone conversations, or her favorite soap opera.

To the woman we are calling the natural Demeter, much of this comes easily or is quickly learned. It is only a nervous Athena mother who reads Dr. Spock so diligently because of her fears of dire failure, or a Hera who dogmatically insists on the "right" way to do diapers. Natural Demeter was never much of a reader, and she certainly doesn't turn to books now that she has her children. She seems to "know" what is needed in most cases; she has a sort of folk wisdom, usually derived from her own Demeter mother. At a deeper level her seemingly tireless supply of nurturance, patience, and devotion to her offspring arises because as mother, every Demeter woman is identified with the archetype of the Great Mother herself. In ways it would never occur to her to articulate she feels herself close to the physical and emotional wellsprings of life itself.

Demeter's world, it must be remembered, is first and foremost the child's world, not the adult one. Primarily she is tuned into the preverbal and preegoic phases in her children, which is to say, their predominantly physical and emotional needs, not their intellectual development. Babies and small children fascinate her for what they are, not for what they will become. What's more, she loves to be identified with their infant level of consciousness. Her total empathy for the hardships of runny noses, overflowing diapers, knocks and scrapes, and so on is quite unfeigned.

The child-adult gestalt of Demeter's consciousness compared to everyone else's is actually reversed. To most adults, children's noises are a background babble they tune out; with Demeter it's the other way around. Many a husband or friend experiences mild consternation when a beaming Demeter greets their news of the new tax breaks, antipollution laws, or a terrific sale at Sears with exactly the same warm exclamation ("Oh, that's wonderful!") that she used moments ago for her toddler's latest creation.

It must be said that the endless resourcefulness, tolerance, and selflessness certain Demeter mothers seem to have acquired after two or three children arouses quite deep skepticism and not a little cynicism in other goddess types. For many women in whom Demeter is absent or deeply buried because wounded, it is tempting to mock the "saintliness" in a natural Demeter woman or look down on what seems to be her mindlessness. It is extremely hard for Athena, Artemis, and Hera types, who all have such highly developed egos and practical-cum-rational ways of functioning, to put themselves into Demeter's egoless frame of mind.

The fact is that mothering has little or no ego rewards. The same old chores have to get done over and over again without an iota of congratulation: baby's meal gets sloshed onto the floor for the ninetieth time and must be cleaned up; the soaking bed must be changed for the hundredth time. And as soon as one child grows out of it, guess what? Yes, there's another on the way, and Demeter starts all over again. And alas, for poor Athena, who measures everything as an achievement, there are no diplomas; sorry, Hera, there's no public recognition for service beyond the line of duty.

What, then, *is* Demeter's reward? Is she really so totally selfless, a saint in aprons? Of course not. If that is what we think, we are forgetting the center of Demeter's consciousness, her growing children. As the myth of Demeter and Kore indicates, Demeter consciousness is dual, it pictures both mother and child, and, as we have seen, it points to the continual pattern of growth and change. Demeter's fulfillment is unquestionably in the wonder of her children, in whom she lives, moves, and has her being. Her greatest satisfaction by far—above any amount of wealth, status, degrees, worldly achievements, power, fame, beauty, or glamor—is to see the lovely fruits of her womb well nurtured and have them grow up into happy young adults.

Naturally there is a side of Demeter that would like her children never to grow up, always to remain with her in the nest—this, we suggested, was why the goddess Demeter tried to immortalize the baby Demophon. But more often than not, Demeter's perpetual longing for children simply means that she will love to keep on having more. (The whole movement toward smaller families and strict birth control in modern society was not instituted by Demeter, but more likely by Athena and Hera.)

When she is bearing and raising children, the Demeter woman is at the very peak of her fulfillment as a mother. She proudly provides new life and hope for her community. In the ancient symbolism of her cycle, she embodies now the fullness of the moon, as well as the summer bursting with fruit and produce. The cup of the life force within her runneth over.

DEMETER'S INFERIORITY COMPLEX

As lovely as this picture of Demeter fulfilled as a mother is, it is far from being a universal one for most modern mothers in advanced Western urban industrial societies. The economic and physical demands of basic survival frequently require that pregnant women work right up to the day of delivery. Prenatal visits to a hospital or clinic focus on the purely physical, never the emotional aspects of the coming birth. The actual birth is often treated not as a natural process but as a medical emergency that requires a bewildering variety of impersonal experts and intrusive technology.

After the nightmare of modern birthing practices—amniocentesis, internal fetal monitoring, drug-induced labor, then caesarean section—which could easily leave her emotionally as well as physically scarred for life, the new mother is often obliged, again for economic reasons, to return to work almost immediately. Unless she is economically privileged, she can rarely afford time off from work for that precious bonding with her newborn baby. More often than not, pregnancy leave is disgracefully limited; no "civilized" country has a worse record than America in this respect.

And if a mother is able to stay at home with her baby—with or without a husband away working—for most of the day, she may find herself feeling horribly lonely, depressed, and desperate in her suburban high rise or small-town apartment house, with few other women to support her or share in the joys and chores of child rearing. To become a mother in most of Western society is, as Germaine Greer points out in her book *Sex and Destiny*, to fall considerably in social and economic status and to become, in many respects, something of an outcast.

Even in something as typically mundane as the television soap operas, having a baby means being out of the game, no longer really a part of the action. The main players in that version of contemporary reality are Athena, Hera, and Aphrodite, with their unending squabbles and competition. Without a strong element of Athena in her makeup to hold it together as a working mother, to become pregnant is for so many women to become sentenced to what has today become Demeter's contemporary prison, the home—where, as soap opera viewers, the very most such mothers can do is to wistfully look back into the world they have lost.

How is it that Demeter's sacred functions have come to be so demeaned and so neglected in the modern world? To answer this question, we must once more look back at the social history of the goddesses in the rise of the West.

In classical Greek times Demeter was unquestionably the closest descendant of the more ancient Great Mother goddesses who were worshipped by different names up to the second millennium B.C. in Egypt, the Near East, and the Mediterranean basin. Why didn't more of this primordial earth power come down to us from the Greeks the way their much lauded creations such as democracy, philosophy, and Greek art have? Part of the answer is that Demeter's kind of goddess energy was much less compatible with the goals of a rising patriarchy. Athena and Hera had much more to offer the men of that era, with their images of dutiful daughter and (more or less) obedient wife. Mothers were needed for the production of children, to be sure, but then as now they were relegated to the home and given little other status.

Despite the widespread and well-attested popularity of her cult in ancient Greece, Demeter was barely mentioned in Homer. True, she was given a position on Mount Olympus, but as with Artemis, hers is clearly a token membership compared with the honor accorded to Hera and Athena by Father Zeus.

Why is this? The answer is relatively simple. The early ascendancy of the Greeks was centered on the city-state of Athens, which was essentially a warrior hegemony. The land around Athens was and is extremely poor for agriculture, and much of their food had to be imported from all over the Greek peninsula. By the end of the Second Peloponnesian War of the fifth century B.C., so much arable land had been impoverished that the Athenians took to piracy and colonization to ensure a steady food supply, according to William H. McNeill's history *The Rise of the West.*

A sharp division slowly arose between the urban gods and goddesses (Zeus, Apollo, Hera, Athena) who reflected the values of a rising warrior patriarchy and the more traditionally rural divinities (Artemis, Dionysus, Kronos, Demeter, Poseidon, and Aphrodite), who were all essentially matriarchal and attached to the land. For the Athenians especially, the tension of this division was symbolized by two of their major religious festivals: one was the Panathenic Festival in honor of Athena, where thousands moved in procession *into* the city to celebrate the warrior patroness and protector of Athens; the other was the celebration of Demeter's Mysteries, when almost the entire Athenian population moved in procession *out of* the city to walk to the then country town of Eleusis.

This tension between the urban and the rural psyche is still with us today at a psychosocial level. In goddess language, this tension could be described in terms of whether we choose to give Athena and Hera or Demeter and Artemis a higher valuation in the ways we live. Since the nineteenth century all over the Western world the majority of the population has moved away from the land. Athena's culture of cities has therefore become the dominant cultural force; today, more than 80 percent of the American population is living in cities.

Demeter, who could be said to rule childbearing, mothering, and agrarian culture, has little power today. Midwives and home births are fast becoming a thing of the past, thanks to the heavily patriarchal structures in the medical profession. Motherhood is viewed more as an accident in the Athenian world than a blessing. Agriculture has been undergoing intensive semi-industrial capitalization for a century or more, breaking up most old country communities. Artemis's wilderness is constantly being destroyed and polluted; she, too, is mostly powerless (see Artemis chapter).

Demeter suffers particularly in the civilized eclipse of the old matriarchal ways that were once well nigh universal in peasant communities in Europe and early America. Individually, representatives of Demeter's way are largely inarticulate and cannot hold their own with educated Athena women who have political influence. The natural Demeter woman is not an intellectual; she neither reads books nor goes to town meetings nor participates in political groups for the most part. She is mostly silent and tongue-tied, therefore, when it comes to protecting her needs and her rights as a mother and primary natural educator of her children in the home environment. The broader identification with the earth and its cyclic values was lost so long ago that neither she nor any but a few of her ecologically minded Artemis sisters would even think to mention it (see Artemis chapter).

Unable to articulate such things, the Demeter woman who adores simply raising children is constantly sentimentalized, patronized, and disempowered by even her feminist sisters, whose stance is predictably Athenian and educated. The kind of schemes that are designed to put mothers back in the work force and make them economically independent of men are primarily Athena's conceptions; they mostly leave the Demeter woman feeling betrayed and pushed around. A Demeter woman, if asked, would choose a minimum of five years' paid work leave to raise her kids. And why not, she might say, in a society that truly honored motherhood?

DEMETER BETRAYED: A POWERLESS ROLE IN PATRIARCHAL SOCIETY

It is tempting, from our earlier caricature of contemporary Demeter and her children, to see her domain as entirely that of the home. But this is an insidiously modern distortion. Naturally a home is an essential part of the secure base that makes child rearing possible and effective, but it is only in relatively recent times that Demeter has been more or less confined there. In most African, Asian, and South American countries and many Mediterranean countries today women and children are still to be seen in the marketplaces, in the fields, and at the heart of their community and social life. Many Third World cities would be unable to function without the widespread involvement in commerce, agriculture, and production of masses of children who dutifully contribute to their extended families in many invaluable ways.

Not so in North America and northwestern European countries. Demeter is far less honored, and her children have been relegated to the home. It is all part of what Germaine Greer, in *Sex and Destiny*, calls "the anti-child thrust of the Western life-style." As many a proud young couple with their first cute baby learn, their old, favorite restaurants suddenly become quite inhospitable when they approach with stroller and diaper bag. Suddenly blue-collar diners and the ubiquitous McDonald's sign become warm and welcoming, whatever our former disdain for fast food before we became parents. By contrast, in restaurants in Italy and Greece, whole families can be seen coming to eat of an evening, and children are welcomed and known by name very often. In rural and small-town Italy, the evening *passeggiata* or stroll before dinner is traditionally a family occasion; often all three generations—children, parents, and grandparents—will be out together almost every evening during the warm months.

But for centuries now, urban Europe and America have been ruled jointly by Athena's Protestant ethic of hard work and achievement as well as by Hera's bourgeois pretensions. Demeter, the mother, and every aspect of rearing children are subtly and blatantly controlled and put down. In areas of social life where they may once have belonged, both mother and child today find themselves effectively ostracized. As Germaine Greer writes,

> Access to the adult world is severely rationed in terms of time, and in any case, what the child enters into is not the adult's reality but a sort of no-man's-land of phatic communication. Mothers who are deeply involved in exploring a developing infant intelligence and personality are entitled to feel that such a generalization is unjust, but even they must reflect that they share the infant's ostracized status. No one wants to hear the fascinating thing that baby said or did today, especially at a party. Mother realizes she is becoming as big a bore as her child and can be shaken by the realization. The heinousness of taking an infant or a toddler to an adult social gathering is practically unimaginable. A baby may be produced and brandished momentarily, but then it must disappear. Otherwise well-meaners begin cooing about its being time for bed; the more a baby chirps and chatters and reaches for necklaces and earrings, the more likely it is to be told it is a poor little thing. Restaurants, cinemas, offices, supermarkets, even Harrods auction rooms, are no place for children. In England, restaurants mentioned in *The Good Food Guide* boldly advise parents to "leave under-fourteens and dogs at home": their object in doing so is to increase their patronage by vaunting their child-free condition. The placing of children on a par with dogs is naughty but nice. (p. 3)

It is as though in being banished along with her children from the greater community, Demeter has been given an extra task—that of keeping and tending the hearth. In goddess psychology we might say that Demeter has been required to take on a role that strictly belongs to another ancient Greek goddess, Hestia (the Roman Vesta). In many ways Hestia represents a most important need in modern women, a need to center themselves at the sacred fire of the hearth, to compensate for all the frantic rushing, getting, and spending required by contemporary life.

Yet we must note that archetypally this is not Demeter's primary function, that she doesn't necessarily belong in the home in this way at all, that her authentic relationship to the life of the community was originally much more dynamic.

In the old farm communities that predated the industrialization of the West, a Demeter woman was happy to be an integral part of the gathering, harvesting, winnowing, storing, canning, preserving, and so on. Her life would be a busy round of preparing and processing food-stuffs and produce, both for her family and for the marketplace. In addition she would traditionally have the task of raising her children and cooking for all.

Hard as this life-style was, she would have been a pivotal and in-dispensable part of the whole economic and social structure of her small community. The Demeter woman of the old agricultural com-munities (along with her more rugged hunter sister, Artemis) had dig-nity, authority, and a broadly fulfilling life. All that has been lost in a society where everything is subservient to the economic demands of the consumer monolith.

The frantic style of urban industrial production, which knows no seasonal cycle, has long since succeeded in breaking up the old patterns of communal family labor. Modern work patterns spread commuters the most absurd distances across our sprawling modern cities. Such obligatory traveling physically alienates husbands, wives, and children for all but a handful of days a year. Meanwhile, brainwashed by two generations of consumerist propaganda, exhausted and demoralized by ferrying their children to and from school, sports meetings, or music lessons, women in the cities and the suburbs have lost all their interest in cultivation, and except in rural states such as Vermont, the old De-metrian arts of food gathering and processing have all but disappeared.

DEMETER'S MOST INTIMATE WOUND: BIRTH RIGHTS DENIED

One might think that if the Demeter woman as mother, natural edu-cator, and producer is thus denied any greater role in the community or society at large, then at least she and those close to her would be allowed the pleasure of bearing children without interference. But alas, not even this function remains sacred in a world of experts who are happy to rob Demeter of yet another time-honored matriarchal skill.

For all the pain and risk that accompany childbirth, the testimony of women everywhere who have borne children is, over and over again, that it is "the greatest event in their life." Bringing a child into the world is surely Demeter's greatest fulfillment and joy. And yet a function that has for millennia been very much the natural province of women has become, in the modern world, increasingly taken over by the medical profession and by men.

The takeover began in the nineteenth century with the professionalization of medicine. Up until then childbirth had been attended mostly by midwives. But most midwives were poorly educated and badly organized politically, a situation that has not changed fundamentally to this day. In America in particular the male medical establishment has worked, with great success, to minimize the power and role of midwives and has turned childbirth essentially into a medical specialty rather than regarding it as a natural process.

Delivery by caesarean section has nearly tripled in recent years. According to a bitter article by Gena Corea in the magazine *Mother Jones* entitled "The Caesarian Epidemic," there is a large movement among obstetricians to make all birth "from above"—by C-section, that is. Traditional vaginal delivery is seen as inferior, unpredictable, and therefore uncontrollable. Two enthusiasts of caesarean birth, Drs. John Suthurst and Barbara Case, recently wrote that "it may well be that during the next 40 years the allowing of vaginal delivery or attempted vaginal delivery may need to be justified in each particular instance" (*Clinics in Obstetrics and Gynecology*, London [April 1975]).

The outlook, then, is grim, and the experience of childbirth, despite the movements associated with Drs. Grantly Dick Read, Fernand Lamaze, and Frederick Leboyer, is one that is increasingly under the control of drugs, intrusive technology, and of course surgical intervention. Granted, as all serious critics of this trend do, that there are indeed legitimate reasons for medical intervention, the general feeling is that things have gotten hugely out of hand. There seems to be less and less possibility of relatively pain-free, joyous, and uncomplicated childbirth, even though this may well be a description of what is in fact both natural and normal. Despite an increase in birthing rooms in many hospitals, the general tendency is to excessively mechanize and depersonalize the birth process and to denigrate the woman in labor. Suzanne Arms's powerful collection of women's hospital experiences, *Immaculate Deception*, should be read by any woman contemplating a hospital birth.

Judy Chicago in *The Birth Project* gives us an excellent summary of the contrast between home and hospital birth clearly biased in favor of Demeter's view of things:

> Those who support home birth find the atmosphere of hospital births dehumanizing, pathological and unnecessary for the great majority of births. The medical profession as a whole has tended to see home births as dangerous. The one study done on comparable populations who chose prepared home birth as opposed to hospital birth found that the infant death rates were about the same for both groups, but that hospital babies suffered about thirty times the number of birth injuries (primarily from the use of forceps), four times as many infections, 3.7 times as many resuscitations (primarily because of the large proportion of births during which the mother is sedated). (p. 196)

The home birth movement, because of deliberate maneuvering to disempower midwives by the medical establishment, seems to be foundering. Alas, as we write, this antagonism has some of the hallmarks of a modern witch-hunt in certain American states. The medical profession so often sounds like the last and worst bastion of patriarchal authoritarianism. An institution theoretically dedicated to the protection of life seems all too frequently concerned only with the protection of its own tarnished power.

As the gentlest of all the goddesses, Demeter can often do little more than suffer in silence at these indignities. She can only hope and pray that as more goddess awareness emerges in our time, her Artemis and Athena sisters will come to her aid on the political and professional front. Perhaps qualified and experienced midwives will one day be restored to their primary and time-honored place beside every laboring mother. Perhaps mothers will rediscover once more the mutual harmony of working together in small shared communities where they can support each other in birthing and caring for children. Perhaps birth will once more be honored as the great woman's mystery that it is. Until that day, the wounded as well as the awakened Demeter deep within every mother can only weep for this great loss.

THE THIRD DEMETER CYCLE: FROM GRANDMOTHER TO GREAT MOTHER

As we were completing this chapter, a synchronistic event happened, which is to say, we became aware of a symbolically meaningful coincidence. An extended family moved into an apartment near our home. It was a young family from India: mother, father, young child—and a *grandmother*, whose job it is to look after the infant boy while her daughter and son-in-law are out working all day.

Meeting this lovely older Indian woman, traditionally dressed in her sari and with the ritual gray marking of older women in the middle of her forehead, reminded us of a missing dimension in the Demeter cycle for the average American and Western family. We have forgotten what an important role the older generation of women can play in the third and last stage that completes the great cycle of a woman's life.

The tradition of the grandparents living with a young family lingers on in many black and Hispanic communities all over America as well as in some families of Italian descent. But as more such families adopt "the American way," these remnants of the older, traditional, extended family styles disappears. Sadly, the American way that becomes their model is predominantly the way of successful Anglos with their Athenian urban values, their relentless Protestant work ethic, and their shrinking and often fragmented nuclear family structure. To be economically efficient, such families must live in smaller and smaller units and spend less and less time close to their parents or their family community as a whole.

For these reasons most harassed young mothers today rarely know the comfort and friendly support of having their own mother around helping to raise the kids and run the household. At one time a young mother could feel confident and secure knowing that she could turn to the older and often wiser figure of her mother whenever crises arose

THE GRANDMOTHERS

They moved like rivers in their mended stockings,
Their skirts, their buns, their bodies grown
Round as trees. Over the kitchen fires
They hoarded magics, and the heavy bowls
Of Sunday bread rose up faithful as light.
We smiled at them, although they never spoke.
Silent as stones, they merely stared when birds
Fell in the leaves, or brooms wore out, or children
Scraped their knees and cried. Within my village,
We did not think it odd or ask for words;
In their vast arms we knew that we were loved.
I remember their happiness at the birth of children.
I remember their hands, swollen and hard as wood;
And sometimes in summer when the night
Was thick with stars, they gathered in the garden.
Near sleep, I watched them as they poured the wine,
Hung paper lanterns in the alien birches.
Then one would take a tiny concertina
And cradle it against her mammoth apron,
Till music hung like ribbons in the trees
And round my bed. Oh, still within my dreams
Softly they gather under summer stars
And sing of the far Danube, of Vienna,
Clear as a flight of wild and slender girls!
                    —Mary Oliver, *No Voyage Out and Other Poems*

in the home. But today such solidarity between the two generations is relatively rare because so many mothers are, and have been, alienated from each other for several generations now.

We believe that this alienation of mothers and daughters can be traced back, at least at one level of society, to the Industrial Revolution in Europe, when many peasant communities were driven from the land to be semienslaved in the industrial cities and when women thereby ceased to be the emotional and productive center of family life. Up to this time, the ties between mothers, daughters, and grandmothers were largely unbroken because they all lived close together in the same village communities. Life for the majority of the population was lived close to the soil, to the animals, and to nature. And even if there were no visible mother mysteries, the great cycle of the seasons was still celebrated in a mixture of old pagan and semi-Christian festivals— winter fire festivals, May Day, harvest home, and so forth.

It was the solidarity between all three generations of women that the Greek Mysteries of Demeter and her daughter, Kore, celebrated. Their continuity was reinforced ritually in the mystical death and re-birth of the corn maiden and her grieving mother, who embodied the greater cycles of the earth and the seasons. What this meant psycho-logically for women who once took part in these ceremonies has been described with great insight by Jung:

> Demeter and Kore, mother and daughter, extend the fem-inine consciousness both upwards and downwards. They add an "older and younger," "stronger and weaker" dimension to it and widen out the narrowly limited conscious mind bound in space and time, giving it intimations of a greater and more comprehensive personality which has a share in the eternal course of things. . . . We could therefore say that every mother contains her daughter in herself and every daughter her mother, and that every woman extends backwards into her mother and forwards into her daughter. This participation and intermingling give rise to that particular uncertainty as regards *time*: a woman lives earlier as a mother, later as a daughter. The conscious experience of these ties produces the feeling that her life is spread out over generations—the first step towards the immediate experience and conviction of being outside time,

which brings with it a feeling of *immortality*. The individual's life is elevated into a type, indeed it becomes the archetype of woman's fate in general. This leads to a restoration or *apocatastasis* of the lives of her ancestors, who now, through the bridge of the momentary individual, pass down into the generations of the future. An experience of this kind gives the individual a place and a meaning in the life of the generations, so that all unnecessary obstacles are cleared out of the way of the life-stream that is to flow through her. At the same time the individual is rescued from her isolation and restored to wholeness. All ritual preoccupation with archetypes ultimately has this aim and this result.

—"Psychological Aspects of the Kore,"
in *Essays on a Science of Mythology*, p. 162

When a woman passes childbearing age, she is psychically ready to become a grandmother. This means she can not only support her daughter in the chores of raising her children but also have a special kind of relationship with her grandchildren and especially her granddaughter. This relationship is not about physical nurturing—that is truly mother's job—but potentially about things spiritual. Because she is one step removed from mother, as it were, she can embody that bridge to the ancestors, to the "old ones."

As she reflects upon her daughters and her grandaughters, she may see the successive phases of her own earlier life. And in reminiscing about her own childhood she may remember her own grandmother with stories of bygone generations. And so the great mystery of generational time that Jung hints at, the fantasies and dreams of the ancestors, the momentary glimpses into the timeless realm of the Mothers, is awakened (see box, "The Grandmothers").

THE FINAL MYSTERY: THE ETERNAL SEED FORM

All this is part of the half-forgotten psychology of the third phase of Demeter's life cycle, as she opens to the Crone, the old wise one within her. It is part of the unwritten inner psychology of menopause. We would speculate that at this deeper level, many of the tribulations of menopause—depressions, marital tensions, hysterectomies—arise because a woman in whom Demeter is wounded yet strong or otherwise unfulfilled is not ready to make the second great transition, to let go of the fecund mother in her and go on to the next phase of Crone, or female elder.

As the last of the three phases of Demeter's life cycle, the Crone will inevitably be closer to the aspect of the Great Goddess who rules the underworld and death, whom we have called the mature Persephone (see Persephone chapter). But strictly speaking it does not seem to us that the Demeter woman herself need ever become identified with this awesome form of Persephone in the final phase unless tragedy or permanent depression overtakes her.

In the myth, we may remember, Demeter the goddess disguises herself as a crone at Eleusis. In grieving for her lost daughter, she shares everywoman's experience of the loss of fecundity, magnifying it so that it is felt by all as the universal barrenness she projects upon the whole earth. In this way she shows to all the depth of rage and grief that can potentially overwhelm any woman when her fruitfulness dies within her and she is faced with the irreversible fact that she is now a Crone. Grief, rage, and loss may therefore erupt as part of a natural transition from the second to the third phase of Demeter's cycle, especially for women in whom Demeter is strong, who made having children the emotional center of their lives.

The Demeter woman who passes menopause without setback strikes us as more likely to encounter the spirit of a different archetypal energy, that of the moon goddess Hecate, who was a kind of helpful mentor to Kore when she descended into the underworld to become Hades' bride.

It is Hecate who helps the mature Kore return from the underworld, bringing with her flaming torches—another major motif of the Eleusinian Mysteries. She can be seen as, first, the symbolic "enlightener" of the young mother when she is reborn from maidenhood, passing from new to full moon. Hecate, according to Carl Kerényi, completes the triad of Maiden, Mother, and Crone. She is thus the wise older woman that the Demeter woman becomes in the completion of her cycle.

Moreover, as Crone and moon goddess, Hecate actually oversees and integrates every aspect of Demeter-Kore's various transformations. This is because she is in fact the Triple Goddess herself and thus the mythic link to the totality of the Great Mother herself. We agree with Kerenyi that this is the more likely reason why the Kore has to spend one-third of her life in the underworld. She must include in her larger consciousness an awareness of death and spirit world, to be sure. But this does not mean that she must become fully identified with this realm and become solely Persephone, queen of the netherworld.

In looking at Demeter's myth we have seen how symbolically the flower cycle of the Maiden yielded to the fruitful cycle of the Mother. Now this must yield to the third and final phase of the cycle, when the fruit becomes the seed. In both transitions there is a psychic death and a deep loss; they are both occasions, therefore, for a certain mourning to occur.

So little is known for sure about what was actually performed during the Mysteries of Eleusis that we have avoided speculating and choosing among the many learned commentaries available. But as our interpretation shows, we do not think that Eleusis was simply about the renewal of agricultural fertility. Agriculture was certainly the symbolic language of the Mysteries, but in our opinion what it points to is the greater mystery of life itself, a mystery that is ultimately couched in feminine agrarian imagery.

On one fact, however, most of the commentators agree: at the culmination of the secret sacred drama that was enacted at Eleusis a single ear of wheat was held aloft in silence. For the initiates this must therefore have been the ultimate symbol of what they were seeking, in some way it was the symbolic reassurance of that which would endure beyond the death of the fruit. The great Indian mystical poet Kabir was surely close to the inner meaning of this act in the following poem (so beautifully translated by Robert Bly, one of our favorite interpreters of the Mother mysteries):

Student, do the simple purification.
You know that the seed is inside the horse-chestnut tree
and inside the seed there are the blossoms of the tree,
    and the chestnuts, and the shade.
So inside the human body there is the seed, and
    inside the seed there is the human body again . . .

It is a common theme in mystical literature that the very tiniest thing, such as a seed or a grain of sand, contains the whole universe. Dame Juliana of Norwich, the medieval English mystic, once had a vision of the All as the size of a hazelnut, for example. This same great lady was also famous for saying that "God is our Mother"—a remark that somehow escaped patriarchal censorship!

What such images surely convey to the initiate, to the grandmother approaching death, and to whoever meditates upon them, is that each part of the cycle contains the whole just as the whole contains the part. When, at the end of her life, a woman finally dies and her spirit goes to the underworld, the Mysteries seem to say that a part of her will nevertheless return embodied in her female descendants. This is not reincarnation in the Oriental sense or as understood by contemporary metaphysics, but more a genetic, ancestral form of eternal return. As T. S. Eliot put it toward the end of his life:

We die with the dying:
See, they depart and we go with them.
We are born with the dead:
See, they return, and bring us with them.
                              —from "Little Gidding," *Four Quartets*

All this can be only dimly hinted at because so much has been forgotten. Our culture has profaned the Earth Mother so extensively that today we risk the worldwide poisoning of our species from pollution of the earth and the air. A poignant example is Eleusis itself: the old shrine, now a tourist curiosity, is surrounded by an industrial seaport with oil refineries that have made it one of the most polluted sites in the whole Mediterranean.

Yet there are hopeful signs of a revival of Demeter consciousness. Books such as Monica Sjöö and Barbara Mor's *The Great Cosmic Mother: Rediscovering the Religion of Earth* are appearing, while teachers such as Starhawk, Jean Shinoda Bolen, and Jean Houston are inspiring women all over the world with their workshops on women's mysteries. Everywhere new generations of young mothers, married and single, are experimenting with new and creative ways of mothering and raising their children in the midst of our complex and fragmented society. Against all odds, and in the face of every imaginable perversion and desecration, the great river of life that is Demeter flows ever onward. Our prayer is that it continues to be felt and honored deep within the body and blood of women everywhere.

PART TWO

INTEGRATING THE GODDESSES

EIGHT

WHICH GODDESS ARE YOU RULED BY? USING THE GODDESS WHEEL QUESTIONNAIRE

In this section we include a self-rating questionnaire to help you discover which goddess influences are most powerful in your life today.

Even if you have already identified yourself (or your partner) from the Goddess Wheel, the questionnaire will help you to focus more precisely on different aspects of goddess psychology in your or your partner's personality.

We don't pretend that this is an objective test, but simply a self-rating scale. It is only accurate to the extent that you are honest with yourself. It will help you assess which goddesses are strong in you (or your partner) and which ones are undeveloped, repressed, or wounded.

INSTRUCTIONS FOR
HOW TO RATE YOURSELF

Women: simply read the six statements in each section. Next rate *how much* or *how little* each statement applies to you and *circle* an appropriate number. The key below explains the number ratings.

Men: simply assess *how much* or *how little* the six statements apply to the woman or type of woman you are most drawn to. Then *circle* an appropriate number based on the rating key.

KEY TO THE SELF-RATING SCALE

3 = Strongly applies
2 = Moderately applies
1 = Mildly applies
-1 = Not true at all

When you have completed the questionnaire, there are self-scoring charts at the end to help you determine your Goddess Profile.

QUESTIONNAIRE

Rating Scale

ONE: *Appearance*   *How I look / How she looks*

A   Since I don't go out a lot, clothes and makeup
      aren't that important to me.   3 2 1 -1
B   I much prefer to be dressed in jeans and
      comfortable shirts.   3 2 1 -1
C   My appearance is rather unconventional.   3 2 1 -1
D   I like to be well, but conservatively dressed and
      use makeup sparingly.   3 2 1 -1
E   I love to make myself up and be attractive.   3 2 1 -1

F   Being well dressed and made up gives me
    confidence to go out into the world.   3 2 1 −1

TWO: *My Body*   *How I feel about it / How she feels about it*

A   I tend not to think about my body.   3 2 1 −1
B   My body feels best when I'm fit and active.   3 2 1 −1
C   I like my body to be touched a lot by those I
    love.   3 2 1 −1
D   I'm often not in my body at all.   3 2 1 −1
E   I find it embarrassing to talk about my body. 3 2 1 −1
F   I love being pregnant / I look forward to being
    pregnant.   3 2 1 −1

THREE: *House and Home*   *What matters to me / What matters to her*

A   I much prefer my home to be elegant and
    impressive.   3 2 1 −1
B   I much prefer the city; an apartment is fine. 3 2 1 −1
C   My home must be warm and have room for
    everyone.   3 2 1 −1
D   I need privacy and space for the things I like to
    do.   3 2 1 −1
E   Wherever I live must be comfortable and
    beautiful.   3 2 1 −1
F   I prefer to live in the country or where I am
    close to parks and open spaces.   3 2 1 −1

FOUR: *Eating and Food*   *Its importance to me / Its importance to her*

A   I eat carefully to keep my body healthy.   3 2 1 −1
B   I like to dine somewhere romantic.   3 2 1 −1
C   I like to eat out a lot and be able to talk. 3 2 1 −1
D   I really enjoy cooking for others.   3 2 1 −1
E   Mealtimes are important family occasions.   3 2 1 −1
F   Eating isn't terribly important to me.   3 2 1 −1

FIVE: *Childhood*   *How I used to be / How she used to be*

A   I had lots of secret games and imaginary worlds. 3 2 1 −1

B	I always ran all the games with my friends.	3	2	1	−1
C	I mostly loved to play with dolls.	3	2	1	−1
D	I always had my nose in a book as I got older.	3	2	1	−1
E	I loved to be outdoors and with animals.	3	2	1	−1
F	I loved changing clothes and playing dress-up.	3	2	1	−1

SIX: Men   *What I need in one / What she needs in one*

A	I want a man who will always excite me sexually.	3	2	1	−1
B	I want a man to protect and spoil me.	3	2	1	−1
C	I like a man who is independent and gives a lot of space.	3	2	1	−1
D	I need a man who will challenge me mentally.	3	2	1	−1
E	I need a man to understand my inner world.	3	2	1	−1
F	I want a man whose position in the world I can be proud of.	3	2	1	−1

SEVEN: Love and Marriage   *What they mean to me / What they mean to her*

A	Marriage only works when there is a higher spiritual connection.	3	2	1	−1
B	Marriage is the foundation of society.	3	2	1	−1
C	Love is all-important; without it my marriage is empty.	3	2	1	−1
D	Love and marriage are fine, so long as I have plenty of freedom.	3	2	1	−1
E	Marriage safeguards my children; love alone is not enough.	3	2	1	−1
F	My marriage sometimes has to be sacrificed for the sake of my work.	3	2	1	−1

EIGHT: Sexuality   *How I am in bed / How she is in bed*

A	It's sometimes hard to let myself go fully during sex.	3	2	1	−1
B	I get turned on very easily by the right man.	3	2	1	−1
C	It sometimes takes me a while to get into my body.	3	2	1	−1
D	I love to give sexually as much as to receive.	3	2	1	−1

E   I'm a bit shy, but I can be very wild.   3 2 1 −1
F   Sex can be ecstatic and almost mystical for me.   3 2 1 −1

NINE: **Children**   *Their role in my life / Their role in her life*
       (If you do not have children, then *imagine* how it would be)

A   I'm happiest when doing things outdoors with my
       kids.   3 2 1 −1
B   My children are the greatest fulfillment of my
       life.   3 2 1 −1
C   I expect my children to be a great credit to me.   3 2 1 −1
D   I choose not to have children so that I can pursue
       my career.   3 2 1 −1
E   I love my kids, but my love life is equally
       important.   3 2 1 −1
F   I love my children and always want to know what
       they're feeling and thinking.   3 2 1 −1

TEN: **Pastimes**   *Types of things I like to do / Types of things she likes
         to do*

A   Metaphysics, tarot reading, astrology, dream
       journal, New Age workshops, personal art and
       rituals.   3 2 1 −1
B   Collecting jewelry, art objects, beautiful clothes;
       fashion, music, theater.   3 2 1 −1
C   Sports, athletics, jogging, camping, fishing,
       sailing, horseback riding.   3 2 1 −1
D   Community involvement, social clubs, volunteer
       groups, local church.   3 2 1 −1
E   Political campaigning, minority group support,
       museums, lecture series, reading.   3 2 1 −1
F   Cooking, baking, gardening, tending plants,
       needlework, weaving.   3 2 1 −1

ELEVEN: **Parties**   *How I am at them / How she is at them*

A   I usually get into political or intellectual
       discussions.   3 2 1 −1

B	I'll often be drawn to people with problems.	3	2	1	−1
C	I much prefer to be the hostess at my own parties.	3	2	1	−1
D	I can't help sizing up the sexiest men in the room.	3	2	1	−1
E	I like to make sure that people have a good time.	3	2	1	−1
F	Parties make me restless so I don't go to too many.	3	2	1	−1

TWELVE: **Friends**   *Their place in my life / Their place in her life*

A	Most of my friends have children the same age as mine.	3	2	1	−1
B	I choose my friends carefully and they are very important to me.	3	2	1	−1
C	I enjoy my latest ideas and projects with both my women and my men friends.	3	2	1	−1
D	I tend to have magical friendships.	3	2	1	−1
E	My friends are mostly the wives of my husband's friends.	3	2	1	−1
F	My men friends are generally more important to me than my women friends.	3	2	1	−1

THIRTEEN: **Books**   *What I mostly have around / What she mostly has around*

A	Cookbooks, craft books, child care books.	3	2	1	−1
B	Serious nonfiction, biographies, coffee table books, travel books, illustrated history.	3	2	1	−1
C	New Age books, psychology, metaphysics, channeled books, I Ching.	3	2	1	−1
D	Sports, fitness, and yoga manuals, animal books, wildlife books, how-to books.	3	2	1	−1
E	Art books, popular biographies, novels, romances, poetry.	3	2	1	−1
F	Politics, sociology, recent intellectual books, avant-garde literature, feminist books.	3	2	1	−1

*FOURTEEN: **The Larger World** My attitude toward it / Her attitude*
        toward it

A   I always try to stay informed about what's going
        on in the world.   3 2 1 −1
B   Politics only interest me for the intrigues behind
        the scenes.   3 2 1 −1
C   I know more about the world from my dreams
        than from newspapers or TV.   3 2 1 −1
D   I rarely know what's going on—or care!   3 2 1 −1
E   It's mostly a man's world, so I leave them to it.   3 2 1 −1
F   It's important for me to play an active role in the
        community.   3 2 1 −1

SCORING: HOW TO DETERMINE YOUR GODDESS PROFILE

1. Cut out or photocopy the Rating Sheet on page 330.

2. Go through the questionnaire, redistributing each of your six ratings for each section among the six goddess columns. You will find the six letters, A–F, arranged under the name of the goddess they belong to.

Simply enter the score you wrote for a particular statement next to its letter.

	Example:	Athena	Demeter	Etc.
		1 = D: 2	1 = C: −1	
		2 = F: 1	2 = A: −1	
		3 = B: 3	3 = C: 1	
		etc.	etc.	

3. Now add up your scores for each goddess column. This will give you a Goddess Quotient for each of the goddesses. Goddesses that are strong in you will naturally be high scores, while undeveloped or disowned goddesses may be low or minus scores.

4. Finally, copy your six Goddess Quotients onto the Goddess Wheel. Now you have a graphic representation of the goddesses within you. This is your Goddess Profile.

GODDESS RATING SHEET

Athena	Aphrodite	Persephone	Artemis	Demeter	Hera
1 = F __	1 = E _3_	1 = C _3_	1 = B _1_	1 = A _-1_	1 = D _-1_
2 = A __	2 = C _3_	2 = D _1_	2 = B _3_	2 = F _3_	2 = E _-1_
3 = B __	3 = E _2_	3 = D _2_	3 = F _3_	3 = C _3_	3 = A _3_
4 = C __	4 = B _3_	4 = F _-1_	4 = A _3_	4 = D _3_	4 = E _3_
5 = D __	5 = F _2_	5 = A _3_	5 = E _3_	5 = C _1_	5 = B _1_
6 = D __	6 = A _3_	6 = E _3_	6 = C _2_	6 = B _2_	6 = F _3_
7 = F __	7 = C _2_	7 = A _3_	7 = D _3_	7 = E _2_	7 = B _2_
8 = C __	8 = B _3_	8 = F _3_	8 = E _2_	8 = D _3_	8 = A _3_
9 = D __	9 = E _3_	9 = F _2_	9 = A _2_	9 = B _1_	9 = C _1_
10 = E __	10 = B _3_	10 = A _3_	10 = C _3_	10 = F _3_	10 = D _2_
11 = A __	11 = D _3_	11 = B _1_	11 = F _1_	11 = E _2_	11 = C _3_
12 = C __	12 = F _3_	12 = D _3_	12 = B _1_	12 = A _-1_	12 = E _-1_
13 = F __	13 = E _3_	13 = C _3_	13 = D _2_	13 = A _2_	13 = B _2_
14 = A __	14 = B _1_	14 = C _3_	14 = D _-1_	14 = E _-1_	14 = F _2_

Totals — _2_   _8_   _8_   _31_   _3_   _22_

When you have added up the totals from each column, enter them
in the Goddess Wheel below.

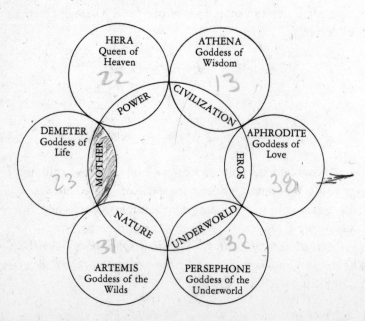

HERA
Queen of
Heaven
22

ATHENA
Goddess of
Wisdom
13

POWER CIVILIZATION

DEMETER
Goddess of
Life
23

MOTHER

APHRODITE
Goddess of
Love
38

EROS

NATURE UNDERWORLD

ARTEMIS
Goddess of the
Wilds
31

PERSEPHONE
Goddess of the
Underworld
32

INTERPRETING YOUR GODDESS WHEEL PROFILE

Now that you have completed the questionnaire and have your Goddess Profile in front of you, what does it mean? What does it tell you about yourself?

In this section we will share with you the stories and profiles of some of the women who have participated in our workshops as examples of how we approach the interpretation of a profile.

Notice, as you study your own profile and the examples below, that a low emphasis in one of the goddess's spheres of influence does not necessarily imply that the goddess is wounded. It is natural for certain emphases to change over the course of a life. Hera rarely manifests in the early years, whereas Artemis is more commonly felt in the first half rather than the second half of life. Aphrodite, however, may come and go throughout your life.

The questionnaire reflects a dynamic process. You are not exactly the same person today that you were two years ago. Because you are constantly changing with experience and new information, your Goddess Profile will be different at different times in your life.

What is important about the questionnaire is not so much the absolute numbers, but the *relationship* between the goddesses of your Goddess Profile. For example, look at Terry's profile (#2): with a 30-point difference in emphasis between Athena and Demeter, there is a strong suggestion that one part doesn't listen to the other. An examination of the issues surrounding work and motherhood will offer her a rich source of understanding and awareness.

In the case of Sara (profile #3), the strength of emphasis for Hera, Demeter, Artemis, and Aphrodite suggests a richly fulfilled life in which the independent and worldly interests of Athena and the cthonic, underworldly meditations of Persephone are notably absent. It was in asking about these two goddesses that we discovered their earlier emphasis. For Sara, the reduced involvement with those goddesses provided an opportunity to allow the others to emerge.

For Mary (profile #4), the 28-point difference between Hera and Persephone, combined with a low emphasis on Aphrodite, suggested to us some unresolved issue that Mary might have with her mother. We were correct.

What women and men in our workshops have learned is that they can use the profile and the goddesses as maps for exploring the inner landscape of the psyche. The objective being to become aware of the strengths and wounds of each of the goddesses, to bring them to consciousness and to work with them to exploit the strengths and heal the wounds.

Goddess Profile #1

Ellen is a thirty-eight-year-old attorney married to a pediatrician. They have two long-awaited children, ages two and four. The family lives in a comfortable, modern house in the countryside outside a large eastern city. Whereas just a few years ago her primary concern had been writing briefs, today Ellen is absorbed by the wonders of growing children, her garden, and a small flock of hens. A few months ago her mother told her that she has cancer and she has since become dependent on Ellen for emotional support. At the time of our workshop, Ellen was experiencing the confusion of not knowing how to relate to her mother, who had always been a strong, domineering sort and was now vulnerable and uncertain.

When she did the self-rating questionnaire, Ellen's goddess profile revealed the following values:

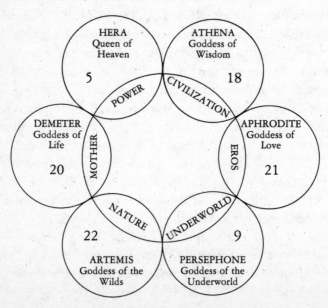

The Goddess Wheel Profile reflects Ellen's strength and confidence in her legal work, enjoyment of motherhood, and pleasure in her peaceful country life. It also suggests an imbalance in what we call the power dyad on the wheel; that is, the dialogue between Hera and Persephone. This dialogue was expressing itself through Ellen's relationship with her mother at the time of the workshop. Since midlife is often the time when we must begin to confront the unfinished business of our early life and come to terms with our mothers, Ellen's experience was a common one. Our suggestion to her was to reflect back over her relationship with her mother in order to complete unfinished emotional business.

In following this suggestion, Ellen undertook the work of Persephone. In so doing, she began a series of journal letters to her mother in which she wrote about things she had never been able to say as a child or teenager. Through this process she began to understand her mother's wounded Hera in the loneliness her mother had always felt in her marriage to Ellen's father. And Ellen began to see how she had learned to imitate her mother's habit of concealing low self-esteem behind a mask of self-confidence and correct behavior. Eventually Ellen was able to emotionally disentangle herself from her mother enough to forgive her for being demanding and critical. As a result she found she was able to give her mother the emotional support she needed while going through extended cancer treatment.

Goddess Profile #2

Terry was forty-two when she came to one of our goddess workshops. A successful free-lance photographer, she spent much of her life traveling throughout the world on assignments, moving easily between her New York City base and some of the wildest places on the planet. Recently her work had taken her to western China, where she had photographed mosques along the ancient Silk Road. She told the group that she had never married and had found even love affairs difficult because of her life-style.

Until about a year ago Terry had never questioned her life choices. After all, she was paid well to do interesting, creative work. During the last several months, however, she had begun to feel depressed and lonely. She was tired of always coming home alone at night to an empty house. Just the week before, she had had a dream of herself alone in a strange city peering into the lighted window of a house and watching a large and noisy family gathered around the dinner table. She awoke, she said, with a feeling of terrible loneliness.

When she filled out the questionnaire, Terry's Goddess Wheel looked like this:

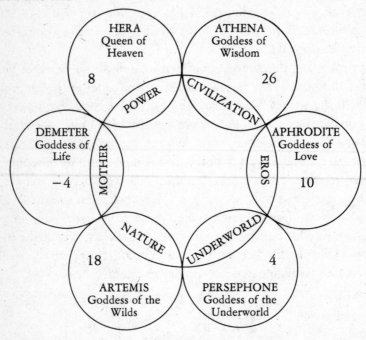

Terry's independence and confidence in both city and wilderness are evident in the relatively high emphasis of Athena and Artemis on her wheel. Because of this strikingly low rating for Demeter and Persephone (−4 and 4 points, respectively), our first questions had to do with the nature of Terry's relationship with her mother (Demeter/Persephone) and her attitudes about children and family life. Terry admitted that she felt a good deal of regret about her childlessness, which she now had to recognize as a permanent fact in her life. She also admitted that her mother had been an alcoholic throughout much of her childhood, leaving Terry burdened with premature domestic responsibilities and a determination not to have a family. At eighteen she had left home and never returned.

The major work suggested by Terry's wheel is a dialogue between Athena and Demeter. Like Athena in the myth, Terry is psychologically motherless. And like the overused sword arm of the warrior, Athena has become very strong in order to compensate for the vulnerability of the motherless little girl who lives inside of Terry. The challenge for Terry is to find a way of bringing Demeter's loving mother energy into her life so that she need not always live the spartan existence of an independent Athena.

Goddess Profile #3

At fifty-four years of age, Sara asserts that her life has never been better. After raising her daughter alone for many years following the end of her first marriage, she now finds herself very happily married to a man who dotes on her and who has awakened her long-dormant sexuality. For twenty years she had struggled with a clerical job she loathed in order to support herself and her daughter. They had been hard, lonely years, during which her relationship with her daughter had been frequently strained, especially following the divorce, when Kitty, her daughter, was ten.

"I can't believe how different my life is now," she told the group in one of our workshops. "Since I met Rick two years ago, everything has changed. For one thing, I have finally been able to quit my miserable job. Rick has really encouraged me to take my time about deciding what I want to do next, so I'm spending most of my time these days working in my herb and flower garden. I always wanted a garden, but never had the time. I'm also learning how to dry my herbs and flowers and use them in cooking and cosmetics. The other thing that's changed is my relationship with my daughter; after years of struggle we are like sisters. I've never felt so happy or so fulfilled."

After completing the questionnaire and reflecting on the wheel, Sara remarked, "If I had taken this ten years ago, when I was forty-four, it would have looked very different. I was lonely, depressed, and overweight. Kitty was twenty and had left home for good, and my mother died. There was nothing in my life except my work and my wretchedness. Looking at this profile, I can see the richness of my life in terms of Aphrodite and Demeter and Artemis."

Sara's Goddess Profile looks like this:

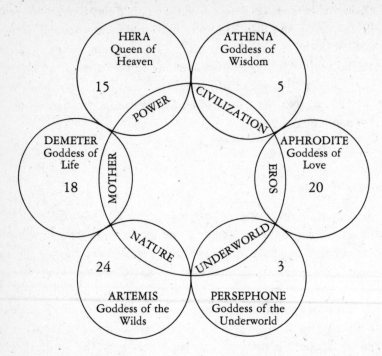

For someone like Sara, who has spent years at lonely and hard work, the emphasis on those aspects of life that have to do with love, abundance, and peaceful contact with nature reflects the healing nature of compensation. At a future time, old unfinished business may surface for completion (Persephone), or a new course of activity may begin (Athena). But for the time being, our suggestion to Sara was that she fully enjoy the well-earned pleasures of her present life.

Goddess Profile #4

For Mary, speaking up in a group and expressing her thoughts is very difficult. Shy and reserved with strangers, she is warm and generous with her friends. At forty-one, Mary is an artist who works with collages and sculpture. She draws inspiration from nature with images of clouds, trees, and mountains. The daughter of a cold and distant father and an alcoholic mother, she decided early in life to avoid marriage and intimate relationships. "The biggest problem," she told the group in one of our workshops, "is not so much loneliness but a feeling of being closed out of the world at large. Most people don't understand my art, so it's hard to make a living. What I need is a gallery or agent who will help me sell my work."

Mary's Goddess Profile looked like this:

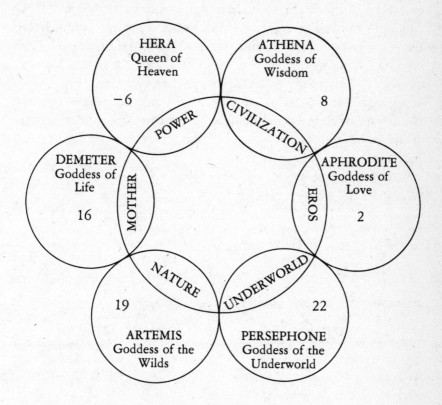

Mary's shyness and sensitivity are evident in her emphasis on Persephone and Artemis and her *de*emphasis on Aphrodite and Athena. Her lack of confidence in the outer world of Hera is evident in the gulf between Persephone (22 points) and Hera (−6 points). We suggested that she look at her attitudes about worldly power and her low self-esteem in that arena. She discovered in a role-play exercise that her attitude toward gallery owners and other people in authority was one of critical judgment exacerbated by a reluctance to engage with people socially. She realized that it is much easier to communicate with people when she "lightens up."

Goddess Profile #5

Joanne is a sixty-eight-year-old grandmother whose widowhood a few years ago exposed her to the work of a hospice. Since then she has become an active volunteer in the program, giving support to the families of the dying. "I was so wrapped up in my husband and our life together that I wasn't much interested in anything else. We raised four children—the youngest is now thirty-six—and ran our own business; Jim was a plumbing and heating contractor and I did the books. When he died of cancer, I thought my world had fallen apart and I was so depressed, I thought I'd die. Then someone suggested that I join a support group for grieving families. Now I help out several families, taking care of children and fixing meals when mothers or fathers are at the hospital. In many ways my life has never been sadder or more fulfilling."

Here is Joanne's Goddess Wheel Profile:

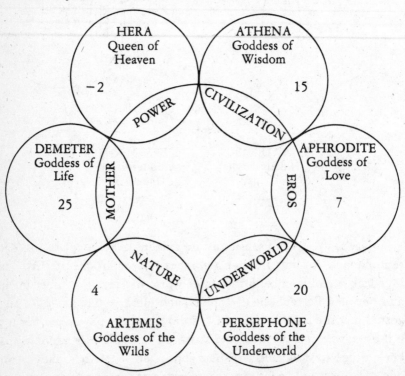

Joanne's commitment to her hospice work and the caregiving she offers grieving families are evident in the emphasis on Demeter (25

points) and Persephone (20). She has brought about much healing for her own grieving heart through this work. But Hera (-2) has suffered. Our suggestion to Joanne was to bring some of the compassionate listening she offered her hospice families to the angry, bereft Hera within herself through journal writing and psychodrama. In following our suggestion she discovered that there were strong emotions that she had never been able to express associated with feeling abandoned by her husband.

RECONCILING YOUR INNER GODDESSES (FOR WOMEN)

RECOGNIZING YOUR DIFFERENT GODDESSES

As you study the major goddesses in part one, you may start to recognize two or even three of them in yourself and in the women in your life, such as your mother, friends, colleagues, and so on. Parts of the descriptions may not fit, of course, but you will probably see how different goddesses have expressed themselves through you at different times in your life. Here, for example, is how women in workshops described phases of their lives using the goddess language:

"I was an Artemis child, on my own, out in the fields mostly, hating to be indoors. But college brought out a lot of Athena in me, and now I always have this push-pull from the city to the wonderful place I bought in the Caribbean a few years ago."

"I was always strong in Aphrodite growing up, and it served me well in the modeling world, but now I'm married to the right mate and want to stay married. I've opened my own modeling agency. I didn't know I had so much Hera in me, but I sure do value it now."

"Having babies was all I ever dreamed about as a kid; you could say that Demeter was always high on my list. And that was right for me, I was never so fulfilled as when all my kids were growing up. But losing my own mother when I was little always gnawed at me in the background. So now that my kids have all left home, I get depressed. I am having to face Persephone's world a lot."

Examples like these of women we know from our own lives point to one obvious fact: that every woman has one or two dominant goddesses in her makeup. It's not likely that she will switch goddesses entirely at a transitional point in her life, but rather that the new phase will open her up to new energies, new perspectives. Her basic energies and goddess perspective will remain, but it will be modified by the particular world she finds herself in as her life changes.

For example, no matter what goddess type we basically belong to, having a baby will take us into Demeter's world, mother consciousness, in one way or another. This is inevitable because, as we might say, Demeter is the archetypal energy that *rules* motherhood. It's her special area.

But if we stop to consider it, every woman can be a mother in six basically different ways. A mother who is fundamentally an Artemis type will be a very instinctive but unconventional mother; clothes and schedules aren't very big priorities, but there will be warmth and strong companionship. She'll want her child to be active and independent, like her. So although she is living out the Demeter phase of her life, she will do it in an Artemesian style.

By contrast, an Aphrodite mother will love to indulge her child with toys, outings, fancy clothes, parties. Her child's appearance will be very important to her; she will also emphasize social skills and getting along with others. Conversely, Hera's style of mothering is based on hierarchy and proper behavior, teaching her children that there is "a right way and a wrong way for everything." It's not hard to see how each goddess functions differently as a mother, despite being firmly in Demeter's realm.

What is important and extremely helpful about this model is that once we have found our fundamental goddess, the one who is present for most of our life, we can see how she influences us at any particular stage. Artemis's experience of childhood is very different from Demeter's or Aphrodite's; Persephone finds adolescence more difficult than Aphrodite or Athena. Hera is just hitting her stride at the age when Demeter and Aphrodite are mourning the loss of their youthful womanhood.

We must all go through the various archetypal and experiential stages of life—infancy, childhood, adolescence, adulthood, and old age. What is relevant to us here is *how* we experience these stages. *How* we experience the various stages of our life indicates, in both subtle and obvious ways, the goddesses being expressed then or now.

In our workshops we use a game to help participants begin to work with the inner goddesses. The game is called "Remembering" (see appendix A) and is a journal exercise in which we make a list of the things that stand out in our memory during the different life stages. When the list is complete, we go through it and identify the goddess who represents that particular experience or attitude. The exercise reveals which goddesses have been emphasized throughout our life and which ones have been avoided, suggesting to us a dynamic interplay among them.

For example, a fifty-one-year-old woman in one of our workshops had the following list for her adolescent years: boats, fishing, swimming, reading in the sun, quarrels with my mother, skinny and flat-chested, heroic daydreams of saving the world. It was immediately apparent in looking at her list that Artemis and Athena were very strong in her psyche and that Aphrodite and Demeter were absent. "This was to change dramatically, however, when I found myself a married mother of three just twelve years later!"

Sometimes the power of a particular goddess type emerges early, sometimes late. If we are endowed with the youthful energy of Athena or Artemis but had to spend our twenties and thirties bringing up a family, we may nevertheless find either of them enormously valuable in the second half of life. Or, in a quite different way, we may find that Hera's mature energy helps us to deal with a very responsible job as a younger woman.

What is important, then, in reflecting back over our own personal histories with each goddess is to discover who is most strongly emphasized and who is missing. It could be that whoever is emphasized is compensating in some way for one who is deemphasized or missing. Is there a pattern that is currently reflected in your life? Have you been aware of certain patterns all along? What do your patterns say about the way you are wounded? Recognizing patterns of unconscious behavior is the first step in the reconciliation and healing process.

MISSING GODDESS ENERGIES

Taking the questionnaire can be very provocative. What are we to make of those two or three goddesses with low or even negative scores? If we are honest with ourselves, we may find that these are areas in ourselves we have yet to explore. It can be a useful practice to read the chapters you skipped and *see if you recognize friends or family who embody your missing goddess energies.*

For example, you may recognize you mother as the local Hera who runs all the women's clubs in your hometown. Or perhaps you have a sister who is really a frustrated Athena, struggling to finish her college education with a husband and kids; she's not a Demeter at all, despite appearances. Perhaps your daughter is a young Artemis, with a room full of gerbils, guinea pigs, kittens, praying mantises, and horse pictures. Perhaps you had a roommate in college who was a shy but incredibly perceptive Persephone. And of course, we all know a few Aphrodites, whether we like their free-and-easy life-style or not. And Demeter? Hard to miss those comfortable, glowing women who always seem to be happily draped with babies.

The goddesses are not only within and around us, their stereotypes can be seen in the soap operas, the daily tabloids, and the latest public sagas being played out in Washington and Hollywood. The goddesses are everywhere, and you can observe them at your leisure now that you have the key. The question to ask yourself is, Which one do I have unfinished business with?

The goddess with whom you have unfinished business is likely to be either the one who has had the least "voice" in your life so far or the one whose voice has nagged at you in the background, the one you don't want to hear. The task here is to discover what your issues are with her and to have it out with her. In our workshops we use a dynamic role-playing game called "Having It Out With Your Shadow" in order to explore some of the fundamental issues between the goddesses; solitary readers can do this as a writing exercise (see appendix A). In your journal or on a large sheet of paper, make six circles, one for each goddess. Inside and around each circle write words or phrases that you associate with that goddess. Reflecting on your diagram, begin to notice the phrases and images that suggest some sort of wound to a particular goddess. Begin to see how the wounds of that goddess influence your life on a day-to-day basis.

THE LIFE CYCLE IN GODDESS PERSPECTIVE: A NEW KIND OF VALUES CLARIFICATION

In describing the goddesses we have often referred to certain fundamental qualities that stand out in each of them; youthfulness, achievement, independence, relatedness, passion, and power have been noted in particular. One way of seeing the emergence and evolution of these qualities is to look at them in terms of a woman's life cycle.

Traditionally a woman's life cycle was divided into three simple stages: *Maiden*, *Mother*, and *Crone*. For obvious biological reasons, until very recently in history Demeter, as mother principle, tended to dominate the middle of a woman's life in most societies. But birth control and education have changed all that. Today the phase traditionally reserved only for Demeter may be just as strongly available to the youthful energy of Artemis or Athena or be expressed in Aphrodite's love of personal contact and relationships. So today, in order to show this rich new development, it seems fully appropriate to show all four goddesses' energies as coequal in the unfolding of the life cycle:

Persephone (as Maiden) *rules childhood, the young girl*

Artemis and Athena *rule adolescence, young womanhood,*
      and transition

Demeter and Aphrodite *rule motherhood, relationships,*
      and maturity

Hera *rules the second half of life, the woman as elder*

Persephone (as Crone) *rules old age and death, the wise woman*

However, to have four goddesses competing for one's loyalties—to say nothing of trying to satisfy Hera and Persephone's demands, if they are your dominant type—can be quite exhausting. But this is precisely the conflict so many women find themselves in and that the Goddess Wheel is designed to illuminate. For this reason we sometimes call it a kind of archetypal values clarification.

Let's take the four goddesses we have bracketed together as most operative today in a woman's life after late adolescence: Demeter, Aphrodite, Athena, and Artemis. In many ways they all seem to be tugging away in almost every woman's psyche—Demeter wants babies, Aphrodite is looking for romance, Athena wants a career, and Artemis just wants to be alone. How do we stop their competing pulls? How do we decide between them?

First, you must decide who has the strongest inner voice, which is to say, who is your dominant type? It's probably obvious to you by now who is your dominant goddess; she's the one whose name appears most often in your Remembering game and is probably the one with the highest score on your Goddess Wheel Profile.

Second, you must look at *outer* influences that are pushing you or pulling you toward one of the realms that belong to the other goddesses. Take a long look at your *mother*, if you can. What is her main type: Demeter, Hera, Persephone? Are you dutifully following out her wishes for you, or are you reacting strongly against her?

If you are an Athena with a Hera mother, you probably have lots of power issues and a need to be out in the world—usually to prove something to your mother, in which case Demeter's world won't attract you and won't seem to serve you directly. On the other hand, if your mother didn't give you much good Demeter nurturing, a part of you probably longs for that in the form of a child. You will need to be very clear about where you stand before you rush into marriage and child-bearing.

But, to reverse it a bit, if you are an Aphrodite or an Athena with a Demeter mother, you may feel duty bound to have children and reproduce that wonderful home you grew up in. All this despite the fact that inside you are really looking for adventures or achievement of one kind or another, activities in which you have to admit, deep down, there isn't much space for children.

Or to reverse it again, you might be a natural Demeter with an Athena mother who insists you go to college, where you slowly come to realize that you are desperately unhappy. You may need simply to drop out and have those longed-for children instead of getting "accidentally" pregnant all the time.

You will also want to look at your *father*. His wishes for you, conscious or unconscious, can have enormous influence. He may have wanted sons but got you and your sisters instead. And secretly he wanted you all to be successful Athenas so that he could have close intellectual companionship. Or, if he's more down-to-earth, his fantasy of you may be of a rugged Artemis buddy to go off fishing and sailing with, again, to replace that son he never had. The question is, What is your legitimate type? Are you molding yourself to please him and betraying your true nature?

Sometimes a young woman will get drawn into the shadow of her father's unhappy sex life, having learned as a child to absorb a lot of his feminine fantasies. She may find herself in adult life behaving promiscuously and come to distrust her true Aphrodite nature, because in fact she is driven, quite unconsciously, by his secret, unexpressed life. Is she really an Aphrodite or not? She will need to look inside to find what is most important to her, which goddess is really her guide.

And beyond your parents you need to look around at the general values of the community you grew up in and how it influenced or distorted your fundamental goddess type. Did you grow up in a college town where Athena women were valued? Or were you always around show-biz people, who expect exaggerated Aphrodite displays in women? Or was landing a respectable mate and having children the top priority for your town—Hera and Demeter values?

These are all *collective* values, a sort of average or norm of the feminine that you may have absorbed. Try to step back and observe how you took them for granted and see if they really fit you or not.

WHICH GODDESS RULES?
SOME EXAMPLES FROM LIFE

In our workshops we encourage women to explore the different goddesses until it is clear who their dominant goddess is. We do this by playing a game called "Everything You Ever Wanted to Know About the Goddess." In this game we create six sections—one for each goddess—in a large circle, forming a Goddess Wheel. Everyone sits in a place on the wheel where she is most comfortable. The participants are then invited to make statements about the goddess in whose place they are sitting. For example, a woman sitting in Demeter's section of the wheel might say, "As Demeter, I love to make cookies with my children and fill my home with good smells." Another, as Athena, might say, "My work keeps me so busy that I don't have time to buy and prepare my meals." A woman speaking for Hera might say, "I don't understand these strange new hairdos kids are wearing nowadays." After every section has been heard from, we invite people to stay where they are but ask questions of someone in another section. Thus a woman in Artemis's section might ask the Aphrodite section, "How can you stand to be around people so much?" The Aphrodite section would be invited to answer the question. Or a person in the Demeter section might ask the Hera section, "Why is it so important to keep the house clean and have everyone sit down to supper together? And why, oh why, must children eat everything on their plates?" To which the Hera section would have many answers.

The game grows more complex and often hilariously funny when people in one goddess section feel compelled to answer a question posed to a different group. To join the dialogue, we ask participants to move to that section; soon everyone is shifting about the Goddess Wheel, experiencing both the asking and the answering in many sections. It does not take long for the recognitions to begin: "Oh, she's just like my sister," or "Wow, does that describe my mother," or "Oh, now I get why I don't like my boss." We learn from each other and slowly we begin to sew together our own personal goddess tapestry.

Here are some examples from our workshops of how women have described their lives in terms of the goddesses:

1. *Margy's Story: An Artemis Discovers Aphrodite*

"My mother was a typically frustrated Hera, always knowing what was best for all of her kids. I never really got on with her from the beginning. She had all these ideas of what a pretty little girl should be, and, well . . . I suppose you could say I was a huge disappointment to her. I guess I was an Artemis most of my childhood and as a young woman. I was always off with the boys, a kind of tomboy myself. I looked up to them, always wanted their approval.

"What got to me most was that in Mother's eyes boys could do no wrong. They were sort of wonderful, doing all the things she never got to do, out there winning and leading, or so she hoped. It was a double standard, I now see, a way of avoiding her own feminine. There were four siblings, actually. I had two older brothers and a younger sister.

"Father was never around. I always felt I disappointed him too. He was right there to offer help when my sister got pregnant, but never seemed to understand me. My sister, Sue, was an Aphrodite from early on, which made Mother mad in a different way, though she did like to dress Sue up when she was a little girl. Sue would come to me when we were teenagers and ask me all kinds of things about sex—I was kind of horrified because it was so different from how I got on with boys. They respected me for my toughness, because I was on various teams, knew a lot about cars, and because I *didn't* seem to care about sex yet.

"College was about the same. You might say I developed a bit of Athena to get by, but I still hung out with the kind of boys who went to racing-car meets and wanted me as a sisterly sort of companion. I had a couple of awkward sexual encounters. The boys were so shy and inexperienced, I concluded the whole thing was overrated. I guess, looking back, I really couldn't let them in. And all those things Sue used to talk about, oral sex and so on, really put me off.

"Aphrodite didn't enter my life till I met Jane. I was working in the city at the time as a computer programmer. Jane was quite a whiz organizational consultant; I met her at a seminar one day. I admired her energy in the marketplace, how she dressed, how she knew all the latest books, music, movies. That was her very successful Athena, which I aspired to, but I didn't quite have the ambition. It just blew me away one evening at her place when she told me what a beautiful woman I was and we just started to make love. That evening totally changed my life. I found myself and my body in a whole new way. I understand my sister, Sue, a little better. Aphrodite was instinctive for her. For me it was quite buried. I had to be initiated.

"Mother hates my relationship with Jane, of course, but Jane is teaching me to stand up to her. I'm just starting to see how little Aphrodite there was in my mother's marriage and, I suppose, how little Demeter. Demeter is still a great mystery to me. Jane and I have been together six years now and we talk of adopting a kid, but we know we are neither of us ready. We nurture each other a lot. It's sad how little Demeter love any of us had as kids. But I value the independence I learned as a child. My Artemis self gives me a lot of strength out there in the world, even if I do feel like a bit of an outsider."

2. Pat's Story: Losing Demeter, Facing Persephone

"Growing up in a family of six kids, you'd think I would have had enough of kids and families. But as the eldest, and my mother an utterly devoted Demeter, I couldn't help just falling into it as a way of life. I was married by nineteen. Bill was a career officer in the air force and seemed very stable and predictable, and I knew I wanted babies of my own, so what was to stop us?

"I had all the kids I was to have by twenty-five, and if it hadn't been for a complication with Kevin, my fifth, I would've had more. But the doctor talked me into having my tubes tied.

Life in the service is great for a Demeter like me. You meet other mothers and their kids so easily, and somehow the air force provides for everything you need.

"At least, so I thought. I hadn't reckoned on Bill. I put on quite a lot of weight during the pregnancies and sat around a lot—too much, you might say. I barely noticed that our sex life had tailed off. It had never been that exciting. At home Bill was rather a shy type. I suppose I was his mother too. But I didn't reckon with his sex needs. I might have guessed when I found a pile of girlie magazines in his workroom one day. But I was still in a dream, surrounded by all my kids.

"The day he announced he had this other woman and that he intended to move out, the bottom fell out of my world. I didn't see it then as any kind of failing in me. I had given him everything. Or so I thought. If I felt rage, I didn't let myself feel it. I have this calm, warm, unflappable exterior. I just carried on as though nothing had happened. But then my drinking started. Just a couple of bourbons to start with. But then, by the time I was dickering with lawyers about settlements, it was up to a quart a week. I tried to carry on as before, but I was depressed, real depressed. I'd sit in front of the tube for most of the day before picking up the kids, smoking and drinking, totally lost in all the garbage. I just wanted to lose myself, that's all. That's how I know Persephone. My kids suffered at that time. I was mean to them, leaning on them one moment, lashing out the next.

"The alimony was decent, but I needed more than that, so I took various secretarial jobs. I was out in the world for the first time, having to support myself. I found I had a talent for organizing and selling and I ended up in a partnership with another woman running a small diner. She put up most of the money, I agreed to manage it. I'd always been a good cook— all that Demeter—but now I was discovering some Hera in me. Before, I used to let my husband run the show.

"Friends pushed me in the direction of AA, and I'm almost there, but it's been real hell. I wish I had understood Aphrodite more and what went wrong. Was I hiding behind all my kids? Did I really think I could go from one big cozy family straight into another? I suppose I never grew up till Bill left. Persephone has been a real teacher for me. I'll never see the world the same way again after my depression and the alcoholism."

3. Trish's Story: From Persephone to Athena and Demeter

"It's so hard to talk about myself. Often I just feel as though I don't exist and that only pain reminds me that I'm real. Making contact with the world has never been easy. You would say I'm a Persephone, probably.

"Even being born made me feel left out, ignored. I was the second twin. They didn't notice I was there. So I came out as a kind of afterthought. That's how I would see my life, as a kind of afterthought. I suppose I must have been a very difficult child.

"Mother was what you'd call an Artemis. We lived in the country, she was absorbed in her plants, her sculpture, and her dogs and her umpteen cats. We got fed now and then, along with the animals! I liked Father much more. He was soft and kind and had his own dreamy life somewhere. I liked to think he understood me, but it was just wishful thinking.

"I was so disconnected from things as a child that even at seven, when a twelve-year-old boy from a nearby family started interfering with me sexually, it didn't fully register. There was a lot of confusion and guilt, of course, but it just made me feel even more alien than ever.

"I froze up even more in adolescence. I lost a lot of weight and I became obsessed with Jesus in a macabre sort of way. I sort of loved the Crucifixion. I can't explain it. It had a sort of sexual aura to it. I kept secret journals, drew elaborate pictures of a Bosch-like sort. I was depressed and not eating much. My parents rightly got me to a psychiatrist, who was extremely kind, but he shook his head when I showed him my drawings and instead tried to talk about boys in a sort of avuncular way. I took all the drugs he prescribed quite docilely and learned to adapt. It was as though there were two mes from then on, one who was here and one who wasn't.

"Looking back on my adolescence, it seems that a part of

me went permanently into the underworld—that's Persephone, isn't it? But it made me understand things from a quite
other perspective. When I made the effort, I could write quite
brilliantly. I started to read more; I loved Emily Dickinson,
Camus, Dostoyevsky, the existentialists. What a strange bird I
was. My Athena was surfacing. I got recognition at school and
found myself naturally propelled into literature and philosophy. I would startle myself by continuing to write incredibly
mature and striking papers. There were times when I simply
wondered where they were coming from.

"College seemed a natural haven for me, so I specialized
in literature, doing my doctoral thesis on Mary Shelley's *Fran-
kenstein*. I had a natural affinity for the gothic imagination,
which I became something of a specialist in. During graduate
school I met Hank, a very gentle and introverted graduate
student of medieval French, whom I eventually married. He
was perfect for me at that time, letting me continue to live in
my cocoon of the imagination. Academic life—we both went
on to become teachers in a small New England college—was
nonthreatening.

"Becoming a mother in my later thirties brought some Demeter to the surface, but not a lot. I tended to be a rather
detached, textbook mother. But I had a very symbiotic attachment to my son, Marc. When my second child died at
eighteen months of a hole in the heart—an early operation
failed—I fell into a morbid depression. I began to feel like
Mary Shelley herself and was quite suicidal for a while.

"Fortunately I found my way to a good Jungian analyst,
who took me through my own gothic underworld, strewn with
the corpses of dead children. I thought I would go mad, but
her wise tolerance and the reading she suggested gave me some
kind of objectivity. When it was over, I started training as an
analyst myself. I am still doing it. It really strengthens the
Athena in me who wants to understand that dark world and
not be sucked into it again."

When a woman starts to tell her story in this way, both she and
the listener or reader notices how important the emergence of certain

goddesses can be at certain points in a woman's life. What a revelation it was for a rather sexually shy Artemis like Margy to encounter Aphrodite in the form of her lover Jane. She was able to effect a connection to her eros nature that many Artemis women struggle with or simply ignore for most of their lives. The ancients would have called such a highly charged moment an epiphany, which is to say, a "shewing" of the goddess as a healer or transformer. (It was precisely this fact that lead Jung to call the archetypes transformers of energy.)

And what a powerful encounter with Persephone for Pat when she fell into depression and drink after her husband left. Living alone and working with AA subsequently forced her to discover that she possessed both some Athena and a lot of Hera when she started to work for herself.

HAVING IT OUT WITH YOUR EXCLUDED GODDESSES

Opposition is true friendship
—William Blake

None of these stories offers magical solutions to these women's wounds or deficiencies, but it was immensely helpful to each of them to be able to recognize their personal patterns as belonging to particular goddesses. Pat had had no perspective at all on how absorbed she was becoming in Demeter's world with all her kids until her husband left her. Margy had begun to take her loner Artemis life-style for granted, until she met her lover.

It was illuminating for each of them to realize how they had been confronting unfamiliar goddesses' energies in their life crises and transitions. We saw how Margy's lover awakened her to all of Aphrodite's lovely gifts. And how, in a different way, Trish found comfort for her depressions and morbid imaginings when she learned to critically reflect on gothic literature and existentialist philosophers, a process that strongly called upon Athena's wisdom and that goddess's ability to objectify complex experiences.

But in addition, simply telling their stories to a circle of women who embody *all the goddesses* was enormously empowering for all three of these women. It helped them to overcome their feelings of alienation and strangeness, to know that their struggles are not theirs alone but ones that connect us to each other in all kinds of heartening ways. Certain women in that particular group shared with Pat and Trish similar stories of their bouts with alcohol and depression. Other women were deeply moved by Margy's revelation of her sexual awakening and later sought her out in person to tell her so. These things happen frequently within the powerful container of the Goddess Wheel.

Sometimes we have found it especially helpful to ritualize the encounter with a wounded or alienated goddess. We might suggest to a woman who is in a workshop who is deficient in, say, Aphrodite, that she go sit and have a quiet dialogue with a woman who strongly incarnates that goddess. This can be an effective start to working with this particular goddess wound. We will have further suggestions of ways to structure your own goddess exchanges.

Exercises such as these are valuable for a very simple reason: when a goddess has been missing or deficient in a woman's life, it may simply be that there has never been a model of that energy to bring it out. A very extraverted Aphrodite woman, for example, can go through life never encountering the Artemis energy in herself because no one in her family ever spent any time alone and she has never been attracted to solitary pursuits. In reality it may take something like a friend talking her into a meditation retreat, or a serious illness for her to have any awareness of the power of solitude. But with the Goddess Wheel it is possible to generate ritual encounters or dialogues with her excluded Artemis self.

Hera women, because they are so strong-willed, often manage to control their lives so as to exclude any intrusions from Aphrodite or Artemis or Persephone. This last one, Persephone's realm, they are particularly afraid of, so their final years and approaching death can be a crucial time for them. But again, with the Goddess Wheel they can play out their fears and prejudices about Persephone in a workshop environment or with a written dialogue.

Often life itself will catapult us into the most intense and agonizing conflicts between the goddesses and their values in ways we may never have previously questioned. Suddenly an Athena mother finds her fourteen-year-old daughter pregnant; where does she stand on the Demeter issue of the sanctity of life, given her own previous history of abortions? Or else it might be the wife of a respected minister who finds herself in a clandestine affair with a widowed parishioner; how does she resolve the screaming match between Hera and Aphrodite going on inside her?

Quite commonly our conflict with a particular goddess may play itself out in the form of some highly charged encounter with a woman or type of woman in our life. What this means, practically speaking, is that there is often important work to do with such women, since they represent goddess energies from which we are alienated or with which we are in conflict.

A place where many a woman will find her excluded goddesses is naturally in her family constellation, where she will recognize them in her mother or her daughter or sister. Perhaps the version of this that is most familiar to women is their relationship to their mothers or their daughters. This can take many forms from the goddess perspective: it may be an Athena daughter alienated from a Hera or a Demeter mother, an Aphrodite daughter at loggerheads with her prudish Artemis mother, or a Demeter mother totally unable to communicate with her Persephone daughter, and so on.

Books like Nancy Friday's *My Mother, My Self* or Vivian Gornick's *Fierce Attachments* have explored the labyrinthine complexities of the mother/daughter relationship with great insight and compassion. They are graphic examples of ongoing life dialogues between the goddesses. Literature, too, has produced some highly charged plots based on this theme; for example, in Marsha Norman's *'Night, Mother* a suicidal Persephone daughter plays out her final dialogue with a bewildered and uncomprehending Demeter mother (see also Videography).

A good movie example of a dialogue between two alienated goddess types is to be found in *The Turning Point*. Here we have a straightforward saga of two women, Emma and Deedee, who take different directions in life. Once a close friend and rival of Deedee's in ballet school, Emma decides to devote herself entirely to dancing, thus giving up all thought of family and children. Deedee, on the other hand, becomes pregnant at this time and, doubting her ability to succeed as a dancer, plumps for a family in suburbia, nevertheless keeping her hand in running a small ballet academy with her husband.

Twenty years later they come together to celebrate the "coming out" of Deedee's daughter, a talented and aspiring young ballerina.

Now the buried rivalry between the two older women erupts, but along with it, barely disguised envy for each other's life-style: career success in one instance, family and children in the other (see box, "Athena and Demeter at Loggerheads"). It is an oft-repeated dialogue between wounded Demeter and wounded Athena, one full of subtle undercurrents and bitter paradoxes.

Deedee has become an isolated but unfulfilled housewife who has really escaped into her Demeter role to avoid the hot-paced ballet world. The ambitious Athena in her has never been properly tested in that highly competitive arena. So this frustrated goddess in Deedee is nursing old grudges and jealousy for her rival, Emma, who was, it seems, more talented than Deedee. Emma, by contrast, has lived out her Athena to the full but at the cost of never experiencing motherhood. In her psyche unfulfilled Demeter is very attracted to Deedee's daughter, Emilia, whom she would like to make her protégée. Deedee instinctively smells the ulterior motive and quite brutally taunts Emma in her most wounded place.

The whole exchange deserves watching on the screen, of course, but our extract gives some idea of its intensity. Its enormous power derives, it seems to us, from the fact that it is indeed the two goddesses who are, so to speak, expressing their larger grievance *through* the two women. Regardless of what career any woman like Deedee has longed for, she can identify with these wounds in Athena, just as every woman who has renounced motherhood will feel Demeter's pangs of regret in this story.

SOME TYPICAL GODDESS DIALOGUES

In our workshops we have observed all kinds of spontaneous dialogues like this breaking out from different sections of the Goddess Wheel. Of course, they don't have the personal detail expressed in *The Turning Point*, but very similar archetypal themes constantly recur. It may be the Athenas challenging both the Artemis and the Persephone women to come out of the closet and show what they really feel, to get more involved in life. It may be a hurt and wounded Aphrodite challenging self-righteous Hera about her empty marriage. It may be Hera angry at Persephone's draining energy from the group with her victim stories.

ATHENA AND DEMETER AT LOGGERHEADS: *THE TURNING POINT*

In this extract Deedee feels very left out when her daughter Emilia shares the spotlight with her old friend and rival, Emma, at a gala benefit. Deedee is also incensed because Emma has offered to be ballet coach for Deedee's daughter Emilia when she eventually moves to New York. Deedee can hardly contain her jealousy, as though the munificent Emma were now "stealing" her daughter and getting all the kudos for her blossoming career. Her jealousy leaps out like so many little green toads, as Deedee puts it:

EMMA: You're trying to blame me for what you did, Deedee, the choice was yours, it's much too late to regret it now.

DEEDEE: The same to you, Emma darling.

EMMA: I don't regret mine.

DEEDEE: Then why are you trying to become a mother at your age?

EMMA: Oh, that's not a little toad, that's a rather large bullfrog. I don't want to be anybody's mother. I think of Emilia as a friend. And one reason I tried to help—stupid me!—I thought it would make you happy if your daughter became what you wanted to be but never could be.

DEEDEE: Meaning you! Is it so lovely to be you, Emma?

EMMA: Well, obviously you think so.

[. . .]

EMMA: Deedee, I'm sick to death of your junk. . . . Just don't blame your goddamn life on me. You picked it.

DEEDEE: You picked it. You took away my choice. You never let me find out if I was good enough.

EMMA: You aren't and you knew it. That's why you married Wayne.

DEEDEE: I loved Wayne!

EMMA: So much so that you said to hell with your career?

DEEDEE: Yes!

EMMA: And got pregnant to prove that you meant it?

DEEDEE: Yes!

EMMA: Oh, you lie to me like you lie to yourself. You got married because you were second-rate. And you got pregnant because Wayne was a ballet dancer, and in those days that meant queer. So you had to prove he was a man, so you had a baby!

DEEDEE: That's a goddamn lie!

EMMA: That's the goddamn truth and you know it! You saddled him with a baby and blew his career, and now that she's grown up and better than you ever were, you're jealous!

[. . .]

DEEDEE: And you're a user. You know that. You always have been for your whole life . . . and now Emilia.

EMMA: How Emilia?

DEEDEE: How Emilia! That was plain five minutes ago upstairs. You were using Emilia so that everybody in the room would say, "Isn't Emma wonderful, isn't Emma marvelous." . . . You know something? You are wonderful. You are truly amazing! It's incredible how you keep going on. You're over the hill and you know it. You're terrified. All you've got are your scrapbooks, your old posters and those stupid little dogs. Well, what are you going to fill in with, Emma? Not my daughter. You keep your goddamn hands off my daughter!

The quarrel degenerates briefly into a quite vicious physical fight. Finally, it seems, the two women can release all that pent-up, seething envy. And as so often in quarrels where there is a deeper connection, they end up laughing, in each other's arms. In William Blake's wise words "I was angry with my friend; I told my wrath, my wrath did end."

When dialogues such as these have arisen in a group setting, huge energy starts to flow back and forth within the sacred container of the Goddess Wheel. Almost everyone gets drawn into the debates with their polarized energy as the goddesses become more forthright in speaking out for their hurts, their convictions, their forgotten wisdom. Sometimes it's as though centuries of cobwebs are being swept away by a fresh wind of utterance.

In the end, of course, every woman must find what dialogue is most pressing in her. But to at least stimulate that process, we offer some reconstructed extracts from some of the more common kinds of exchanges the Goddess Wheel generates.

HERA AND PERSEPHONE: THE PSYCHE VERSUS THE "REAL" WORLD

Most of us rarely realize how much we are stuck in our own goddess perspective until we are confronted with a very different view of the world. No two goddess perspectives are quite so far apart as that of Hera, with her seemingly unshakable confidence in how the "real" world operates, and that of Persephone, with her almost flippant rejection of such matters in favor of "inner" realities.

In the following exchange an older Hera woman decided she had had enough of a young Persephone woman's "psychic drivel," as she called it. A Hera woman's presence at a goddess workshop is, incidentally, a relatively rare event since, as a rule, she doesn't approve much of psychology, but when she does attend one, she is often the occasion for considerable fireworks.

H (HERA WOMAN): May I say something? I have been listening to you, young lady, talk about these Tarot cards and how you use them with your clients and how you pick up their "energy" and work with their dreams and so on and so forth. I don't think I've ever heard such psychic drivel. This is all fantasy. You're just keeping all those poor people believing in some never-never land. What they need is good, down-to-earth advice about jobs and money and family.

P (PERSEPHONE WOMAN): I find your energy extremely negative and I think you are being very patronizing—maybe I should say "matronizing"! Have you ever had a reading? Have you ever studied your dreams? I think you'd be very surprised.

H: I wouldn't dream of wasting my money on such things. As for dreams, we all know that's just the brain ticking over while we're asleep. My son is at college studying psychology; he says the brain is just a machine, and I think he's right.

P: Surely you don't think that what's studied in colleges is the whole of psychology? What about analysis, meditation, hypnosis?

H: Oh, they're just fashions that come and go. They don't do a scrap of good. Most people's problems are cured by good hard work, if you ask me. All this brooding about your subconscious or whatever—it's morbid and it's self-centered.

P: I don't think you've heard a word I or the other Persephone women here have been saying. Our lives have been significantly changed by meditation practices and talking to our guides. You don't seem to have any idea what it is to trust an inner guide. My guides are never wrong.

H: Well, dear, I trust my husband, my lawyer, and my bank manager—and that's about all I need.

Clearly there was no resolution to be had here, with a Hera who was so rigidly identified with the given social structure of her world and external authorities like her husband, college professors, bankers, and so on. But as other members of the Goddess Wheel group later pointed out to them, Persephone is often just as dependent on authorities and "pulling rank" as Hera. The only difference is that Persephone's authorities are spiritual and discarnate, or else gurus—figures equally hard to argue with. And as one observer pointedly remarked, both Hera and Persephone throw their weight around when they want to. Wielding power, whether worldly or psychic, is a major concern for both of them. The difference is that this Hera was more out front and direct, whereas the Persephone woman was using power very subtly yet in a way that was every bit as dogmatic and unyielding.

HERA AND APHRODITE ON LOVE AND MARRIAGE

Hera doesn't always get away with trying to play one-up in Goddess Wheel workshops, authoritarian as she may sound. Once in a while another woman will get to her wounded place, as the following dialogue shows.

No more archetypal opposition exists, of course, than the one between Hera, standing for marriage, monogamy, and fidelity, and Aphrodite, who is totally dedicated to the proposition that love and passion transcend all social and personal considerations. This may sound like the stuff of soap operas, but this exchange is representative of one that many women in our workshops deeply need to have, regardless of which goddess they are closest to.

H (HERA WOMAN): I've been listening to you [an Aphrodite woman in the group] talk about how you had an affair with that married man for so many years, and it really makes me *mad*! Did you ever stop to think what you were doing to that poor wife?

A (APHRODITE WOMAN): What do you know about that "poor wife"? Did you ever meet her? Look, I knew lots about her, how she never wanted to sleep with Fred, how she clung to him, how he stuck in there for the children.

H: But if it hadn't been for you, they might have worked it out together. In any case, I think he had a lot of guts sticking up for his wife and children. That's something you just don't understand—faithfulness!

A: To the contrary. I would say I'm faithful in my own way. Actually I could say I'm a lot more faithful than you; I'm faithful to my true feelings. You seem prepared to sacrifice real feelings just to hold together some *ideal*, the perfect family, and to hell with feelings and happiness! That's what gets me about your type of marriage—it's phony! It's hypocritical.

H: It sounds as though you think you have some God-given mission to go around rescuing men from rotten Hera wives. In the past that used to be called marriage wrecking. Now you want to glamorize it as "open marriage" and all that baloney.

I think you and all you Aphrodites are really jealous of our stability and happiness and deep down you want to destroy it.

A: Well, there's maybe some truth in that. My mother sure hated my sexuality when I was a wild teenager. I guess I said, "Screw you, Mother, and your stuffy marriage." I suppose I must admit that; I *am* still angry at her. She's a Hera, all right. . . . But if you're a Hera, too, help me understand why Aphrodites like me are so threatening. It's not just our marriage wrecking, as you call it. What about your sexuality?

H: There's nothing wrong with my sex life, thank you very much!

A: That just sounds like, "Mind your own business." Look, I've been pretty frank about my sexuality in this workshop. I think you are just hiding. You do a lot more pretending than you'd like to admit.

H (*now in tears*): It's not fair. I try *so* hard. I've always tried so hard. I did exactly what my mother wanted me to. I married the right person. We had everything, everything. It was all so perfect. . . . But now, it's so empty, so mechanical. I don't really know if he loves me. Not in that way. For all I know, he could be sleeping with someone like you. (*More tears*) I just don't know him any longer.

A (*coming over to comfort* H): You know, you're a lot more like me than you think. I can see that side of you. I bet you were pretty hot stuff once.

H (*torn between a grimace and a smile*): I don't think you know how lonely it is inside.

A: Oh, yes I do, I really do. (*They hug, both in tears now.*)

In most of our workshops Hera starts out by being superior and gets attacked by the other goddess types. So many women see Hera in their mothers that a Hera in a workshop is going to bear the brunt of all their pent-up gripes. And the only way Hera knows how to defend herself is to become even more superior. But, as this dialogue shows, there is nearly always a chink in her armor when it comes to her marriage. This is inevitable; she is, to adapt Marion Woodman's felicitous book title, "addicted to perfection." And since no one can be perfect, she will often crumble when put in touch with her imperfections. This is actually very valuable for her. She needs to come down a little from the Olympian superiority of her phony perfect marriage and be human. Here Aphrodite got through to her and was able to be compassionate with a woman very like her own Hera mother.

APHRODITE AND ARTEMIS ON SEX AND SENSUALITY

Nothing is more deceptive than appearances and nothing brings out goddess differences faster than talking about how we look and feel about our physical selves. In the following extract a somewhat overweight Aphrodite woman found herself intrigued by an Artemis woman's description of how she related to her body.

ART (ARTEMIS WOMAN): I really don't know how I'd live if I didn't jog and do my dance classes regularly. I just feel so good when my body is really fit. Lovemaking, work, everything is so vibrant. I love my body's tautness.

APH (APHRODITE WOMAN): For me it's just the opposite. I like to melt when I make love. I can't imagine having all those taut little muscles everywhere. I can stand some aerobics maybe, but jogging sounds like boot camp to me. All that discipline would get in the way in sex. I simply wouldn't be able to let go.

ART: But lovemaking isn't about letting go for me. It's an incredible dance, an ecstatic intertwining of energies. Orgasm is a kind of explosion.

APH: I hope I'm not missing something! I'm much more interested in being touched and fondled and pampered. It gives me such a rush when he's really turned on by how my body looks and feels to him. And don't you love all that gushy romantic stuff, dinners, music, the right dresses?

ART: You know, I don't really think about that much. People, men especially, tell me I'm very attractive to them, but it really doesn't mean much to me. I don't pay that much attention to clothes, though I know what I like. I don't really understand your interest in all that romance and seductiveness. Frankly it rather embarrasses me. I guess deep down I'm a bit shy—but that doesn't mean I can't get really turned on. You make me realize I'm much more in control of my body than you.

APH: Hmm. I have to say, listening to you, that I must simply *inhabit* my body in a quite different way from you. I suppose you could say I'm very sensual. And I'm always fantasizing about nice things my body would like.

ART: I don't think I really fantasize much in that way. Wild adventures, certain kinds of encounters with men where I'm very active (*blushes*), but I don't give too much energy to my body as such when it comes to sex. I've never understood those women's magazines, beauty salons, and all that. It's not that I disapprove. I just don't seem to belong there. It's all too self-conscious for me.

Most of the other goddess types in the group could identify with one side or the other of this dialogue, although some of the Persephones had no idea what either were talking about. Instead, they tried to describe their sexuality entirely in spiritual terms, which completely baffled everyone else. But the observers of the Artemis-Aphrodite exchange who were most intrigued were the *men* in the group. It was a revelation to them to see and hear two manifestly attractive women reveal how they experienced their bodies so differently. They had to admit that their own projections about beauty and sex could easily be wildly off the mark.

DEMETER AND PERSEPHONE ON HAVING CHILDREN

We saw in the extract from *The Turning Point* how deeply the issue of having or not having children can affect an Athena whose life energy is taken up by her career and how difficult this is for every woman in whom Demeter *and* Athena are equally strong. But the Goddess Wheel has more than once brought out other and even more agonizing issues concerning children, among them abortion, miscarriage, infertility, and unwanted children. Women in whom Demeter is strong and fulfilled are frequently more than a little naive about the feelings of others in this painful area. This was the case in the following dialogue.

D (DEMETER WOMAN): You've been awfully quiet during all this talk about babies and motherhood. Does it upset you?

P (PERSEPHONE WOMAN): Not really, not any longer. It's hard to talk about for me . . . it's all so painful, even though it's over. I just feel lousy about myself when it comes to mothering.

D: I know how you feel, dear; I've failed my kids in lots of ways. . . .

P (*quietly*): I doubt if you really know what I feel (*sighs deeply*).

D: Can you tell us a bit? I don't even know if you have kids or not, you've said so little.

P (*fighting back tears*): You think you've failed. Well, that's almost an understatement for me. My mother remarried when I was ten. You might call her a real Aphrodite; she always had men around. They used to tease me.

D: So, what happened?

P: Well, this one she married, he came into my bedroom when I was fourteen. I kind of liked him, and well . . . then it all happened. He made love to me. It went on for several months till Mom found out. She kicked him out. But the damage was done. I was pregnant.

D: Oh, you poor thing.

P: "Poor thing" nothing! Mom and the social worker made me have it. We were Catholic, you see. It was like a punishment. I hated her during that pregnancy. And I suppose I hated the baby. It wasn't so easy when he was born. Then he was adopted. It was a little boy. I think about him still, how he is, what it would be like to find him. He comes to me in my dreams all the time. I feel I know him. I tried to tell that stupid psychiatrist I had to see for years. Finally I just clammed up. What does he know? What does anyone know? . . . So, yes, you could say I feel like a failure as a mother!

D: I just want to hold you, that's so, so terrible. I just can't imagine.

P: No, exactly. Most people can't imagine. That's why I say

nothing. It was *my mother*, damn it, who forced me into giving it away. That's why I can't talk about mothering. I just don't believe your kind, I just don't believe it—sorry!

D (*bewildered*): I don't know what to say. I'm sorry too.

Dialogues like this—particularly around Persephone issues of loss, abandonment, or death—often have no resolution. Demeter needs to come out of her cozy and rather self-absorbed cocoon once in a while, and no one can get to her more than an unhappy Persephone. Demeter's impulse to rescue, to make it all right, to nurture, is of course very laudable in its place, but it is not the appropriate response to everything.

This Demeter got more than she bargained for when she invited the silent Persephone into the discussion. She was genuinely shocked by what she heard, never having been in a position of not wanting children and certainly never having conceived of hating one. So Persephone educated her a little about the underworld.

Being drawn out by Demeter was good for Persephone too. It brought to the surface a lot of bitterness that she had been nursing silently. She saw how she had been comparing herself negatively to successful mothers and really taking it all on. Healthy rage at the betrayal by her own mother was beginning to emerge even in this short exchange.

ATHENA, ARTEMIS, DEMETER, AND PERSEPHONE ON CHANGING THE WORLD

The Goddess Wheel gives ample opportunity not just for dialogue but theoretically for six-way exchanges. It rarely gets that diffused in practice, since most women will become identified with one pole or another of a debate. Here is an excerpt from a "quadrologue," in which the issue was less personal than the preceding ones but equally intense. It began as a discussion about life-styles and values, but the underlying dynamic that emerged had more to do with fundamental—which is to say, archetypal—differences of orientation to the world and to relationships.

ATH (ATHENA WOMAN): I think the only way we're going to effect any change in this society is if we all take some responsibility and fight for what we want. Look at what we've done in our city: women's health care centers, representation for women at state level, legislation of nondiscriminatory wage structures—real, solid changes.

ART (ARTEMIS WOMAN): That's great, and I'm sure we all applaud it. But I think if we put all our energy into political change, our life-style suffers. I think women need to experiment with whole new community structures *away from the cities*. They're decaying so fast, they're a bottomless pit. Small towns, maybe, but forget the cities.

D (DEMETER WOMAN): I kind of agree with you. I'm just not temperamentally inclined toward politics, but I think that I can contribute to the quality of life in my immediate community, *with my family*. If I get it right there, my children will spread it and so on.

ATH: Yes, but the family and community structures are breaking down everywhere, the economic indices make it quite clear—

ART: Oh, come off it, Athena, don't start all that "our studies have shown" stuff again. You admitted earlier that you live alone, with no mate or family, so this is all theory.

ATH: Yes, but you *can* legislate change—

P (PERSEPHONE WOMAN): May I say something? I'm a counselor, and I've been through my own crazy family scene and one failed marriage—I raise my eight-year-old daughter alone. I'm so far removed from political action that it sounds unreal to me, but people's pain is very real. I hear it every day, and it has very little to do with wage structures or even family love. It has to do with being real and with alienation. Yeah, sure, a bit more money, more jobs, birth control, and so forth will help, but that's all surface. People are just so, so alone—they just need a bit more honest being with each other. I'm sorry, Athena, it's none of my business, but all this political activity is a cover-up. You're alone, and I would say you are in pain.

ART: That's why I think we've got to start with fundamentals. I don't think your proposals are really radical, Athena.

They're nothing more than Band-Aids. The whole rotten structure is about to tumble down. Why bother shoring it up? Get
out of the cities.

ATH: But don't you see, that's where the power, the influence, is. Societies change from the center, not the periphery.

D: Maybe it's just a matter of perspective, but my center
is the home—what did some poet say, "Home is where you
start from?"

Obviously this dispute is not going to end with any simple agreement, but it did air a lot of strong feelings. Terms such as *introverted*
and *extraverted, conservative* and *liberal* seem barely adequate to convey
the highly complex and quite contrasting sensibilities these women
brought to their debate.

When the patriarchy suppressed the Goddess, it left the lesser goddesses bitter, wounded, and divided. The consequence, from which we
have been suffering ever since, is that women have had to exist deeply
alienated from themselves and from the core of their feminine being.
Dialogues such as those quoted actually begin to heal the dividedness
within the Great Goddess herself. We therefore recommend dialogue
as the first step toward reconciling ourselves, both outwardly as women
and inwardly as complete beings.

Knowing that all the lesser goddesses are connected primordially
to the Great Goddess, we come to realize what an act of redemption
it is for us to allow them the opportunity to come together; to tell their
stories, to have their say, and to listen compassionately to one another.
And the miracle is that they can come together either *within* us, as
individual women, or *between* us, in groups, when we explore their
patterns and conflicts in our lives and relationships. The Goddess
Wheel then becomes a tiny mirror of the greater world. If inner or
small-group dialogue can bring understanding and healing on a small
scale, the same is possible on a much larger scale. The dynamics operating are identical.

When we as women can see how deeply our differences and inner
strife derive from the wounded and disempowered goddesses, we can
use the Goddess Wheel as a powerful tool for feminine values clari-

fication. By listening compassionately to one another and to our shared struggles to become whole, we are also able to become fully differentiated as modern women, better able to face a complex and demanding world.

Men, too, listening to these often passionate psychodramatic debates, have been able to arrive at radical new understandings of their partners, colleagues, mothers, daughters, and sisters. In the next chapter we show how the goddess can also help men understand *their* reactions and roles in the complex and ancient dance of the sexes we are calling goddess psychology.

LIVING WITH
THE GODDESSES
(MOSTLY FOR MEN)

The great question that has never been answered, and which I have
not been able to answer despite my thirty years of research into the
feminine soul, is: What does a woman want?
—Sigmund Freud

WOMEN: AN ETERNAL MYSTERY
TO MEN

Despite all the powerful advances wrought by feminism and psychology, most men still agonize over Freud's celebrated question, What do
women really want? Possibly it is not given for men to really know.
Perhaps men must always live with this great and tantalizing puzzle.
Nevertheless we have found that goddess psychology can help many
men come a little closer to the complex heart of this mystery.

For a start, we believe that there is not one, but at least six ways
to pose this question—six ways corresponding to each of the different
goddess types, and then as many combinations as the goddess energies
need to weave within the psyche of any individual woman. Just the

fact that we can, with a little close attention, recognize more than one goddess in every woman may help us realize that of course there is no one or simple answer to this perplexing question. If anything, Freud's mistake was to want to generalize too broadly.

Let us take, for example, the old pat answer that every woman wants *love*. Even such a safe-sounding answer takes on a whole new meaning if we run it by all six goddess types. Aphrodite wants love of course, but does the kind of love she wants—sensual, ecstatic, passionate—suit all the goddesses? Certainly not Hera. Hera wants a rather different kind of love—devoted, reverential, faithful, kind, perhaps, but not especially sensual; that's simply not Hera's style. She likes to be put upon a pedestal, to be looked up to, honored for her authority, her opinions, and her person. Above all, Hera wants a man to fully concretize his love for her in a marriage that will make her both well respected as his wife and also prominent in their community.

And what kind of love does Persephone want? Something much more spiritual, tinged with mystical rather than the sensual ecstasy Aphrodite seeks or with Hera's material and social requirements. The Persephone woman wants her man to enter into a communion with her that is not entirely of this world. There is for Persephone a certain longing for the ineffable that will never be satisfied by Hera's splendid estates or even Demeter's lovely children.

Demeter's needs for love are different again. She wants to be loved for her capacity to give. In many ways, because of her huge capacity for mothering and nurturing, she almost feels she is love itself, giving not only to her children but to all and sundry. She might even say she doesn't need love because there is already so much of it in her life, reflected in the happiness of her children. But then, as we saw in her chapter, she may be so busy giving out that she is deeply needy inside and has forgotten how to ask.

As for Athena and Artemis, it is far from certain that love would be the first thing to spring to their minds, if they were asked Freud's famous question. Recognition, achievement, equal rights, justice, independence, to be left alone, or a healing vision of the earth and mankind—any or all of these could easily be named by either or both of them as more important than love. They are both so idealistic, forever seeing beyond themselves to the larger picture. Relationships do not feature strongly for them; in fact, they are more than a little shy of intimacy. So the whole issue of love conjures up ambivalence and un-certainty for them. They would usually rather set the whole business to one side and get on with the practical matters at hand. If we ask an Athena woman about love, we are more likely to elicit a philosophical discussion or a brilliant epigram, but not necessarily a personal re-joinder. Artemis is likely to find the question embarrassing and even distasteful.

Yet even revising Freud's question to What do each of the god-desses want? doesn't go far enough. Just recognizing single goddess types in the women we know is only the beginning of understanding goddess psychology. As we have emphasized from the first chapter, *every woman has all of the goddesses within her, but in different proportions.*

So when we ask the question of an individual woman, we might hear several often quite contradictory answers all at once. For example, we might think that a particular woman shows every sign of putting all her energies into being out in the world in a successful job. But then, with a sigh, she may admit, "What I really want is children." What we are hearing is the back-and-forth of her inner dialogue between Athena and Demeter, dialogues that are described in chapter 9. It is tempting to take sides in this often excruciating dialectic, but it is more often just as helpful to acknowledge and support the very process of dialogue. In the end, a woman has to know her own truth as a dynamic tension of these different inner voices we call the goddesses.

THE GODDESS AND HER CONSORTS

As we showed in the separate chapters on the goddesses, each indi-vidual goddess, on the evidence of her myths, is attracted to (or repelled by) a different type of mate, lover, or companion. These myths can give women today helpful clues for understanding how these god-desses, which live in varying proportions within them, influence their relationships with men. This works the other way around as well: knowledge of these archetypal patterns of relating can help modern men get some perspective on what different types of women expect regarding husband, lover, or friend.

Men reading this chapter may be helped by first completing the questionnaire to sort out which goddess types they are predominantly attracted to. Then they may wish to go on to the major chapters corresponding to their highest scores. But here, for handy reference for both men and women readers, we offer summaries of the six patterns of relationships we have identified as belonging to each of the goddesses, following the order of the Goddess Wheel.

Once again, we hasten to remind you that no woman is exclusively one goddess—this is not like sun-sign astrology, in which one is fixed as an Aries or a Scorpio. Rather, every woman has within her a complex mixture of all of the goddess types, which she may or may not recognize.

Nevertheless, one or two goddesses will inevitably stand out more strongly than others. So it is probably best for men and women to start with these more obvious character traits and attractive features. As a man starts to understand the goddess types, he may be able to actually reflect back to her certain goddess features a woman is only partially aware of. In this way he may be an important factor in awakening that side of her. But each man first needs to be conscious of what a woman's more conscious expectations of him are and where they originate. This is where goddess psychology can be extremely helpful.

ATHENA AND MEN

Athena is an intellectual. She tends to respect only those men whose muscle is mental, not the macho hero type. This is where she is distinctly different from Aphrodite. True, in Greek myth Athena was a patroness of heroes, but it was their cunning, inventiveness, and daring she most loved—Ulysses was one of her favorites in this respect. Such qualities are shared by many ambitious young men living in the cities today. Athena was also a goddess of crafts, what the Greeks called techne, which means "making." So, practical men who are creative in science, technology, and research are appealing to the modern Athena woman.

If she is drawn to academic life or to politics or to publishing, an Athena woman will usually want a companion who is in tune with her interests and her bright, inquiring mind. Although there isn't any precise mythic background for this, we believe that modern Athena is strongly attracted to the qualities of Hermes—known to the Romans as Mercury—the messenger of the gods. Hermes is sometimes seen to stand for the intellect, mind, and communication in general. This would today include all the media—journalism, television, radio, writing, publishing, advertising—as well as the academic world, research, and political campaigning. Mercurial men in this world can easily reflect and share Athena's own intense mental activity. To take another example from our workshops:

> Sally met Don at a lecture on Central American politics while they were both in law school. Sensing a kindred spirit in each other, they began attending many lectures, as well as concerts and films together; to prepare for exams, they formed a study group. After law school they found jobs in different firms, but in the same large city. Although they slept together a few times during the years of their friendship, they never lived together or seriously considered marriage. "It was more that we were the best of friends," Sally told the group. "We could talk to each other about anything; we kept each other intellectually honest by constantly challenging each other. It was a terrible loss to me when Don was killed by a drunk driver; I don't think I'll ever have a friend who understands me so well. I still miss him even though it has been five years since he died."

Athena is always adventurous and competitive and likes men with the same qualities. She is stimulated by debate and, as with Sally and Don, likes to both challenge and be challenged. Her mate, if she marries at all, will always need to be available for her as a mental sparring partner. Constantly keeping up with new films, plays, music, political developments, and the latest research makes her an avid reader who needs someone with whom she can intelligently discuss views, reviews, and opinions. Sometimes her career takes her into business investment or some international organization where she will move among diplomats, public servants, and politicians. She will value a mate or close friend with whom to mull over the intrigues and intricacies of these complex worlds.

Relationships as such are not especially intriguing to her, nor is the idea of marriage and family in traditional terms. If she marries, it will be to a colleague or to someone in an urbane, fast-paced career in many ways similar to her own. She is therefore not looking for a family man to have children with. If she does have children, they will most likely be experienced as a burden and a restriction to her initially, until she has gotten them squared away in school for part of the day. Citing feminist principles, she will want her husband to sacrifice an equal part of his career to raising their children. Traditional roles and values will come under heavy fire at this time, unless she experiences an unexpected surge of Demeter's mothering energy that removes her from her mental and career preoccupations. Later, when her children get older and more articulate, she may be a good friend to them, but things could be tough for a few years. Her mate will have to be very flexible and tolerant during these early years of her motherhood.

As often as not, Athena women prefer to stay single, devoting most of their creative energies to their careers or their creative work— writing, researching, editing, organizing, campaigning, painting, designing, and so on. Much of their sexual energy becomes quite sublimated into their work, and they will often be happy with purely platonic relationships with men.

For reasons we explore more fully in her specific chapter, Athena will also be strongly sexually attracted to older men. It is part of her Zeus complex, an idealization of father figures, that is mirrored in the Greek myth by Athena's closeness to her father. A modern Athena woman may well have had a very impressive father whom she idealized and to whom no younger man ever quite matches up. Or she may have had a very disappointing father, for whom she compensates in her imagination, always looking for certain ideals in men that can never be realized.

Either way the capacity of certain distinguished men to be a fatherlike authority will often deeply impress her. For this reason, it is not uncommon for an unmarried Athena woman in her twenties or thirties to have a long and quite deep relationship with an older, usually divorced man who mirrors an idealized Zeus. It is often an opportunity to explore part of her Aphrodite nature. A woman in one of our workshops, Anne, told this story about her affair with a much older man:

"I was twenty-five when I met J. He was a very successful international banker who managed investments for his multimillionaire clients. I'll never forget the first time I met him. It was an art gallery opening that I had been sent to cover by the paper I was then working for. My first impression of him was of a man of supreme self-confidence and sophistication. He was wearing a beautifully tailored suit with a silk shirt; his thick, gray hair was in striking contrast to his tan face. He seemed both youthful and mature. When I asked if I could photograph and interview him for my paper, he declined but invited me to have a drink with him after the opening. That night was the beginning of an affair that lasted three years and spanned more than a dozen countries. He was forty years older than I, but his energy was greater than most men half his age."

APHRODITE AND MEN

There is more to be said about Aphrodite and her relationships with men because they are more important to her and she usually has more of them than either Athena or Artemis.

Aphrodite likes her men to both look and act strong. She likes leaders, adventurers, powermongers, athletes, sportsmen, even what other goddess types tend to look down on as the jock or macho male. In Greek myth she has a passionate affair with Ares, the war god and epitome of the warrior type. Muscle, and the determination and strong will that produce it, deeply appeal to the Aphrodite woman, much more than brains or a steady income. She admires adventurous, outgoing, well-traveled men of the world; all the qualities that add up to what in her chapter we call the phallic-narcissistic male, the man with a strong ego and a healthy self-love. Or, to put it in cruder, but nevertheless appropriate terminology, a man with balls.

Since she is also a goddess of beauty, she will also admire handsome and sophisticated men of fine tastes and with a certain worldliness. Nothing melts an Aphrodite woman more than candle-lit dinners and soft music. She loves gifts, glamorous rendezvous, and any opportunity to dress dazzlingly. Any man courting an Aphrodite might as well come to terms right away with her need to be the prima donna. Hollywood and the tabloids like to portray Aphrodite women around playboys and millionaires. James Bond, though predominantly a stereotype for men, embodies many of the qualities appealing to Aphrodite in his urbanity, his charm, and his restless adventuring.

A man cannot be Aphrodite's lover or husband if he doesn't basically feel good about himself, which is to say his power, his ability to achieve, his fundamental masculinity. All this will be reflected in bed, when his phallic self-confidence will be fully tested by Aphrodite. No amount of education or money will impress an Aphrodite woman if a man cannot perform comfortably in his body, which, as far as she is concerned, is also where the foundations of his feeling self will be. As we said in her chapter, this goddess wants the heart—nothing less will satisfy her—and her favored man will need to be fully open to his own capacity for sensuality, beauty, and love in all its forms.

The Aphrodite woman brings out the extremes in the man she loves. She challenges a man to be his most heroic and masculine in the outer world and, at the same time, to find his most feminine and tender self in his intimate relationship with her. The Aphrodite spirit has often appeared in warrior cultures, such as ancient Greece and Rome, as a kind of balance to the predominantly warmongering spirit of the times. Venus-Aphrodite was often allegorized by the Romans as the loving and peaceful complement to fiery Mars, their war god. In medieval Europe, at the time of the brutal Crusades, she appeared as the patroness of the troubadours, playing a major inspiration in the courtly-love movement, which served to soften and civilize the crude arts of war.

The Aphrodite woman loves to bring out the other side of the overachiever, the fighting man, namely his sentimentality, his softness, his passion. Yet she never matronizes or smothers such a man; it is always the mystery of his phallic maleness that she worships. She adores encouraging him to truly lose himself in the great act of love so that she can merge with his ecstatic explosion of energy in the transcendent moment of orgasm.

By her very example of total erotic abandon, Aphrodite teaches a man to be what D. H. Lawrence called "love-submissive" to the woman he loves. When a man can, like Tristan, give himself "utterly to love," he undergoes, in the moment of orgasm, a kind of death. The French, self-appointed experts in such matters, call this *le petit mort*—"the lesser death"—in which a man and woman momentarily lose themselves to a greater power and are reborn. It is one of Aphrodite's mysteries; one of the ways in which she opens the heart to the divine Eros, who, the Greeks say, created all.

Every man should realize that there is much to challenge him about an Aphrodite woman's indulgence in the arts of eros. It is almost fair to say that often she is as much in love with love itself as she is with her individual lover. The god Eros was often far from constant, spreading his arrows far and wide. So a man needs a strong ego to suffer Aphrodite's changing affections. She may love for an evening, a year, or a lifetime, but never predictably. Her ways are not ruled by social convention, like Hera, nor do mental pacts or shared ideals mean much to her, as with Athena. Aphrodite will open as many hearts as she breaks, as Peter, one of our workshop participants recounted:

> "My marriage had been going downhill for some time and I had taken to working late and hanging out with workmates rather than going home. I met Jane in a bar one evening. She was a semisuccessful actress who said she had regular work in a modeling agency. She was away a lot on modeling assignments and must have had lovers all over the place, I later began to realize. At any rate, when she came on to me that night and took me back to her apartment, I thought my circuits would blow. I realized I had never really known what lovemaking was about till then.
>
> "As you might guess, it accelerated the breakdown of my marriage. I became quite obsessed with Jane and she with me. I had never known any woman who seemed to be so inside me, so warm and affectionate, so utterly natural in bed. She must have loved seeing me blossom after the depressed state she first found me in.
>
> "I more or less lived for her for six months, while my divorce papers went through. I was walking on air much of the time. Then, one day, Jane came back from some photographic assignment in the Caribbean and announced flatly that she had met this older man with a business down there who had offered her a job, and so on. I got the message—like I had been punched hard in the belly! I packed my bags and left. It took me months to get over it. I went to the heights and to the depths, but I sure learned a lot."

Aphrodite stands for passion in relationships; in its original sense, passion also meant suffering. The man who is drawn to Aphrodite must therefore be prepared to undergo a certain amount of pain—from separation, loss, jealousy, hurt, rejection—when he commits himself to the way of the heart. These are some of the trials that the old medieval romancers saw as part of the initiation of the true knight of love. Aphrodite often demands of a man that he become strong by first becoming weak, that he experience the woundedness of his own immature feeling nature before he is truly worthy of love. In knowing his own feeling nature, he is also discovering his inner feminine self, his inner goddesses.

We mentioned that as well as her role as goddess of love, Aphrodite was a goddess of beauty and hence the spiritual matroness of all the arts. So men who are painters, sculptors, poets, dramatists, novelists, and musicians will always gravitate to the Aphrodite woman, because she has such a natural intuitive understanding of the inner ideals they are trying to express in their creations. The Aphrodite woman knows more deeply than the other goddess types what it is for a man to bring forth his soul in the creative act. She also knows what Jung saw so clearly, that a man's soul is essentially feminine. So Aphrodite understands not just how to open a man's heart but also how to mirror it back to him in the beauty and harmony of his creations, how to be his *femme inspiratrice*, his muse, the unfailing inspiration of his soul.

PERSEPHONE AND MEN

Since the Persephone woman's life is actively geared toward the understanding of spiritual matters—occultism, metaphysics, messages from "the other side," healing, and mysticism—she wants a male partner who is a spiritual seeker like herself, someone who is genuinely sympathetic to the idea and reality of spiritual influences. Men who are mostly extraverted—achievers and materialists—will rarely be attractive to her, nor she to them. Since so much of her energy is focused on the nonphysical, the sensual concerns of Aphrodite will be of secondary interest to her; eros only exists for her as a pathway to the spirit, not the other way around.

The Persephone woman will often have deeply conflicting feelings about men. She may harbor half-buried childhood abuses or a seemingly innate suspicion that men are betrayers and somehow dangerous. As a result she will be inclined to keep her distance from most of the opposite sex throughout childhood or adolescence. Later, when she feels more confident that she is in charge of things, she will choose relationships with introverted, spiritually inclined men who are quite soft and gentle, with a certain feminine quality of protectiveness.

> Lewis had already been part of a spiritual studies group for several months when Janet joined the group. A shy and unathletic man, he had been interested in such subjects as astrology and numerology since high school. Then his esoteric studies had provided him with an outlet for his solitariness. The son of a loud, domineering father, he had vowed never to treat women as he had so often seen his mother treated. Janet was attracted to Peter for his gentleness and seriousness of purpose.

Deep down Persephone treats all relationships with a degree of trepidation. She has an acute antenna to pick up warning signals of difficulty and conflict. In fact, she so loathes conflict that she will use all her mediumistic talents to foresee it and her conciliatory and sweet nature to smooth over things long before they reach any kind of explosion point.

Because of this underlying and almost habitual fear, the Persephone woman is in fact quite manipulative in all her relationships with both men and women. She sees herself as looking only to orchestrate harmony and good feeling, to see all things "in the light," but in fact her excessive emphasis on the light is usually a denial of any darkness, any negativity whatsoever. She actually succeeds in driving dissension and any expression of anger or violence underground. By expecting similar "positive thinking" from the man she has chosen to trust, she may often, for the very best of motives, be suppressing his individuality and his masculinity. In extreme cases, what she may not see is that her mate is in many ways as totally in her power as the henpecked husband of an overbearing Hera.

Relationships that are satisfactory to Persephone may have a strong illusory quality to them that she will not be aware of. Because of the intense web of psychic preoccupations that she obsessively shares with her lover or mate, she will often help create a distinct psychic *folie à deux* between the two of them. The common focus that binds them— a common metaphysical training, some shared spiritual path—is extremely seductive because they do indeed speak the same language. An Athena woman, by contrast, would probably insist on a separate teacher from that of her mate so that she could debate the different systems, but not so Persephone.

Because of her chronic lack of boundaries she can easily feel herself totally absorbed by her loved one's psychic issues, which she makes very much her own. The result is that he will often be profoundly grateful and moved by her uncanny insights into his inner self. While this spiritual love affair is at its height, the two of them will find themselves endlessly discussing and exchanging the subtlest of insights and spiritual nuances. He will be enraptured by this woman who sees so deeply into his soul. When this happens, there is for the man an almost egoless bliss in the fusion of their two psyches, a kind of mystical union with her in which she becomes the soul mother of his inner evolution.

Such a symbiotic relationship may last for a while, but sooner or later it will become intolerable for a man's ego and he will have to withdraw in one way or another. Sometimes quite out of the blue, wild rages will appear, bringing distress and then estrangement. Inevitably they will leave the Persephone woman herself feeling misunderstood and bitterly betrayed. This is all the negativity that they have agreed to deny, suddenly surfacing. She needs to see how, quite unconsciously, she has set herself up as a kind of psychic mother to him as her divine child. They have together been enacting the part of the Persephone myth where the goddess gives birth to the child of the mysteries, deep in the underworld.

Archetypally, this child would be Dionysus, the god who dies and is reborn through the mother. In religious terms he represents the eternal quality of the spirit, the principle of life perpetually renewing itself. In Greek art the young Dionysus is usually represented as very soft and effeminate, almost androgynous. As a child, he is frequently surrounded by women nursemaids; as a young man, he is pursued by ecstatic women followers, the maenads, who, according to the myth, kill and sacrifice him.

Clearly the model of Dionysus as companion of the Persephone woman is no easy model for any man to adopt in their relationship. For one thing, the myth suggests that he must either remain a child or else constantly sacrifice himself to the greater power of the mother principle. No man can carry this archetype for long without severe mental disturbance—Dionysus was in fact a god of ecstatic madness.

Such a relationship, we believe, really says more about Persephone's intercourse with the mysterious power of the spirit than with any actual man. One of Persephone's greatest challenges is to clearly distinguish between the inner guide and the outer friend. Only then will she be fully ready for proper relationships. Often this will take the help of a trained guide or teacher.

Even then Dionysus only represents one side of the masculine dynamic Persephone must deal with in her inner and outer lives. For just as Dionysus represents the principle of life, Hades, lord of the underworld, represents the principle of death, to whom Persephone is eventually married in the myth. Sooner or later the Persephone woman must encounter the shadowy Dark Lord in order to be fully initiated into his mysteries.

Sometimes Persephone will mistake the kindly persona of a man with quite serious psychopathic traits and find herself trapped in a nightmare relationship based purely on power and brutality. Whether it is the result of his growing alcoholism, depression, unemployment, postwar traumatic-shock syndrome, or sheer perversity, she is suddenly face-to-face with her own worst fears of violence, abuse, and even possible death. She has drawn to her an incarnation of Hades and a no-exit hell of destructiveness. Perhaps there was briefly a time when she sentimentally thought she could help and cure him, just as he genuinely saw in her understanding and salvation, but that moment has barely passed before she realizes in horror just how trapped she is.

At thirty-six, Brad had never married and seemed to have difficulty maintaining a steady relationship with women. For a while he had a homosexual lover, but that had not worked out either. When he first saw Melanie, she was feeding the ducks on the pond at the town park. For days he returned to the pond at the same time in hopes that she would reappear. When at last she came again, he managed to overcome his shyness and talk with her. During the following weeks they met often at the pond and then went to a nearby coffee shop to talk. Brad found in Melanie a sympathetic listener who seemed to understand the pain of his lonely and tormented childhood as the only son of a psychotic mother who had rejected him from birth and a distraught father who did not have time to attend to the emotional needs of a small boy. A few months after they met, Brad asked Melanie to move into his apartment with him and she agreed. All seemed well with them, and Melanie actually believed that her influence was helping Brad erase the pain of his childhood. Then she discovered that she was pregnant. Anticipating Brad's enthusiasm, Melanie prepared a special dinner to celebrate their good news. But instead of reacting positively to her news, Brad blew up. He smashed the plates and glasses and raged at her for her carelessness. Melanie felt that her world had fallen apart; two weeks later, following an abortion, she moved out of his apartment and in with a friend. "I was terrified," she told the group in a workshop. "He suddenly changed from this sweet, loving guy to a madman. He reminded me of my father and the hell of my own childhood."

Not every Persephone woman will go through this if she is lucky, but she may not escape periods of her life when she will find herself hearing about or being close to accidents, suicides, terminal illnesses, or sudden death of one kind or another. She is, in some ways, a kind of lightning rod for fatal happenings and disasters. If she can accept this and work with this dark energy, instead of being just a victim to it, she might find her way to the deep satisfaction of nursing, hospice work, counseling the dying, or psychotherapy that works with deep trauma. She might well marry a doctor, a surgeon, or another therapist—a professional colleague with whom she can share and objectify the world of suffering, tragedy, and death that she seems constantly drawn to and that she is uniquely endowed to understand.

ARTEMIS AND MEN

Most of the time the Artemis woman does not think or care too much about relationships with men—or relationships as such. Aphrodite's candle-lit dinners mean little or nothing to her; Persephone's search for a soul mate with compatible vibrations cuts little ice with her. Probably the most independent of the goddesses—closely followed by Athena—she prefers to do most things by herself; in fact solitude is in itself enormously attractive to her.

Artemis's predominant activity in ancient myth was solitary hunting in the forests. Today an Artemis woman still loves the forests, the wilderness, the open sea, the great untouched world of nature. Today hunting has become a dominant metaphor for her fixed, tireless, energetic drive to pursue some goal or target. Like her closest sister, Athena, Artemis is an achiever: she likes to get things done, whether it be a nature conservancy project, getting a wildlife magazine started, or running a marathon.

If Artemis tolerates having a man around, he has to be, like her, a doer, an achiever, an outdoor type; someone who is happy being absorbed in practical activities, concrete projects that keep him physically preoccupied. The one male that Artemis of myth allowed close to her was her brother, Apollo (see also Artemis chapter). He, too, was a hunter and was known for a somewhat aloof and distant disposition. Actually, the Artemis woman will prefer the kind of man who, like Apollo, keeps a certain emotional distance. She respects such self-containment and the way he gets on with his own projects and activities. When he is undemanding and independent in this way, she can derive a lot of pleasure from having him doing things alongside her.

Nevertheless, the Artemis woman's attitude to men may seem rather puzzling at first. She will be perfectly happy with a man or a group of men going on a pony trek in the wilderness or being part of a crew of men on a sailing trip. She wants to be treated as no different from the men; indeed she will be insulted if she is patronized or treated as less physically competent. And yet—here is the part that baffles men—while she does genuinely admire men who are taciturn and competent, she would probably be just as happy with a group of women with similar outdoor interests!

Any man who wants to show off his endurance, his physical prowess, or his toughness to an Artemis woman is in for ego-deflating disappointment. The Artemis woman has all those skills herself. What, she might say, do they have to do with having a male body? The answer is, of course, nothing if you are a fit, active, and resourceful Artemis who is yourself forever busy doing, making, training, fixing, climbing, racing. The man who wants his pectorals admired is really looking for an Aphrodite woman, not an Artemis. Aphrodite does indeed love beautiful bodies and rippling muscles for their visual and sensual qualities, though she has little interest in the athletic activities that produce them—except, perhaps, to maintain her own figure as she grows older.

It may help men to look a little more closely at the resemblances and differences between Artemis women and Aphrodite women. Both can be very physically attractive to virile, active men. On the surface they both seem to care a lot about their bodies, generally keeping trim figures. And they both seem very comfortable in their bodies, too: Aphrodite will be naturally graceful and grounded in hers, while Artemis has a lithe, supple ease of movement. They both love to dance, love rhythm and music. Many a male has been driven to near distraction by the eroticism of their free dance movements. But right here in the dance there is a major difference: Artemis dances for herself; Aphrodite dances for both herself and her partner. Aphrodite's dance could well lead to the bedroom, it is a part of the courtship ritual for her. But Artemis will want to dance alone on into the night, oblivious of anything, except perhaps the moon.

Everything that Aphrodite does in dressing and taking care of her body is highly self-conscious. She is always aiming for effect. Basically she wants to make herself attractive to a man, which is why she spends so much time in front of mirrors. Artemis, on the other hand, loathes mirrors; she probably doesn't even own one. Her eros is so totally self-containing that it does not really need a partner to complete the energy circuit. Attracting men plays little or no part in her psychic makeup. This is why she rarely dresses in any but practical ways. Courtship behavior is quite unimportant and alien to her nature.

Because of all this, the Artemis woman is better off, as we have hinted, with men who are themselves emotionally self-contained and who are in fact contentedly introverted. Artemis will do just fine with men who are farmers, craftsmen, artists, researchers, or writers, as well as fellow wilderness explorers, sailors, or adventurers like herself. Men who need mothering, spiritual understanding, or ego support had better go seek out Demeter, Persephone, or Aphrodite.

Artemis will want in a male sexual partner a man who is free of all narcissistic needs, and who demands little of her, save that she is always free to come and go as she wishes. Shyness and reserve about sex in a man are very acceptable to Artemis. She herself never wants to be rushed, often preferring to take the initiative in such matters. She is extremely modest and secretive about this mystery of mysteries and is utterly unimpressed by male displays of machismo or bragging. Yet she respects a man who, like her, can be spontaneously in touch with and unself-conscious about his instinctive sexual nature.

As we speculated in our Artemis chapter, this goddess's true partner in sex may well have once been the ever-phallic nature god Pan. Now, there is a challenge to men; to let go of the many layers of our masculine persona built up through centuries of heroic patriarchy and return to the natural wild man within us!

DEMETER AND MEN

The Demeter woman has much to give in any relationship. Giving and loving are practically synonymous to her. A man who wins her favor will feel himself exceedingly lucky and proud of such a woman. She has seemingly endless reserves and is so in touch with the deepest needs of others that he cannot but feel loved and fully nurtured emotionally by her.

If a Demeter woman is so in touch with what others want and need, what does she herself want and need of her man? For one thing, solid financial support; her man must be a strong and steady provider. Since the Demeter woman has, for several centuries now, been cut off from the immediate production of food and sustenance, she is deeply dependent upon her mate as a primary source of material resources.

In the days when most of the population lived on or close to the land, a Demeter woman would be supremely fulfilled, living and laboring as part of the cycle of planting, tending, harvesting, preserving, and feeding. Nowadays most of those direct functions are denied to her, so she needs money that can be converted into material goods with which to nurture her family. Although circumstances may force her to take work in an office or factory, she usually much prefers to be at home with her children. This is made possible in the modern world by a working husband who fulfills the role of provider.

Since Demeter focuses so strongly on the home and the family, the actual means by which her mate provides for her is relatively un-important. He can be anything, from a banker to a bus driver to a disc jockey, just so long as he brings home the paycheck. In that respect she is utterly different from that other power in the home, Hera, who is extremely interested in her husband's work and status in the outside world because it reflects upon her. A man who marries a Demeter woman expecting her to take a close interest in his career and give constructive feedback will be quickly disappointed once the first babies appear. If he is looking for a business partner in a wife, it is really Hera he should have married.

Intellectual distinction is in itself of no more interest to Demeter than is business acumen. From her perspective they are both means to the end of material security and plenty. A man who is a writer or college professor could well marry a warm, comfortable Demeter, but he will have to seek intellectual companionship with his collegues. The most he will usually get from a Demeter as he announces his latest article or professorship is, "That's lovely, dear. I'm so glad for you." She is unlikely to want to read the article or know the title of the professorship. For sympathetic support of this nature, a man would need an Athena or a Hera as his wife.

Any man who marries a Demeter woman should bear in mind that the true center of her world is in every way her home and her children. And we mean "center" in a way few men really comprehend. Nothing, absolutely nothing comes before her passionate devotion to the feeding and raising of her children. Her husband's work, even if he is president of a huge corporation or a world-famous actor, is essentially peripheral to her. The outer world becomes decreasingly important in exact pro-portion to how far it is from her home or her children. This is why a man may feel somewhat disturbed by that sweet, but glazed smile that often comes over her face when he talks about his work or politics or sports. All that is far away and really quite trivial to her—"men's games," she might call them to another Demeter friend.

Since the Demeter woman is first and foremost a mother, it is hard for her not to see most, if not all men, as sons, rather than adult males. She does, of course, have a fantasy of a grown man, too, but it's a rather sentimental picture of a young hero type who bravely overcomes the obstacles of the world to return home faithfully to his beloved wife laden with prizes. This view of men naturally mirrors her own inexperience in the greater world. It remains immature just so long as she never extends her horizons beyond the home—developing her Athena or Hera side, for instance. Nevertheless for the man who manifests the qualities of the youthful hero, Demeter has boundless love and admiration.

From the man's viewpoint the Demeter woman can fulfill deep needs for home and security. The cozy picture of home life replete with apple pies, golden retrievers, and Thanksgiving family dinners we know so well from the media and from the artist Norman Rockwell is part of the contemporary yearning that many men feel for Demeter. Men will shackle themselves to dull and repetitive jobs for their whole lifetime in order to gain this. But unfortunately they will often fail to mature emotionally, the pull of mother and home being essentially regressive.

Consciously or unconsciously, what many such men are seeking in the emotional warmth and security of a Demeter woman's love is primarily mothering. In these relationships they will frequently confuse such longing with their sexual needs. This is not altogether surprising, since Demeter is generous with her eros as with everything. But in fact they may at a deep level really want to be another one of Demeter's children, albeit one with grown-up privileges! Some are even prepared to pay the price of having their more worldly and seemingly manly achievements gently "matronized."

More often than not, the Demeter woman's mate will tend to lead a kind of double life: one lived with other men and work colleagues and one lived with his wife and family at home. Such men enjoy having a separate male world of their own, because it fulfills a need in them to perpetuate a kind of eternal adolescent bonding with other men like themselves. It also protects them from the often overwhelming power of the mother archetype experienced in their mate. A part of such a man never fully outgrows his youth in emotional terms; he remains, instead, quite deeply attached to his wife as a mother figure.

Sometimes a Demeter will be attracted to a somewhat older, solid, taciturn male, who is something of a father figure to her. He will tend to be a practical person—an engineer, builder, carpenter, gardener, mechanic—in Jungian typology a sensation type, one who has many earthy qualities, a maker and a doer. He appeals deeply to the part in Demeter that herself wants to be taken care of as a child but that rarely gets expressed. We might almost call him an Earth Father, though this is a rarely seen archetype in our culture. Possibly he belongs to the old farm cultures that disappeared with the drift to the cities. In those times the farmer and his wife lived more or less securely close to the great cycles of the earth and reproduction. So much of this has been lost, as we pointed out in Demeter's chapter, but a part of the old longing is there in many Demeter women, just as there still remain many men who manifest this solid, grounded quality that complements her extremely well.

HERA AND MEN

Since so much of our chapter on Hera is about her difficult and complex relationship with her husband and her sons, we do not need to repeat ourselves here. Nevertheless, it may be worthwhile to recapitulate certain key points and to look at Hera a bit more from the point of view of the man's psyche.

The Hera woman looks primarily to marriage and partnership to satisfy her main ambitions, which are status and power. While love and children may come into her calculations, they are not nearly so important as they would be to an Aphrodite or a Demeter woman. Like Demeter, she wants a man who is a solid provider for her family, but it is essential that he be someone important in the community, not just a breadwinner. In contrast to Demeter, who sees almost everything in terms of what is good for her children and who can be quite self-effacing in public, Hera wants to be looked up to as the wife of a man known and well-respected in the larger world. She wants to be someone, not just the little woman at home.

Hera likes ambitious and powerful men. She will always gravitate toward men with potential for leadership and with executive skill; later in life she will be seen to have instinctively chosen successful corporate managers, bankers, or politicians when she was young. But it doesn't matter, to begin with, whether they are intellectuals or practical types, provided they rise to the top of their chosen professions and wield power and influence. She will therefore require her intellectual husband to be more than just a professor; she will have college presidency picked out for him. Likewise she will expect her practical mate to do more than just invent new gardening implements; she'll want him to turn his skills into a highly profitable company.

For a man with such ambitions she can be the most devoted and loyal of mates. She wants to share her husband's struggles all the way to the top and to feel that she is an integral part of them. If he forms his own company, she will probably want to be on the board. She will not like a very independent man who goes his own way in his career and expects her to follow her own, as the husband of an Athena or an Artemis woman might do. "Partnership" for the Hera woman speaks of much more than just marriage; it means mutually shared life goals.

It goes almost without saying that the Hera woman will not tolerate wimps, laziness, or the kind of dependency that Demeter may well foster in her husband. Woe betide the man who makes all sorts of promises to a Hera wife and then never makes good on them. She will make his life a misery, henpecking him almost to death. She expects courage, perseverance, and tenacity from her mate; weakness on his part will make her blood boil.

Superficially a young Hera woman may seem a bit like a Demeter woman in her initial devotion to children and the home, but this is never her main focus. As the children grow up, she'll look for more and more involvement in the community or her husband's career—and rightly so, since this is where her power instincts will best be satisfied. If her husband mistook her for a warmly docile nest-building Demeter when he first married her, he will now be in for a big shock. All his masculinity will be shaken to the roots as she challenges him to abandon that youthful mother dependency and find the masterful Zeus in himself. Many marriages founder at this point, the husband seeking out affairs with younger women to mend his fractured ego, the Hera wife becoming possessed with fury that her mate will not live up to the potential she has always seen in him.

The man who chooses to live with a Hera woman must therefore be prepared for what can truly be a lifelong and often painful experiment in partnership, in which he ceases to be fully individual from the time he marries. He and his Hera wife are from that moment on a unit, in which she becomes a part of him and he a part of her. A certain loss of ego is required for such a man, but the gains he can expect if he fully opens himself to a loving Hera are immeasurable. It is only when he tries to keep his own power to himself and not share it that the sort of quarrelsome marriage the Greek Zeus and Hera had will ensue. If both partners can stick with the hurts and abuses that inevitably come with any power struggles, they will both come out, as the years pass, with much stronger and fuller personalities.

Something of the intense psychological transformation this may entail is described in the poem we quoted by William Carlos Williams in the Hera chapter. Here instead we end with one of our favorite poems on the quasi-mystical merging that can happen in a good marriage; it is by a Chinese woman poet (Kuan Tao-sheng) of the thirteenth century:

> You and I
> Have so much love,
> That it
> Burns like a fire,
> In which we bake a lump of clay
> Molded into a figure of you
> And a figure of me.
> Then we take both of them,
> And break them into pieces,
> And mix the pieces with water,
> And mold again a figure of you,
> And a figure of me.
> I am in your clay.
> You are in my clay.
> In life we share a single quilt.
> In death we will share one coffin.
> —from *The Orchid Boat: Women Poets of China*,
>   translated by Kenneth Rexroth

HONORING THE CHANGING SEASONS OF A WOMAN'S LIFE

As we remind women in chapter 9, "Reconciling Your Inner Goddesses," it is most important to honor the many faces of the goddesses as they emerge in different periods of any woman's life. This is important for men too. However much we men want the woman we fell in love with to stay that way all her life, it is unrealistic and more than a little naive from the perspective of goddess psychology.

The portraits of individual goddess types and their relationships are necessarily limited and somewhat artificial. Women go through all sorts of changes in their lives in the modern world. The goddesses a woman knew well in adolescence—Athena or Artemis, say—may be gone by her mid-twenties, when having a family brings out quite new understandings and other energies—perhaps Demeter or Hera.

Men need to be tolerant of what in modern women's process of self-discovery we call the seasons of a woman's life. These are the seasons that correspond to the natural emergence of different goddesses at different times in a woman's life cycle, as well as goddesses that appear as if by fate; Persephone may present herself as a result of a death or serious accident or illness.

When men talk freely about women in our workshops, they often admit that the woman they fell in love with shocked them by suddenly becoming transformed into someone they hardly knew. They thought they had married an Artemis, with that love of the outdoors, long hikes, sailing trips, and so on, but now they can't get her out of the house. Why? Possibly Demeter is emerging, and, in her predominantly taciturn Artemesian way, the woman doesn't think to tell them.

Most men see or at least project a lot of Aphrodite onto the woman they eventually marry. This is natural. Our whole society encourages the Aphrodite ritual of "falling in love," which we then legalize and sanctify by Hera's more permanent institution, called marriage. The afterglow of Aphrodite's honeymoon ecstasy may last months and sometimes years, but nothing will extinguish the waning fires of eros quicker than a pregnancy.

Perhaps there is no more difficult transition for a new husband to make than when the Aphrodite they see in their beloved slowly but surely begins to fade and is overtaken by a very different image, that of Demeter. That lovely slim waist expands, those firm young breasts now hang like ripe fruit as she transforms into the unmistakable bursting rotundity of the Great Mother. The overflowing eros of the honeymoon days starts to dry up, often in both of them. Her libido even seems to disappear into her in some mysterious way. What is happening is that all the eros energy previously directed outward onto him is now transmuting into Demeter energy; it has gone underground, to feed the new life incubating within her.

When a man first falls in love and Aphrodite rules his heart, he is perhaps seen by the woman he loves as a powerful phallic, heroic male. But now, as she finds the tremendous generative power that belongs to Demeter, he may in subtle ways shrink in her consciousness and become less powerful, more diminutive in her eyes. The man's sexual needs may arouse instead her mothering eros and undermine his sense of maleness, reducing him to feeling more dependent, less phallic. This is the reason why so many men have extramarital affairs during their wife's pregnancy. Emergent Demeter deeply threatens their masculine identity, shrinking it to that of a little boy, so men feel driven to reassert themselves at this time.

The best way for a man to avoid this is first to recognize it. The second thing that every man needs to do at this time is to find his even stronger father energy. *This* is what an expectant wife needs from him now—Earth Father strength and protection. She is now planted firmly in Demeter; the man should be the containing garden for her emergent growth. He must change with her. This could be the first major lesson for any man in learning to flow with the seasons of the goddess. Maybe Aphrodite will return for him as she regains her original figure, but equally she may live with Demeter's ample body for many years as she pays homage to the wonders of that goddess.

Another difficult emergent goddess for many men to recognize and acknowledge in their wives is Hera. Since Hera only fully emerges in maturity, a man may manage to avoid noticing her presence in his mate in the early days of their marriage. This fine woman he married may have strong opinions and ideas about raising the children, running the household, and how to celebrate family holidays, and he rarely objects. After all he is caught up in his rising career and may feel more than a little guilty that she is always at home, apparently sacrificing her career for the family they both want.

But now, as their children are racing through adolescence, that strong will and forcefulness he always admired in her seems to be getting out of hand. She's more argumentative, a bit interfering in those difficult business decisions, and he gets more than a little irritable. She seems to be on his case a lot, and he may suddenly find his eros wandering. Younger women seem increasingly attractive—they're more admiring of him for one thing! What such a man is seeing, if he cares to look, is the portentous emergence of his wife's Hera, and with it all the huge problems and challenges of the real season of that goddess's life: maturity.

The biggest challenges in the marriage are just beginning. A man now has to learn to share power, supporting the tremendous abilities his wife has but envisioning her fully out in the world, not just at home or running the golf club socials. A whole new person is emerging, one who doesn't have time to flatter his once tender ego anymore but who, instead, puts him on the line more and more. He can always retreat into flattering affairs that beckon with lovely Aphrodites or young, uncommitted Athenas, but he will really be running away. He married Hera as his true lifelong partner, even if it feels like an unconscious mistake twenty years later. But there was no mistake, just long-term planning by his unconscious mind! Hera is now emerging to challenge him to find his own maturity.

Sometimes it is a quite different goddess who emerges in the second half of life. The tireless Demeter wife who had been utterly absorbed in the children's growth and development now finds she wants to go back to college, even though she feels deeply inadequate scholastically. Her Athena side never got much support in high school and she dropped out of college; she wasn't the scholarly type then. But now certain things have really begun to grab her intellectually and she sees a whole career pattern emerging—social work, community nursing, teaching in a Waldorf school, for example. As her husband, a man can help her overcome her feelings of inferiority so that she can get through college successfully this time. It may mean that he has to take over a lot of the household chores now. Demeter is no longer around to get his supper; she's at the community college four days and two nights a week and studying most weekends!

Another perplexing shift for certain men is when they have been married to or living with either an Athena or an Artemis woman for a long time when suddenly these independent and resourceful women discover their unexplored Aphrodite nature. They might have thought they had a perfect setup: neither of them wanted children but opted instead for intellectual and creative companionship, parallel careers, a wonderful network of friends, plus carefully chosen watering places for their equally busy life-styles. Sex was good, when they could grab it, but it was never the most compelling thing in their relationship, they'd have to admit.

But now, quite suddenly, this bright and energetic companion or wife has discovered the joys of sex as she has never known them before. Her liberated mind finds ways around monogamous values, and she is busy indulging in not one but several affairs. Aphrodite has struck with a vengeance, and she's transformed the woman so that she's suddenly less serious, more open, and more appealing than ever. Her sensuality has blossomed in a whole new way, and a man can feel somehow dowdy and left out. Their old parallel and somewhat mental relationship styles have taken a serious tumble. Perhaps the lesson is that it is time to look for what is missing in his own eros, to come down out of the headier heights he has inhabited for so long and loosen up a bit.

To honor all these changes that the woman he loves is going through over the years is surely a great challenge for any man. It is easy to react to them by turning tail and setting out to find another partner. Sometimes this may even be appropriate; the partners may indeed have outgrown each other, and a man may have nothing new in him to complement the new energies emerging in the woman. But more often, to arrive at this conclusion is to fail to accept the possibility of change in oneself as a man.

All men have in them heroes, lovers, fathers, leaders, listeners, protectors of one kind or another and it is never asking too much to make the long overdue sacrifice of the whining little boy that prevents their emergence. When a man is strong in his masculine self he can also face the goddesses within him. And here men have an even bigger challenge than women. For just as the goddesses have lain suppressed and dormant in women so too have they slept in all but the most exceptional and creative of men for millennia.

When the goddesses start to awaken in men—usually this happens in strong attractions where women mirror back certain goddess qualities—they will not be easy to accept to begin with. A man who suddenly finds how much a small baby brings out his mothering instinct (Demeter) may be quite embarrassed at first. So may a man who discovers a talent for designing women's clothes (Aphrodite) or an ability to channel psychically (Persephone). But once a man is strongly in touch with one of the goddesses within him, others will slowly emerge and his own dialogues, not unlike those of women, can begin.

If men can learn to flow a little more with their own changing seasons, they can learn to participate in the truly wonderful reawakening, the healing, and the renewal of the goddesses going on around them. Nothing quite like it has happened before in human history—and it needs conscious male energy to really succeed.

PART THREE

SOME CONCLUSIONS

ELEVEN

THE
TRANSFORMATIONS
OF THE GODDESS

*To us of the West, these things are mysteries only dimly sensed. We
cannot speak of them with certainty, but at the same time we cannot
ignore the fact that modern poetry and art and the dreams and
phantasies of many people today agree with the myths and religious
teachings of the past. The symbols, which appear today, and their
development, show that a movement is taking place beneath the surface
of consciousness, which resembles in a fundamental way the movements
which have been immortalized in the teachings of the past. They tell
of a path for renewal which is new in our day but old in actual fact,
a path of redemption through the things that are lowest, which is the
fundamental teaching of the moon religions, and of the worship of the
feminine principle.*
—M. ESTHER HARDING,
WOMEN'S MYSTERIES, ANCIENT AND MODERN

PLUS ÇA CHANGE...

Not long ago the *Utne Reader*, which reprints what it calls "the best of
the alternative press," did a major feature entitled "What's With Feminism These Days?" (May/June 1987). The front cover was a witty
cartoon by Lynda J. Barry summarizing the state of affairs of feminism
as the editors and contributors saw it in 1987. The graphic shows a
perplexed modern young "everywoman" being throttled by a banner
around her neck that stretches from 1967 to 1987. The banner, clearly
symbolizing the women's movement, is being pulled in different directions by two smaller women. The one on the left, presumably the
feminist, is trying to pull the banner—and the head around which it is

399

wrapped—*back* to 1967. The other is tugging the 1987 end of the banner.

What fascinates us about this depiction of modern women's plight is that the two embattled women are also mouthing slogans about what "everywoman" wants—and the slogans correspond exactly to all the concerns of our goddesses, with the exception of Persephone, who has learned to keep her mouth shut about her apocalyptic visions. Thus the feminist in the cartoon is saying of "everywoman":

- She wants absolute independence!! Who needs men?!
- She wants an exciting and socially responsible career!
- She wants equal rights!
- No nukes!

The other woman, who is opposing the feminist, is saying the following about "everywoman":

- She wants a foxy and successful husband!!
- She wants a lovely home and two totally excellent children!
- She wants red spiked heels and a perfect body!
- More calcium!

Readers of this book will have no trouble discerning the concerns of Athena and Artemis in the slogans of the feminist. As for the other, more traditional woman, it is clear that she is speaking for Hera, Demeter, and Aphrodite.

A magazine image such as this is just one sad reminder of how alienated, fractious, and powerless the goddesses are today in both the inner and the outer worlds of modern women. *Plus ça change, plus c'est la même chose* ("the more it changes, the more it stays the same"), as the French say. For when a priestly consensus among the ancient Greeks created the celebrated "departmental" pantheon of gods and goddesses on Olympus, they may simply have been responding to the diversity of their religious practices. But whatever the original intent, the effect of splitting the ancient Mother Goddess into various specialized roles under a supreme father god, Zeus, was to set up a divide-and-rule strategy that guaranteed an inferior place to feminine values from that time onward.

And if by feminine values we include, in even the broadest definition, a concern with social services, education, and child care, housing and urban development, we find that the United States has devoted less than 1 percent of its 1988 federal research and development budget to these areas. By contrast military research and development received 71 percent of the budget; health, 9 percent; agriculture, 2 percent; and natural resources and the environment, 2 percent. (Source: *Jobs for Peace*, Boston, 1989). With figures such as these, we can only wonder once more if the Hopi Indian prophecy of a "world out of balance"— *koyaanisqatsi*—is not the most accurate assessment of our present condition. A military-technological patriarchy is more firmly in control than ever; the poor betrayed, the feminine in disarray.

Nevertheless, there are signs that however limited and powerless it may be politically, goddess consciousness is growing everywhere. No one should underestimate the extent to which the feminist movement has changed public consciousness of women's issues on a world scale. The very existence of women's studies departments in universities everywhere and the level of media debate in the mainstream press and stimulated by magazines such as the *Utne Reader* and talk shows like Oprah Winfrey's speaks of an unprecedented tide of change. No matter that the goddesses within and without are arguing and complaining; the point is that they are being heard, that their long silence has finally been broken, and that, divided or not, they are making us all aware that theirs is a common cause.

WHAT, THEN, MUST WE DO?

In part two of this book we have outlined ways in which both men and women can become aware of the powerful influences of the Goddess in their lives. We have suggested ways to use journal writing, meditation, goddess games, and discussion with friends to encourage expression of the voices of the goddesses.

Where we begin our work on the Goddess Wheel is unimportant— there is no beginning or end to a circle. What matters is that we start by affirming which goddess energies are strong in us so that we can begin to build healing alliances with those that are weak or seemingly absent.

If, like us, you have a strong Athena voice, you will probably read books and endlessly discuss the different aspects of life. But if you are more comfortable with Demeter, you might be more inclined to quietly reflect on the differences in your daughters, your own feelings about your education, your sexuality, and so on than read a book about these subjects. As a Persephone you may want to communicate with your other goddesses in your dreams or call them up in meditations or rituals. As an Aphrodite, you may want to bring your women friends together in some sort of social gathering to swap stories.

Since Hera's concern is with the family, if you are a woman strongly influenced by Hera, you might start by reflecting on all the women in your family—sisters, daughters, grandmothers, aunts—and see how different they are or were from yourself and also see how they mirror some aspect of your unlived goddess selves.

If the solitary impulse of Artemis is strong in you, you may need to overcome your tendency to separate yourself from the world and challenge yourself to spend more time with women whose strongest goddess influence is different from your own. Persephone women, too, need to challenge their tendency to become isolated from ordinary reality by retreating into private meditation.

It may help to visualize yourself sitting in the Goddess Wheel as a large circle of comfortable chairs, slightly divided into six clusters. Place yourself where you feel strongest or most at home. Now imagine other women you know sitting in the other places, women who came to mind while you were reading this book as well as women you have imagined in literature or movies. Whether you like them or not, try to just allow them to be there. They are the images of all the other goddess parts of yourself or your larger feminine community. You may find that you have strong things to say to some of them, and certainly there are some you would rather avoid altogether, but try to allow the wheel to contain them all. Remember the words of the poet G. K. Chesterton: "we are all in the same boat in a stormy sea / And we owe each other a terrible sympathy." The "boat" is the Wheel, the Great Mother herself; she has the power to contain and hold together all the fragments.

This and other exercises for both individual and group process are described in appendix A. They are tools with which we can all begin or continue the extraordinary process of facilitating awareness of the emergent goddess. Sometimes the process will bring with it unbidden feelings and impulses: a Demeter woman might decide to go back to school for a nursing degree; an Artemis woman might fall in love as her connection to Aphrodite becomes stronger. Critical inner voices that diminish our sense of self-esteem may reveal themselves to us as the repetitive refrains of Hera as articulated by the authoritative women in our lives ("You should never wear pants, they make your hips look too wide.") or the depressed tones of Persephone when she says things like, "It doesn't matter what I do, no one will notice anyway," and so on.

For many women, one of the signs of the emergence of goddess energy is strange dreams in which an animal or animals play an important role. In the ancient shamanic traditions, animals came in dreams as powerful allies. For us in the modern world, these animal helpers have lain dormant for many centuries. But they are returning and bringing with them powerful assistance if we pay attention to our dream life. One such animal helper is the snake. The ancient companion of the Great Mother, the snake carries messages about the subtle energies of the earth. Turtles, bears, horses, and raccoons are all common animal helpers that bring subtle assistance through our dreams.

Another vivid image of how the reemergence of goddess consciousness might appear was given by the California artist Norma Churchill. The first of her extensive series of encounters with an underworld snake king began with an image of a huge female figure beneath the surface of California reaching up toward the city of San Francisco, sending shock waves from beneath the earth. It was of course a psychically perceived image of Gaia, the Great Mother, awakening from within and beneath; the serpent king was her consort and divine emissary. We would be wrong to literalize the earth tremors as a prediction of an earthquake, however. In fact many of the Persephone predictions that emanate from California regarding impending earth upheavals probably tell us far more about the tragic ungroundedness of so many wounded Persephone women than they do actual geophysical events.

These and many other emergent goddess images may seem puzzling and even a little frightening on first encounter. In our Artemis chapter we remarked on the bloody Death Mother images that seem to torment the imaginations of certain directors of Hollywood horror movies. These belong to a long lineage of gothic images of the dark feminine that first began to surface in the poetry and stories of the German, French, and English Romantic writers of the eighteenth and nineteenth centuries: brides of Dracula, Lamia and Medusa figures, Keats's "belle dame sans merci" (woman without mercy), and so on. Painful and frightening as they may seem, the enormously repressed feminine consciousness needs to express them in order to become whole. In Jungian terms, they represent the shadow or dark side of the Mother, who brings death, miscarriage, abortion, and bloody demise. The fierce side of Demeter that emerges in her rage and grief when she loses her daughter is a reminder of this; she brings drought, starvation, disease, and death when not honored.

And even when we have allowed some of our personal images of the goddesses to surface and begin to hear their lost voices, we must not expect benign, comforting goddess platitudes and gentle homilies. The goddesses are angry and wounded after centuries of neglect, distortion, and subjugation. Like the cartoon we described from the *Utne Reader*, the current state of communication between the goddesses is extremely heated and disputatious. This is by no means bad or regrettable, since there is a lot of energy generated by dispute and thus a lot of potential for new awareness. As we quoted William Blake earlier, "opposition is true friendship." So we need not be afraid of the arguments, anger, and distress of the goddesses as they erupt in us. We recommend the video of *The Turning Point* for a useful model of the cathartic venting of pent-up feelings long suppressed.

There is much that needs to get said as well as done as the goddesses and their primordial power are allowed to surface once more. Three thousand years of varying degrees of vilification, misrepresentation, and persecution have left oceans of unexpressed frustration for the collective feminine in us all. It is a momentous task of rehabilitation and healing that can hardly be underestimated. It is no wonder the *Utne Reader* cartoon has "everywoman" being throttled; women have become so used to being silenced, they are quite conditioned to silencing themselves! But it need not happen this way. The dynamic container and transformer we offer in the Goddess Wheel can be a way of both understanding, expressing, and eventually, with much work, of reconciling the divided feminine and rebuilding a more balanced society.

CONVERGENT AND DIVERGENT GODDESSES

It may indeed take many generations before new patterns evolve among women that heal and reconcile the alienation and imbalances we have described in the individual goddess chapters. The present situation has taken centuries to develop, both socially, politically, and psychologically, so it would be naive to expect it to be corrected in a short time. Nevertheless we want to conclude by noting some of the more hopeful symptoms of change we see manifesting as the goddesses emerge and transform the lives of contemporary women. For, now that we have begun to understand the dynamics that have separated women from themselves and their true power for so long, we can also see the strengths they have in common—strengths that can build new visions and alliances that may one day recreate the now sadly eroded foundations of our whole social structure.

It seems to us that it is only by restoring the feminine principle to its true parity with the masculine spirit in all aspects of life and human relationships that the planet and the human race can avoid the cataclysms and the misery that the patriarchy, with its greed for military control, its thoughtless depletion of the earth's resources, and its cruel disregard of the children of the Third World—including the Third World that is growing within both the cities and the countryside of North America—is bringing about. A return to matriarchal consciousness entails honoring the Goddess beneath, above, and around us, as earth, as creation, as life itself. It means a harmonious sharing of power for the benefit of the whole. It means an attitude of celebration of life in its infinite variety.

SOME EMERGING ALLIANCES: STRENGTHS AND WEAKNESSES

When the Constitutional Convention met in Philadelphia in 1787 to articulate a Constitution for the United States, its convenors drafted a document worthy of the highest vision of Athena.

We the people of the United States, in order to form a more

perfect Union, establish justice, insure domestic tranquility, provide for the common defense, promote the general welfare, and secure the blessings of liberty to ourselves and our posterity, do ordain and establish this Constitution for the United States of America.

The first words of the preamble, "We the people of the United States" describe the source of power conferred by the rest of the document. Of its statements of purpose, the principle of "promoting the general welfare" has been one of great importance in the twentieth century for upholding social legislation. But such large visions are not easily attained, as those who have participated in the many civil rights movements of this century can attest. As many women excited by the promise of feminism in the sixties have found, few of the ideals that seemed to be within reach have in fact materialized; women today are, in fact, poorer and lonelier than they were twenty years ago. From the broader perspective of goddess psychology it may well be that most feminists were still internally caught up in Athena's old psychic pattern of "divide and rule" and hence were deeply alienated from their own constituency—other women.

As the *Utne Reader* cartoon graphically demonstrates, the feminism of the sixties and seventies has largely been a coalition between Athena and Artemis women to the exclusion of the needs and concerns of the other goddesses. In fact, the major principle that has united and strengthened Athena and Artemis women is the common factor we observed in our goddess dyads: *independence*. For feminists have commonly demanded, as part of the equal rights they seek in pursuing their lives and careers, relative independence from men. And even when they have wished to become mothers, many Artemis and Athena women have chosen to do so without male support. Relationships with the opposite sex, then, have remained low on the feminist list of priorities.

Unfortunately such single-minded insistence on an independent life-style has seriously alienated many Athena and Artemis feminists from the majority of women who represent a major psychological dimension of the feminine, namely the dyad of love that belongs to Demeter-Aphrodite. For the fact is that in pursuing their hard-bitten intellectual political goals and community experiments they have often lost sight of the eros that binds the individuals in any society together. And that eros has to be found in intimate human relations with one's mate, one's children, and one's community.

There has often been a waspishness and a shrillness among feminist Athenean debates about politics or sexuality that tells more about the wounded areas of their authors than about the subject in question. Andrea Dworkin's diatribes characterizing all male sexuality as nothing but a form of oppression border on fanaticism and do little justice to the deeply satisfying experience of Aphrodite's blessings that millions of women have discovered in perfectly traditional forms of heterosexual relationship.

The vitally important Artemesian area of eco-feminism, known popularly as the Green Movement, is urgently concerned about planetary pollution. One would think that with such a momentous common cause—the very continuance of the life of the earth—there would be tremendous energy for solidarity and action. But alas, some of the disputes we read of between the Marxist and the "spiritual" wings of the movement seem to us excessively acrimonious and do little credit to their participants.

But few issues have lost the feminists more support among the broader population of women than their attitudes to Demeter's realm of motherhood. Nothing is more difficult and indeed fundamental among all the disputes between the goddesses than the one between Athena/Artemis and Demeter regarding the role that being a mother should or should not play in any woman's life. But unfortuately it has been a largely one-sided debate, because one of the Demeter woman's greatest areas of inferiority is often around her lack of interest in the intellectual matters of Athena. Demeter women rarely write books and articles about women's matters, nor (because of the demands of her family) can she easily attend meetings or workshops where her feelings might be expressed and her opinions heard. The urgently important things that Demeter has to say go unheard because she is so wounded in Athenean matters. And on the receiving end, Athena women often fail to hear Demeter's cries for recognition because Athena herself can be so wounded in her Demeter function—as we show in our chapter on Athena.

A woman who has struggled with the integrating of Athena and

Demeter energies is Sylvia Ann Hewlett, who writes about her struggle in her book *A Lesser Life*:

> The biggest problem has been the women's movement's atti-
> tude toward motherhood. Many feminists have alternately ig-
> nored, reviled, and lashed out at motherhood, and in doing so
> the movement has alienated its main constituency. The great
> majority of women have children at some point during their
> lives, and few of these women ever cease to love their sons
> and daughters. For the majority of mothers, their children con-
> stitute the most passionate attachment of their lives. It is absurd
> to expect to build a coherent feminist movement, let alone a
> separatist feminist movement, when you exclude and denigrate
> the deepest emotion in women's lives. (p. 15)

Here is Demeter talking from the heart of the matter. Alas, the women's movement suffers from a major blind spot, a conspicuous lack of mother love. In goddess psychology the reason is clear: Athena women who are wounded in their own experience of mothering cover up their pain by donning the heavy heroic armor of the warrior goddess, devoting themselves to serious political causes and adopting essentially independent life-styles when they can safely protect their vulnerability. Painful as the dialogue is, if the women's movement is to heal the greater wound, its Athena sisters must first look at their alienation from Demeter in terms of their relationships with their own mothers.

Artemis women tend to be more indifferent to Demeter than alien-ated from her. They tend to cherish their isolation and independence so much that they find it hard to imagine themselves as part of the chaos of a multigenerational family. But precisely here is one of Ar-temis's greatest challenges: to tolerate and nurture the needs of those more vulnerable and dependent than she is.

Every political and social movement, once it has a large following, tends to get caught up in the seductive narcissism of its own rhetoric and its own success. It is particularly hard for Athena women who spearhead the movement to see how their intellectual brilliance and political success sets them apart from Demeter, Aphrodite, and Per-sephone women. These other goddess types rarely read or write radical journals or attend political meetings, so they are rarely heard in the public arena. It is a valuable part of the healing of the goddesses that writers like Sylvia Ann Hewlett come along and articulate their concerns for them or that Betty Friedan tries to bridge the gulf between work and motherhood in her broad-minded and sympathetic work *The Second Stage*.

When asked how they see feminists, both Demeter and Aphrodite women (as well as many Hera and Persephone women in our experience) describe them as "clannish," "elitist," "aloof," and "intellectual." Even if such reactions do betray considerable feelings of inferiority among the critics, these descriptions are nevertheless symptomatic of a tendency to self-isolation among the Athena-Artemis feminist alliance, despite the fact that the spirit of Athena-Artemis has changed the face of modern social consciousness in recent years as no other emergent factor in the awakening of the Goddess has.

THE CHALLENGE OF THE NEW FAMILY

But if some individual Athena and Artemis women are beginning to confront the wounded and insecure Demeter they carry within them, American society as a whole, whether feminist or not, still ignores two of its greatest and most cynical affronts to Demeter: the lack of any statutory rights to paid maternity leave and the failure to provide even minimal social services for working single mothers who increasingly are sinking into poverty. When we look at this scandalous issue, we see another wounded goddess in the background: Hera, the guardian of marriage, family, and community.

For hand in hand with so many Athena women's alienation from Demeter and motherhood goes a deep ongoing battle with Hera. As we suggested in our chapter on Hera, many Athena women who find successful careers after a college education are escaping from mothers who are wounded Heras. For such mothers, marriage and motherhood became one long imprisonment as well as a perpetual source of bitterness and rage. Cut off from the fatherworld, from which they desired power for themselves but had no way of attaining it, they left their daughters with a false and subservient model of marriage and a desolate picture of motherhood. Not surprisingly, many women who grew up with such mothers have deeply rejected the very institution of marriage itself and are loathe to look at any issue that relates to it.

What we are suggesting is that the ongoing battle between Athena and Hera suggests that old styles of marriage are slowly decaying. The ever-growing divorce rate, the contempt for marriage of many Athena women, and the profusion of alternative, noncommitted experiments in sexual relationships during the 1970s and early 1980s have undermined the foundations of the institution of marriage as we have known it, despite the current increase in marriages and the vocal conservatism of Hera apologists for the old way, exemplified by the Moral Majority.

But this may not be a bad thing. What is happening is that everywhere there are many marriages where one or both of the partners brings children from a previous marriage to create a whole new and complex blended family. From the often artificial and stifling isolation of the traditional, nuclear family, a modern kind of extended family seems to be emerging; a whole new social pattern of the family that poses immense creative challenges to the Hera in every woman who remarries. How to share power, privileges, and love among "my," "your," and "our" children raises new issues about parenting and power sharing in the domain of Hera. If she can let go of her traditional expectations, she may find herself presiding over a revolution in the very nature and role of the family for future generations.

REGAINING THE BODY, RECLAIMING THE EARTH

As the two goddesses historically closest to the source of patriarchal power, Athena and Hera both suffer similarly in their alienation from Demeter as Earth Mother and Aphrodite as expert in matters of eros and the heart. This alienation is most painfully manifested as an alienation from oneself as body, as earth, as matter. Athena's birth from the head of Zeus and Hera's identification with the "head of state" too often leave them identified with matters of mind and disliking their bodies. Here is the origin of the aloofness and intellectualism that so intimidate the other goddess types. If an Athena daughter grows up with a Hera mother, the problem can be seriously compounded.

In our experience of the movements and awakenings of individual women we have known, we have found that Aphrodite's energy is often the gentlest and easiest way for both Athena women and Hera women to reconnect with the natural cycles of the body. A powerful transformer, Aphrodite can soften the heroic armor Athena unconsciously carries around and help open up her heart as well as her mind. For Hera, Aphrodite can bring brightness, tolerance, and a whole new sense of relationship to her life.

It goes almost without saying, from Aphrodite's perspective, that what has been missing for so long for Hera and Athena, in their intense attachment to family, career, and patriarchal ideals, is the language of the heart. Athena's aloneness and insecurity make it difficult for her to indulge in the fleeting pleasures of the moment that Aphrodite so exults in. And Hera has had her head so filled with received traditions, correct standards, pedigrees, and snobbery that she has forgotten how to take life and people exactly as they are. Aphrodite (who was *pandemos*, "of the people") has much to teach both Athena and Hera about charm and the common touch and about her communal, down-to-earth warmth and enjoyment of simple pleasures.

We realize that Aphrodite's vision of things is profoundly problematic and disturbing to people raised with traditional attitudes about sexuality and the body. The idea that the body is sacred and that the earth, as Mother of all life, is the source of all that is divinely beautiful runs counter to nearly two millennia of patriarchal, antimaterialist conditioning. Any Athena or Hera woman who truly opens to Aphrodite may find herself mentally reiterating deeply ingrained injunctions about her body, her sensual impulses, and her ideas of what is offensive. Very often, when Athena and Hera truly appraise their self-denigrating attitudes toward their bodies and the whole business of pleasure, they discover that these ideas are simply received attitudes, not ones derived from personal experience with eros.

LOVE'S BODY:
APHRODITE AND DEMETER

In writing about the dyad of love in the Goddess Wheel and about Aphrodite and Demeter in their respective chapters, we found ourselves returning again and again to the great mystery of the *embodiment* of the feminine: the body as vessel that wondrously contains growing children, as source of life and nourishment in Demeter, and the body as the magical locus of pleasure, beauty, and ecstasy in Aphrodite. "Naked came I out of my mother's womb, and naked shall I return thither," Job says in the Bible, referring to the great cycle of life. Though the Bible does not name her, the "mother" to whom Job knew he would return is, of course, the earth.

For the Greeks she was primordial Mother Earth, Gaia or Ge, who was mother and grandmother to all of the gods and goddesses we speak of in this book and many more in Greek myth. Psychologically, she speaks to the ultimate principle of embodiment as matter, sacred in and of itself. How she fecundates herself as Aphrodite, how she reproduces herself as Demeter, how she covers the earth with every kind of life form as Lady of Beasts and Lady of Plants, are all mysteries of the embodiment of living, growing, and expiring forms.

It has been the thesis of feminist critics of modern science from Simone Weil to Evelyn Fox Keller that the analytic masculine mind has essentially desacralized nature, matter, substance, and the body and sought to dominate, control, and subdue it from the "higher" perspective of what was first called "spirit" and, since the Renaissance, more simply "mind."[1] Having abstracted intellectual forms from the substance in which they inhere, scientific thinkers attained a certain godlike insight into the structure of reality. This has allowed them, by means of these complex formal intellectual patterns called theories and principles, to manipulate the material order and reimpose new and "improved" ways upon it. Science has been able, not without a certain hubris, to re-create the world after its own designs.

This extraordinary achievement has brought with it almost unbelievable power. The discovery and use of nuclear energy and the development of genetic engineering and space technology are truly wondrous in themselves. But in the end, as the products of the purely masculine rational mind, these achievements inevitably carry with them a certain contempt for matter, for the body, and for the

---

[1] See Evelyn Fox Keller, *Reflections on Gender and Science*. We are grateful to Cheryl Southworth for bringing this book to our attention.

whole natural order, which, in strict metaphysical terms, corresponds to the "feminine" dimension of reality.[2]

The seeds of this contempt for the body and for the material realm were strongly present in the early decades of Christianity, as we saw in our Aphrodite chapter, and they have come to infect the whole consciousness of the West. In fact it is doubtful whether the magnificent enterprises of modern science and technology could have arisen without the prior despiritualization of the feminine as *mater*/matter that Christianity has wrought. The recent ability of humans to create life in laboratory situations, as in recombinant DNA, is typical of a contempt for matter as *materia*—symbolically the "mother" of life—and the natural process of selection and adaptation.

Science can only experiment with nature if she is viewed as dead matter, a conglomeration of "atoms," "things," or "objects" without soul or spiritual force. Thus the scientific mind has successfully placed us "outside" of nature and has further reinforced our persistent cultural alienation from the body, which emerged in the beginnings of the Christian era. It is from this larger perspective that critics of the repression of the feminine (such as Susan Griffin, in her heartrending poetic vision *Woman and Nature*, and Carolyn Merchant, in her scholarly book *The Death of Nature*) are exposing the abysmal levels to which our hatred of the Aphrodite and Demeter dimension of the feminine has sunk. And it is only from such a perspective that we find ourselves able to understand the mentality of female as well as male gynecologists who wish to surgically redesign "natural" childbirth and turn it all into mechanized caesarean delivery. Or that we can understand the cynical pornographic exploitation of women's images and the crude trafficking in female sexuality that has grown to huge proportions in the latter part of this century.

The authors do not pretend to know what it will take for contemporary women and men to restore Aphrodite to her full dignity in the current cultural climate, in which the forces of Christian reaction are as strong as ever. It takes only one experimental film, such as Martin Scorsese's *The Last Temptation of Christ*, in which Jesus entertains

[2] For a unique historical critique of the metaphysical presumptions of modern science, see Seyyed Hosein Nasr's *Man and Nature*. London: George Allen and Unwin, 1976.

fantasies of the sexual life he never lived, for fundamentalists to start picketing the movie theaters.

Yet we believe that Aphrodite women, who are secure and confident in their bodies and in their sexuality, can teach the other goddesses a fundamental kind of trust in themselves, letting them know that their natural sensuality and impulses are not sinful, but a divine gift. Aphrodite has much to teach us about receptiveness, vulnerability, sensitivity, and forbearance—all the subtle fragrances of the flowering of eros when it arises between two people.

But we realize how hard it is for the Aphrodite woman to survive in the modern world and not be sucked into the many games and exploitative ventures that surround eros. The media have grown so accustomed to feeding the mass appetites with images of beautiful women and superficial love stories that it is seldom that Aphrodite is able to speak out for herself and not simply be a mouthpiece or a puppet in the endless manipulation of male fantasy images. Possibly, as more women actresses find their way into directing or writing this may change.

One heartening story of an exploited Aphrodite woman who found self-respect and a renewed dignity in Athena's world caught our eye in a 1988 issue of the New York *Daily News*: Endesha Ida May Holland had been working the streets as a prostitute since she quit school in ninth grade to support her family. She had been arrested thirteen times by the age of eighteen. In the early sixties, following a black man who seemed like a potential "trick" into a building, she found herself in a civil rights office during Dick Gregory's food airlift to Mississippi to encourage blacks to register for the vote.

In her words, "I looked in the door and saw for the first time in my life a black woman typing on a typewriter. I couldn't imagine black people typing. It really was impressive and even more so because she wasn't looking at the keyboard. Then the worker I was trying to turn a trick with opened the door and asked if anyone could read and write. Somebody pushed me forward, and I went in and started signing people's names and how much food they were going to get."

The civil rights worker encouraged Holland to get a high school equivalency diploma, which she did. At the University of Minnesota she earned a bachelor's and then a master's degree and finally a Ph.D. Today she is a tenured professor of black studies at the State University of New York at Buffalo. She has written five plays and was at work on two more. One of them, *Delta*, was on tour at the time in New York State.

THE CHALLENGES OF POWER

Many Persephone women may have found it surprising to read in our overview of the Goddess Wheel that we see them as sharing the power dyad with Hera. Isolated in subtle ways from the larger community, they often feel weak and ineffective. In extreme cases they feel themselves victimized by forces beyond their control. Most Persephone women usually experience themselves as the very opposite of powerful. Yet if they pursue practices such as channeling, psychic readings, and healing of various kinds, as many are now doing, they are in fact wielding enormous power—not the worldly power that runs institutions or political movements in the way of Athena or Hera, but power nevertheless.

The deeply materialist world of mass culture views with contempt such practices as astrology, psychic readings, creative visualization, healing affirmations, and aura balancing. Persephone and her intuitive skills are not accorded the status of "powers" by orthodox thinking. The American Psychological Association, for example, has steadfastly refused to officially recognize parapsychological research as a scientific discipline. As for the mainstream media, they rarely miss an opportunity for "psychic bashing" or trivializing the New Age. Yet as remarkable pioneers like Drs. Elisabeth Kübler-Ross, Stephanie and Carl Simonton, and Bernie Siegel have demonstrated, thought forms have the power to heal; imagery and the spirit play a central part in the process of the transformation of both psychic and physical life.

Channels, psychics, and other spiritual teachers constitute a large segment of the New Age movement, a place where many Persephone women have recently begun to feel quite at home. Yet even as a rapidly growing movement in its own right, the New Age community still remains well outside of academia and is scorned by the scientific establishment and more traditional religious groups. Such widespread institutional rejection only serves to reinforce Persephone's sense of alienation.

Part of the reason why Persephone is still so deeply rejected in Western culture lies in the prevailing orthodoxy of materialist science and psychology. With a dogmatism worthy of the medieval church, the scientific establishment and most academic psychologists confidently deny any psychic factors at work in the universe. Another reason is the fear of the occult and of Satan that is regularly voiced by fundamentalist Christians. But possibly the strongest reason is the historical one that we alluded to in our chapters on both Persephone, Aphrodite, and Artemis—namely the medieval horror of witchcraft.

It is hard for us today to imagine the pure terror and loathing that the medieval churchmen held for so-called witches. Yet for several centuries, as the historical records testify, women with psychic powers, women with wanton or loose sexuality, women who lived alone on the fringes of society, women who healed with herbal remedies, and even skilled midwives were widely believed to be in league with the Devil. This predominantly male paranoid fantasy of the witch led, as we know, to some of the most appalling persecution in the history of any civilization. The psychic consequences, as Jung would say, have not entirely gone away.

When any individual or group is persecuted or victimized, it learns to feel powerless and guilty for what it may or may not have committed. This is undoubtedly what happened to the millions of Persephone-Artemis women in the late Middle Ages who were healers, midwives, shamanesses, seers of one kind or another, or simply local eccentrics. Collectively, as a result of the painful experience of many generations, such women learned to think of themselves and their gifts as wicked and that to practice their skills in any way was a deformation of God's law. Psychic powers in women in particular were thus totally outlawed and demonized by the patriarchs of the medieval Church. As a society we still operate under the influence of this old prohibition, which has never, one might say, been taken off the books.

Although spiritualism, Madame Blavatsky's extremely influential Theosophical Society, and the nineteenth-century occult revival in France did much to restore the psychic or mediumistic woman to a quite respectable, if somewhat eccentric, place in ordinary society, the old Christian paranoia still lingers on in patriarchal consciousness, disguised as rationalistic contempt.

There is no question, as Norman Cohn concluded in his remarkably researched *Europe's Inner Demons*, that whole picture of the medieval witch-casting spells and consorting with the Devil is a paranoid projection of a gynophobic Church. But this does not mean that these victimized women did not have other, quietly kept secrets. In fact, many of the medieval women who were persecuted were probably shamanesses and psychic healers, practitioners of the deeply misunderstood and maligned art of Wicca—"the way of the wise." As we are finally beginning to realize, these women had to operate well outside the bounds of Christian orthodoxy, probably practicing healing arts not unlike those that many Persephone women are recovering today in New Age centers and rediscovering among traditional native shamanic traditions of North and South America and elsewhere—what we might call the lost Artemis-Persephone connection.

The cultural isolation in our society of Persephone as psychic healer, medium, and seer and of Artemis as shamaness has complex roots, therefore. The result of this isolation has been a residual lack of social status in the larger community and a nagging inferiority that she feels about her gifts and interests. We see the growth of New Age communities and centers such as Findhorn in Scotland, Omega Institute and the Open Center in New York, as well as healing centers such as Esalen Institute in California, as enormously important in restoring to Persephone and Artemis women some of their true power and dignity as healers and spiritual helpers.

It has been hard for the Persephone woman to feel powerful without a social group or community to support her and give her self-esteem and status. In the ancient world, priestesses had respected status in serving the gods and goddesses in their temples. Even today in those remaining tribal cultures that have not been eroded by Western "civilization," the medicine man or woman, the shaman or shamaness, continues to play a central role in the overall psychophysical health of the community. Realizing this, therefore, more and more Persephone women are today restoring their self-respect and security by forming their own communities, centers, and groups that specialize in psychic matters and popular metaphysics.

Valuable as such communities are in the short run, however, the biggest challenge we see for Persephone women is to find communities that diversify the energies of the different goddess types. Communities inhabited solely by Persephone women do not work well, we have observed, because the spiritual and psychic dimension gets overemphasized, and practical, down-to-earth matters get enmeshed in unrealistic and often grandiose "messages" from the other side. Frequently when a Persephone woman gets to run her own community, her power shadow, Hera, emerges with quite royal presumptions from the opposite side of the Goddess Wheel! There is always in the Persephone woman the temptation to make portentous, prophetic statements to compensate for her feelings of powerlessness. What she fails to realize is that her pronouncements will be taken literally by her spiritual followers, who are still deeply in awe of the unaccustomed archetype of the High Priestess.

Demeter's realism, Artemis's physical awareness, and even Athena's critical evaluation are particularly needed in any healing or metaphysical community to complement and ground Persephone's visions and revelations. Many Persephone women derive much benefit from spending time with Native American or African or South American spiritual teachers and from visiting their communities, where they can observe a fully respected spiritual leader or healer in a social group. This is one of the ways that the Artemis spirit within Persephone may help her rediscover wholesome, ancient models outside the hothouse of Western psychic traditions, whose esotericism is often sadly lacking in the rich soil of authentic traditional transmission.

In traditional societies, such as those of Africa, Indonesia, or Native America, the personality of both shaman and shamaness is a complex mixture of Persephone vision, Artemesian skill, and Demeter containment. In other words, the goddess energies in traditional healers are integrated, having never suffered the kind of fragmentation they did in Western society, which we have described throughout this book. In these cultures we see a model for a powerful healing alliance between Persephone, Artemis, and Demeter, one that could potentially occur for modern women as well. For all three goddesses need to be present in a woman in order for her healing and regenerative powers to flourish; together they can strengthen one another in this triple alliance.

Above all, the isolated Persephone woman of our culture can benefit from the confident grounding and centering that belongs to Demeter's awareness of the body as earth reality. Without the confidence that comes with Demeter, she cannot trust her descent to the underworld realm and her safe return to this-worldly reality. Unless Demeter is fully embodied in her, she can easily be tempted to live entirely with and for her spirits.

Conversely the Artemis woman who has not developed her Persephone-like sensitivity tends to become accustomed to solitude and to overcompensate with excessive concern for the extraverted, physical aspects of survival. She can experience considerable psychic expansion as she contacts more of Persephone's inner vision of things. Demeter, on the other hand, needs Artemis to free her from the cozy restrictions of home and small-town life and to reconnect her with the greater natural world of Gaia. And Demeter, too, needs to be reunited with her lost Persephone inwardness, to remember the mysteries of death-in-life and life-in-death that together they once knew at Eleusis.

ARTEMIS, DEMETER, AND GAIA

In earlier parts of this book we have characterized the modern Artemis woman as a loner. For many Artemis women, however, the motive is not so much to be alone as to experiment with alternative ways of living on the land and in community. This movement is evident in the many farm communities, lesbian communities, and women's cooperatives that have grown up in recent years in remote areas all over this and other countries.

Perhaps it is this drive for new and better communities that is behind the attraction to Marxism among many eco-feminists. Perhaps, too, we can hear it echoed in the ancient legends of the communities of Amazon women. The movement to create new communities expresses a visionary life-style that is fundamentally loving and respectful toward the earth and all living things. Many Artemis women have rediscovered something of what they long for among Native American people. And some Artemis-Persephone visionaries have initiated highly creative experiments in bringing together representatives of more than one traditional culture to share their insights and ways of living with white ex-urbanites. Joan Halifax's Ojai community in California is one such experiment in living.[3]

[3] For further examples of innovative community experiments, see Corinne McLaughlin and Gordon Davidson's *Builders of the Dawn: Community Lifestyles in a Changing World.*

Communities inspired by Artemis unassisted by other goddess energies tend to be somewhat rugged and austere, however. There is, of course, an important place for spiritually based communities that emphasize simplicity and even asceticism, where Artemis can flourish, but they must, by their very nature, exclude the softer awareness of nurturing and family life that belongs to Demeter consciousness. We raise the question, therefore, of whether there could not be more in the way of alliances between Demeter and Artemis in the creation of new forms of community. One successful, but almost unique experiment in this kind of integration is the Farm, founded by Stephen and Ina May Gaskin. This is a self-sufficient agricultural community in Tennessee, famous, too, for its pioneering work in community midwifery.[4]

In the recent history of Western society, Demeter has mostly contributed from the background. As we pointed out in her chapter, economic and social change has largely confined her to the home. But she, too, needs to find her place once more in the larger community, perhaps with Artemis as her ally. For, in addition to healing our disrupted ecologies, Artemis and Demeter can work together to help to restore our fragmented communities. What Demeter can provide, if she can find her voice once more, is her holistic vision of the entire cycle of the human family, which is fundamental to a broader-based community.

Demeter consciousness desperately longs to bring all three generations—mother, children, and grandparents—together *in a single community*, just as Artemis instinctively knows that any such community has to be rooted productively, not destructively, in the environment around it. Here ecology and family, Artemis and Demeter could be united in a common vision of a wholesome relationship to the earth that nourishes the human community, both physically and spiritually. This is one of the most important alliances among the goddesses that could possibly take place, because it would so creatively reengage with the unifying earth principle, Gaia, the Earth Mother herself.

In our survey of all six of the goddesses we are tempted to say that the most common wounds they share revolve in the end around alienation from the mother and isolation from any true community. And as we keep seeing, ideally the nurturing Demetrian family and the larger

---

[4] See Ina May Gaskin's *Spiritual Midwifery*.

community should be a mutual support to each other. We might say therefore, that the healing of the mother function and the healing of the community must, to be effective, go hand in hand.

How this may happen for us each as individuals obviously will require all kinds of permutations in order to reconcile, merge, and integrate the different goddess energies within us. We have only been able to sketch here and in earlier chapters a few of the more common movements we have observed. But wherever we start from, it is important to remember that just as the upholder of all life is Gaia, the Great Mother, so our own bodily self is the "mother" or matrix of all that is unconscious, unformed, and wanting new life within us. And the different, multifaceted expressions of this urge to life make up the inner community of goddesses who live within us. It may take time to notice and accept all of them, but they will be there silently waiting. Somewhere deep in this place within us all the goddesses ultimately meet.

How the goddesses come to us to energize and inform different aspects of our life remains a mystery. But we can become a part of this mystery if we will only sit quietly with ourselves, listen, and ask for guidance. In their different and unique ways they have abundant blessings and gifts to give to us—gifts we can bring creatively into our lives and our interactions with others. As you come to know them, you will hear them in your own way. We would like to end here with a prayer to each of them as they have guided our reflections and meditations:

From Athena may we be granted wisdom, a passion for truth, and a desire for justice for all beings.

From Aphrodite may we be blessed with the joys of sensual ecstasy, a delight in our bodies, and the knowledge that in our eros nature we touch the divine.

From Persephone may we receive vision and profound understanding of the veiled mysteries of the greater realities beyond our earthly being.

From Artemis we ask for the fervent and abundant energy to protect the precious natural world and its endless benefices and that we find the ways to live with all beings in peace.

From Demeter we pray for the assurance that the life force will nourish us at every level of our being for as long as our task on earth requires.

And from Hera may we receive the full power of the feminine will to become the cocreators with the masculine in all that we choose in our shared destinies as women and men.

The Blessings of the Goddess!

GAMES GODDESSES PLAY

INNER WORK WITH THE GODDESSES: JOURNAL WRITING, ACTIVE IMAGINATION, AND ARTMAKING

In this section we offer some suggestions for engaging with the goddesses within that you can do on your own. It is helpful to keep a journal during your work with the goddesses; in it you can enter dreams, thoughts, and reflections that mark the process of engaging with your dominant and deemphasized goddesses, as well as drawings and dialogues. If the process of inner work is unfamiliar to you, we urge that you find (borrow or buy) *The New Diary: How to Use a Journal for Self-Guidance and Expanded Creativity*, by Tristine Rainer, and *Inner*

Work: Using Dreams and Active Imagination for Personal Growth, by
Robert A. Johnson.

GAME 1: REMEMBERING

In your journal, make a list of the important events that stand out
in your life so far. If the list becomes very long, you might want to
break it down into three sections: childhood, adolescence, and adulthood. Opposite each event, write the name of the goddess that you
associate with that time in your life, for example:

Broke my leg falling out of a tree	Artemis
Learned Morse Code	Athena
Buried pet canary in the garden	Persephone
Fell in love—I was fifteen	Aphrodite

When your list is complete, look back over it to discover the themes
and patterns. Did one goddess stand out over the others at some time
in your life? Or over an extended period? Is she the same goddess who
is dominant or absent today? What do these patterns and themes say
about you in terms of the six goddesses?

Now do the same exercise again, but instead of listing events from
your own life, list the turning-point events from someone else's life,
such as your mother's. Looking at this second list, how does it compare
or contrast with your own? What sort of picture or story emerges from
this person's goddess themes? What do these two profiles suggest about
your relationship with this other person?

GAME 2: TYPECASTING

On a sheet of paper or in your journal, make list headings for each
of the six goddesses. Under each heading, list all the women you can
think of that you know personally who represent or manifest obvious
aspects of that goddess. Be sure to include your mother, your aunts
and grandmothers, your female bosses and colleagues, your friends,
your daughters, and so on. When finished, look back over your list.
What is your first impression? It it balanced or lopsided? Are there

any surprises? Is there a pattern or theme similar to the patterns in "Remembering" (game 1).

GAME 3: FIND YOUR MISSING GODDESS

Perhaps it is now obvious to you which goddess(es) are deemphasized in your life. These are the one or two goddesses whose scores are low on your self-rating questionnaire, whose names don't show up much in your own "Remembering" game (game 1) or who are represented by people with whom you have difficulty dealing in "Typecasting" (game 2). When you have identified your one or two deemphasized goddesses, write their names as list headings. Now write below them everything you can think of about that goddess, especially the qualities that you like the least. Now look at your list; reflect on these characteristics as aspects of yourself that together describe what Jung called the shadow. What does your shadow look like? What sort of person is she?

GAME 4: HAVING IT OUT WITH YOUR SHADOW

Begin this game by first imagining the person to whom all your most unwelcome characteristics belong. Personify her: give her a name and imagine what she looks like and how she dresses. Be as specific as you can.

Once you have imagined your shadow, you can confront her with the things about her with which you take issue, whether they be her attitudes about food or politics, her housekeeping habits, her appearance, her values, whatever. A good way to begin having it out with your shadow is to write her a letter articulating all the things you have thought or felt but never had a chance to say.

After you've said your piece, reflect back on what you have written. Does your shadow have any reply?

GAME 5: MAKING FRIENDS WITH YOUR SHADOW IN DIALOGUE AND IMAGERY

A dialogue is simply an imaginary conversation in which you gain insight about an aspect of yourself that you personify as another person.

The purpose of the dialogue is to come to know more about the other person (in this case your shadow) and to form a sympathetic relationship with the other, imaginary person. Try to approach the game with the attitude that this other character has something of value to teach you about yourself. For instance, she may have reasons for acting or thinking as she does.

As you imagine your shadow goddesses, try to visualize what they look like, what sorts of physical characteristics they possess. As they come into focus, draw them with colored pens. Or look for pictures in magazines that remind you of your shadow goddesses. Glued to a circular piece of poster board, these images form a mandala upon which to meditate and add new images as you find them. Pay attention to the changes in your attitudes toward the character portrayed by your shadow goddess.

GAME 6: MASKMAKING

You will need the help of a friend for this process, and you will need to have certain supplies at hand:
- A hair net
- Petroleum jelly
- Fast-setting plaster gauze, the kind used by doctors to set broken bones (available from surgical supply stores and some pharmacies)
- Scissors
- Towel
- Tissues
- A pan of warm water
- White glue
- Acrylic paints and decorations of various sorts

Begin by pinning your hair out of the way with a hair net or clips, then smear your face liberally with petroleum jelly to keep the mask from sticking to your face. Meanwhile, have your friend cut plaster tape into four-inch pieces. Now lie down on the floor with your head on a towel and pieces of tissue over your eyes and eyebrows (so that your eyelashes and eyebrows aren't pulled out when the mask is removed). Your friend should dip the strips of plaster tape into the warm water, remove the excess, and lay the pieces on your face, covering all of it with two or three layers of wet tape. Your eyes and mouth should be covered but not your nostrils—you must be able to breathe!

After the face is fully covered, allow the plaster to set for about twenty minutes. When you can scrunch your face inside the mask, it is ready to be removed. Remove the mask and set it aside to dry completely (two to three hours, or one hour in a warm oven).

When your mask is dry, cut out the eyes, and paint the raw edges with a mixture of white glue and water (so that bits of plaster do not get into your eyes when you put on the mask). Your mask is now ready to paint and decorate in the image of one of the goddesses (such as your most or least favored goddess). You can add things such as feathers, ribbons, glitter, leaves, and so on to further express the goddess you are imaging.

GROUP EXERCISES FOR WORKING WITH THE GODDESSES

Working with a group offers opportunities for dynamic interaction through role-playing games and psychodrama; it is a powerful complement to the introverted journal and maskmaking processes. The first three games are played with everyone finding her or his place of strength on the Goddess Wheel. Begin these games by dividing your space (the room or part of the room you are in) into six sections, one for each goddess.

GROUP GAME 1: THE SPOTLIGHT GAME: EVERYTHING YOU EVER WANTED TO KNOW ABOUT THE GODDESSES . . .

Have everyone move to the section of the Wheel designated for the goddess with whom she (or he) is most at ease. This is your opportunity to ask Hera why she always has to be right or question Aphrodite about her self-indulgence or Persephone about her "voices." The game begins with one person asking a question that is directed to the people sitting in that goddess's section of the Wheel. For example, a woman sitting in Aphrodite's section (her place of strength) might ask the Artemis group, "Why do you like to run around in the woods, getting all sweaty and bug-bitten?" Anyone in the Artemis section can respond to this question, speaking as the representative of the goddess. Thus a dialogue begins. As more questions are asked, the exchanges become alternately heated, humorous, intense, and revelatory. Anyone wishing to be involved in a dialogue, say between Athena and Demeter, must move to sit in one of their sections on the Wheel if they are not there already. Thus people are invited to leave their original place on the Wheel and move to a place where they can join the dialogue and express an opinion. In this way you get to feel what it is like to be identified with goddesses other than your strongest or easiest choice.

GROUP GAME 2: PLANNING GODDESS RITUALS

As with "The Spotlight Game" (game 1), this process begins with everyone finding her or his place of strength on the Wheel. The task set for each of the six groups is to separately prepare some sort of ritual that is suggestive of the goddess they represent. The ritual may be the creation of a group altar (with objects found nearby, such as leaves, pine cones, stones, and flowers for Artemis), or a dance (with sensuous music for Aphrodite), or a cornucopia of flowers and vegetables (for Demeter), or anything else the group can devise in a short amount of time. Each of the six groups offers their ritual to the other five.

GROUP GAME 3: AFFIRMING THE GODDESS

Beginning with everyone in her place of strength on the Goddess Wheel, have each person in each of the six sections write an affirmation of the goddess, such as "As Demeter I am in tune with the cycles of the seasons" or, "I enjoy talking with animals" as Artemis, or "I am wise in the ways of the world" as Hera. Now go around the Wheel and have everyone say her affirmation aloud to the whole group.

DYADS

Dyads offer possibilities for exploring personal relationships through role-playing and supportive listening. For dyad exercises, find a partner and agree between you who is "A" and who is "B." Sit facing each other with knees nearly touching.

GROUP GAME 4: "I HAVE A PROBLEM WITH THIS PERSON . . ."

In this game you will each have the opportunity to express yourself to someone with whom you have a relationship problem, as role-played by your partner. Begin with "A" describing to "B" in terms of the goddess the person with whom she is having or has had a problem (let's call this person "C.") For example, if as "A" you find yourself in repeated power struggles with your boss at work, you would describe him or her as a Hera type who always has to be right. Continue describing "C" until "B" has a sense of his or her personality.

Now "A" begins to talk to "B" *as though* "B" were "C": "My trouble with you, _____, is that you never listen when I try to talk to you." "B" should try to respond as "C": "What do you mean I don't listen?" Allow the exchange to continue for three to five minutes, then stop, thank each other and reverse roles, with "B" describing to "A" someone with whom he or she is having difficulty and so on.

When both in the dyad have had their turn, take another ten minutes or so to process together what you both learned about your relationships from the exercise.

GROUP GAME 5: "HOW I RELATE TO MEN . . ."

This exercise is an opportunity to examine how you relate to men in terms of the goddess.

Decide who is "A" and who is "B." Before you begin, take a few moments to reflect over what you know about yourselves and your relationships with men. Do you relate as sparring partners as Athena? Erotically or romantically as Aphrodite? Do you treat them like little boys as Demeter?

"A" begins by talking about himself or herself in relationship with men in terms of the Goddess, free-associating about the ways in which one or two goddesses inform the nature of these relationships. "B" should simply listen, without saying anything, noticing themes and patterns in the narrative.

Stop after three to five minutes, thank your partner and reverse roles, with "B" talking and "A" listening. When "B" is finished, take another ten or fifteen minutes to discuss the themes and patterns revealed by the narrative.

GROUP GAME 6: "HOW I RELATE TO WOMEN . . ."

As with game 5, "How I Relate to Men," this exercise offers an opportunity to explore the archetypal nature of your relationships with women.

Begin by deciding who will be "A" and who will be "B." Now follow the same format as "How I Relate to Men" (game 5), with "A" and "B" taking turns talking about their relationships with women in terms of the goddesses.

A BRIEF HISTORY OF
GODDESS PSYCHOLOGY

We don't pretend that we have "invented" goddess psychology. We have simply given a name, an accessible form, and a new approach to feminine psychology that has been developing for over a generation. Our aim has been mainly to summarize and synthesize the brilliant and inspiring work that others have done, organizing it around the archetypal images of six of the major Greek goddesses.

Nevertheless, since we do make use of concepts of matriarchy and patriarchy, and throughout this book we base many of our interpretations on ideas prevalent among Jungian and feminist writers, it might satisfy our more discriminating Athenean reader to put this ill-defined field into some kind of order. We offer here a brief sketch of how it developed, to supplement our main bibliography.

What follows, then, is an annotated bibliography of the major writers, researchers, and theorists who have sought to reinterpret both psychology, sociology—and inevitably politics and religion—through the eyes of the gods and goddesses. (*Note*: all dates given are of the first publication of a work in its original language; full publication details are given in the bibliography.)

The first major work to question the idea that monogamy and the patriarchal family are the natural foundations of all human society comes from the Swiss anthropologist and cultural historian J. J. Bachofen in *Das Mutterrecht* (1861; major passages appear in an English translation of Bachofen's selected writings in *Myth, Religion and Mother Right*, edited by Joseph Campbell, 1967). Bachofen believed, on the basis of the interpretation of mostly Greek and Roman myths, that there have been three stages in human society: a period of sexual promiscuity that he called cthonic hetaerism; the development of gynocracy or rule by women, that is, true matriarchy; and patriarchy.

Bachofen's work was enormously influential, seeding investigations in ethnography, anthropology, and sociology for several generations to come. Even Engels's work, *The Origins of the Family, Private Property and the State* (1884), bears its influence. Sir James Frazer's vast work, *The Golden Bough* (1890), does not address matriarchy explicitly, but gathers substantial amounts of data on the Mediterranean and Near Eastern cults of the Mother Goddess and her son-lover consort.

Jane Ellen Harrison's classic *Prolegomena to the Study of Greek Religion* (1902) looks at Greek religion in terms of the social transition from matriarchal to patriarchal structures; her approach bears the mark of both Frazer and Bachofen.

The first major application of mythological material toward the understanding of psychological processes is in C. G. Jung's *Symbols of Transformation* (1912). Here, in analyzing the fantasy contents of a case of schizophrenia, he finds copious parallel mythological motifs of the Great Mother Goddess, her Divine Son, and the Hero journey into the unconscious. Here, for the first time Jung develops the idea of a mother *archetype* that transcends the individual image of the mother. He also explores the profound psychological implications of the Dual

Mother Goddess who dwells in our unconscious minds as both Life and Death.

Robert Briffault's voluminous work *The Mothers* (1927) modifies Bachofen's original postulation on the existence of pure matriarchies and instead amasses huge amounts of contemporary anthropological data about the role and place of women, of marriage, and of sexuality in primitive societies and early Western cultures. Inspired by both Bachofen and Briffault, as well as Freud, Jung, and Frazer, German writer Helen Diner published *Mothers and Amazons* (c. 1930), later subtitled *The First Feminine History of Culture*. This remains a controversial and speculative book, however, tending to amplify all of Bachofen and Briffault's inaccuracies.

By the end of the thirties Jung had attracted to him a number of scholars and psychologists who extended and developed much of his work. His proposal to base all of psychology upon the structure of archetypes bore fruit in many fields, including science and religion. Using Briffault's findings about the Moon Mother goddess and menstruation, for example, Jungian analyst Esther Harding produced her psychological study *Women's Mysteries* (1955).

A close association between Jung and the Hungarian classicist Carl Kerényi led to four major papers, later known as *Essays on a Science of Mythology* (1949). Of these, both Kerényi's and Jung's papers on the Kore or Maiden have been a major inspiration to many writers on the goddesses, including the present authors. Kerényi's German mentor, W. F. Otto, wrote a fine study of the spiritual meaning of Greek religion, *The Homeric Gods* (1929, trans. 1974), which has also inspired two generations of Jungians and, recently, many archetypal psychologists.

Erich Neumann, another of Jung's close associates, returned to Bachofen's ideas in *The Origins and History of Consciousness* (1949). Neumann took Bachofen's original theory of *social* evolution and adapted it to a *psychological* model for the evolutionary development of individual consciousness from matriarchal through patriarchal stages, using mythological parallels. Neumann also adds the intermediary stage of the Hero, thus making his book a major reworking of Jung's *Symbols of Transformation*.

Shortly afterward, Neumann published his indispensable cross-cultural, psychological analysis of the Mother archetype, *The Great*

Mother (1955). In it he presents an exhaustive collection of illustrations and examples of the Mother Goddess motif from the Paleolithic to Christian times, covering symbolic and iconographic variations from a wide range of ancient and contemporary cultures. Further developing Jung's concept of the Dual Mother, he also isolates specific *aspects* and functions of the Great Mother, namely: the Lady of Beasts, the Lady of Plants, the archetypal Feminine as Sacred Vessel of Transformation, the Feminine as Priestess and Shamaness, the Goddess as Wisdom (Sophia). These are the major dimensions of the archetypal feminine that we address in this book.

In a brilliant summation of the growing Jungian understanding of feminine psychology, Toni Wolff, Jung's closest associate for many years, wrote the short paper "Structural Forms of the Feminine Psyche" (1956.) This "sketch," as she called it, has had wide-ranging influence, not least upon the present authors. In it, Wolff distinguished four major female types: the *Mother* and her opposite, the *Hetaira*; the *Amazon* and her opposite, the *Medium*. Wolff briefly alluded to Greek parallels to this fourfold schema, but did not develop them.

Essentially, what we do in this book is subdivide the Amazon type into thee categories—Hera, Athena, and Artemis—and create two slightly different pairs of opposites. We feel this is fully justified, both in terms of Neumann's helpful, but by no means rigid sixfold classification in *The Great Mother* and in the light of the growing complexity of the Amazon psyche as we observe it more and more in contemporary women.

Quite independently of all this Jungian exploration in the forties and fifties, Robert Graves wrote his magnum opus, *The White Goddess* (1948), which focused mainly on rich Celtic sources of matriarchal culture. Shortly after, he complemented this picture with his idiosyncratic and controversial dictionary, *The Greek Myths* (1955). His footnotes, very much in the spirit of Jane E. Harrison half a century earlier, are a treasure trove of information about matriarchy and patriarchy, early Greek religion and society, and the complex interaction of the peoples of the ancient world.

The feminist awakening of the late sixties produced a series of powerful manifestos and critiques of patriarchal society, both as it is today and as it developed historically. Betty Friedan's *The Feminine Mystique* (1963), Kate Millet's *Sexual Politics* (1970), and Germaine

Greer's *The Female Eunuch* (1970) were among the most widely read, but a whole revolution of values was under way that produced new political forms, new art, new literature, new music, and new educational and social institutions. In short, a whole new subculture of the feminine had been born, which allowed women of all persuasions to become politically, socially, and spiritually active and self-aware in a fashion unprecedented in Western history.

A lovely tribute to the rebirth of feminine culture was Judy Chicago's extraordinary project to commemorate the great feminine spirits of all ages on painted china plates and embroidered table runners. Her record of the project, *The Dinner Party* (1979), became a miniature Who's Who of the feminine in history.

Books like Simone de Beauvoir's *The Second Sex* (1949), which had attracted only intellectual curiosity on its first appearance in English (1953), now became manifestos. The patriarchal distortion of every kind of social institution came under attack: Mary Daly's *Beyond God the Father* (1973) proposed a radical critique of Christianity; Phyllis Chessler's *Women and Madness* (1972) deplored the sorry record of sexism in psychiatric treatment of women; Adrienne Rich's *Of Woman Born* (1976) reexamined motherhood; Suzanne Arms's *Immaculate Deception* (1975) exposed the callousness of routine hospital childbirthing practices; and Susan Griffin's *Woman and Nature* (1978) gave a passionate visionary critique of the patriarchal exploitation and abuse of nature and women's bodies. These and many more created a whole new climate of opinion and debate about "the feminine."

During the seventies and eighties many new spokeswomen for radical approaches to feminine spirituality appeared, ranging from radical Christians such as Rosemary Ruether, in her *New Woman, New Earth* (1975), to self-confessed pagans such as Starhawk, in *The Spiral Dance* (1979), and Margot Adler, in *Drawing Down the Moon* (1979). In addition, Merlin Stone's *When God Was a Woman* (1978) and Charlene Spretnak's *Lost Goddesses of Early Greece* (1978) contributed to the growing interest in the goddesses and further challenged official patriarchal assumptions about both history and spirituality. In an attempt to summarize the whole range of thinking in this area, Barbara Walker produced her monumental *Woman's Encyclopedia of Myths and Secrets* (1983).

More and more feminists have recently become open, though not uncritically, to Jung. Among women academics and psychologists there have been efforts to integrate Jungian and feminist thinking, in particular *The Changing of the Gods* (1979), by Naomi Goldenberg, and *Feminist Archetypal Theory*, by Estella Lauter and Carol Schreier Rupprecht (1985). These writers have been strongly influenced by the "revisioned" view of Jung presented as "archetypal psychology" by James Hillman. Hillman's seminal *Myth of Analysis* (1972) and *Re-visioning Psychology* (1975) make a powerful case for a "polytheistic" psychology, based upon a plurality of gods, myths, and archetypes. A valuable discussion of this kind of thinking is to be found in David Miller's *The New Polytheism* (1974.)

The anthology *Facing the Gods* (1980) is a representative collection of papers on archetypal psychology by Hillman, Kerényi, Murray Stein, Miller, and others on Athena, Hephaistos, Artemis, and more. Many of these papers are taken from Hillman's influential journal *Spring*, which has published other major writings on the gods and goddesses. These works have set a new standard for looking at the feminine, at individual psychology, and at cultural patterns by virtue of the sophisticated interpretive tool that archetypal psychology makes available.

Many other recent and important books are also part of this trend to see psychology and our culture through an archetypal understanding of gods, goddesses, and myths as inspired by Jung and later followers and revisionists; among them we would mention the following, in no particular order: Christine Downing's *The Goddess* (1981); Penelope Shuttle and Peter Redgrove's *The Wise Wound* (1978); Nor Hall's *The Moon and the Virgin* (1980); Sylvia Brinton Perera's *Descent to the Goddess* (1981); Edward C. Whitmont's *Return of the Goddess* (1982); Jean Shinoda Bolen's *Goddesses in Everywoman* (1984) and Marion Woodman's *Addiction to Perfection* (1982) are two of the most popular and influential works in making the idea of a psychology based on inner experience of the Goddess available to a larger audience.

Finally, mention should be made of three influential articles that appeared in the seventies: one was Philip Zabriskie's "Goddesses In Our Midst" (1974) and the other two were a much-quoted interview with Robert Bly in *East West Journal* entitled "The Great Mother and the New Father" and his important essay "I Came Out of the Mother Naked" in *Sleepers Joining Hands* (1973). For many years Bly has run invitational conferences that have done much to stimulate all kinds of intellectual and artistic creativity around the goddesses and the emergent feminine.

SELECTED
BIBLIOGRAPHY

* These books have excellent bibliographical and other resource information.

[ ] Denotes original dates of publication.

I. GREEK MYTH AND RELIGION: BASIC SOURCES AND COMMENTARIES

Anonymous (trans. Charles Boer). *The Homeric Hymns*. Dallas: Spring, 1979 [1970].

Bly, Robert. "On the Great Mother and the New Father." *East West Journal*, August 1980.

———. *Sleepers Joining Hands*. New York: Harper & Row, 1973.

*Bolen, Jean Shinoda. *Goddesses in Everywoman*. New York: Harper & Row, 1984.

Burkert, Walter. *Greek Religion*. Translated by John Raffan. Cambridge, Mass.: Harvard University Press, 1985.

Cantarella, Eva. *Pandora's Daughters*. Translated by Fant. Baltimore: The Johns Hopkins University Press, 1987 [1981].

Downing, Christine. *The Goddess*. New York: Crossroad, 1981.

*Eliade, Mircea. *A History of Religious Ideas*, 3 vols. Chicago: University of Chicago Press, 1978.

Godolphin, F. R. B., ed. *Great Classical Myths*. New York: Modern Library, 1964.

Grant, Michael. *Myths of the Greeks and Romans*. New York: New American Library, 1962.

Graves, Robert. *The Greek Myths*, 2 vols. New York: Penguin, 1979 [1955].

Guthrie, W. K. C. *The Greeks and Their Gods*. Boston: Beacon, 1950.

Hamilton, Edith. *Mythology*. New York: New American Library, 1942 [1940].

Harrison, Jane Ellen. *Prolegomena to the Study of Greek Religion*. London: The Merlin Press, 1962 [2d ed., 1907].

———. *Mythology*. New York: Harcourt, Brace and World, 1963 [1924].

———. *Themis: A Study of the Social Origins of Greek Religion*. Cambridge, England: Cambridge University Press, 1927 [1912].

Hesiod. *Theogony*. In *Hesiod and Theognis*, translated by Dorothea Wender. London: Penguin, 1973.

Homer. *The Odyssey*. Translated by E. V. Rieu. London: Penguin, 1946.

———. *The Iliad*. London: Penguin, 1950.

Jung, C. G., and Carl Kerényi. *Essays on a Science of Mythology*. Princeton, N.J.: Princeton/Bollingen 1969 [1949].

Kerényi, Carl. *The Gods of the Greeks*. New York: Thames & Hudson, 1979 [1951].

Meyer, Marvin W., ed. *The Ancient Mysteries*. New York: Harper & Row, 1987.

Nilsson, Martin P. *A History of Greek Religion*. New York: Norton, 1964 [1952].

Otto, Walter F. *The Homeric Gods*. Translated by Moses Hadas. New York: Thames & Hudson, 1979 [1929].

Ovid. *Metamorphoses*. Translated by Innis. London: Penguin, 1946.

Rohde, Erwin. *Psyche: The Cult of Souls and the Belief in Immortality Among the Greeks*, 2 vols. Translated by Hillis. New York: Harper & Row, 1966 [1920].

Slater, Philip. *The Glory of Hera: Greek Mythology and the Greek Family*. Boston: Beacon, 1968.

Spretnak, Charlene. *Lost Goddesses of Early Greece: A Collection of Pre-Hellenic Mythology*. Boston: Beacon, 1981 [1978].

II. GENERAL WORKS ON THE GODDESS AND THE FEMININE

1. Anthropology, History, and Historical Fiction

Bachofen, J. J. *Myth, Religion, and Mother Right*. Edited by Joseph Campbell. Princeton, N.J.: Princeton/Bollingen, 1967 [1861].

Bernal, Martin. *Black Athena: The Afroasiatic Roots of Classical Civilization*, 3 vols. New Brunswick, N.J.: Rutgers University Press, 1987.

Bradley, Marion Zimmer. *The Firebrand*. New York: Simon and Schuster, 1988.

Briffault, Robert. *The Mothers*. Abridged and introduced by Gordon Rattray Taylor. New York: Atheneum, 1977 [1927].

Brindel, June Rachuy. *Ariadne: A Novel of Ancient Greece*. New York: St. Martin's Press, 1980.

———. *Phaedra: A Novel of Ancient Athens*. New York: St. Martin's Press, 1985.

de Riencourt, Amaury. *Sex and Power in History*. New York: Delta, 1975.

Diner, Helen. *Mothers and Amazons*. New York: Doubleday/Anchor, 1973 [c. 1930].

Frazer, Sir James G. *The Golden Bough*. New York: Macmillan, 1922 [1890].

Gimbutas, Marija. *The Goddesses and Gods of Old Europe*. Berkeley, Calif.: University of California Press, 1974.

Graves, Robert. *The White Goddess*. New York: Vintage Books, 1958 [1948].

James, E. O. *The Ancient Gods*. New York: G. P. Putnam's, 1960.

Patai, Raphael. *The Hebrew Goddess*. New York: Avon, 1967.

Pomeroy, Sarah B. *Goddesses, Whores, Wives and Slaves*. New York: Schocken, 1975.

*Sjöö, Monica, and Barbara Mor. *The Great Cosmic Mother: Rediscovering the Religion of the Earth*. New York: Harper & Row, 1987.

Stone, Merlin. *When God Was a Woman*. New York: Harvest/Harcourt, 1976.

————. *Ancient Mirrors of Womanhood*, 2 vols. New York: New Sibylline Books, 1979.

Thompson, William Irwin. *The Time Falling Bodies Take to Light*. New York: St. Martin's Press, 1981.

2. *Contemporary Feminism*

Daly, Mary. *Beyond God the Father: Toward a Philosophy of Women's Liberation*. Boston: Beacon Press, 1973.

de Beauvoir, Simone. *The Second Sex*. New York: Knopf, 1952 [1949].

Demetrakopoulos, Stephanie. *Listening to Our Bodies*. Boston: Beacon, 1983.

Friedan, Betty. *The Second Stage*. New York: Summit, 1981.

————. *The Feminine Mystique*. New York: Dell, 1963.

Greer, Germaine. *The Female Eunuch*. New York: Bantam, 1970.

Keller, Evelyn Fox. *Reflections of Gender and Science*. New Haven: Yale University Press, 1985.

Kolbenschlag, Madonna. *Kiss Sleeping Beauty Goodbye*. New York: Doubleday, 1979.

Millett, Kate. *Sexual Politics*. New York: Avon, 1970.

*Morgan, Robin, ed. *Sisterhood Is Powerful*. New York: Vintage, 1970.

Ruether, Rosemary. *New Woman, New Earth*. New York: Seabury, 1975.

*Wynne, Patrice. *The Womanspirit Sourcebook*. San Francisco: Harper & Row, 1988.

3. Jungian and Archetypal Psychology

Bly, Robert. "I Came Out of the Mother Naked," *Sleepers Joining Hands*. New York: Harper & Row, 1973.

*Bolen, Jean Shinoda. *Goddesses in Everywoman*. New York: Harper & Row, 1984.

Castillejo, Irene. *Knowing Woman*. New York: Harper & Row, 1974.

Colegrave, Sukie. *The Spirit of the Valley*. Los Angeles: J. P. Tarcher, 1979.

Goldenberg, Naomi. *The Changing of the Gods: Feminism and the End of Traditional Religions*. Boston: Beacon, 1979.

Hall, Nor. *The Moon and the Virgin*. New York: Harper & Row, 1980.

Harding, M. Esther. *Women's Mysteries, Ancient and Modern*. New York: Harper & Row, 1978 [1951].

Hillman, James. *Re-Visioning Psychology*. New York: Harper & Row, 1975.

————. *The Myth of Analysis*. New York: Harper & Row, 1978 [1972].

Hillman, James, ed. *Facing the Gods*. Irving, Tex.: Spring, 1980.

Hillman, James, et al. *Fathers and Mothers*. Dallas: Spring, 1982.

Jung, C. G. *Symbols of Transformation*. Princeton, N.J.: Princeton/Bollingen, 1954 [1912].

————. *Aspects of the Feminine*. Princeton, N.J.: Princeton/Bollingen, 1982.

Jung, C. G., ed. *Man and His Symbols*. New York: Doubleday, 1964.

*Lauter, Estella, and Carol Schreier Rupprecht. *Feminist Archetypal Theory*. Knoxville, Tenn.: University of Tennessee, 1985.

Miller, David L. *The New Polytheism*. With appendix by James Hillman, Irving, Tex.: Spring, 1981 [1974].

Neumann, Erich. *The Great Mother*. Princeton, N.J.: Princeton/Bollingen, 1955.

————. *The Origins and History of Consciousness*. Princeton, N.J.: Princeton/Bollingen, 1954 [1949].

Stern, Karl. *The Flight From Woman*. New York: Farrar, Strauss, 1965.

Ulanov, Ann. *The Feminine in Jungian Psychology and Christian Theology*. Evanston, Ill.: Northwestern, 1971.

Von Franz, Marie-Louise. *The Feminine in Fairy Tales*. Irving, Tex.: Spring, 1974.

Whitmont, Edward C. *Return of the Goddess*. New York: Crossroad, 1982.

Wolff, Toni. *Structural Forms of the Feminine Psyche*. Zurich: C. G. Jung Institute, 1956.

Zabriskie, Philip. "Goddesses in Our Midst." *Quadrant* 17 (1974).

4. *Anthologies, Reference, and Resources*

Barnstone, Alki and Willis, eds. *A Book of Woman Poets*. New York: Schocken, 1980.

*Chicago, Judy. *The Dinner Party*. New York: Anchor Press/Doubleday, 1979.

Christ, Carol P., and Judith Plaskow, eds. *Womanspirit Rising: A Feminist Reader in Religion*. New York: Harper & Row, 1979.

Cosman, Carol, Joan Keefe, and Kathleen Weaver, eds. *The Penguin Book of Women Poets*. New York: Penguin, 1979.

Johnson, Robert A. *Inner Work: Using Dreams and Active Imagination for Personal Growth*. New York: Harper & Row, 1986.

Rainer, Tristine. *The New Diary: How to Use a Journal for Self-Guidance and Expanded Creativity*. Los Angeles: J. P. Tarcher, 1978.

Ruether, Rosemary Radford. *Womanguides: Readings Towards a Feminist Theology*. Boston: Beacon, 1985.

*Walker, Barbara G. *The Woman's Encyclopedia of Myths and Secrets*. New York: Harper & Row, 1983.

Washburn, Penelope, ed. *Seasons of Woman*. New York: Harper & Row, 1982.

*Weigle, Marta. *Spiders and Spinsters*. Santa Fe: University of New Mexico, 1982.

*Wynne, Patrice. *The Womanspirit Sourcebook*. San Francisco: Harper & Row, 1988.

III. THE SIX MAJOR GODDESSES: REFERENCES AND FURTHER READINGS

Chapter Two: Athena: Warrior Woman in the World

Fynn. *Mister God, This Is Anna*. New York: Ballantine, 1974.

Hall, Nor. *Those Women*. Dallas: Spring, 1988.

Hennig, Margaret, and Anne Jardim. *The Managerial Woman*. New York: Anchor/Doubleday, 1977.

Jung, C. G. "Psychological Aspects of the Mother Archetype." In *Four Archetypes*. Princeton, N.J.: Princeton/Bollingen, 1970 [1959].

Kerényi, Carl. *Athene: Virgin and Mother*. Translated by Murray Stein. Zurich: Spring, 1978.

Leonard, Linda. *The Wounded Woman*. Boulder, Colo.: Shambhala, 1983.

Lichtenstein, Grace. *Machisma: Women and Daring*. New York: Doubleday, 1981.

Moffat, Maryjane, and Charlotte Painter. Part 2: "Work," of *Revelations: Diaries of Women*. New York: Random House/Vintage, 1974.

Morgan, Robin, ed. *Sisterhood Is Powerful*. New York: Vintage, 1970.

Panichas, George A., ed. *The Simone Weil Reader*. New York: David McKay, 1977.

Pearson, Carol, and Katherine Pope. *The Female Hero in American and British Literature*. New York: Bowker, 1981.

Perlingievi, Ilya Sandra. "Strokes of Genius," in *Ms*. Sept 1988 [on Sofonisba Anguissola].

Petroff, Elizabeth Alvilda, ed. *Medieval Women's Visionary Literature*. New York: Oxford University Press, [For Hrotsvit of Gandersheim.]

Pisan, Christine de. *The Book of the City of Ladies*. New York: Persona Books, 1982.

Warner, Marina. *Joan of Arc: The Image of Female Heroism*. New York: Alfred A. Knopf, 1982.

Weil, Simone. *Selected Essays, 1934–43*. London: Oxford University Press, 1962.

Woodman, Marion. *Addiction to Perfection: The Still Unravished Bride*. Toronto: Inner City, 1982.

Chapter Three: Artemis: The Heart of the Lonely Hunter

Adler, Margot. *Drawing Down the Moon*. Boston: Beacon, 1981.

Andrews, Lynn V. *Medicine Woman*. San Francisco: Harper & Row, 1981.

Auel, Jean. *The Clan of the Cave Bear*. New York: Crown, 1980.

Bly, Robert, ed. *News of the Universe: Poems of Twofold Consciousness*. San Francisco: Sierra Club, 1980.

Dillard, Annie. *Teaching a Stone to Talk*. New York: Harper, 1982.

Ehrenreich, Barbara, and Deirdre English. *Witches, Midwives, and Nurses: A History of Women Healers*. London: Writers and Readers Publishing Cooperative, 1973.

Fox, Matthew. *Original Blessing: A Primer of Creation Spirituality*. Santa Fe: Bear, 1984.

Griffin, Susan. *Woman and Nature: The Roaring Inside Her*. New York: Harper & Row, 1978.

Kerényi, Carl. "A Mythological Image of Girlhood: Artemis" (1949). In James Hillman, ed. *Facing the Gods*. Irving, Tex.: Spring, 1980.

LaBastille, Anne. *Women and Wilderness*. San Francisco: Sierra Club Books, 1980.

LaChapelle, Dolores. *Earth Wisdom*. Silverton, Colo.: Finn Hill Arts, 1978.

Lawick-Goodall, Jane van. *In the Shadow of Man*. Boston: Houghton Mifflin, 1971.

Lichtenstein, Grace. *Machisma: Women and Daring*. New York: Doubleday, 1981.

Lovelock, James. *Gaia: A New Look at Life on Earth*. New York: Oxford University Press, 1975.

Mahdi, Louise Carus, Steven Foster, and Meredith Little, eds. *Betwixt and Between: Patterns of Masculine and Feminine Initiation*. La Salle, Ill.: Open Court, 1987.

Malamud, Rene. "The Amazon Problem." In *Facing the Gods*, edited by James Hillman. Irving, Tex.: Spring, 1980.

Merchant, Carolyn. *The Death of Nature*. New York: Harper & Row, 1980.

Michel, John. *The View Over Atlantis*. London: Garnstone Press, 1969; revised, updated edition: *The New View Over Atlantis*. New York: Harper & Row, 1983.

Mowat, Farley. *Woman in the Mists: The Story of Dian Fossey and the Mountain Gorillas of Africa*. New York: Warner, 1987.

Paris, Ginette. *Pagan Meditations: Aphrodite, Hestia, Artemis*. Dallas: Spring, 1986.

Petroff, Elizabeth Alvilda, ed. *Medieval Women's Visionary Literature*. New York: Oxford University Press, 1986. (For Hildegard of Bingen and Juliana of Norwich.)

Schumacher, E. F. *Small Is Beautiful*. New York: Harper & Row, 1975.

Spretnak, Charlene, and Fritjof Capra. *Green Politics: The Global Promise*. Santa Fe: Bear and Company, 1986.

Starhawk. *The Spiral Dance: A Rebirth of the Ancient Religion of the Great Goddess*. New York: Harper & Row, 1979.

Stratton, Joanna L. *Pioneer Women*. New York: Touchstone, 1981.

Stroud, Joanne, and Gail Thomas. *Images of the Untouched*. Irving, Tex.: Spring, 1982.

Thompson, William Irwin, ed. *Gaia: A Way of Knowing*. Great Barrington, Mass.: Inner Traditions Lindisfarne, 1987.

Ywahoo, Dhyani. *The Voices of Our Ancestors*. Edited by Barbara Du Bois. Boston: Shambhala, 1987.

Chapter Four: Aphrodite: Golden Goddess of Love

Bedier, Joseph, ed. *The Romance of Tristan and Iseult*. Translated by Hilaire Belloc and Paul Rosenfeld. Pantheon, New York, 1945.

Boswell, John. *Christianity, Social Tolerance and Homosexuality*. Chicago: University of Chicago, 1980.

Cohn, Norman. *Europe's Inner Demons*. New York: Basic Books, 1975.

De Rougement, Denis. *Love in the Western World*. New York: Pantheon, 1956.

Friedrich, Paul. *The Meaning of Aphrodite*. Chicago: University of Chicago, 1978.

Goldberg, B. Z. *The Sacred Fire*. Secaucus, N.J.: Citadel Press, 1974.

Grigson, Geoffrey. *The Goddess of Love*. New York: Stein and Day, 1977.

Janus, Sam, and Barbara Bess. *A Sexual Profile of Men in Power*. New York: Prentice-Hall, 1977.

Jung, C. G. *Psychological Types*. Princeton, N.J.: Princeton/Bollingen, 1971 [1921].

Kensington Ladies' Erotica Society. *Ladies' Home Erotica*. Berkeley: Ten Speed Press, 1984.

Lawrence, D. H. *Sons and Lovers*. London: Heinemann, 1913.

Marin, Peter. *Provence and Pound*. Berkeley: University of California, 1976.

Moffat, Maryjane, and Charlotte Painter, eds. Part 1: "Love," of *Revelations: Diaries of Women*. New York: Random House/Vintage, 1974.

Pagels, Elaine. *Adam, Eve and the Serpent*, New York: Random House, 1988.

———. *The Gnostic Gospels*. New York: Random House, 1979.

Paris, Ginette. *Pagan Meditations: Aphrodite, Hestia, Artemis*. Dallas: Spring, 1986.

Qualls-Corbett, Nancy. *The Sacred Prostitute: Eternal Aspect of the Feminine*. Toronto: Inner City, 1988.

Rouselle, Aline. *Porneia: On Desire and the Body in Antiquity*. New York: Blackwell, 1988.

Russell, Bertrand. *Marriage and Morals*. New York: Liveright, 1929.

Sanford, John A. *The Invisible Partners*. New York: Paulist Press, 1980.

Summers, Anthony. *Goddess: The Secret Lives of Marilyn Monroe*. New York: Macmillan, 1985.

Taylor, Gordon Rattray. *Sex in Society*. New York: Vanguard Press, 1954.

Welwood, John, ed. *Challenge of the Heart*. Boston: Shambhala, 1985.

Wilder, Thornton. *The Woman of Andros*. New York: Harper, 1958.

Young, Wayland. *Eros Denied: Sex in Western Society*. New York: Grove Press, 1964.

Chapter Five: Hera: Queen and Partner in Power

De Rougement, Denis. *Love in the Western World*. New York: Pantheon, 1956. [For Books V and VI.]

Fellini, Federico. *Fellini on Fellini*. New York: New Directions, 1976.

Kerényi, Carl. *Zeus and Hera*. Princeton, N.J.: Princeton University Press, 1975.

Lawrence, D. H. *Fantasia of the Unconscious*. London: Heinemann, 1923.

Leonard, Linda Schierse. *On the Way to the Wedding*. Boston: Shambhala, 1986.

Lewis, C. S. *Till We Have Faces*. New York: Harcourt, Brace, Jovanovich, 1956.

Moffat, Maryjane, and Charlotte Painter. "Part III: Power," of *Revelations: Diaries of Women*. New York: Random House/Vintage, 1974.

Regan, Donald. *For the Record*. New York: Harcourt Brace Jovanovich, 1988.

Sanford, John A. *The Invisible Partners*. New York: Paulist Press, 1980.

Stein, Murray. "Hera, Bound and Unbound," *Spring* (1977).

Stern, Karl. Chapter 8: "Hedda and Her Companions," of *The Flight From Woman*. New York: Farrar, Strauss, 1965.

Welwood, John, ed. *Challenge of the Heart*. Boston: Shambhala, 1985.

Wilde, Oscar. *The Importance of Being Earnest*. In *Plays*. London: Penguin, 1954.

Williams, Tennessee. *Suddenly Last Summer*. In *Four Plays*. New York: Signet, 1968, [1958].

Woodman, Marion. *Addiction to Perfection: The Still Unravished Bride*. Toronto: Inner City, 1982.

Young-Eisendrath, Polly. *Hags and Heroes: A Feminist Approach to Jungian Psychotherapy With Couples*. Toronto: Inner City, 1984.

Chapter Six: Persephone: Medium, Mystic, and Mistress of the Dead

Adler, Margot. *Drawing Down the Moon*. Boston: Beacon, 1981.

Berry, Carmen Renee. *When Helping You Is Hurting Me*. New York: Harper & Row, 1988.

Bradley, Marion Zimmer. *The Firebrand*. New York: Simon and Schuster, 1987.

Bryant, Dorothy. *The Kin of Ata Are Waiting for You*. New York: Random House, 1971.

Chessler, Phyllis. *Women and Madness*. New York: Doubleday, 1972.

Demetrakopoulos, Stephanie. *Listening to Our Bodies*. Boston: Beacon, 1983.

Ehrenreich, Barbara, and Deirdre English. *Witches, Midwives, and Nurses: A History of Women Healers*. London: Writers and Readers Publishing Cooperative, 1973.

Garrett, Eileen. *Many Voices: The Autobiography of a Medium*. New York: G. P. Putnam's, 1968.

Hillesum, Etty. *An Interrupted Life: The Diaries of Etty Hillesum 1941–1943*. Old Tappan, N.J.: Washington Square Press, 1981.

Hillman, James. *The Dream and the Underworld*. New York: Harper & Row, 1979.

Jacobi, Jolande, ed. *Paracelsus: Selected Writings*. Princeton, N.J.: Princeton/Bollingen, 1958.

Jung, C. G. *Psychology and the Occult*. Princeton, N.J.: Princeton/Bollingen, 1977.

Klimo, Jon. *Channeling*. Los Angeles: Jeremy P. Tarcher, 1987.

Kübler-Ross, Elisabeth. *Living With Death and Dying*. New York: Macmillan, 1981.

Lagerkvist, Pär, *The Sybil*. New York: Vintage, 1958.

Lewis, C. S. *Till We Have Faces*. New York: Harcourt Brace Jovanovich, 1956.

Neumann, Erich. "On the Moon and Matriarchal Consciousness." In *Fathers and Mothers*, edited by Patricia Berry. Zurich: *Spring*, 1973.

Nikhilananda, Swami, trans., *The Gospel of Sri Ramakrishna*. New York: Ramakrishna-Vivekananda Center, 1942.

Perera, Sylvia Brinton. *Descent to the Goddess*. Toronto: Inner City, 1981.

Rohde, Erwin. Translated by W. B. Hillis. *Psyche: The Cult of Souls and the Belief in Immortality Among the Greeks*, 2 vols. New York: Harper & Row, 1966 [1920].

Walker, Barbara. *The Crone: Woman of Age, Wisdom, and Power*. New York: Harper & Row, 1985.

Wolkstein, Diane, and Samuel Noah Kramer. *Inanna, Queen of Heaven and Earth*. New York: Harper & Row, 1983.

Chapter Seven: Demeter, Mother of Us All

Arms, Suzanne. *Immaculate Deception*. New York: Houghton Mifflin, 1975.

Berger, Pamela. *The Goddess Obscured: Transformation of the Grain Protectress From Goddess to Saint*. Boston: Beacon, 1975.

Berry, Patricia. "The Rape of Demeter/Persephone and Neurosis." *Spring* (1975).

Bombeck, Erma, *Motherhood: The Second Oldest Profession*. New York: McGraw-Hill, 1983.

Chicago, Judy. *The Birth Project*. New York: Doubleday, 1985.

Demetrakopoulos, Stephanie. *Listening to Our Bodies*. Boston: Beacon, 1983.

Gaskin, Ina May. *Spiritual Midwifery*. Summertown, Tenn.: The Book Publishing, 1980.

Greer, Germaine. *Sex and Destiny*. New York: Harper & Row, 1984.

Hall, Nor. Chapter 4: "Mothers and Daughters," of *The Moon and the Virgin*. New York: Harper, 1980.

Kerényi, Carl. *Eleusis—Archetypal Image of Mother and Daughter*. Princeton, N.J.: Princeton/Bollingen, 1967.

Meyer, Marvin W., ed. Chapter 2: "The Greek Mysteries of the Grain Mother and Daughter," of *The Ancient Mysteries*. New York: Harper & Row, 1987.

Rich, Adrienne. *Of Woman Born*. New York: Norton, 1976.

Shuttle, Penelope, and Peter Redgrove. *The Wise Wound*. London: Penguin Books, 1978.

Sorel, Nancy Caldwell. *Ever Since Eve*. New York: Oxford University Press, 1984.

Walker, Barbara. *The Crone: Woman of Age, Wisdom and Power*. New York: Harper, 1985.

Wasson, R. Gordon, Carl A. P. Ruck, and Albert Hoffman. *The Road to Eleusis*. New York: Harvest/Harcourt, 1978.

IV. OTHER WORKS MENTIONED

Hewlett, Sylvia Ann. *A Lesser Life: The Myth of Women's Liberation in America*. New York: William Morrow, 1986.

Friday, Nancy. *My Mother/My Self*. New York: Delacorte Press, 1977.

Gornick, Vivian. *Fierce Attachment*. New York: Farrar, Strauss & Giroux.

McLaughlin, Corinne, and Gordon Davidson. *Builders of the Dawn: Community Lifestyles in a Changing World*. Shutesbury, Mass.: Sirius Publishing, 1986.

Thompson, William Irwin. *Darkness and Scattered Light*. New York: Doubleday/Anchor, 1978.

VIDEOGRAPHY

Video rental stores are a rich source of information about the goddesses. In this section we have listed feature films readily available on video cassette that reflect the six goddesses. Also listed are films that demonstrate a dialogue between two or more of the goddesses. We offer these films as suggestions of where to begin to look for the goddesses; we are sure that you will discover many more examples if you look for them. The goddesses, after all, are everywhere!

ATHENA

Broadcast News (CBS/Fox)
A brilliant young producer (Holly Hunter) sets out to groom a good-

looking but empty reporter (William Hurt) for the job of anchorman and has to deal with her affections too.

The China Syndrome (Columbia)
Jane Fonda plays a reporter investigating a melt-down at a nuclear power plant.

Educating Rita (RCA/Columbia)
Rita is an English working-class woman who desperately hungers for an education. To escape her dreary life as a hairdresser, she enrolls in college. With Michael Caine.

House of Games (Orion)
An intriguing psychological thriller in which nothing is as it appears: a famed psychiatrist (played by Lindsay Crouse) is drawn into the dangerous underworld of the con artist.

Julia (CBS/Fox)
A true story of loyalty, courage, and love, *Julia* is playwright Lillian Hellman's tribute to her friend. The story relates to an incident when, at Julia's request, Hellman smuggled money through Nazi Germany to help secure freedom for Jews. With Jane Fonda, Vanessa Redgrave, Jason Robards, Jr., and Hal Holbrook.

Network (MGM/UA)
Faye Dunaway plays a ruthless vice president of programming for a network TV station.

Norma Rae (CBS/Fox)
Sally Field plays Norma, a textile worker whose life is changed by a union organizer when she overcomes her fears of management reprisal and joins his cause.

Plenty (Thorn EMI)
The clash of attitudes in the post–World War II world between a strong-willed resistance fighter (Susan, played by Meryl Streep) and her spineless husband leads to the destruction of Susan's sanity and her husband's career.

Silkwood (Embassy)
Meryl Streep as a divorced woman who speaks out against the safety

hazards of a plutonium plant. Based on the true story of Karen Silk-wood.

An Unmarried Woman (CBS/Fox)
Jill Clayburgh plays Erica in a comedy set in the "liberated" seventies about a woman who must "rediscover" herself when her husband leaves her.

APHRODITE

Anna Karenina (Metro-Goldwyn-Mayer)
Greta Garbo and Frederic March in Tolstoy's epic story of unrequited love set in nineteenth-century Russia and Venice.

Camila (Embassy)
The tragic love story of a young Catholic socialite from Buenos Aires and a Jesuit priest.

Carmen (Media Home Entertainment)
Passion and flamenco dancing.

Gentlemen Prefer Blondes (Twentieth Century–Fox)
Marilyn Monroe and Jane Russell play showgirls on a quest for love, romance, and money.

Gone With the Wind (MGM/UA)
An extravaganza, with Vivien Leigh as Scarlett O'Hara and Clark Gable as Rhett Butler.

Indiscreet (Republic)
Ingrid Bergman and Cary Grant in a love affair between an internationally renowned actress and a deceitful NATO official.

Madame Bovary (MGM/CBS)
A tragedy about a nineteenth-century French woman's revolt against conventional society in her search for passion and novelty.

An Officer and a Gentleman (Paramount)
Debra Winger and Richard Gere in a steamy love story with the rigors of the navy's officers' candidate school as the background.

Pretty Baby (Paramount)
A young Brooke Shields plays a twelve-year-old prostitute married to an older man.

Ryan's Daughter (MGM/UA)
The hopeless love and public shunning of an Irish girl who falls in love with a German officer during World War I.

Same Time Next Year (Universal)
Ellen Burstyn plays a young married woman who falls in love with a married man (played by Alan Alda) whom she meets by chance in a motel. As they continue their affair every few years at the same motel, we watch them change and grow, neither giving up his or her marriage.

Some Like It Hot (Twentieth Century–Fox)
A romantic satire of the Prohibition Era, with Marilyn Monroe, Tony Curtis, and Jack Lemmon.

The French Lieutenant's Woman (Twentieth Century–Fox)
Meryl Streep plays a woman ostracized by Victorian society after being abandoned by her French lover.

PERSEPHONE

The Bell Jar (Vestron)
Based on the semiautobiographical novel by poet Sylvia Plath, this is the story of a young woman who suffers a nervous breakdown in her effort to achieve personal and professional goals.

Black Narcissus (Video America)
A haunting film about the isolation, madness, spiritual failures, and sexual frustrations that overwhelm five missionary nuns in a Himalayan convent; with Deborah Kerr and Jean Simmons.

Black Orpheus (CBS Video)
The legend of Eurydice and Orpheus comes to life in a tragic and passionate meeting at the Mardi Gras carnival in Rio.

Carrie (MGM/UA)
Sissy Spacek plays Carrie, a naive and lonely teenager who discovers

that she has the witchlike power to avenge herself against her teenage persecutors.

Days of Wine and Roses (Warner)
Lee Remick and Jack Lemmon play a young couple caught in the trap of alcoholism.

Extremities (Paramount)
Farrah Fawcett plays a young woman who narrowly escapes a brutal rapist only to have him return to finish what he started. She fights back and eventually overcomes him.

Frances (Thorn)
Jessica Lange as Frances: at sixteen she was an award-winning high school student; at twenty-three a rising stage and screen star; at twenty-seven a chain of events led to her arrest and eventual involuntary committal to a mental institution. Based on the true story of Frances Farmer.

Harold and Maude (Paramount)
An unforgettable story about a wealthy, death-obsessed teenager who falls in love with a free-spirited octogenarian, played by Ruth Gordon.

I Never Promised You a Rose Garden (Warner)
Kathleen Quinlan plays an emotionally disturbed teenager trapped in a vivid fantasy world she has created as an alternative to the realities of her confused home life.

Long Day's Journey Into Night (NTA Home Entertainment)
Katharine Hepburn, Sir Ralph Richardson, Jason Robards, Jr., and Dean Stockwell in Eugene O'Neill's autobiographical account of his explosive home life. Katharine Hepburn plays a drug-addicted mother.

'Night, Mother (MCA)
Sissy Spacek and Anne Bancroft in a harrowing study of a mother's attempt to stop her daughter from committing suicide.

Nuts (Warner Bros)
Barbra Streisand plays a prostitute who has killed a man and is being examined by the court to determine her competency to stand trial.

Psycho (MCA)
Anthony Perkins plays Norman Bates in this classic Hitchcock thriller about a psychotic young man who is obsessed by his dead mother. Janet Leigh plays his victim.

ARTEMIS

Aliens (CBS/Fox)
Sigourney Weaver plays a fierce Amazon woman of the future, out to protect her threatened child from space monsters.

Among the Wild Chimpanzees (National Geographic)
Documentary film about Jane Goodall's extraordinary work with primates.

The Clan of the Cave Bear (CBS/Fox)
Daryl Hannah plays Ayla, a Cro-Magnon woman orphaned as a child and raised by Neanderthals who do not understand her advanced intelligence. Exiled by them, she eventually becomes leader of the Cave Bear clan.

Dressed to Kill (Warner)
A pyschiatrist is faced with a murderous puzzle: the sudden, hideous slaying of one of his patients with a straight razor stolen from his office. With Michael Caine, Angie Dickinson, and Nancy Allen.

Gorillas in the Mist (CBS/Fox)
Sigourney Weaver plays Dian Fossey, the Kentuckian who abandoned the outside world to live with and protect mountain gorillas in the rain forest of Rwanda.

Killing Heat (Key)
Karen Black plays an independent woman living in South Africa who decides to abandon her career to marry a struggling jungle farmer.

National Velvet (MGM/UA)
Elizabeth Taylor as an English schoolgirl in love with horses.

Out of Africa (MCA)
Visually beautiful, this film is based on the life of writer Isak Dinesen. Born Karen Blixen in 1885, Dinesen was a Danish aristocrat who re-

belled against bourgeois values and operated a coffee plantation in Kenya.

Red Sonja (CBS/Fox)
Brigitte Nielsen plays the ultimate female warrior, Red Sonja, who avenges the murder of her family by wicked Queen Gedren.

DEMETER

Country (Touchstone)
Jessica Lange embodies the resolute spirit of American farmers as she fights to keep her land and hold her family together in this wrenching account of an Iowa farm family faced with bankruptcy.

Eleni (Embassy Home Entertainment)
The true story of a mother's love and a son's revenge. Set in 1948 in Greece, this is the story of an ordinary woman driven to extraordinary actions out of love for her children, and of her son's revenge against her murderers.

I Remember Mama (Media Home Entertainment)
A sentimental, nostalgic re-creation of a Norwegian immigrant family's struggles at the turn of the century.

Mask (MCA)
Cher plays the devoted mother of Rusty, a teenager whose disfigured face resembles a bizarre mask. Based on a true story.

Places in the Heart (CBS/Fox)
A nostalgic evocation of life in director Robert Benton's Texas home-town during the Depression. Sally Field plays the mother.

Raggedy Man (MCA)
Sissy Spacek plays a lonely mother of two young sons who struggles for love in a small Texas town in the 1940s.

Rosemary's Baby (Paramount)
A melodrama about a baby sired by the Devil. With Ruth Gordon, John Cassavetes, and Mia Farrow as the mother-to-be.

The Turning Point (CBS/Fox)
When her daughter joins the National Ballet, Deedee (played by Shirley MacLaine), a dance teacher who might have been a star had she not married, and Emma (played by Anne Bancroft), a renowned ballerina with an empty personal life, must confront the choices they made years before.

HERA

Cleopatra (Twentieth Century–Fox)
Elizabeth Taylor portrays the queen of Egypt, a woman consumed by her ambition to rule the entire civilized world.

A Doll's House (MGM/UA)
Ibsen's examination of middle-class women's dominance by their husbands. Julie Harris plays Nora, and Christopher Plummer plays her husband.

The Importance of Being Earnest (Paramount)
One of the great drawing-room comedies of all time, this is the story about Jack, a lovestruck suitor whose fiancée can only love a man named Ernest. With Michael Redgrave, Margaret Rutherford, and Edith Evans (playing Lady Bracknell).

Juliet of the Spirits (Embassy)
Federico Fellini's film about a bored housewife who starts to have visions when her husband is unfaithful to her. She discovers for herself a much fuller life.

Macbeth (RCA/Columbia)
Roman Polanski's brilliant version of Shakespeare's nightmarish vision of ambition and violence.

Ordinary People (Paramount)
Mary Tyler Moore plays an upper-middle-class wife whose "ordinary" existence is shattered by the death of her oldest son.

Scenes From a Marriage (Columbia)
Ingmar Bergman's exploration of a twenty-year marriage; with Liv Ullmann and Erland Josephson.

Suddenly Last Summer (RCA/Columbia)
A poet dominated by his mother is horribly murdered in the Galápagos Islands. The mother attempts to commit her niece (Elizabeth Taylor) to a mental institution for revealing the truth of the incident.

The Taming of the Shrew (RCA/Columbia)
Shakespeare's look at male chauvinism and women's lib in the sixteenth century. A battle of wits between husband and wife, with Elizabeth Taylor and Richard Burton.

Terms of Endearment (Paramount)
The story of the relationship of a mother and daughter over a thirty-year period. With Debra Winger, Shirley MacLaine, and Jack Nicholson.

Witness for the Prosecution (CBS/Fox)
Mystery melodrama, with Marlene Dietrich as the defendant's wife.

GODDESSES IN DIALOGUE

The following films feature two or more of the goddesses and their relationships with each other.

Cat on a Hot Tin Roof (MGM/UA)
Hera, Demeter, and Aphrodite lobbying for power in the family hierarchy.

Gone With the Wind (MGM/UA)
Athena, Aphrodite, and Demeter themes interweave in this epic.

Hannah and Her Sisters (Orion)
Demeter, Persephone, and Aphrodite sisters in Woody Allen's social comedy set in Manhattan.

Juliet of the Spirits (Embassy)
A shy Hera's odyssey via Persephone to Aphrodite's world.

Rosemary's Baby (Paramount)
Innocent Demeter sucked into Persephone's world as sacrificial victim.

Suddenly Last Summer (RCA/Columbia)
Hera and Persephone/Aphrodite in a power struggle over Hera's son.

The Turning Point (CBS/Fox)
Demeter and Athena in conflict.

ABOUT THE AUTHORS

Jennifer Barker Woolger is a psychotherapist and teacher who has worked with women, teenagers, and children for over twenty years. She is an award-winning videographer and President of Laughing Bear Productions, a multimedia education company.

Roger J. Woolger, Ph.D., is a Jungian analyst and author of *Other Lives, Other Selves,* a definitive account of past-life therapy. English by birth, he received his training in psychology and comparative religion at Oxford and London universities and is also a graduate of the C. G. Jung Institute in Zurich. He has been a Visiting Professor at Vassar College, the University of Vermont, and Concordia University in Montreal. The Woolgers travel frequently throughout the United States to speak and conduct their popular goddess workshops. They make their home in upstate New York.

Twelfth Night, 197
"Typecasting," 424–25

Ulysses, 143, 151, 373
Unconscious mind, 36, 231–37, 253, 263–64, 296
Underworld, 232
  Persephone as goddess of the, 9, 36, 228, 230, 232–34, 250–51, 254
Unmarried Woman, An, 65
Utne Reader, 399–401, 404, 406

Valerie's Week of Wonders, 289
Van der Post, Sir Laurens, 252
Van Dyke, Anthony, 57
Venus, *see* Aphrodite and Aphrodite woman
Verney, Dr. Thomas, 296
Victim, eternal sacrificial, 247–51
Victoria, Queen, 176, 191, 193
Videography, 452–61
View Over Atlantis, The (Graves), 125
Vindication of the Rights of Women, A (Wollstonecraft), 57
Virgin goddesses, 38, 46, 54, 94, 97, 111
Virgin Mary, 155, 157, 158, 172, 275–78
Visual arts, 36
Voices of Our Ancestors, 129
Von Stuck, Franz, 160

Wagner, Richard, 156, 159
Waiting for God (Weil), 77
War and Peace (Tolstoy), 146
"Warning," 265–66
Warrior, 41
Wasson, R. Gordon, 276

Webb, Beatrice, 191
Webb, Sidney, 191
Weil, Simone, 412
Wells, H. G., 143
"What's With Feminism These Days," 399
When God Was a Woman (Stone), 115–16, 150
When Helping You Is Hurting Me (Berry), 243
Whitmont, Edward C., 3, 7
Whole Earth Catalogue (Brand), 123
Wicca, 125–27, 262, 417
Wife beating, 183–84, 185
Wilde, Oscar, 160, 178, 214–15
Williams, Tennessee, 214, 215
Williams, William Carlos, 223–25
Wills, Gary, 190
Winfrey, Oprah, 401
Winter's Tale, The, 160
Wise Wound, The (Shuttle and Redgrove), 260, 291
Witchcraft, *see* Shamanism
Witch-hunts of Middle Ages, 58, 110, 127, 157–59, 262, 416, 417
Wolff, Toni, 142, 143, 198–99, 203, 231, 232
Wollstonecraft, Mary, 57
Woman and Nature (Griffin), 74, 124, 413
Women and Wilderness (LaBastille), 94–95, 122
Women in Love (Lawrence), 87, 215
Women's movement, 5, 58, 399–401, 406–9
  Artemis woman and, 118;
  Athena woman and, 71–75, 407, 408

PERMISSIONS ACKNOWLEDGMENTS
(*continued from copyright page*)

Harper & Row, Publishers, Inc.: Excerpts from: *Goddesses in Everywoman* by Jean S. Bolen. Copyright © 1984 by Jean Shinoda Bolen, M.D.; *The Dream and the Underworld* by James Hillman. Copyright © 1979 by James Hillman. Reprinted by permission of Harper & Row, Publishers, Inc.; Excerpts from "Getting There," "Mary's Song," and "Lady Lazarus" by Sylvia Plath. Copyright © 1963 by Sylvia Plath. From *Ariel* edited by Ted Hughes. Copyright © 1961, 1962, 1963, 1964, 1965 by Ted Hughes. Rights in the United States administered by Harper & Row, Publishers, Inc. Rights in all other territories administered by Olwyn Hughes. *Ariel* published in London by Faber & Faber Ltd. Reprinted by permission of Harper and Row, Publishers, Inc. and Olwyn Hughes.

Inner City Books: Excerpt from *Addiction To Perfection: The Still Unravished Bride* by Marion Woodman. Reprinted by permission of the publisher, Inner City Books.

John Johnson Limited: "Warning" from *Rose in the Afternoon* by Jenny Joseph, Dent, 1974. Copyright © Jenny Joseph. Reprinted by permission of John Johnson Limited, London.

Alfred A. Knopf, Inc.: Excerpt from *The Second Sex* by Simone de Beauvoir, translated by H.M. Parshley. Copyright 1952 by Alfred A. Knopf, Inc. Reprinted by permission of the publisher.

Liveright Publishing Corporation: Excerpt from "somewhere i have never travelled, gladly beyond" from *Viva*, poems by e. e. cummings, edited by George James Firmage. Copyright 1931, © 1959 by e.e. cummings. Copyright © 1979, 1973 by the Trustees for the e.e. cummings Trust. Copyright © 1979, 1973 by George James Firmage. Reprinted by permission of Liveright Publishing Corporation.

Mother Jones magazine: Excerpt from an article appearing in *Mother Jones* magazine in July, 1980. Copyright © 1980 by the Foundation for National Progress. Reprinted by permission of *Mother Jones* magazine.

New Directions Publishing Corporation: Poem of Kuan Tao-sheng from *Women Poets of China* by Kenneth Rexroth. Copyright © 1972 by Kenneth Rexroth and Ling Chung; "Come into Animal Presence" from *Poems 1960–1967* by Denise Levertov. Copyright © 1961 by Denise Levertov Goodman; "The Ivy Crown" from *Collected Poems Vol. II, 1939–1962* by William Carlos Williams. Copyright 1955 by William Carlos Williams. Reprinted by permission of New Directions Publishing Corporation.

Pendle Hill Publications: Excerpt from *Two Moral Essays: Draft for a Statement of Human Obligations and Human Personality* written by Simone Weil, edited by Ronald Hathaway, Pendle Hill Pamphlet 240, Pendle Hill Publications, Wallingford, Pennsylvania 19086, 1981.

Penguin Books Ltd: Excerpts from *The Iliad* by Homer, translated by E.V. Rieu (Penguin Classics, 1950). Copyright 1950 the Estate of E.V. Rieu. Reproduced by permission of Penguin Books Ltd.

Princeton University Press: Excerpts from *Essays on a Science of Mythology: The Myth of the Divine Child and the Mysteries of Eleusis*, Bollingen Series 22, written by C.G. Jung and C. Kerényi, translated by R.F.C. Hull. Copyright 1949, © 1959 by Bollingen Foundation. New material copyright © 1963 by Princeton University Press.

The Ramakrishna-Vivekananda Center of New York: Excerpts from *The Gospel of Sri Ramakrishna* as translated into English by Swami Nikhilananda and published by The Ramakrishna-Vivekananda Center of New York. Copyright 1942 by Swami Nikhilananda.

Schocken Books: "Sappho's Hymn to Aphrodite" from *Sappho and the Greek Lyric*

GODDESS
WITHIN
SEMINARS

Jennifer and Roger Woolger offer a variety of seminars, workshops, lectures, and festivals on the goddesses, on Jungian psychology, and on past-life therapy. They are sponsored by Laughing Bear Productions, a multimedia education company that specializes in video, film, writing and teaching projects.

For further information about their work, please write to:

Laughing Bear Productions
5 River Road
New Paltz, NY 12561